WAGNER'S RING

A Listener's
Companion & Concordance

Wagner was fond of this engraving, which hung over the desk in his Dresden apartment in the 1840s. The German artist Peter von Cornelius fashioned it in 1821 for the title page of a new edition of the epic poem *Das Nibelungenlied.*

The engraving depicts (left to right, top to bottom): Siegfried wrestling with Brünnhilde, Siegfried's marriage to Kriemhild, the Burgundians' return from war with the Saxons, the battle in King Etzel's hall, King Etzel brooding on his throne, and Siegfried departing from Kriemhild for the hunt. Courtesy the British Library.

WAGNER'S
RING

A Listener's
Companion & Concordance

J. K. HOLMAN

AMADEUS PRESS
Reinhard G. Pauly, General Editor
Portland, Oregon

Music examples used by permission of G. Schirmer, Inc. (ASCAP).

Excerpts from Deryck Cooke's *An Introduction to Wagner's "Der Ring des Nibelungen"* used by permission of The Decca Record Company Limited.

Excerpts from the translations of *The Ring* by Salter and Mann used by permission of Mr. Lionel Salter, Mrs. William Mann, and Deutsche Grammophon GmbH.

Woodcuts by Susan Perl used by permission of Erica Merkling.

Library of Congress Cataloging-in-Publication Data

Holman, J. K.
Wagner's Ring : a listener's companion and concordance / J. K. Holman.
p.   cm.
Includes bibliographical references (p.   ), discography (p.   ) and index.
ISBN 1-57467-014-X
1. Wagner, Richard, 1813–1883. Ring des Nibelungen.
2. Wagner, Richard, 1813–1883. Ring des Nibelungen—Concordances.
I. Title.
ML410.W22H65   1996
782. 1–dc20   96-1829
                                                       CIP
                                                        MN

Printed in Singapore

AMADEUS PRESS
The Haseltine Building
133 S.W. Second Avenue, Suite 450
Portland, Oregon 97204-3527 U.S.A.

For Diana

All these years,
all in one—

Sieglinde and Brünnhilde,
Freia and Fricka

CONTENTS

Foreword
9

Preface
11

Introduction
15
How to use this guide,
with an overview of the major translations

CHAPTER ONE
Background
23
Mythological sources of the Ring *operas,*
a chronology of their creation and of Wagner's life,
and the genesis of Bayreuth

CHAPTER TWO
The Story
45
The four plots delineated,
presenting characters and actions as Wagner directed

CHAPTER THREE
The Music
103
How the story of The Ring *is told through music*

CHAPTER FOUR

The Characters

171

Each character's ancestry in myth and role in the music dramas

CHAPTER FIVE

Concordance

243

The first concordance to The Ring *in English,*
an alphabetical listing of key words
and of every appearance of each term in the four operas

Appendix

371

Staging The Ring,
a closer look at the motive Woman's Worth,
the chain of possession of the ring,
and the characters' fates

Discography

403

Selected recordings, cast lists, and timings

Notes

420

Bibliography

426

Annotated guide to helpful books in English

Photo Credits

435

Index

437

FOREWORD

A FRENCH authority on Wagner wrote in the preface to his important new book on the music dramas, "Of course I have not read all that has been written about Wagner—one human life would not suffice for that."

His name was Lavignac, and he was writing in Paris in 1897!

Lavignac might have been both dismayed and delighted to learn that the great mass of books and articles he was referring to a century ago has become merely the tip of today's iceberg. Yet I venture to say that the book you have in your hands now will prove not merely unique among all those works, but uniquely useful, in more ways than one.

As I sat down to write this brief foreword to the impressive manuscript that would become this book, I was shocked to realize that there had been a time when I had looked forward to—or, less ambiguously, anticipated—hearing my first performance of a Wagner opera with something close to dread. As a young player in string ensembles I had found playing in quartets, above all, to be the most satisfying of musical experiences. Wagner seemed far removed from that world, and his reputation for massive works built out of something called leitmotifs was forbidding.

But I also recall that I enjoyed my first encounter with *The Ring* without being able to name a single one of those leitmotifs. And as I heard more and more of this revolutionary work, I knew that my pleasure in it would grow even greater if I could dig deeper into both the work and its background. Well, it happened that an invitation to write and narrate the Metropolitan Opera's *Ring* cassettes enabled me to spend large parts of three years immersed in this magnificent creation and in the fascinating ways in which its creator achieved his miracle. The result was what I had hoped for, an even more intense—and lasting—enjoyment.

The key to that enjoyment was getting as close as possible to the composer's genius—his thinking, his intentions, both in his drama and in his music. As

Alexander Pope said in a sadly neglected couplet, "The perfect judge will read each work of wit, with the same spirit that its author writ." For Pope, *wit* meant not so much cleverness as intellect—originally, *wit* meant "mind." Indeed, his thought becomes different, clearer, if we read the couplet in the spirit with which it was written.

And this is not a matter of purism. I'd no more want to see the goddess Fricka enter, as Wagner indicated, in a chariot drawn by fake rams than I'd like to see Cleopatra played by the boy actors of Shakespeare's day. Nevertheless, for me, the richest experience of *The Ring* comes with Wotan and Fricka in a mountain pass, not a spaceship, and the Rhine Daughters swimming, not sitting in easy chairs chewing gum, as I once saw them.

It is that striving for Wagner's intentions that I enjoy so much in the Met's current production and that I find so valuable in Jim Holman's approach.

I do have one regret—that I did not have his book by my side as I was plunging into my *Ring* studies, although it will be good to have on hand from now on, if only for the decidedly helpful chapter on the characters and the wonderful concordance. In addition to Holman's knowing surveys of the text, the music, the background, and the scholarship of *The Ring*, he enables us with those chapters to find quickly the various places in the opera where, say, Brünnhilde appears, or even that elusive character, Loge, or all the references to the sword or the spear.

In short, this is a valuable new tool for mining the rich depths of an unparalleled work.

Peter Allen
New York

Peter Allen, since 1975 host of the Texaco–Metropolitan Opera Saturday broadcasts, is the author-narrator of cassettes on Wagner's Ring *operas produced by the Metropolitan Opera Guild.*

PREFACE

AT THE END of *The Rhinegold,* or the other three *Ring* operas for that matter, we sit in a state of emotional shock. We are in the grip of a theater experience as intense as we are ever likely to have, exposed to everything that is beautiful and difficult and hateful in life. We have been connected with all we have longed for and with the presentiment of inevitable disappointment.

These reactions are not unusual; they typify experiences documented by *Ring* listeners over and over for more than a century. For George Bernard Shaw, Thomas Mann, Friedrich Nietzsche, C. S. Lewis, and countless others, there is always this immersion into the deepest world of human feeling.

Visceral, passionate emotion was precisely what Wagner was after. His voluminous explanations of his own art, generally confusing and often contradictory, were remarkably coherent on the essential points, among them that "the essence of drama is knowing through feeling."[1] Spontaneous emotions, he said, are by nature closer to the truth than rational reflection; he cogently described his artistic intentions as "emotionalizing the intellect."[2]

Much has been written about this antirational, even mystical element in Wagner's art—its uncanny power to move us, its exploration of the human subconscious, its evocation of our most primal ambitions and fears. Yet pure feeling was an end, not a means; Wagner, like every master in art, reaches us by craft, by artistic—artificial—manipulation. Drawing on disciplined theories and musical-dramatic practices, he was relentlessly systematic in achieving seemingly natural results.

Wagner's expressive power is in fact no mystery at all: it stems from the unique musical language that he fashioned to communicate drama. It is a tonal, harmonic language that is unusually explicit and verbal. For listeners willing to learn the vocabulary, *The Ring* becomes a vast, intricate—but above all comprehensible—conversation and an inexhaustible source of both intellectual and emotional pleasure. The present work, I hope, will widen that circle of listeners.

This book is deliberately nontechnical. Its intellectual underpinnings, if any, can be found in Deryck Cooke's *The Language of Music.* Cooke convincingly defends the notion that "music functions as a language of the emotions."[3] He articulates what we all know intuitively, that harmony and tonality have enabled western music since the Renaissance to bring about a shared emotional response. It is no wonder that Cooke is also among the most knowing analysts of Wagner's music, a supreme achievement in the expressive language of tonal harmony.

I have been trying to understand that language for thirty years, solely for the pleasure of it. There were milestones: a *Twilight of the Gods* at the old Met in 1963; Merrill Knapp, the dean of students, who taught the Wagner course because none of the brightest lights of Princeton's music department wanted to; most of all, the hours spent in 1967 with Solti's *Ring,* earphones, and the vocal scores.

This book began with a suggestion from my wife, Diana, an enthusiastic Proustian. Her frequent use of Terence Kilmartin's *A Reader's Guide to Remembrance of Things Past,* "a guide [for those] daunted or bewildered by the profusion of characters, themes and allusions,"[4] led her to suggest that a similar work might be welcomed by the growing number of *Ring* listeners.

A few others agreed, especially M. Owen Lee, professor of Classics at the University of Toronto. Father Lee is well-known to opera listeners for his Metropolitan Opera radio broadcasts; his enormously popular talks on *The Ring* were published in 1990 as *Wagner's "Ring": Turning the Sky Round.* Father Lee's kindness and unexpected encouragement made me brave.

Over the past two years, a number of people have read the manuscript and made it better. Chief among these is Rena Charnin Mueller of the music department of New York University. As a result of Rena's candid and sometimes painful tuition, many technical misstatements and misjudgments have been avoided; those that remain do so in spite of her.

I have also benefited from the suggestions of Roman Terleckyj, the award-winning director of production at the Washington Opera; Lionel Salter, perhaps most admired for forty years of musical programming at the BBC and whose translations are an important basis of this book; and Speight Jenkins, the general director of the Seattle Opera and a brilliant Wagner producer.

Additional insights were provided by Adams Holman of the music research department of the New York Public Library; Blaine Marshall, an editor at *Civilization* magazine; and Gabrielle Steers, an authority on nineteenth-century German literature. Hilary Shaw provided diligent and artful editorial advice.

A number of institutions have helped in extraordinary ways, most of all the Metropolitan Opera. The Met has permitted me to use a large number of stage set photos from that company's magnificent *Ring* of the late 1980s. In particular, I would like to thank Peter Clark of the press department; Robert Tuggle, head of the archives; and Richard Wagner, head of the costume department.

Rolf Langenfass, the gifted Austrian costume designer for that same Met *Ring*, has graciously permitted me to use his wonderful design sketches.

William K. Tell, Jr., and Michael Keenan of Texaco, always generous friends, have given me their substantial support throughout the project.

Other opera companies contributed to my survey of postwar *Ring* productions, including the Lyric Opera of Chicago, the Seattle Opera, the Washington Opera/Kennedy Center for the Performing Arts, the English National Opera, the Wiener Staatsoper, the San Francisco Opera, and the Châtelet/Théâtre Musical de Paris.

Special thanks are extended to Peter Emmerich and the Bayreuther Festspiele for permitting a comprehensive look at postwar Bayreuth productions, photographs of the Festspielhaus, and other materials.

I also appreciate the cooperation of the Performing Arts Reading Room staff, Music Division, Library of Congress, Jon W. Newsom, acting chief.

For his vision and wisdom I thank Dr. Reinhard Pauly, general editor at Amadeus Press. His support and encouragement have been steadfast since he first looked at a partial manuscript in 1993.

That manuscript has been turned into a book by Eve Goodman, its editor. For her unrelenting professionalism, patience, and friendship, I am sincerely grateful.

Finally, I would remember Carol Odlum. Her unexpected death from cancer, in the midst of editing this book, saddened me, her colleagues at Amadeus, and all who knew her.

J. K. Holman

INTRODUCTION

THE PURPOSE of this book is to provide English-speaking listeners, audiences, and readers with a basic guide to the four operas of Richard Wagner's *The Ring of the Nibelung.* Of this huge work we will ask the seemingly simple questions *who is who?* and *what happens?* Newcomers to *The Ring* may take some satisfaction in knowing that even Wagner scholars cannot answer these questions with perfect recall or, indeed, complete agreement.

We will look at *The Ring* as Wagner created it, probing its surface and its depth in great detail and with as much objectivity and as much fidelity to Wagner's directions as possible. This close look may well prepare us to ask *why?* and *what does it mean?* But a fascinating journey precedes such questions, a journey for which this book provides an exhaustive guide and the first-ever concordance to key words in the translated texts.

To explore *The Ring* as Wagner created it does not necessarily engage us in the interpretive debates. Even revisionist *Ring*s are more fairly judged and sometimes better appreciated against a strict-constructionist background. (In revisionist interpretations of *The Ring,* which include most *Ring* performances today, directors and designers stray far from the composer's directions.) In fact, the starting point for any journey into *The Ring* is a world of myth and a context of gestures, motivations, and even topography that Wagner explicitly set down for its performance.

While understanding Wagner's German texts and even his idiosyncratic nineteenth-century poetry has enormous value, it is not a prerequisite for enjoying the masterpiece. Since the first performance of *The Ring* in 1876, it has been admired by vast numbers of people who neither read nor speak German, and its

English-speaking audience continues to grow. American and British opera houses, performers, critics, and scholars have made historic *Ring* contributions from the earliest days, and the English-language literature on *The Ring* is broad and rich. Excellent translations are also available, and these are discussed below.

The time is right for a comprehensive, in-depth guide and reference for English-speaking readers. By design, hardly a word of German will be found here. These explorations will lead readers into *The Ring* by way of four basic avenues: its story, its music, its characters, and, finally, its principal words. Each approach offers its own perspective on *The Ring*; together they provide a unique companion to the tetralogy.

Because nobody writing about Wagner can suppress personal views for long, my own interpretations inevitably enter into some of the discussions in this book, especially in the commentary on the characters in chapter 4, and to a lesser extent in chapter 3, on the music. More important, references to a wealth of *Ring* analyses by other interpreters can also be found in these pages.

The Contents

In chapter 1, three short sections present the mythological sources on which Wagner based the operas, a chronology of the composition of *The Ring* juxtaposed against other important events in Wagner's personal and creative life, and a brief history of the Bayreuth theater and festival during Wagner's lifetime.

Chapter 2 tells the stories. Extended plot synopses provide a comprehensive blueprint of the action. All the characters and actions appear here as Wagner directed, without interpretation.

Of course, few of us would have any interest in Wagner's story, characters, or theories were it not for his surpassing achievements as harmonist, polyphonist, instrumentalist, orchestrator, and musical architect. A central assumption here is that the deepest meaning of *The Ring* lies in its music, so that chapter 3 focuses on how the *Ring* story is told through music.

Among the principal tools Wagner developed to convey meaning are the musical themes and fragments commonly called leitmotifs or motives. Simple labeling of motives has in the past been misleading and counterproductive: motive hunting undervalues the technical depth of the music and obscures the intuitive comprehension that Wagner intended. On the other hand, ignoring the motivic fabric would be akin to looking at a master painting without considering the brushwork. Thus we will focus on the dramatic (rather than musicological) significance of the motives and how they help tell the story of *The Ring*.

Chapter 4 gives us a sense of each character's place in the music drama. The discussion identifies the twenty-five characters or character groups, covering each character's mythological sources, relationships to the other *Ring* dramatis personae, appearances in the story, and music.

For those who wish to look more closely at Wagner's use of words or indeed see what the characters have to say about any key terms in these operas, please turn to chapter 5, the first exhaustive concordance to *The Ring* in English. The concordance holds a powerful mirror to the text: it is an alphabetical index of all principal words, with every occurrence of each key word shown in its context in the dramas. Thus the concordance can illuminate how Wagner used certain words— and the images, contrasts, and memories they elicit—to weave the story. Dedicated *Ring* scholars and newly devoted readers alike should find the concordance a surprising and valuable tool.

The Appendix adds useful information while stopping somewhere short of a trivial pursuit.[1] It includes a brief review of postwar stagings of *The Ring;* a detailed account of one important musical motive, Woman's Worth; the chain of possession of the ring; and a summary of each character's fate. These are followed by a selected and annotated bibliography and discography.

Throughout the text, the individual operas of *The Ring* are referred to as:

R   *The Rhinegold (Das Rheingold)*
V   *The Valkyrie (Die Walküre)*
S   *Siegfried (Siegfried)*
T   *Twilight of the Gods (Götterdämmerung)*

The first three titles are easily translated, but the final one has been translated in various ways, including *The Twilight of the Gods, The Dusk of the Gods, The Downfall of the Gods,* and *Night Falls on the Gods.* Although none of these does full justice to the sense and feel of the German, I have used the word *twilight* because it is widely accepted and it does suggest the sense of passing associated with this evocative time of day. I do not use the initial definitive article *the* (and neither does Wagner) because its use might convey a more specific or prosaic twilight than should be sensed.

Acts are given in Arabic numbers (1, 2, 3), scenes in small Roman numerals (i, ii, iii). Thus, the first scene of the second act of *Siegfried* becomes S-2-i.

The *Ring* Texts and Their Translations

Like other aspects of *The Ring,* the texts (or librettos or poems) present huge challenges and special rewards to their audiences. Wagner remains the most prominent among the small number of opera composers to write their own texts, and he considered the poems to be especially germane to the music and to the operas as a whole.

Around the time Wagner began writing his sketches for *The Ring*, he was also articulating his mature artistic theories, including his commitment to what Wagner scholar Barry Millington has called the "absolute equality of poetry and music." Wagner believed that the "text should be projected intelligibly. To that end he developed a new kind of vocal line that faithfully reflected the verbal accentuations, poetic meaning, and emotional content of the text."[2] Whatever the literary quality of his librettos—and critics range far and wide on this subject—Wagner's approach to the words and their relationship to the music deeply influenced the final shape of *The Ring*.

The full *Ring* text is not only the longest in opera but arguably the most elaborately constructed as well. From 1843 to 1848, Wagner intensely researched primary sources and secondary nineteenth-century materials on German and Scandinavian mythology. For the next four-and-a-half years (June 1848 to December 1852) he constructed the prose scenarios, the prose sketches, and finally the poems for the *Ring* operas (see "Mythological Sources" in chapter 1).

The subject matter of *The Ring* is highly conceptual. As the late *Ring* analyst Deryck Cooke put it:

> The truth is that in *The Ring*, the text is important to the understanding of the whole in a way that it is not in *Tristan* or *Parsifal:* we have to comprehend and connect the concepts expressed by the text before we can give ourselves spontaneously to the musical expression of the emotions which lie behind these concepts. *The Ring* is unique amongst great musical stageworks in having at the core of its emotional music-drama a text which is almost as much a "play of ideas" as a work by Ibsen or Shaw.[3]

Unfortunately, the fact that the *Ring* texts are so important does not make them more comprehensible. To the contrary, in Cooke's words, Wagner's "'play of ideas' has proved opaque to our intellects . . . . We are always still puzzling over its meaning when we leave the theater."[4]

Wagner's poetic style contributes to this problem. Complex ideas are expressed in language deliberately shaped by Wagner's effort to recreate, as Wagner scholar and translator Stewart Spencer says,

> the language of the heart, as spoken by the "folk" [which Wagner hoped would] appeal directly to the stultified hearts of his nineteenth-century listeners and rekindle the emotions he felt had been extinguished by modern civilization: the right sound, in phonological and musical terms, would evoke a spontaneous resonance in the audience without the need for the intermediary of rational thought processes.[5]

To achieve this effect, Wagner reached back to stylistic elements from the *Poetic Edda,* the anonymous Scandinavian poems written between 1150 and 1250, which are among the key sources of *The Ring*'s story. Chief among the poetic devices he borrowed was *Stabreim,* an alliterative meter whose principal feature is an insistent repetition of the initial consonant within groups of words. Here is a famous example from Siegmund's Spring Song in *The Valkyrie* (V-1-iii):

> Winterstürme wichen
> dem Wonnemond,
> in mildem Lichte
> leuchtet der Lenz;
> auf linden Lüften
> leicht und lieblich,
> Wunder webend
> er sich wiegt.

Even without knowing German, the listener can readily hear much of what Wagner intended in the text. Andrew Porter, British music critic and translator of *The Ring,* points out how much more compelling is the sound of Alberich's cry in R-iv ("Zertrümmert! Zerknickt!") compared to the English rendering ("Destroyed! Crushed!").[6] Sometimes, however, Wagner had to force this phonological enhancement—for example, to find clusters of words beginning with the same consonant—and this "counterfeited style," as Spencer notes, "all too often proves an obstacle to our understanding of the poem."[7]

Finally, even in paraphrase, the story of *The Ring* is elusive if not confusing. Quite beyond its conceptual and stylistic aspects, it contains vast amounts of information often conveyed elliptically or by implication. Even highly knowledgeable readers still find new or forgotten meanings, motivations, and details at each rereading of the text.

The conflicting demands of retaining meaning, literalness, meter, alliteration, archaic vocabulary, historical flavor, and most important, a complementary relationship to the music render any perfect *Ring* translation impossible. Thus it is understandable that despite numerous efforts over the past century, no definitive English translation has emerged.

At the end of the nineteenth century, Frederick Jameson's translations were adapted to the vocal scores transcribed for piano by Karl Klindworth, a noted piano student of Liszt, and Wagner's friend and frequent piano accompanist. These translations and the Klindworth transcriptions have survived in the United States in the G. Schirmer Vocal Scores. Today we find the Jameson translations largely incomprehensible, but, incredibly, they still from time to time strike closest to the sound and sense Wagner intended.

Andrew Porter translated *The Ring* on behalf of the Sadler's Wells Opera (now called the English National Opera) for that company's historic *Ring* production in the early 1970s. Porter modestly notes that his translation "was made for singing, acting, and hearing, not for reading."[8] To this end, Porter made an elegant effort toward more contemporary language that would also enhance—as Wagner intended—the phonological aspects of meter and alliteration, and the relationship of the words to the music.

Porter is the clear choice for *Ring*s sung in English, but since such productions are rare and his prose is more relaxed, he is—ironically—much more widely read than sung. In addition, Porter's introduction to the published version of his translation offers an insightful discussion of *Ring* translations.[9]

In 1993 Stewart Spencer published a new translation. Spencer's goal, unlike Porter's, was not to fashion an English text to be sung, but rather to improve on earlier translations by simultaneously advancing the causes of both literalness and meaning. Spencer's work may well emerge as a standard translation.

Spencer also "offers an authoritative edition of the German text,"[10] although there has never been a major controversy about a correct *Ring* text as there has about other librettos in the opera repertory. In fact, Spencer's work is all the more valuable for including key parts of the text Wagner ultimately rejected and rewrote. Spencer's 180 "Notes on the Translation" are fascinating for those wishing to probe deeply into the art of *Ring* translation.

The translations used throughout this book are by Lionel Salter (*The Rhinegold*, 1968; *Siegfried*, 1970; and *Twilight of the Gods*, 1969) and by the late William Mann (*The Valkyrie*, 1967). These excellent translations, especially Salter's, are both comprehensible and literal. These are factors of particular relevance to the concordance (chapter 5) because its value as a reference and research tool is enhanced by the closest possible correlation between the German and English words. Salter and Mann have largely managed to avoid archaic usages like those in Jameson's Edwardian idiom while generally retaining the German meter and preserving many alliterative effects.

Listeners are most likely to encounter the Salter and Mann translations. They were issued with Herbert von Karajan's Deutsche Grammophon recordings of 1967–1970, and they accompany Georg Solti's Decca compact discs (the LPs were originally issued with Peggie Cochrane's translations). The Solti and Karajan recordings have become the closest we have to standard *Ring* recordings.

Furthermore, the Salter and Mann translations accompany the Böhm/Philips and Boulez/Philips compact disc sets, produced from live recordings made at Bayreuth in the 1970s, as well as the Janowski/Eurodisc set of 1980 and the

Levine/Deutsche Grammophon recordings of the late 1980s. The Boulez/Philips videotapes use the Salter translations (including *The Valkyrie*), while the Haitink/EMI CDs of 1988–1991 use the Mann translations exclusively. Neither the compact disc reissue of the Furtwängler/EMI recording of 1953 nor the Krause/Foyer set recorded live at Bayreuth in the same year is accompanied by any translation.

CHAPTER ONE

BACKGROUND

Mythological Sources

IN CREATING the story of *The Ring*, Wagner drew on an enormous number of Norse and Germanic mythological sources. He cannot have read the Scandinavian sagas in the original Old Icelandic, and even for the German myths he relied heavily on secondary sources—plays, poems, stories, and academic works written in Germany during his own lifetime. He consumed these voraciously.

Wagner's prodigious effort was typical for him. He consistently researched and exploited his source materials as fully as any composer ever has, yet his research for *The Ring* was exceptional even by his standards. The dramatist was determined to arrive at the most effective time and place and characters for communicating his musical and nonmusical ideas.

The period after the completion of *Lohengrin* (1845–1849) was one of unprecedented ferment in Wagner's emerging artistic, aesthetic, and political (but not overtly musical) theories. Confronted with the various attractions of historical (Frederick Barbarossa and Jesus of Nazareth) versus mythic (Siegfried) themes, he finally turned to the latter. Wagner biographer Robert Gutman:

> Concluding that, because it was addressed to the understanding, history was unsuited to drama, he saw in myth, arising from the pathos of man, the only material meet to stir emotions in the theater, a frankly sensuous purpose, which, in his judgment, alone justified the stage.[1]

The old myths and sagas provide powerful dramatic vehicles. Wagner came to see, in the words of Deryck Cooke, the extraordinary power of myth as "humanity's intuitive expression, in symbolic form, of the ultimate truths about its own nature and destiny."[2] The northern mythologies invite audiences to tap directly into a profound cultural memory, filled with evocative archetypes and symbols. They remove us from inhibiting time- and place-specific associations, and project a symbolic vision of the universal human problems Wagner was exploring.

At the same time, the myths provide an especially apt passage into the inner and intuitive dimensions of life. For many audiences, the psychological constitutes *The Ring*'s most enduring level of meaning, rendered in terms of the inner drives and attributes ascribed to the ancient gods and heroes. We might note in passing how clearly Wagner foreshadowed Freud in this. It is no accident that Robert Donington's Jungian study, *Wagner's "Ring" and Its Symbols*, is among the most illuminating and convincing of the many *Ring* interpretations.

But *The Ring* is not a series of mythological stories set to music. As a creative reformer, Wagner set out to communicate his own artistic, political, spiritual, and other points of view. He did not hesitate to select, reorder, ignore, combine, compress, and restyle the sources, or to invent new events and actions.

The result is that Wagner's *Ring* text is a modern piece; audiences continue to find the conflicts and issues it raises to be thoroughly contemporary. Nevertheless, the characters and most of the episodes have specific sources. Recognizing these traditions will help us probe the meaning of *The Ring*.

The Norse and Germanic sagas reflect the oral traditions and pre-Christian religion of Teutonic tribes that roamed northern Europe and Scandinavia during the first millennium.[3] Their conversion to Christianity, often coerced, caused them to turn away from, or even suppress the worship of the pagan gods.

Some scholars, including Cooke, have speculated that the northern mythologies, and hence Wagner's story, may have some historical basis.[4] A fifth-century chronicle, *Lex Burgundiorum*, tells of the Burgundians, based in the Rhine Valley, who were led by a man named Gunthaharius and defeated in 437 A.D. by Attila's Huns. Attila himself died in 453, possibly in the arms of his bride, Ildico, who may have murdered Attila to avenge her kinsman, Gunthaharius.

Cooke believes this tale was transformed, before the Middle Ages, into a short narrative poem or lay and then combined with other lays about Siegfried and Brünnhilde as the basis for the Nibelung stories. In any case, in the twelfth and thirteenth centuries literary efforts sought to preserve the pre-Christian stories: although only a few manuscripts survived, these sparked an eighteenth-century revival which ultimately inspired Wagner and others.

In 1755, a manuscript of the epic poem *Das Nibelungenlied* was discovered and published, soon establishing itself in German academic and literary circles. In the first years of the nineteenth century, while German Romantics idealized the Middle Ages and German nationalists squirmed under French domination, the *Nibelungenlied* became a sort of German national epic, and in 1844 F. T. Vischer called for a German national opera based on it. Scholars also borrowed from other sagas: the encyclopedic efforts of the brothers Jacob and Wilhelm Grimm were particularly noteworthy.

Popular interest in the myths was rekindled in the 1840s—once again in connection with the move for German political unity—in new commentary, poems, plays, and even an opera (Heinrich Dorn's *Die Nibelungen,* first performed in 1854). In no way, therefore, did Wagner discover the myths underlying his own work. He did understand their vast potential, however, and began to research the sources in 1843 and 1844 while he was Court Kapellmeister at Dresden. He frequently borrowed from the Royal Library there, as well as beginning a personal collection of relevant volumes.[5]

Wagner's commitment to the Nibelung story was intimately connected to the development of his mature artistic theories and practices. By the end of 1848, before he had fled Germany into political exile and before he had realized a musical style beyond *Lohengrin,* he had completed both the first prose sketch for the entire *Ring,* which he called "The Nibelung Myth as Scheme for a Drama," and the poem for *Siegfried's Death* (the original name for *Twilight of the Gods*). By the end of 1852 he had completed all four librettos and the major essays, "Art and Revolution," "The Art Work of the Future," "Opera and Drama," and "The Wibelungs."

ULTIMATELY, Wagner drew heavily from five primary mythological sources —*Das Nibelungenlied, Thidriks Saga af Bern,* the *Poetic Edda,* the *Volsunga Saga,* and the *Prose Edda*—as well as many lesser ones.

Das Nibelungenlied is a German epic poem, thought to have been written anonymously in Austria around 1200 A.D. It focuses on the story of Siegfried, as told in *Twilight of the Gods,* after his arrival at Gunther's palace: his marriage to Gunther's sister, Kriemhild; his wooing of Brünnhilde for Gunther; his giving Brünnhilde's ring to Kriemhild; and his murder by Hagen while hunting. The poem also includes Hagen's narration of Siegfried's slaying a dragon and winning the Nibelung hoard from two royal brothers. The poem goes on to tell of Gunther and Hagen's army fighting in Hungary, which is of no relevance to *The Ring.*

Elizabeth Magee, Deryck Cooke, and others have demonstrated that the *Nibelungenlied* was a lesser influence on *The Ring* than was once thought. While its vast popularity made it a natural starting point for Wagner, it covers only the end of the *Ring* story. Moreover, Wagner eventually lost interest in its medieval, chivalric style and context in which, for example, Siegmund and Sieglinde were sophisticated, royal personages, king and queen of the Netherlands.[6] Stylistically,

Wagner found what he wanted in the more primitive world and language of the Scandinavian, rather than the German, sources.

Thidriks Saga af Bern is a Norwegian prose narrative, based on German sources, written in Bergen around 1260 to 1270. The story covers much the same material in Siegfried's story as the *Nibelungenlied* but also includes episodes from the hero's early life, roughly equating to the first two acts of Wagner's *Siegfried*.

The three remaining sources, which are Scandinavian, were composed in Iceland, then a Norwegian colony, between 1150 and 1270. The *Poetic Edda* is a series of anonymous poems collected between 1150 and 1250. An important innovation of the *Poetic Edda* was the use of *Stabreim*—unrhymed lines containing alliteration on the beginning consonants of words—which Wagner adapted as the most distinctive poetic device in his own texts. The *Poetic Edda* relates to Siegfried's life, but it also includes elements important to *The Rhinegold*: how Loki (Loge) and Odin (Wotan) steal gold and a magic ring from the dwarf Andvari and use them to pay off a debt to a father and two brothers. One brother, Fafnir, kills both his kin and turns himself into a dragon to protect the hoard.

The *Volsunga Saga*, an anonymous prose narrative written in Iceland between 1200 and 1270, tells the stories of Siegmund and Sieglinde that we also encounter in Wagner's *The Valkyrie*. It contains many other dramatic details adopted by Wagner as well, such as the reforging of Siegmund's shattered sword by Siegfried.

The *Prose Edda* was written by Snorri Sturluson (1178–1241), an Icelandic nobleman, politician, and adventurer. The only medieval source of known authorship, it was written two centuries after Iceland's conversion to Christianity, perhaps in part to preserve a record of the old mythology. Its stories of the gods, rendered in an unusually vivid and sophisticated literary style, provided Wagner with background material for *The Rhinegold*.

Magee's research has been especially useful in showing how much Wagner drew on secondary sources, including contemporary academic and popular writings. He found the Grimm brothers' efforts helpful, but he also drew on other sources, including Friedrich Baron de la Motte Fouqué's dramatic trilogy *Sigurd der Schlangentödter* (Sigurd the Dragonslayer), Karl Simrock's complete translation of the *Poetic Edda* and his six-volume *Heldenbuch* (Book of Heroes), and F. J. Mone's reference work *Untersuchungen zur deutschen Heldensage* (Investigations into the German Heroic Sagas).

In *The Ring*, Wagner compressed and arranged these hundreds of stories and characters, often conflicting and in diverse styles, into an integrated, compelling poetic text—his greatest achievement as dramatist. Without ever losing touch with their mythological roots, the characters engage us both as convincing, distinct individuals and as archetypes and symbols of the subconscious.

In addition to the works of Magee and Cooke, *The Wagner Operas* by the eminent Wagner biographer and critic Ernest Newman provides a coherent summary of the changes Wagner made in the stories after he had completed his first prose sketch in 1848.[7]

Chronology of Wagner's Life and *The Ring*

Creating *The Ring* occupied Wagner, on and off, for about thirty years—from the early 1840s until the final notes were put to paper in 1874—and through August 1876 as he rehearsed and staged the first full performance of the cycle. This is the longest time span for the composition of any major piece of western music; *The Ring* as we know it was affected in many ways by the passage of so much time.

The years 1848–1852 were, in the words of Ernest Newman, Wagner's "long spell of intellectual and spiritual indigestion,"[8] a period of intense ferment and change in the composer's artistic life. During these years, he wrote no music[9] but articulated ideas and theories about music and drama which shaped not just the *Ring* operas (he wrote the *Ring* librettos at this time) but his other mature masterpieces as well *(Tristan and Isolde, The Mastersingers of Nuremberg,* and *Parsifal).* Though in exile and without apparent prospects, he also set forth ambitious plans for his own theater and for a *Ring* festival. Thus despite a hiatus in composing, Wagner emerged in 1853 as mature artist, prepared to begin work on the music for *The Ring.*

THE TEXTS

Wagner set forth the concept for the *Ring* story in a sketch, "The Nibelung Myth as Scheme for a Drama," in October 1848. Although he wrote the sketch in the proper dramatic order, Wagner composed the individual poems in reverse order of performance.[10] Just two weeks after completing the Nibelung sketch, he finished a prose plan for *Siegfried's Death,* later entitled *Twilight of the Gods.*

Agreeing with friends that the project would benefit from a description of earlier events in the hero's life, Wagner wrote the poem for *Young Siegfried,* which later became simply *Siegfried.* The *Valkyrie* text provided further information about Siegfried's Volsung forbears and the events leading to Brünnhilde's punishment. Wagner also felt that an introductory opera, *The Rhinegold,* was needed to depict the theft of the gold and the basic dilemma of the gods. Especially because of the central position of Wotan in the first three operas, we should keep in mind that Wagner started with the story of Siegfried.

He completed *The Rhinegold* poem in November 1852 and ultimately subtitled the entire *Ring* "A Festival-Stage-Play To Be Produced on Three Days and a Fore-Evening." He first read the four poems to a circle of Swiss friends in December 1852 and published a private edition of them in February 1853.

During this period Wagner also wrote the essay "The Wibelungs," described by Gutman as "a determined but confusing attempt to organize and clarify his reading and thinking on the Rhenish myths of Siegfried and the Nibelung hoard and their relationship to German history."[11] Wagner came to argue that myth, not history, was the proper stuff of music drama, and in order to demonstrate an impressive intellectual evolution toward that position, he later claimed that "The Wibelungs" predated the *Ring* writings. Recent scholarship has shown, however, that Wagner wrote "The Wibelungs" early in 1849, *after* both "The Nibelung Myth as Scheme for a Drama" and *Siegfried's Death.*[12]

As Wagner transformed his artistic persona during the years 1848 to 1852, he also changed and expanded his concept for *The Ring*. New characters, events, and information led to extensive revision of the texts, and he continued to add, delete, and revise as he put the texts to music over the ensuing two decades. Gutman has written, "Especially in the final two dramas, fascinating stratas of the cycle's literary formation lie pell-mell like abandoned rock in an exhausted quarry."[13]

The consistency of the texts is remarkable under these circumstances. Outright errors are exceedingly rare. In S-2-iii, for example, Mime incorrectly chides Alberich: "The giants tore [the ring] from your timorous hands!" when, in fact, it was Wotan who wrenched the ring from the Nibelung in R-iv. In T-1-i, Hagen advises Gunther that the Nibelungs have become Siegfried's slaves, a preposterous notion unsupported elsewhere in the texts. *Ring* advocates who are convinced the cycle is without flaw have sometimes tried to rationalize such discrepancies, which are more likely the unwitting failure of the poet to reconcile all revisions.

More complex and ambiguous are the questions of motivation and meaning raised by many of the characters' statements and actions. These have perplexed audiences ever since Wagner's friends first read the poems, and they still do.

Wagner's conventional optimism toward life changed significantly between his thirtieth (1843) and sixtieth (1873) years, and he adjusted *The Ring* accordingly. Among other fundamental changes, he altered the fate of the gods themselves. In the first sketch of 1848, Siegfried is the hero who *redeems* the gods. After restoring the ring to the Rhine and declaring Alberich and the Nibelungs to be free again, Brünnhilde brings the slain hero to Wotan in Valhalla: "One only shall rule, All-Father, Glorious One, Thou. This man I bring you as pledge of thy eternal might; good welcome give him, as is his desert!"[14]

As early as an 1851 revision, Wagner had replaced this happy and rather tidy conclusion with the necessary downfall of the race of gods—in the words of Ernest Newman, "not the eternal establishment of the power of the Gods but their annihilation by their own willing of that end."[15] However Brünnhilde's concluding peroration in T-3-iii may be interpreted, Wagner rewrote it frequently into the 1870s, making revisions even after the final text was published in 1872.[16]

Wagner's change of heart and mind has been examined in detail and ascribed to many things—his conversion to the philosophy of Schopenhauer, his exile from his homeland, even the *coup d'état* of Louis Napoleon at the end of 1851, which disappointed the revolutionaries of 1848 (like Wagner) and helped restore the old order in France. Wagner himself, when asked why the gods must perish if the gold is to be returned to the Rhine, responded defensively and evasively: "I feel that, at a good performance, the most simple-minded spectator will be in no doubt as to that point. . . . The necessity of this downfall springs from our innermost feelings, as it does from the innermost feelings of Wotan."[17]

Wagner's answer was also revelatory, for it shows how he intended to communicate to his audience an experience that was deliberately emotional, not rational. His response also sheds light on the resolution of a central issue throughout his *oeuvre*: the relationship between poetry and music. He began from a clear premise about the primacy of words, and he obstinately clung to this notion throughout his life. Yet as his music became more expressive, his arguments became more tortured and less convincing. He may have been the only one not to see how clearly, as Newman put it, "the musician in Wagner ruled the poet."[18]

THE MUSIC

In *My Life*, Wagner tells a story about a trip to Italy in September 1853 designed to refresh body and soul. Short of funds as usual, despondent without musical inspiration, and weakened by dysentery, he staggered into a hotel in La Spezia. Falling into

> a kind of somnolent state . . . I suddenly felt as though I were sinking in
> swiftly flowing water. The rushing sound formed itself in my brain into a
> musical sound . . . . These broken chords seemed to be melodic passages of
> increasing motion, yet the pure triad of E-flat major never changed. . . . I at
> once recognized that the orchestral overture to *The Rhinegold*, which must
> have lain latent within me, though it had been unable to find definite form,
> had at last been revealed to me.[19]

Scholars give general credence to the notion that the *Ring* music followed this incident. As Gutman states, "What for years had been fermenting deep in the unconscious was rising to the surface. . . . [After La Spezia, Wagner] was ready to give musical shape to his universe of water, vapor, and fire."[20]

In just four months, *The Rhinegold* was completed. *The Valkyrie* followed close behind, during the last six months of 1854. Wagner composed the first two acts of *Siegfried* from September 1856 to July 1857. Musical innovation continued throughout this period; indeed, the extent of Wagner's tinkering with the texts is overshadowed by the scope of his musical invention.

The Rhinegold represents a stunning break with Wagner's earlier musical output. *The Valkyrie* has an even more seamless motivic momentum, so self-assured, ripe, and melded with text that *The Rhinegold* sounds tentative and incipient by comparison. The process continues into *Siegfried*'s first two acts, where, according to opera analyst Charles Osborne, "Wagner [is] at his most lyrical [and the] score is the most joyous and orchestrally colorful of the entire tetralogy."[21]

And then for twelve years, no *Ring* music at all.[22] After composing the second act of *Siegfried*, Wagner turned to other matters. Various reasons are cited for the extended interregnum: the composer's growing weariness with the creative burden of the *Ring* project, his skepticism that the cycle could ever be staged, his need for money, his relationship with Mathilde Wesendonck, and a growing artistic imperative to compose the erotic and revolutionary *Tristan*. Gutman also suggests that "perhaps [Wagner] believed himself unready to depict musically the goddess turned woman,"[23] the Brünnhilde of S-3.

Between 1857 and 1869 Wagner tasted both the substantial patronage of King Ludwig II of Bavaria and a greatly enhanced reputation throughout Europe. There had been serious discussions about a Wagner theater to be built in Munich. And during this period he wrote not only *Tristan* but also the Paris *Tannhäuser* revisions and *The Mastersingers of Nuremberg*. In March 1869, idyllically happy with Cosima at Triebschen, Wagner turned back to *The Ring* to compose Act 3 of *Siegfried* with enthusiasm and even deeper dramatic powers. He began *Twilight of the Gods* later that year and finished in 1872.

Both music and text in *The Rhinegold* are marked by a relatively straightforward and unadorned exposition. The actions and emotions of the characters are causative and logical, virtually inevitable given the circumstances that motivate and constrain them. The action is intensely compressed and largely external; there are no long monologues and only glimpses of the yearning emotionalism and introspection of the subsequent operas. The story moves resolutely to its conclusion in a declarative and unsentimental manner reminiscent of the Greek dramas which so influenced Wagner (see "Origins," page 37).

As revolutionary as the music of *The Rhinegold* is, it is clearly an early version of Wagner's mature style. At times, Wagner seems to be feeling his way toward what has come to be called "endless melody" or "continuous music," music unbroken by self-contained numbers such as arias. Here also are references to the more conventional, even melodramatic romanticism of his earlier works. The motivic exposition is especially linear—a clear, largely sequential introduction of musical ideas.

By contrast, Act 3 of *Siegfried* bursts upon the listener, exultant with creative energy and release. Nowhere else in *The Ring* are the players drawn more deftly. The daunting challenge to paint the woman Brünnhilde musically is brilliantly accomplished. Hers is not the only descent from godhood so realized, for Wotan, too, appears at last in all his human majesty and weakness.

In *Twilight* Wagner's musical development runs its fullest course. Audiences and critics find its text the least credible in *The Ring*. Many are unconvinced or confused by the resort to magic potions and mistaken identities as dramatic devices of crucial importance. Siegfried's failure as hero and man is perplexing after so much preparation and promise.

The music of *Twilight* sweeps these concerns aside. Its textures are dense, and motive is piled on top of motive—hinting, combining, evolving. It is a triumph of music over poetry, for the music achieves a credibility and meaning virtually independent of words. As Newman has commented, "It would be impossible to make the tissue of *Das Rheingold* intelligible without the voices: but the orchestral part of *Götterdämmerung* would flow on with hardly a break if the vocal part were omitted."[24]

CHRONOLOGY

The following basic chronology looks at *The Ring*'s creative history relative to other milestones in Wagner's life and work, but of course readers are cautioned that even the historical facts—that Wagner wrote the texts and then wrote the music—can be misleading. Before the La Spezia epiphany and even before he took to writing the poems, for example, Wagner was conceptualizing the music for *The Ring*, the new music. In fact, the rhythms and structures of the texts were often shaped by musical ideas already notated by the composer, rather than the other way around. Bryan Magee, among the most prescient of contemporary Wagner critics, claims, as Wagner did, that "the initial seed germ from which each of his works sprang was musical . . . a vague yet insistent intimation of a possible sound-world that did not as yet exist."[25]

Dates in boldface designate *Ring*-related (and Bayreuth Festival–related) entries.

22 May 1813	Wilhelm Richard Wagner is born, Leipzig. His mother is Johanna Rosine Pätz Wagner. His legal father is Carl Friedrich Wagner, who dies 23 November 1813. His real father may be Ludwig Geyer, whom Johanna marries 28 August 1814. The family moves to Dresden.[26]
February 1815	A daughter, Cäcilie, is born to Johanna and Ludwig Geyer.

1821	Ludwig Geyer dies.
1822	Wagner enrolls in school as Wilhelm Richard Geyer.
1823	Shows early interest in Greek mythology and history.
Fall 1826	Mother and sisters Rosalie, Klara, Ottilie, and Cäcilie move to Prague. Wagner stays in school in Dresden.
1827	Leaves Dresden for Leipzig; changes his surname from Geyer to Wagner.
1828	Encounters Beethoven's music; begins composition lessons, Leipzig.
1829	Composes first piano sonatas and a string quartet.
1830	Writes piano arrangement of Beethoven's Ninth Symphony.
1831	Studies music briefly at Leipzig University.
1832	Concert Overture is performed in Leipzig. Symphony in C Major is performed in Prague. Writes other compositions and first opera libretto, *Die Hochzeit* (The Wedding).
1833	Writes libretto for first opera, *Die Feen* (The Fairies). Becomes chorus master in Würzburg.
1834	Completes composition of *Die Feen*. Begins work on *Das Liebesverbot* (The Ban on Love). Meets actress Minna Planer. Becomes music director at the Magdeburg theater.
1835	First visit to Bayreuth, in search of talent for Magdeburg.
29 March 1836	First performance of *Das Liebesverbot*.
24 November 1836	Marries Minna Planer, Königsberg.
1837	Becomes music director at Königsberg. Begins libretto of *Rienzi*. Marital and financial problems. Takes up new post as theater director in Riga.
1838	Conducts in Riga.
1839	Flees Riga creditors with Minna. Stormy voyage to London via Norway inspires idea for *The Flying Dutchman*. Arrives Paris.
1840	Completes *Rienzi*. Meets Liszt.
July–November 1841	Composes *The Flying Dutchman*.
20 October 1842	With Meyerbeer's help, *Rienzi* is premiered, Dresden, and is a great success.
2 January 1843	First performance of *The Flying Dutchman*, Dresden.
February 1843	Appointed Royal Saxon Court Conductor. Begins to study the Nibelung sources at the Royal Library and to amass his own collection of the sources.
July 1843–April 1845	Composes *Tannhäuser*.
October 1845	First performance of *Tannhäuser*, Dresden.
Summer 1846	Sketches *Lohengrin* music.
March 1847	Reads Aeschylus' *Oresteia*.

January 1848	His mother dies.
May 1846–April 1848	Composes *Lohengrin*.
June 1848	Publishes "A Project for the Organization of a German National Theater for the Kingdom of Saxony." Joins the radical political organization, the Vaterlandsverein. Meets Jessie Laussot.
4 October 1848	Completes first prose sketch, "The Nibelung Myth as Scheme for a Drama."
20 October 1848	Completes prose plan for *Siegfried's Death* (later entitled *Twilight of the Gods*).
November 1848	Completes poem (text, libretto) for *Siegfried's Death*.
February 1849	Revises poem of *Siegfried's Death*.
Early 1849	Publishes the essay "The Wibelungs." Develops sketch for an opera, *Jesus of Nazareth*.
May 1849	Participates in the Dresden uprising, flees Germany under indictment for treason, settles in Zurich.
July 1849	Writes "Art and Revolution."
November 1849	"The Art Work of the Future" is published.
February 1850	"Opera and Drama" is published.
March–May 1850	Affair with Jessie Laussot, Bordeaux. Returns to Minna in Zurich.
August 1850	Liszt produces first performance of *Lohengrin*, Weimar.
10 May 1851	Completes first prose sketch for *Young Siegfried* (later *Siegfried*).
24 May–1 June 1851	Writes prose plan for *Young Siegfried*.
3–24 June 1851	Writes poem for *Young Siegfried*.
November 1851	Completes first prose sketch for *The Rhinegold* and first prose sketch for *The Valkyrie*, Acts 1 and 2.
February 1852	Meets Mathilde Wesendonck.
Early 1852	Writes prose sketch for *The Valkyrie*, Act 3.
23–31 March 1852	Writes prose plan for *The Rhinegold*.
17–26 May 1852	Writes prose plan for *The Valkyrie*.
1 June–1 July 1852	Writes poem for *The Valkyrie*.
15 September–3 November 1852	Writes poem for *The Rhinegold*.
October–December 1852	Revises *Young Siegfried and Siegfried's Death*.
October 1852	Decides on final title: *Der Ring des Nibelungen*, "A Festival-Stage-Play to be Produced on Three Days and a Fore-Evening."
15 December 1852	Completes the *Ring* poems.

February 1853	Publishes a private edition of the *Ring* poems.
5 September 1853–14 January 1854	Composes *The Rhinegold*.
October 1853	Meets Cosima Liszt, age fifteen, Paris.
28 May 1854	Completes composition of *The Rhinegold*.
28 June–27 December 1854	Composes *The Valkyrie*.
Fall 1854	Reads Schopenhauer.
March–June 1855	Conducts in London. Meets pianist and future accompanist Karl Klindworth.
23 March 1856	Completes orchestral score of *The Valkyrie*.
16 May 1856	Prepares sketch for an opera, *Die Sieger* (The Victors).
22 September 1856–30 July 1857	Composes *Siegfried*, Acts 1 and 2.
April 1857	Moves with Minna to the Wesendonck estate at Asyl, near Zurich. In August, newlyweds Cosima and Hans von Bülow visit.
9 August 1857	Interrupts *Ring* composition for twelve years.
November 1857–May 1858	Composes "Wesendonck Lieder."
December 1857–July 1859	Composes *Tristan and Isolde*.
7 April 1858	Minna intercepts incriminating letter to Mathilde, leaves Asyl.
August 1858–March 1959	Wagner leaves Asyl for Venice. Completes second act of *Tristan* there on 18 March.
September 1859–August 1860	In Paris conducts concerts and revises *Tannhäuser*.
15 July 1860	Is granted political amnesty in all Germany except Saxony.
13–24 March 1861	Revised version of *Tannhäuser* performed in Paris, withdrawn after three tumultuous performances.
11 May 1861	Wagner hears *Lohengrin* for the first time, at a Vienna Opera rehearsal.
28 March 1862	Is granted political amnesty by King of Saxony, visits Saxony.
April 1862	Composes Prelude for *The Mastersingers of Nuremberg*. Conducts first performance on 1 November, Leipzig.
November 1862	Last meeting with Minna, Dresden.
26 December 1862–11 January 1863	Conducts extracts from *The Ring*, Vienna.
February–April 1863	Undertakes successful concert tour, St. Petersburg, Moscow.

25 March 1864	Evades creditors and debtor's prison, Vienna; flees to Switzerland.
3 May 1864	Is summoned to Munich by the new King of Bavaria, Ludwig II. First meeting 4 May.
July 1864	Begins affair with Cosima von Bülow, Munich.
10 April 1865	A daughter, Isolde, is born to Wagner and Cosima.
10 June 1865	First performance of *Tristan and Isolde*, Munich.
July 1865	Begins autobiography, *My Life*.
August 1865	Completes poem for *Parsifal*.
December 1865–April 1866	Scandal over his relationship with Cosima forces removal from Munich for Switzerland. Establishes house at Triebschen.
25 January 1866	Minna dies.
17 February 1867	A second daughter, Eva, is born to Wagner and Cosima.
24 October 1867	Completes composition of *The Mastersingers of Nuremberg*.
March 1868	Ludwig II breaks off negotiations for a Wagner theater in Munich.
21 June 1868	First performance of *The Mastersingers of Nuremberg*, Munich.
November 1868–April 1871	With Cosima at Triebschen.
8 November 1868	Meets Nietzsche.
1 March 1869	Resumes composition of *Siegfried*, Act 3. Completes *Siegfried* on 14 June.
6 June 1869	A son, Siegfried, is born to Wagner and Cosima.
22 September 1869	Ludwig stages first performance of *The Rhinegold*, Munich, against Wagner's wishes.
2 October 1869–5 June 1870	Composes Act 1 of *Twilight of the Gods*.
26 June 1870	Ludwig stages first performance of *The Valkyrie*, Munich, against Wagner's wishes.
18 July 1870	Cosima divorces von Bülow, marries Wagner on 25 August.
25 December 1870	Has concert piece, *Siegfried Idyll*, played for Cosima, Triebschen.
5 February 1871	Completes full score of *Siegfried*.
March 1871	Ludwig orders Wagner to produce *Siegfried* in Munich.
April 1871	Visits Bayreuth in search of Festspielhaus, or festival theater, location.
24 June–19 November 1871	Composes *Twilight of the Gods*, Act 2.
4 January–10 April 1872	Composes *Twilight of the Gods*, Act 3.

1 February 1872	Executive committee founded in Bayreuth to supervise organization of the festival.
22 May 1872	Festspielhaus foundation stone is laid, Bayreuth.
10 November–15 December 1872	Travels in search of *Ring* performers.
April 1873	Undertakes concert tour to raise funds: Hamburg, Berlin, Cologne, Kassel, Leipzig. These and other trips during 1873 do not raise enough to fund the festival.
20 February 1874	Bayreuth Festival funding crisis is solved by gift from Ludwig II.
28 April 1874	The Wagners move into new home, "Wahnfried," Bayreuth.
21 November 1874	Completes final score of *The Ring*.
February–April 1875	Undertakes fundraising tours for Bayreuth. Begins *Ring* rehearsals.
2 August 1875	First hears orchestra play in the Festspielhaus, Bayreuth.
Winter 1876	Receives $5000 from U.S. Independence celebration committee for composing "Centennial March."
August 1876	Affair with Judith Gautier.
13–17 August 1876	First public performance of the complete *Ring*, Bayreuth, followed by two additional cycles, through 30 August.
September–December 1876	Recuperative holiday in Italy is interrupted by fundraising tour of Italian cities in effort to cover festival deficit.
May 1877	Concert series in London.
August 1877–January 1882	Composes *Parsifal*.
September 1877	Announces plan for a music school in Bayreuth, which is not realized.
1878	Neumann stages *Ring* cycle, Leipzig.
31 March 1878	Agreement with Munich Treasury solves Bayreuth Festival financial crisis.
Summer 1878	Final break with Nietzsche.
25 December 1878	Private performance of the Prelude to *Parsifal*, Wahnfried.
1879	Works on composition of *Parsifal*.
4 January–30 October 1880	Is in Italy with family.
10 November 1880	Has last meeting with Ludwig II, Munich.
29 March 1881	Helps Neumann stage a *Ring* cycle in Berlin; suffers possible heart attack after final curtain. Health problems delay composition of *Parsifal*.

November 1881–April 1882	Is in Italy with family, returning to Bayreuth on 1 May.
13 January 1882	Completes composition of *Parsifal*.
22 July 1882	First performance of *Parsifal* at the second Bayreuth Festival. Fifteen additional performances through 29 August.
September 1882	To Venice.
13 February 1883	Wagner dies, Palazzo Vendramin, Venice. Funeral at Bayreuth, February 18.

Bayreuth

Wagner's ideas for a Nibelung opera and for a new national theater devoted to his own works, indeed for reforming German art as a whole, were inextricably linked. These plans, outrageously ambitious at the time, took shape in the late 1840s; they were fully realized at the same time and place more than twenty-five years later.

ORIGINS

The Bayreuth Festival grew out of Wagner's view that German art had become corrupt. His prescriptions for curing this condition, and his most important theoretical essays, were written and published in 1849–1850 at the start of his political exile in Switzerland. Among these was "A Project for the Organization of a German National Theater for the Kingdom of Saxony."

During this period Wagner composed no music, but he was working on *The Ring*. As we have seen, he completed the first prose sketch, "The Nibelung Myth as Scheme for a Drama," in October 1848 and the first draft of the entire *Ring* poem in December 1852.

Like other reformers of the time, Wagner found artistic ideals in Greek tragedy, in which all arts—drama, music, and dance, had been combined. The Greek works had an ethical, instructive purpose and were often directly based on the eternal truth of myth. In Wagner's view, Germany's cultural decline had reached a nadir, especially in opera, the most "frivolous, vulgar, socially exclusive and contentless" of the contemporary arts.[27]

Opera, said Wagner, was in need of revolution. He conceived of a new "total art work" (in German *Gesamtkunstwerk*) in which drama, music, and dance would once more be mutually supportive and which would deal with only the most serious issues of the day. Wagner said he would build on the sublime achievements of Shakespeare and Beethoven to create such works, which he described in all their musical, theatrical, cultural, and spiritual detail. Reflecting Germany's mythological heritage, his new music dramas would redeem the German people and culture.

Wagner's plan included a new theater designed and administered for the sole purpose of performing these works of the future. In 1851 he wrote, "I shall erect a theater by the Rhine, and I shall send out invitations to a great dramatic festival . . . I shall stage the whole cycle in the course of *four* days."[28]

THE TOWN OF BAYREUTH

Wagner first visited Bayreuth in 1835. As the twenty-two-year-old music director at the theater in Magdeburg, he was traveling through Germany seeking operatic talent. Bayreuth is in Franconia, northern Bavaria, about 130 miles north of Munich, and thirty miles northeast of Nuremberg. Bayreuth's only cultural attraction before Wagner was its baroque theater, built in the middle of the eighteenth century for the Margrave Wilhelmine, sister of Frederick the Great. Its huge stage, the deepest in Germany, made a strong impression on Wagner in 1835.

Sex and politics affected the eventual selection of Bayreuth as much as artistic considerations. Wagner's visible though illicit relationship with Cosima, the illegitimate daughter of Liszt and the wife of Hans von Bülow—a friend, admirer, and conductor and tireless advocate of Wagner's works—created a substantial scandal in Munich in 1864. Soon after Wagner and Cosima arrived in the Bavarian capital, anti-Wagner feelings were stirred up by those who opposed Wagner, who envied his support from Ludwig II, or who simply wanted to embarrass the king for political purposes. Deliberately misleading Ludwig about their liaison, Wagner and Cosima fled the poisoned atmosphere of Munich for Switzerland in 1865.

The real process of finding a home for the new theater and festival began in the late 1860s. By that time, Wagner's reputation had been established by the successes of *Tristan and Isolde* and *The Mastersingers*. His support from Ludwig, beginning in 1864, had encouraged him to believe that his remarkable ambitions could actually be realized. Plans for a Wagner theater in Munich were drawn up by Wagner's architect friend, Gottfried Semper. The size and cost of Semper's design, however, discouraged Ludwig's ministers, and even Ludwig.

Moreover, king and composer were to have a falling out over Wagner's financial excesses, the eventual strain of the von Bülow affair, and Ludwig's determination to stage the already completed *Rhinegold* and *Valkyrie* in Munich, without waiting for the two unfinished *Ring* operas, the Wagner theater, the Wagner festival—or Wagner. The king, as copyright holder, had a legal right to stage the works; despite Wagner's bitter resistance, each was performed three times in June–July 1870. Hoping for a fiasco, Wagner brooded at his home in Triebschen, Switzerland, but the premieres were a great success.

Wagner's attention was thus focused on the need for a *Ring* theater and festival with an administrative and political structure, outside Munich, that he could control. The rise of Prussia favored Bayreuth. Prussia's power and influence had clearly eclipsed Bavaria's by the late 1860s, and Prussia's *de facto* leadership of the German states was confirmed by the victory over France in 1870–1871. Bayreuth's location between Munich and Berlin seemed to represent a geographical middle ground from which Wagner might play Prussia and Bavaria against each other for support, although in the end neither the Prussian Kaiser Wilhelm II nor his minister Otto von Bismarck was of much help.

Wagner and Cosima visited Bayreuth in April 1871. They immediately saw that the Margrave's theater was too baroque for the reformist purpose and primitive ambience of *The Ring* and that it had too few seats. Despite interest from other cities in and outside of Germany, they nevertheless pressed ahead in selling the festival scheme, including a new theater, to the town elders. Wagner painted a picture of national glory to be associated with his plan. He told them Bayreuth would become the new and independent capital of German thought—"a sort of Washington of art."[29] The town leaders welcomed the proposal with enthusiasm, shrewdly anticipating the prestige and revenues it would ultimately bring.

The Bayreuth town council contributed the theater site just north of town, atop a little green hill. In April 1872, with construction of the theater's foundations already underway, Wagner moved to Bayreuth with Cosima and the children, where he at once became the town's most famous citizen. The cornerstone of the new theater was laid on Wagner's fifty-ninth birthday—22 May 1872.

FINANCES

Finding the money to pay for constructing and equipping the theater and for establishing the festival's administration, costumes, crews, and casts was more daunting for Wagner than composing *The Ring*. The problem of spending too much money and having to raise more was a central and constant fact of Wagner's life. He developed an enormous talent for begging, wheedling, and demanding loans from others—and for not paying them back.

His fundraising efforts for Bayreuth were Herculean. In just the six months from November 1872 to April 1873, he visited:

Würzburg Frankfurt Darmstadt Mannheim Darmstadt Stuttgart Strasbourg Wiesbaden Mainz Cologne Düsseldorf Hanover Bremen Dessau Leipzig Bayreuth Dresden Berlin Hamburg Schwerin Berlin Bayreuth Cologne Kassel Leipzig Bayreuth.[30]

Wagner societies were established all over Germany to raise funds. Even so, funding was insufficient; Ludwig saved the project with eleventh-hour contributions in 1874.

THE HOUSE

Semper's plan for the unbuilt Wagner theater in Munich was adapted to the Bayreuth location by the architects Carl Brandt and Otto Brückwald. In order to save money, Brandt and Brückwald eliminated much of the ornamentation of the original Semper design, using less expensive materials—wood, brick, and canvas rather than the original marble and stone—for the internal structure and external finish.

Drawing on his knowledge of other theaters, especially the theater in Riga, Wagner was intimately involved in the design, and the Festspielhaus remains a spectacular achievement. The acoustics of the house, considered perfect by generations of festivalgoers, are attributed to the arrangement of the seats, the absence of side boxes, and the plaster of the interior walls and the ceiling canvas. (Cheaper building materials thus provided unintended benefits.) The fanlike

Bayreuth: the Festspielhaus interior. Patrons enter from six doorways on each side; there is no center aisle.

arrangement of identical, uncomfortable wooden seats also had a democratic purpose; Wagner intended to do away with social stratification within the audience by eliminating different classes of seats.

The most prominent feature in the theater was Wagner's innovative treatment of the sunken orchestra, which he called the "mystic abyss." He placed the front of the orchestra pit lower than normal, below stage level, from which point it slopes even further down and under the stage. The strings were positioned in the front, the louder horns and winds lower at the back. An inwardly curved cowl was wrapped around and above the front of the pit, and an adjustable sound screen was placed at the front of the stage. Thus the sound projected first backward onto the stage, then out into the hall.

This severe suppression of orchestral sound means that the singers are audible to a degree found in few, if any, other major houses. Wagner was equally concerned, however, with the visual effect. He did not want viewers to be distracted by the gestures of the conductor or musicians, nor to see them as a realistic point of reference that would compromise the artificial sight perspectives on the stage.

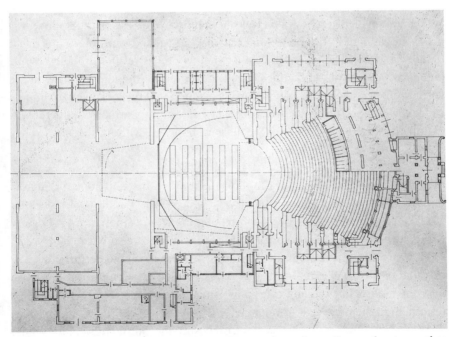

The fanlike seating plan, with no side boxes, focuses viewers' attention on the stage rather than each other.

AUDITORIUM   STAGE

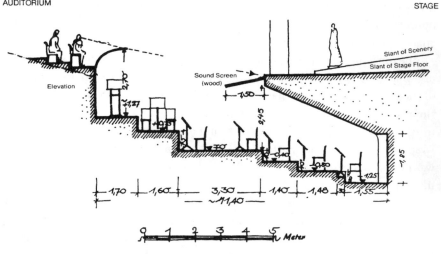

Wagner placed the conductor and orchestra out of the audience's view, but singers have trouble seeing him, too. There is no prompter's box.

The design of the orchestra pit was not so much a concession to the singers as it was an element in Wagner's "total art work" in which beautiful singing, clear diction, and believable acting were as vital as orchestral performance. While audiences, musicians, and critics have widely praised the unique clarity of the vocal acoustics, a few *Ring* conductors have found that the arrangement unduly suppresses orchestral clarity and, especially, power; the German conductor Wilhelm Furtwängler even tried to have the cowl removed, without success.[31]

THE FIRST FESTIVAL—1876

In addition to the challenges of fundraising for his work and constructing the Festspielhaus, Wagner was consumed by a wide range of additional tasks after 1871, not the least of which was completing the composition of *The Ring*. He wrote the final notes and text of *Twilight of the Gods* in November 1874.

He also took personal control of securing singers who could perform this new material of unprecedented difficulty. He assembled an orchestra of the finest instrumentalists in Germany, most of whom agreed to play for expenses only, a testament to their respect for Wagner.

Wagner dominated rehearsals of the orchestra (most observers credit Wagner as a conductor without equal) and of the singer/actors; he supervised the stagehands, the property crew, the set and costume designers, the ticket sellers, and anyone else connected with the festival. Today most opera companies are unable to mount new productions of an entire *Ring* cycle; the bravest typically introduce a new production of only one opera per season. The challenge of staging four revolutionary works in one season in 1876 is difficult to imagine.

The sources give a clear picture of Wagner himself at the center of every activity during the six weeks of rehearsals: sliding down Alberich's rocks, demonstrating Sieglinde's embrace of Siegmund, and teaching the Rhine Daughters how to "swim," the singers how to sing Wagner, and the orchestra how to play his music. Witnesses recount that he even stood on his head to keep spirits up during a period of drooping morale: "He is director, producer, coach, conductor, singer, actor, stage manager, stage hand and prompter."[32]

A glittering audience attended the first cycle: among the notables were Kaiser Wilhelm, King Ludwig, Emperor Dom Pedro II of Brazil, and Nietzsche. Leading composers of the day also came, including Bruckner, Gounod, Grieg, Liszt, Saint-Saëns, and Tchaikovsky.

The performances themselves, by all accounts, were mixed. The orchestra played superbly—Wagner had done well to bring the best musicians to Bayreuth and rehearse with them for weeks—although afterward he was sharply critical of the conductor, Hans Richter.

Wagner was satisfied with most of the singers but generally disappointed with the visual aspects, the Brückner brothers' scenery in particular. Some special effects were successful, notably the swimming Rhine Daughters, but the technical innovations involving light and steam only hinted of their potential. Great mirth greeted the dragon: it had been made in London, and not all the pieces arrived in time for the performance. Many rough edges of the first cycle were smoothed in the subsequent two; Wagner was enraged that further reviews hardly noted the improvements.[33]

Critics readily noticed innovations that created a thrilling intimacy between audience and the stage: the perfect sight lines, the unseen conductor and orchestra, the removal of the prompter's box, and the darkened auditorium.

Yet abysmal food, inadequate housing, arduous travel, the long walk up the Green Hill, the summer heat, the general lack of amenities in the provincial town—all these complicated the proceedings and dampened the general enthusiasm. Many attendees could not summon the necessary stamina and faded away before the final performance.

Ticket sales further eroded the original ideal. The need for funds had obliged Wagner to give up the notion that tickets would be distributed without charge to the common people, who would come out of high regard for his art. Instead, the precedent of high prices was established from the beginning, and many Bay-reuthers scalped complimentary tickets for the first cycle, creating a reputation for expense without enhancing festival coffers.

The first cycle was sold out, but many tickets remained for the second and third.[34] In any case, by the close of the festival Wagner was profoundly depressed, whether from exhaustion, a sense of anticlimax, or the performances' many shortcomings and the criticisms leveled at them. He let it be known that he con-sidered the German people unworthy of the great gift he had made available to them.

The financial results of the first festival were catastrophic. In view of the huge deficit, plans for 1877 were dropped. It was not until 1882 that a second festival was held, devoted entirely to the premiere and fifteen additional performances of *Parsifal.* Toward the end of the final performance, Wagner struggled into the pit, took the baton from Hermann Levi, and conducted the opera to its conclusion. The composer died the following February.

CHAPTER TWO

THE STORY

THE LONG and complex tale of *The Ring* is peculiarly elusive: even experienced Wagnerians need to refresh their memories at times and in so doing commonly encounter previously unnoticed or perhaps forgotten nuance, detail, or motivation.

There is no substitute for reading and rereading the texts with care, whether in German or English, but the synopses that follow provide a thorough grounding in the *Ring* story. The story is presented here as Wagner wrote it, without interpretation or explanation. Based strictly on the librettos and on Wagner's stage directions, these synopses convey the most important thoughts and utterances of the players and describe their significant actions and gestures. And finally, Wagner's set descriptions, accompanied by photographs, offer us a clear picture of the physical appearance of the stage.

It is primarily in their fidelity to Wagner's texts and directions that the synopses in this chapter differ from the many *Ring* summaries written over the past century. Most often I have closely paraphrased the characters' words rather than broadly summarizing them. I have also quoted the statements that best convey the color and flavor of character and story.

Wagner was no ordinary dramatist or director, and he left us with a wealth of guidance, often very specific, on the scenery, physical actions, and emotional gestures he wanted. Thus the visual aspects—the scenery and stage directions—receive careful attention here. Wagner was not inflexible in these matters; he directed only one *Ring* cycle, in 1876 (although he "assisted" Angelo Neumann's

1881 Berlin staging of the cycle), and during rehearsals he was at times open to suggestions.

A strict reading of Wagner's stage directions is not an idle exercise; it reveals how much they clarify and enhance the words and music. These instructions are often changed or ignored today, despite Wagner's overriding objective that all elements, audible and visible, should support and illuminate each other.

Photographs of stage sets in this chapter are taken from the Metropolitan Opera's *Ring* production from the late 1980s and early 1990s, a production that stages the action in settings materially consistent with Wagner's directions. (See "Staging *The Ring*" in the Appendix.)

As throughout this book, all text quotations are from the translations by Lionel Salter (*The Rhinegold, Siegfried,* and *Twilight of the Gods*) and William Mann (*The Valkyrie*). Set and stage directions are from *The Ring of the Nibelungen Vocal Scores,* which since 1904 have been published in the United States by G. Schirmer, Inc., and which employ the translations of Frederick Jameson. The Schirmer scores come from the authorized vocal scores published by B. Schotts Söhne in 1900 as arranged for the piano by Wagner's accompanist, Karl Klindworth.

THE RHINEGOLD

Scene i
48
At the Bottom of the Rhine
The Three Rhine Daughters · Alberich

Scene ii
49
An Open Space on a Mountain Height near the Rhine
Wotan · Fricka · Freia · Fasolt · Fafner · Donner · Froh · Loge

Scene iii
52
The Subterranean Caves of Nibelheim
Alberich · Mime · Wotan · Loge · Nibelungs

Scene iv
53
The Same Open Space on a Mountain Height
Alberich · Wotan · Loge · Fricka · Donner · Froh · Freia · Fasolt · Fafner · Erda
Nibelungs · Rhine Daughters

The Voices

THE RHINE DAUGHTERS
Woglinde · Soprano
Wellgunde · Soprano
Flosshilde · Mezzo-Soprano

Alberich, a Nibelung dwarf · Baritone

THE GODS
Wotan, leader of the gods · Baritone
Fricka, wife of Wotan · Mezzo-Soprano
Freia, Fricka's sister, goddess of love · Soprano
Donner, Freia's brother, the storm god · Baritone
Froh, Freia's brother, the fair god · Tenor
Loge, half-god of fire · Tenor

THE GIANTS
Fasolt · Baritone
Fafner · Bass

Mime, a Nibelung, Alberich's brother · Tenor
Erda, the Wala, the eternal wise woman and Earth Mother · Mezzo-Soprano

Scene iv

Scene i

At the bottom of the Rhine—greenish twilight, lighter at the top with water moving swiftly from right to left, a gloomy mist below. Rocks jut up everywhere. Darkness at the sides indicates deeper fissures.

The first Rhine Daughter, Woglinde, circles gracefully, sporting joyfully in the depths: "Weia! Waga! Waft your waves, ye waters! Carry your crests to the cradle! Wagalaweia! Wallala weiala weia!"

She is joined by her sisters, first Wellgunde and then Flosshilde, who warns the other two to do a better job of guarding the gold. They play like fish, darting among the rocks.

Alberich, a Nibelung dwarf, emerges from a dark chasm below and watches the maidens with increasing excitement. He calls out to them, or any one of them, to come to him to "frisk and frolic." The maidens swim down to take a look at the repugnant intruder, and Flosshilde tells her sisters: "Guard the gold! Father warned us of such a foe." But seeing that Alberich's intentions are only amorous, she laughs at her fears.

They decide to teach Alberich a lesson for his lascivious effrontery. Woglinde tells him to come close but easily avoids his clumsy groping. Wellgunde calls to him but rejects the swarthy, sulphurous dwarf. Flosshilde, too, leads him on only to mock him mercilessly. Each rejection is punctuated with the maidens' derisive laughter.

It is Alberich's turn to hurl insults: "Worthless, sly, sluttish, dissolute wenches! Do you feed only on fraud, you faithless brood of nymphs?" They scold him, but he vows to have one of them.

A glow begins to penetrate the waters from above, gradually focusing, in a dazzlingly bright gleam, on the gold resting on a high rock—a magical, golden light spreads through the water. The three maidens with joy and reverence liken this to a female sun waking the male gold.

Alberich asks what gleams in the water. The Rhine Daughters upbraid him for not recognizing the Rhinegold, and they invite him to sport with them in its splendor. When he asks if the gold has any purpose beyond their games, Wellgunde reveals its fateful secret: "He who from the Rhinegold fashioned the ring that would confer on him immeasurable might could win the world's wealth for his own."

Flosshilde scolds her sisters: their father had told them this secret and ordered them to guard the treasure diligently. But her sisters reassure Flosshilde, reminding her that "only he who forswears love's power, only he who forfeits love's delight, only he can attain the magic to fashion the gold into a ring." They are sure

that no person could reject love, least of all the lascivious dwarf. Flosshilde is persuaded and once again calls to the gnome to swim with them joyfully in the
golden glow.

But Alberich has decided that if he cannot win love, he might nevertheless
gain lustful pleasure through the power of the ring. He approaches the gold,
warning the Rhine Daughters, "Mock on then! The Nibelung nears your toy!"
They scream in sudden fear: love has made him mad.

With a final spring Alberich reaches the summit and takes hold of the gold:
"Are you still not afraid? Then coquet in the dark, brood of the waters! I will put
out your light, wrench the gold from the rock, forge the ring of revenge; for hear
me, ye waves: thus I curse love!"

He tears the gold from the rock with terrible force and plunges with it hastily
into the depths, where he disappears. The nymphs cry for help, diving down after
the robber as darkness falls.

Alberich's mocking laughter is heard from the lowest depths.

Scene ii

*The rocks have disappeared in the darkness, and the stage is filled with black waves
that seem to sink downward, creating the impression that the theater is rising. The
waves gradually become lighter and change into clouds and then a fine mist,
which in turn dissolves to reveal an open space on a mountaintop. Wotan and
Fricka are sleeping on a flowery bank.*

*The dawning day brightens the stage and illuminates a castle with glittering
pinnacles on the top of a cliff in the background. A deep valley, through which the
Rhine is presumed to flow, separates the cliff from the foreground.*

Fricka wakes and, seeing the castle, wakens her dreaming husband. He opens his
eyes and admires the completed castle: "The gods' stronghold superbly soars . . . .
As in my dreams I desired it, as my will directed, strong and fair it stands on show,
sublime, superb structure!"

Fricka angrily calls his attention to the bargain he has made with the giants for
building the castle—the pledge of her sister, Freia. She would have prevented the
bargain had she known of it, but the women had not been told. She is appalled at
the men's thirst for power.

Wotan tells her to pay no heed to the price. Fricka admits that she, too, wanted
the castle, but only as a stately dwelling to keep Wotan home and to end his roaming. He knows she wanted to see him confined at home, but to win the world he
must roam and will not give up the sport.

She rebukes him for "staking love and a woman's worth" against "idle toys of might and dominion." He reminds her that for her love he has put an eye at risk, and that he values women even more than she likes: he has never intended to give up Freia, who now enters fleeing the pursuing giants.

Although Wotan reassures Fricka once more, he asks if she has seen Loge. She berates Wotan for putting his faith in "that trickster" who has harmed the gods in the past and who counseled Wotan to make the disastrous bargain for Freia. But Wotan now relies on Loge's craft and cunning to deliver Freia.

Fasolt and Fafner, of gigantic stature and armed with clubs, enter, seeking Freia as payment for their labors, as agreed. Wotan tells them that he was only joking about the wage and that they should name some other fee. Fafner scoffs at his brother for trusting the gods. Fasolt warns Wotan about breaking his word—"What you are, you are only by contracts"—and he chides the gods: "How foolishly you strive for towers of stone, and place in pledge woman's beauty."

Fafner ridicules Fasolt for his genuine infatuation with Freia. He has no use for her but knows the gods depend on her to tend the golden apples that will keep them youthful: they will waste away without her. Fafner wants to take her away from them.

Freia again calls for deliverance, and this time her brothers, Froh and Donner, rush in to save her. As Donner swings his hammer and approaches the giants, Wotan stretches his spear between them: "Hold, hothead! Violence avails nought! My spearshaft protects bonds: spare your hammer's haft."

Just in time, Loge comes up out of the valley. Wotan chastises him for leaving him in this predicament. Loge feigns innocence and broadly praises the castle built by Fasolt and Fafner, pointedly confirming that they have satisfied their part of the contract.

Exasperated, Wotan warns Loge not to betray his trust, since he is Loge's only friend among the gods. He agreed to pledge Freia only because Loge promised to find an alternative. Fricka, Froh, and Donner vilify the evasive Loge, but Wotan reminds them Loge's advice is more valuable the longer he delays in giving it.

Finally Loge tells his story. He has roamed the world to find a substitute for Freia but has found only one man willing to give up love and womankind. Rejected by the Rhine Daughters, he says, "Night-Alberich" has renounced love to gain the Rhinegold. The maidens bemoan their loss and seek Wotan's help in regaining it. Wotan explodes: he is in trouble himself; how can he help others?

Fasolt grudges Alberich the gold; the Nibelung has already done much harm to the giants. Fafner worries that the Nibelung will plot great mischief if he gains the power of the gold.

Loge confirms that a ring forged from the gold "would bestow supreme power and win its master the world." Wotan says he has indeed heard rumors of the gold and its potential power.

Fricka wonders if the gold could equally serve as a woman's adornment, and Loge assures her that the bright ornaments could ensure a husband's fidelity. Impressed, Fricka is the first to suggest the possibility that Wotan himself might secure the gold.

Wotan now says it would seem wise for him to control the gold. He asks Loge how he could learn to forge the ring of power. Loge tells Wotan this is easy: by renouncing love. Wotan turns away in ill humor. Loge says Wotan will not renounce love, but in any case, it is too late: Alberich has already forged the ring and gained its power.

Now the gods are not merely interested; they are alarmed by a mortal threat. Wotan determines to secure the ring without renouncing love himself. But how? "By theft!" says Loge. "What a thief stole, you steal from the thief."

He urges Wotan to bring Alberich to justice by returning the gold to the Rhine Daughters, but Wotan again dismisses the idea. Fricka adds that she does not even want to hear of that watery brood that has, to her sorrow, seduced many men.

But Fafner has also been listening to Loge's tale. He takes Fasolt aside and assures him the gold is worth more than Freia, for it is the path to "eternal youth." Fafner tells Wotan the giants will accept the Nibelung's gold in place of Freia.

Wotan rebuffs the insolent demand. The giants take hold of Freia and say they will hold her ransom until that evening when they will return. If the gold is not given over then, Freia will be forfeit forever. They rush her away to their domain, Riesenheim.

Froh and Donner begin to pursue the giants, but a pale mist fills the stage and the gods appear pale and wan.

Loge realizes what has happened: the gods wither without Freia's apples! He is unaffected; he is only half as godlike as the others and to him Freia was always niggardly with the precious fruit. But he knows that for the others, Freia's bounty is vital; without her apples the race of gods will grow old and die.

Wotan at last shakes himself awake and orders Loge to go with him to Nibelheim. For the third time Loge pleads on behalf of the Rhine Daughters, but Wotan wants to hear no more of them. Wotan does not even want to pass by the Rhine to reach Nibelheim, so Loge suggests they go through a cleft in the rocks. He disappears into a crevice from which a sulphurous vapor immediately begins to rise.

Wotan bids the others wait until evening when he will return with the gold. Fricka, Froh, and Donner bid him farewell and good luck, and Wotan, too, disappears into the cleft.

Scene iii

As Wotan and Loge enter the cleft, its sulphurous vapor spreads over the stage and the remaining gods are lost to view. The mist turns into a black cloud that rises from below so that the theater seems to sink. A rocky chasm emerges.

A ruddy glow shines in the distance, to the clamor of the Nibelung smiths. A subterranean chasm appears with clefts running off on all sides.

Alberich enters from a side passage, dragging his brother, Mime. He demands to know if Mime has finished making the magic helmet, or Tarnhelm, as ordered. The terror-stricken Mime avoids the question but accidently drops the metalwork, which Alberich grabs.

Alberich tests the helmet by invoking its power to make the wearer invisible: the helmet works, and he takes advantage of it to smack Mime violently. Still invisible and now even more lethal with the Tarnhelm, Alberich exultantly warns all the Nibelungs that he watches everywhere, though he cannot be seen; he is truly Lord of the Nibelungs! He leaves the stage to Mime.

Wotan and Loge arrive. They hear Mime moaning, and Loge offers to help. Mime tells them about Alberich's ring and the enslavement of the Nibelungs. Gone is the time when they happily made trinkets for their women; they are now forced by the power of the ring to mine a new hoard of gold each day. Mime had hoped to secure the Tarnhelm's magic for himself so that he could free himself and enslave Alberich, but he could not have guessed the Tarnhelm's power.

Loge and Wotan laugh at Mime's sad story. Wotan encourages Loge in his cunning against Alberich, and again Loge promises to free the Nibelungs from their misery.

Alberich returns, whipping his Nibelung slaves before him as they pile up the gold they have mined and fashioned for him that day. He notices Wotan and Loge, and drives Mime back into the Nibelung pack.

Alberich draws the ring from his finger, kisses it, and displays it threateningly: "Tremble with terror, abject throng: at once obey the master of the ring!" With howls and shrieks, Mime and the rest scatter in all directions.

Alberich now turns roughly to Wotan and Loge, accusing them of coming to Nibelheim out of envy. Loge chides Alberich for his unfriendliness—in the past have not Loge's flames warmed him and fired his forge? Alberich, noting that his one-time friend now consorts with the race of gods, expresses faith only in Loge's faithlessness and defies them all.

Loge flatters Alberich for his great wealth, but Wotan wonders what use it can be in a place like Nibelheim. Alberich, confident in his power to increase the golden hoard, openly reveals his plan: with the power of the ring and the gods' natural greed, he'll have the gods themselves in his "golden grasp! As I renounced love, all living things shall renounce it! . . . For gold alone you shall hunger. The dwarf will take his pleasure with your pretty women . . . Beware! . . . the Nibelung horde [will rise] from the silent depths to the daylight!"

Wotan is enraged by this blasphemy, but Loge continues to flatter Alberich and asks how the Nibelung can safeguard the valuable ring. The dwarf confidently assures Loge that the Tarnhelm makes him safe, even from Loge, but Loge will not believe in it until he sees its magic.

Boastfully, Alberich turns himself into a giant serpent. Loge feigns terror, and Wotan has a good laugh at the trick. But, says Loge, he doubts that Alberich can also make himself tiny—a clever way to avoid danger. Alberich, falling into the trap, takes the shape of a tiny toad.

At Loge's urging, Wotan immediately puts his foot on the toad; Loge seizes the Tarnhelm, and Alberich reappears, squirming under Wotan's foot. Loge quickly ties him up; dragging the violently struggling Alberich, Loge and Wotan disappear into a cleft to begin the climb back up.

Scene iv

The scene changes until the open place on the mountaintop appears again, still shrouded in a pale mist.

Wotan and Loge emerge from the cleft dragging Alberich, their bound prisoner. They mock his dream of world dominion; he rails against the thieves and vows vengeance.

Loge reminds Alberich he cannot take revenge until he is free, informing him that he must relinquish the golden treasure as ransom. Alberich is appalled but agrees, telling himself that all he really needs to keep is the ring. Loge unties Alberich's right hand so that he may touch the ring to his lips and secretly murmur the command that will summon the Nibelungs and the gold.

To Alberich's great humiliation, the Nibelungs climb up out of the cleft before their captive master. They pile up the gold. Holding out the ring once more, he commands them to return to the pits, warning that he will follow close behind. The Nibelungs cower as if struck, then rush back into the cleft.

Alberich demands the return of the Tarnhelm, but Loge says that it, too, is forfeit. Alberich again suppresses his rage, knowing that if he keeps just the ring, he can force Mime to fashion another magic helmet.

Loge asks Wotan if he is satisfied, but now Wotan demands the ring, too. "My life, but not the ring!" Alberich shrieks, suddenly desperate. Wotan ridicules Alberich's claim of ownership, asking if the Rhine's daughters willingly gave him their gold.

Frantically Alberich accuses:

> Thief, do you throw on me the blame for what you so dearly desired? How gladly you yourself would have robbed the Rhine of its gold had you so easily found the way to forge it! . . . Take heed, haughty god! If I sinned I sinned only against myself: but you, immortal one, sin against all that was, is and shall be if you recklessly seize my ring!

Wotan has heard enough and violently tears the ring from Alberich's finger. Alberich cries out: "Crushed! Shattered! Of wretches the wretchedest slave!"

Wotan contemplates the ring, which will now make him the mightiest of mighty lords. He slips the ring onto his finger.

With Wotan's consent, Loge unties the dwarf and urges him to go freely on his way. Alberich raises himself, laying down his curse in a demented rage:

> Am I free now? Truly free? Then thus I give you my freedom's first greeting! Since by curse it came to me, accursed be this ring! . . . Whoever possesses it shall be consumed with care, and whoever has it not be gnawed with envy! . . . Its owner shall guard it profitlessly, for through it he shall meet his executioner! Forfeit to death, faint with fear shall he be fettered; the length of his life he shall long to die, the ring's master to the ring a slave, until again I hold in my hands what was stolen! Thus, in direst distress, the Nibelung blesses his ring! Keep it now, guard it well; my curse you cannot escape!

He disappears into the cleft.

The stage lightens. Loge spies Fafner and Fasolt returning with Freia. In the dispersing mist Fricka, Froh, and Donner are again visible; they approach Wotan. The misty veil remains at the back, concealing the castle.

Fricka asks Wotan if he brings good news, and Loge points to the gold. Froh welcomes the fresh breezes that return with Freia. Fricka moves to embrace her sister, but Fasolt stops her: they have guarded her honorably and now claim the ransom.

Wotan points out that the gold lies ready. Fasolt says the pain of leaving Freia is so great that she must be blocked from his view by the heaped-up treasure. Wotan agrees that Freia's form will be the measure. Fafner plants the giants' clubs on either side of Freia, and Loge and Froh begin to pile the gold between them.

Fricka reviles Wotan for this latest humiliation at the hands of the ignorant giants. Unable to contain his rage, Donner again threatens the giants, but Wotan intervenes once more to keep the peace. When the gold is piled up, Fafner says he still spies Freia's golden hair behind the hoard and demands that the Tarnhelm be added to the pile to block out the sight. Like Alberich before him, Wotan gives up the Tarnhelm.

Now Fasolt examines the pile. Still seeing Freia's eyes through a tiny opening, he cannot tear himself away from her. Fafner spies the ring on Wotan's finger and demands that it be used to fill the crack.

Wotan is aghast. Loge tells the giants that the gold belongs to the Rhine Daughters, to whom Wotan will return it. Wotan again rejects any such obligation, no matter what Loge has promised, and vows to keep the ring. Fafner, Fricka, Froh, and Donner all appeal to Wotan, but he steadfastly refuses to give up the ring.

The stage has grown dark. A bluish light breaks from a rocky cleft in which a woman suddenly becomes visible. She stretches out her hand: "Yield, Wotan, yield! Escape from the ring's curse. To dark destruction irredeemably its possession dooms you."

Wotan asks the woman who she is. She answers: Erda, the eternal world's first ancestress. She has borne three daughters, the Norns, conceived before the start of time, who nightly tell Wotan what Erda sees. This day, though, she comes herself because of the dire danger: "All that is shall come to an end. A dark day dawns for the gods: I charge you, shun the ring!"

Struck by her words, Wotan asks to know more, but she answers: "I have warned you enough: reflect in fear and dread!" She sinks back down. Wotan, anxious to learn more, rushes after her, but Froh and Fricka throw themselves in his way and hold him back.

Donner tells the giants to come back; they will be given the gold. All look attentively at Wotan. After deep reflection, he rouses himself and brandishes his spear as he comes to a bold decision. He calls to Freia to join the gods and tosses the ring onto the hoard.

The giants free Freia, who joyfully rushes to the gods' welcoming embraces.

Immediately Fafner has begun to collect the treasure. Fasolt asks for his share, but Fafner claims that Fasolt longed more for Freia than for the gold; thus Fafner will retain the greater part.

Fasolt appeals to the gods for justice. Wotan turns away with contempt, but Loge advises Fasolt to give Fafner the treasure yet keep control of the ring. Fasolt throws himself on Fafner, grabbing the ring for which he gave up Freia.

Fafner says: "Hold it fast in case it falls!" and strikes down Fasolt with his staff. He tears the ring from his dying brother: "Now blink at Freia's gaze: the ring you will not touch again!"

For a long moment the gods stand in horror as Fafner quietly resumes packing the hoard. At last Wotan reflects: "Terrible now I find the curse's power."

Loge ironically notes Wotan's luck—his enemies kill themselves for the ring he has given up. But Erda's words still fill Wotan with dread; he says he must go down to her and learn how to end this fear.

Fricka caresses her husband cajolingly, asking if the noble fort beckons its new owner. He replies gloomily: "With unclean wages I paid for that building!"

Donner clears the air. Climbing a high rock and swinging his hammer, he summons the sultry mists to gather into a storm cloud around him. He disappears in an ever-darkening thundercloud. The sound of Donner's hammer striking the rock is heard, followed by lightning and a thunderclap.

From the storm cloud Donner calls to Froh to point the way to the castle. The clouds suddenly disperse; at the feet of Donner and Froh a rainbow bridge stretches radiantly across the valley to the castle, which glows in the light of the setting sun. Froh points to the bridge, inviting the gods to "boldly tread its terrorless path."

For a time, the gods speechlessly contemplate the glorious sight. Wotan wonders at the castle's splendor and reflects on the long day's events: "From morn to eve, in care and anxiety, not lightly was it won."

And then Wotan is seized by a great thought. He salutes the castle and names it Valhalla. He bids Fricka enter with him, safe from terror and dread. When Fricka asks what the name means, he replies that the meaning will become clear if that which "my courage found for me . . . lives on victorious."

Loge remains apart from the gods. To him, they are hurrying to their end. He is almost ashamed to be associated with them and would like to transform himself into flickering flames to burn them. "I'll think it over: who knows what I'll do?" He starts to join the gods.

But as the group approaches the rainbow bridge, the voices of the Rhine Daughters are heard from the valley below, lamenting the lost gold and asking the gods to return it.

Wotan orders Loge to tell the accursed nymphs to stop annoying them.

Loge calls down to them: "Hear what Wotan wills for you. No more gleams the gold on you maidens: henceforth bask in bliss in the gods' new radiance." The gods laugh and proceed across the bridge.

From below, the maidens have the last word: "Now only in the depths is there tenderness and truth: false and faint-hearted are those who revel above!"

THE VALKYRIE

Act 1

58

The Interior of Hunding's Dwelling

Scene i

Siegmund, Sieglinde

Scene ii

Siegmund, Sieglinde, Hunding

Scene iii

Siegmund, Sieglinde

Act 2

61

A Wild, Rocky Place

Scene i

Wotan, Brünnhilde, Fricka

Scene ii

Brünnhilde, Wotan

Scene iii

Siegmund, Sieglinde

Scene iv

Siegmund, Brünnhilde

Scene v

Siegmund, Sieglinde, Hunding, Brünnhilde, Wotan

Act 3

66

On the Top of a Rocky Mountain

Scene i

The Eight Valkyries, Brünnhilde, Sieglinde

Scene ii

Wotan, Brünnhilde, the Valkyries

Scene iii

Wotan, Brünnhilde

The Voices

Siegmund, a Volsung, son of Wotan (in the form of Volse) · Tenor
Sieglinde, Siegmund's twin sister · Soprano

Hunding, a Neiding, Sieglinde's husband · Bass
Wotan, leader of the gods · Baritone
Brünnhilde, a Valkyrie, daughter of Wotan and Erda · Soprano
Fricka, wife of Wotan · Soprano
The Valkyries, warrior daughters of Wotan · Sopranos and Contraltos
Gerhilde, Ortlinde, Waltraute, Schwertleite, Helmwige, Siegrune, Grimgerde, Rossweisse

Act 1, Scene iii

Act 1, Scene i

The curtain rises at the end of the storm prelude to reveal the inside of a wooden dwelling, the trunk of the great World Ash Tree in the center. At the left, steps lead up to an inner room; at the right, a hearth and a storeroom. At the back, a great entrance door, with a smaller door set into it.

As the storm subsides, Siegmund enters the house; he is exhausted from flight and unable to go further. He must rest here no matter whose hearth this is.

Thinking her husband has returned, Sieglinde enters from the inner room and is surprised to find the stranger. Siegmund wakens with a cry for water, and she provides a drinking horn. As he hands the horn back, he looks at her with growing interest. Who has provided such relief? he asks. She belongs to Hunding, she says, and invites him to stay. Siegmund says that, unarmed and wounded, he will not worry her husband.

He brushes aside her concern for his wounds. He has fled only because his spear and shield were shattered by a pack of enemies who have pursued him through the storm. But now, as she has refreshed him, his tiredness has fled and the sun shines on him again.

Sieglinde fetches a drink of mead. He offers her the first drink, and as they share it, they look on each other with increasing warmth. Nevertheless, he tells her that bad luck pursues him; to spare her, he must leave. She stops him, impulsively urging him to stay since he cannot bring bad luck into a house where it already lives. She drops her eyes in shame and sadness.

Deeply moved, Siegmund tells her he will await Hunding. She slowly raises her eyes to his, and during a long silence, they look upon each other with deepest emotion.

Act 1, Scene ii

Sieglinde is startled to hear Hunding leading his horse to the stable. She opens the small door and Hunding appears, armed with shield and spear. As he crosses the threshold, he sees Siegmund and stops, casting a questioning look at Sieglinde.

Sieglinde explains that she found the exhausted stranger and refreshed him as she would any guest. Siegmund pointedly asks if he would scold his wife for this. Hunding responds that his house is inviolate and warns Siegmund to treat it so. Handing his armor to Sieglinde, he orders her to serve him and Siegmund the evening meal.

As Sieglinde prepares supper, Hunding looks keenly at both of them. He is astonished at their resemblance, especially the "snaky shiftiness" in their eyes. Hiding his surprise, he asks Siegmund what rough travels have wearied him. When Siegmund says he has been chased through the storm along unknown paths, Hunding tells him he has reached Hunding's house and that his wealthy kinsmen, who guard his honor, reside close by to the west.

He asks the stranger to reveal his name, but Siegmund only looks thoughtfully before him. Sieglinde, standing next to Hunding, gazes at Siegmund with interest. Noticing this, Hunding embarrasses Sieglinde by saying that if Siegmund is afraid to honor his host with this information, then he should confide in his wife: "look how greedily she questions you!"

Gazing at Sieglinde, Siegmund tells his story. He can't be called Peaceful or Cheerful; Woeful would be more like it. His father was Wolf. He was called Wolf-cub and had a twin sister. After hunting one day, father and son came home to find their home burned, the mother slaughtered, and the sister missing. Chased by the same enemies who attacked their home, they defended themselves bravely in the wild woods. But they became separated during a fight; later Siegmund found only an empty wolfskin.

Drawn to the world of men and women, Siegmund left the forest but was always unpopular; whatever he thought right seemed wrong to others. "I ran into feuds wherever I found myself." He should be called Woeful because "woe is all I possess."

Asked how he became disarmed, Siegmund tells of a young woman who, forced by her family into an unwanted marriage, called out for help. Hearing her plea, Siegmund rushed to her defense and killed her brothers. Her kinsmen attacked them both. He defended her against all comers until his spear and shield were broken. The girl was killed, and Siegmund fled.

Sieglinde has listened with great sympathy, but Hunding now realizes that Siegmund is the very enemy he has been pursuing that day. He tells Siegmund that he is safe for the night but to prepare to fight in the morning, even though he knows Siegmund is weaponless.

Sieglinde steps between them, but Hunding orders her to fix his nightly drink and retire. After pausing in deep thought, Sieglinde prepares the draught, shaking some spices into it. She looks at Siegmund and tries to direct his gaze to a sword hilt buried in the trunk of the ash tree. Siegmund looks at her fixedly but misses her meaning.

Hunding drives her from the room with a violent gesture. Picking up his weapons, he warns Siegmund to be armed for battle in the morning. He follows Sieglinde into the bed chamber and locks the door behind him.

Siegmund is left alone.

Act 1, Scene iii

The hall is lighted only by a dull glow from the fire. Siegmund sinks onto a bench and broods silently for some time in great agitation.

He calls out for the sword his father, Volse, once promised he would find in his hour of need. Now he has met a woman who draws him to her in longing but who is "captive to the man who mocks my defenselessness. Volse, Volse, where is your sword?"

The logs in the fire fall together, and the light from the flames strikes the hilt of the sword buried in the ash tree; Siegmund asks what gleams so brightly and whether it is the blazing gaze of the radiant Sieglinde. The glow fades and darkness returns, but the fire in his heart burns on.

To his joyful surprise, Sieglinde softly returns. She tells him that she has drugged Hunding's drink so that Siegmund might have time to escape. She will also show him a weapon: "O if only you could get it! I could acclaim you as the noblest of heroes."

She tells him that on her wedding day, an old, one-eyed stranger had entered and thrust a sword into the tree. The blade would belong to whoever could pull it out; many tried, but none could do it. Now she knows that Siegmund was intended to come both to claim the sword and to avenge her misery.

Siegmund embraces her: he is that sacred friend she has longed for, and he will avenge her dishonor.

The great door suddenly swings open to reveal a glorious spring night, the full moon illuminating the young pair so that they can now see each other clearly. Siegmund draws her next to him on the bench.

He tells her it is the spring that has come into the room. "Winter storms have vanished before Maytime." In gentle light, on balmy breezes, it wends its way through woods and meadows. Dispelling winter and storms, spring conquers the world. It was love that attracted the spring. Like brother and sister, husband and wife, "love and spring are united."

Sieglinde responds: "You are the spring for which I longed in the frosty winter time." She knew, when she first saw him, that he belonged to her. She hangs in rapture on his neck and gazes into his face.

Looking closely at each other in the bright moonlight, they recognize for the first time how much they look alike. As they speak, they realize how much they sound alike. She asks if he is really called Woeful; was not Wolf his father? Siegmund says he was Wolf only to his enemies—his real name was Volse.

Then, she says, her excitement rising, he is a Volsung, and the sword is his. "So let me name you by the name I love: Siegmund (Victor)—so I name you."

Siegmund takes both name and sword. "Notung (Needy), I name you, sword. . . . come from your scabbard to me!" He draws the sword from the tree and displays it to the ecstatic Sieglinde as a wedding gift. He will take the fairest of women far from the enemy's house into the springtime. With the sword he will protect her.

"I am Sieglinde who longed for you: your own sister you have won and the sword as well." She throws herself on his breast, and he exults: "Wife and sister you'll be to your brother. So let the Volsung blood increase."

He embraces her passionately.

Act 2, Scene i

A wild, rocky place. A gorge at the back. From a high ridge of rocks, the ground slopes down to the front.

Wotan and Brünnhilde stand together, fully armed, and Wotan brandishes his spear. He tells Brünnhilde to prepare for Siegmund's coming fight with Hunding and to ensure the Volsung's victory. In high spirits, Brünnhilde leaps from rock to rock: "Hojo toho! Hojo toho!"

Looking into the gorge, she warns that Wotan's wife Fricka approaches, furiously driving her ram-drawn chariot. Loving warfare but not domestic skirmishes, Brünnhilde says she is glad to leave her father in the lurch, and leaves.

Fricka arrives, approaching Wotan purposefully. Wotan does not look forward to the confrontation: "The old storm, the old trouble! Yet I must take a stand."

Fricka immediately complains that Wotan has been avoiding her and says he must help her: Hunding has prayed to her to avenge the wrong done to him by the monstrous Volsung twins. Wotan sees no error in spring's having united them in love. She reminds him that "it is about marriage, a holy vow, vilely flouted, I am complaining." As guardian of marriage, she must answer Hunding's appeal.

Wotan says he does not think much of a marriage without love and suggests this is none of Fricka's business. She responds that even if he can condone adultery, can he also tolerate incest between brother and sister? He advises her to accept events that may never have occurred before and to bless the twins' union.

She viciously attacks his degrading commitment to the Volsungs and his vulgar mating with a human to produce them. She accuses him of abandoning his own race and everything he used to value. Though he has often been unfaithful, at least up to now he has required that the uncouth Valkyries, and even his favorite, Brünnhilde, respect her as sovereign. But his posing as Volse and mating with a lowly human to father the twins—in this he has abased himself in deepest disgrace.

Wotan tries a different, and fatal, argument: she must understand that "the crisis calls for a hero" who can freely accomplish what the gods cannot. Fricka exposes Siegmund as Wotan's creation and agent; he has no independent or free will. She confronts Wotan with the fact that even Siegmund's adversity, like the sword meant to extricate him, was put in place by Wotan. Wotan gloomily accepts the flaw in his own plans and is defeated.

Fricka insists that he remove his protection, as well as Brünnhilde's and the magic sword's, from Siegmund. The god is overcome by a feeling of his own powerlessness.

Brünnhilde exuberantly returns, but sensing the confrontation with Fricka has gone badly, she turns away and slowly leads her horse into a cave. Fricka demands Wotan's oath to give up the Volsung, which he bitterly gives.

As she withdraws, Fricka passes Brünnhilde and haughtily explains that her father will tell her what he has decided. She rides quickly away.

Act 2, Scene ii

Brünnhilde anxiously approaches Wotan, who is brooding gloomily. In a fitful outburst, he despairs that he has been caught in his own trap and is "the least free of all men."

Brünnhilde asks him to confide in her, but he fears that if he reveals his inner-most thoughts, he will lose his grip on his own will. Loyal Brünnhilde tells him that she is so much a part of him as to be part of his will itself; talking to her, he speaks only to himself.

In a long monologue, Wotan reveals his plans and hopes—now frustrated and doomed.

When the pleasures of young love waned, Wotan says, he longed for power. Power was won, but still he yearned for love.

Alberich forged the ring of power. Wotan took it by trickery but did not return it to the Rhine Daughters; rather he paid the giants with it for building Valhalla.

At Erda's urging, he gave up the ring. Yet still longing to know more of her wis-dom, he pursued her deep into the earth, where he wooed and seduced her and learned her secrets. But she exacted a fee: she "bore me you, Brünnhilde. With eight sisters I brought you up." (These grew up to be his warrior maidens, or Valkyries. They are also called wishmaidens in *Siegfried* and *The Valkyrie*.)

Wotan's aim was to avert the end of the gods. To strengthen the gods against their enemies, he sent the nine Valkyries to amass a host of heroes, brave men the Valkyries would spur on to battle to hone their strengths. In death they would be brought to Valhalla to protect the gods.

Erda warned Wotan that the end will come if Alberich ever recovers the ring, for the dwarf could use its power to turn the heroes against the gods and Valhalla. Fafner guards the ring, but Wotan cannot attack him because of the bargain he struck as payment for Valhalla. Thus Wotan became "ruler through treaties; by my treaties I am now enslaved."

Only one person could do what Wotan could not—a hero whom he has never helped, who would do the deed out of his own needs. But how can Wotan create a free agent to do what he desires? Wotan can only create subjects to himself; the free man must create himself. Regarding Siegmund, "it was easy for Fricka to spot the trick . . . I must yield to her will."

Brünnhilde asks if he will deprive Siegmund of victory against Hunding. Feel-ing the weight of Alberich's curse, Wotan says he must forsake what he loves, betray Siegmund who trusts him. "Away, then with lordly splendor . . . Let it all fall to pieces, all that I built. . . . Only one thing I want now: the end, the end!"

Erda has warned that the end will be near when Alberich begets a son. Wotan has heard that the Nibelung seduced a mortal woman with money, and a son now stirs in her womb. Thus loveless Alberich has a son, and Wotan must abandon his own son who was born of love. "Then take my blessing, Nibelung's son. What deeply revolts me I bequeath to you, the empty glory of divinity: greedily feed your hate on it!"

Wotan orders Brünnhilde to fight for Fricka and Hunding, against Siegmund.

She balks; she knows that Wotan loves Siegmund and that she must therefore protect him.

Wotan warns her not to provoke "the crushing spark of my rage . . . Remember what I commanded. Siegmund shall die. This is the Valkyrie's task."

Wotan storms away; Brünnhilde is left confused and alarmed. She must obey her father. Arming herself, she turns away slowly. She looks into the gorge and sees that Sieglinde and Siegmund are approaching in full flight. She goes back into the cave.

Act 2, Scene iii

The twins appear on the rocky ridge, Sieglinde in full, desperate flight. Siegmund catches up with her and embraces her with gentle force. She has rushed away "from blessed delight." He urges her to rest, to rely on him.

She gazes at him rapturously, throwing her arms around his neck, but then starts up in sudden terror. Wild-eyed with fear, she tells him to escape from her and the curse upon her. Unwanted marriage with Hunding has dishonored and disgraced her. "My body has died . . . I bring shame on my brother, disgrace on the friend who won me." Siegmund assures her that Hunding will pay for her disgrace with his life, and she will be avenged.

She hears the horns of Hunding's host and their dogs. She gazes madly before her. She imagines the hounds tearing at Siegmund's flesh. Finally, she falls senseless into Siegmund's arms. He sinks down, cradling her head in his lap, and tenderly presses a long kiss on her brow.

Act 2, Scene iv

Brünnhilde leads her horse out of the cave and approaches Siegmund gravely. After watching Siegmund for a long moment, she calls his name.

Siegmund asks who she is, "so fair and grave." She tells him that only those doomed to die in battle can see her; whoever looks on her is fated to leave this life.

Siegmund looks long and searchingly into her eyes. He bows his head, then looks up again with resolution. If he must die, where would she take him? To Valhalla and the Lord of Battles, she says. He asks if only Battlefather (Wotan) is there; she assures him that other heroes will embrace and welcome him. Will he see Volse, his own father? He will.

Will he be welcomed there by women? She says that many beautiful maidens live there in splendor. Wotan's own daughter will gladly attend to him.

Siegmund now recognizes that she is Wotan's holy daughter and asks one more thing: Will he find his sister and bride there? Brünnhilde says Sieglinde must stay behind; he will not see her in Valhalla.

Siegmund bends over Sieglinde and kisses her gently. Then he tells Brünnhilde to greet Valhalla for him and to greet Wotan and Volse and all the heroes and lovely wishmaidens (Valkyries), too. He will not follow her.

Brünnhilde is uncomprehending; Siegmund has seen the Valkyrie's glance and therefore must follow. Siegmund responds that he will stay wherever Sieglinde is, in pleasure or sorrow. Brünnhilde's gaze cannot force him to follow her.

Brünnhilde assures him death will force him: today Hunding will kill him. It will take more than Hunding, he says, because he who gave Siegmund the sword has promised him victory. But she tells him that this very same person has decreed his death and will take the power away from the sword.

He asks Brünnhilde to be quiet so that she does not waken and terrify Sieglinde. He bends over her tenderly but turns back to Brünnhilde in an outburst of grief. Sieglinde is betrayed, and his own pledge to defend her is empty: "Oh shame on him who made my sword, if he decreed shame for me, not victory. If I must die I shall not go to Valhalla. Let Hell hold me fast!"

Brünnhilde still does not understand: how can this ill-starred woman mean more than the "everlasting bliss" of Valhalla? Siegmund looks at Brünnhilde bitterly: "cruel, unfeeling maiden . . . of Valhalla's frigid joys please do not speak to me."

Deeply moved, Brünnhilde begins to understand Siegmund's human, exalted love and sorrow. She offers to protect Sieglinde. Siegmund abruptly rejects the offer; he and no other will touch her while she lives.

Brünnhilde says Siegmund must confide Sieglinde to her care, because his sister is pregnant. But Siegmund draws the sword and points it at Sieglinde; if the sword will not fell his foe, then it will take the lives of Sieglinde and the unborn child. He raises the sword against them.

Brünnhilde is won over. They all shall live; she will alter the fight's outcome. The sword will not fail him, and the Valkyrie will protect him. In ecstatic excitement, Brünnhilde says they will meet again on the battlefield; she rushes off with her horse into the gorge.

Siegmund looks after her exultantly.

Act 2, Scene v

The scene has darkened. Heavy storm clouds sink down to cover the background.

Listening to Sieglinde's breathing, Siegmund is grateful for the deep sleep that subdues her sorrow and pain. Laying her gently on the rock, he kisses her forehead in farewell: "Sleep on now until the battle has been fought and peace brings you joy."

He hears Hunding's horn, rises resolutely, and draws his sword: "He who calls me must now make ready; what he deserves I will grant him. Notung will pay him his due." He hurries to the pass at the back of the stage and disappears into the storm cloud in a flash of lightning.

Sieglinde has a terrible nightmare, recalling the day her home was burned and mother slain. She springs awake amid thunder and lightning, and finds Siegmund gone. She stares about her in terror; the stage is almost veiled in the black thundercloud.

Nearby, Hunding's horn is heard again, and his voice calls out to Siegmund to stand and fight, boasting of Fricka's support. Siegmund, still unseen, calls to Hunding to reveal himself: he is no longer unarmed, and Hunding cannot hide behind Fricka.

Sieglinde calls on the men to stop, to murder her first, and she rushes back toward their voices. She is staggered by a brilliant flash of light which illuminates the fight. Brünnhilde has appeared, floating above Siegmund and protecting him with her shield: "Strike him, Siegmund! Rely on your sword."

As Siegmund prepares to strike Hunding, Wotan appears in a reddish light, standing over Hunding and holding his spear in front of Siegmund: "Get back from my spear; to pieces with the sword." Brünnhilde shrinks back in fear as Siegmund's sword snaps. Hunding plunges his spear into the defenseless Siegmund, who falls dead. Sieglinde collapses with a cry, as if lifeless.

Both lights disappear. Brünnhilde gathers the fragments of Siegmund's sword and lifts Sieglinde onto her horse: "Quick, to my horse, and I will save you." They disappear.

The cloud parts to reveal Hunding. Wotan is also seen, leaning on his spear and gazing sadly at his son's corpse. He turns to Hunding: "Be off, slave. Kneel before Fricka; tell her that Wotan's spear avenged what caused her shame. Go! Go!" Wotan waves his hand with contempt, and Hunding falls dead.

Wotan lashes out in a terrible rage: "As for Brünnhilde, she will regret her crime. Terribly her rashness will be punished when my horse overtakes her in flight." He disappears in thunder and lightning.

Act 3, Scene i

The summit of a rocky mountain. A pine wood on the right, the entrance to a cave on the left. The back view opens onto other peaks. Occasional storm clouds drive past.

Four Valkyries—Gerhilde, Ortlinde, Waltraute, and Schwertleite—stand on the highest peak. The Valkyries are assembling, each to carry a fallen hero to Wotan in Valhalla. Helmwige arrives, then Siegrune, and finally Rossweisse and Grimgerde.

After much banter about their horses and the fallen heroes, the eight are ready to depart, but they look for the ninth—Brünnhilde, bearing Siegmund, the fallen Volsung. Waltraute says they must wait for her; Battlefather would be angry if they arrived without her.

They watch in astonishment as Brünnhilde and her horse, Grane, approach in the sky at a furious gallop, bearing not Siegmund, but a woman. Some of the Valkyries rush off to help as Grane brings Brünnhilde and Sieglinde to ground in the pine trees. They return with Brünnhilde, who is leading Sieglinde.

The Valkyries excitedly ask what has happened. "Give me protection," Brünnhilde says, "in my great distress . . . . The father of battles is pursuing me." They cannot believe her, but she tells them to look toward the north. Ortlinde and Waltraute spring up to look, reporting a thunderstorm coming toward them from that direction.

They ask about the woman with Brünnhilde, and she tells them about Siegmund's death and her flight with Sieglinde. Again she asks for protection, appealing to six of the Valkyries by name; none will help her defy Wotan.

The Valkyries cannot comprehend that Brünnhilde has disobeyed Wotan. The black thundercloud comes closer, they can hear the wild neighing of Wotan's steed.

Sieglinde now speaks. She tells Brünnhilde that her only desire now is death, and she wishes she had been left behind to die with Siegmund. She will curse Brünnhilde if she does not honor Sieglinde's earnest plea to kill her.

Brünnhilde tells Sieglinde she must live because she is carrying Siegmund's child. Sieglinde starts violently at the news, then glows with sublime joy. She, too, appeals to the other Valkyries to save her and her child.

The other Valkyries urge Brünnhilde to flee with the woman; they dare not help her. Brünnhilde decides to stay behind to face Wotan, to give Sieglinde time to escape. The Valkyries describe a forest stretching to the east, where Fafner has changed himself into a dragon to guard the Nibelung ring and treasure. Brünnhilde thinks it would shelter Sieglinde from Wotan's anger: he dislikes the place and stays away from it.

As Wotan draws near, Brünnhilde tells Sieglinde she must persevere because:

> The noblest hero in the world, woman, you are carrying in the shelter of your womb. Keep for him the strong sword's fragments. From his father's battlefield I luckily brought them. He will forge them anew and one day wield the sword. Let me give him his name. "Siegfried," joyous in victory.

Deeply moved, Sieglinde responds:

> Oh, mightiest of miracles, most glorious of women. I thank you for your
> loyalty and holy comfort. For him whom we loved I will save the dear child.
> May the reward of my thanks one day smile at you. Farewell, luckless
> Sieglinde blesses you.

Sieglinde, carrying the sword fragments, flees in haste. The thunderclouds surround the height, and a fiery light glows on the right. Wotan's voice is heard: "Stop, Brünnhilde!" Offstage, Wotan dismounts and comes toward them in a brilliant firelight; the Valkyries surround Brünnhilde to hide her.

Act 3, Scene ii

Wotan enters in a terrible rage, looking for the law breaker, Brünnhilde. When the Valkyries continue to conceal her, he warns them to "shrink from her; she is cast aside forever, even as she has cast aside" her own worth.

They plead for Brünnhilde and beg their father to soften his anger. He rages at the "soft-hearted gaggle of females" who weep and wail when he punishes disloyalty. He tells them what she has done: only with Brünnhilde did he share his innermost thoughts and intentions. Now she has "openly scorned her master's orders, and taken up arms against me, though only my wishes brought her to life. Do you hear, Brünnhilde? . . . Do you hide in terror from your accuser?"

Brünnhilde, humbly but firmly, walks out from the group of Valkyries and stands before Wotan. "Here I am, father: pronounce your punishment."

Wotan tells her she has brought on her own punishment. She has defied his will, his orders, his shield, and his fate. He tells her that her Valkyriehood is over, that she is cut off from the gods and banished from his sight.

He says he will confine her here on the mountain. He will lock her in defenseless sleep so that any lowly mortal who finds her can waken and capture her.

The Valkyries, horrified at the punishment, crowd around Brünnhilde. They plead with Wotan to spare her such disgrace and to let them share Brünnhilde's shame. Wotan asks if they have not heard what he has ordered. "The flower of her youth will wither away. A husband will win her womanly favors. To this domineering man she will belong henceforward. She will sit by the fire and spin, the topic and butt of all jokers." The Valkyries must shun her or share her fate.

Brünnhilde sinks to the ground with a cry. The Valkyries recoil from her in horror. Wotan orders them to flee. They rush into the woods to their horses, riding off in thunder and lightning.

The storm subsides. Fine weather returns. It is twilight.

Act 3, Scene iii

For a long time, Brünnhilde lies at Wotan's feet. She raises her head a little: have her actions justified her being shamed, debased, and dishonored? She asks him to explain what she has done to make him threaten to abandon her.

Brünnhilde explains her actions. She disobeyed his order because, when he accepted Fricka's point of view, he became his own enemy. Brünnhilde knew one thing: that Wotan loved Siegmund. She understood the dilemma that caused him to oppose Siegmund.

He angrily asks how she could understand his situation and still dare to protect Siegmund. Brünnhilde says she is Wotan's eyes, and saw, in his dilemma, what he could not see. She went to Siegmund to warn him of his death, but she was instead persuaded by his noble defiance, born of his love for Sieglinde. "One man's love breathed this into my heart . . . and faithful to you inwardly I disobeyed your command."

Wotan, filled with bitterness, says she did the deed he wanted to do but of necessity could not. While Brünnhilde was sweetly learning the power of love, Wotan had to turn against himself, to force himself to turn against love. In agony, rage, and sorrow, he had made this decision, and "in the ruins of my own world I would end my endless sadness."

And so, he says ironically, she can now let her heart continue to guide her. By opposing his intentions, she has renounced him, and he can never share his innermost thoughts with her again.

Brünnhilde says she understood "only one thing: to love what you loved." But if he disgraces her, he would be disgracing himself also, for she was once part of him. Therefore, he must not permit an ordinary mortal to win her.

Wotan says he cannot choose the man who will find her. Brünnhilde says she knows the greatest hero will yet be born to the Volsungs: Sieglinde is carrying the "holiest of issue" and the fragments of the sword which he made for Siegmund.

But Wotan will not hear of the Volsungs; he is finished with them, too. His decision is made. He must now travel far away. The punishment must be exacted.

Resigned to her punishment, Brünnhilde asks for only one thing: "Let my sleep be protected by terrors, so that only a fearless unrestrained hero may one day find me here on the rock." On her knees, she begs with him to surround the rock with a blazing fire that will frighten cowards away.

Wotan is overcome. He raises Brünnhilde and looks deeply into her eyes: "Farewell, you bold, wonderful child! You, my heart's holiest pride. . . . If I must lose you whom I loved, laughing joy of my eyes: then a bridal fire shall burn for you, as it never burned for any bride! . . . For only one shall win the bride, one freer than I, the god!" Brünnhilde sinks in ecstasy on Wotan's breast. He holds her in a long embrace.

She throws her head back and gazes into his eyes as he says: "That radiant pair of eyes . . . for the last time let them delight me today with farewell's last kiss! May their star shine for that happier man: for the luckless immortal they must close in parting. For thus the god departs from you, thus he kisses your godhead away!"

He kisses her eyes for a long moment. She sinks back in his arms, unconscious. He gently carries her to a mossy mound under a fir tree. He lays her down, closes her helmet, and covers her body with her own shield. He turns away but looks back sorrowfully.

Then he strides resolutely to a large rock, pointing his spear: "Loge, listen! Harken here! As I found you first, a fiery blaze . . . I conjure you! Arise, magic flame . . . Loge! Come here!"

He strikes the rock three times with his spear. A flash of flame issues from the rock, which swells to an ever-brightening fiery glow. Flickering flames break out. At Wotan's direction, the flames circle the rocks in a sea of fire, finally enclosing the entire scene.

Wotan holds out his spear again to cast his spell: "Whosoever fears the tip of my spear shall never pass through the fire!"

Wotan slowly turns to go but looks back once more at Brünnhilde. Then he disappears through the fire.

SIEGFRIED

Act 1
72
A Cave in the Forest of Neidhöhle
Scene i
Mime, Siegfried
Scene ii
Mime, The Wanderer
Scene iii
Mime, Siegfried

Act 2
76
Depths of the Forest of Neidhöhle
Scene i
Alberich, The Wanderer, Fafner's Voice
Scene ii
Siegfried, Mime, Fafner, the Wood Bird
Scene iii
Mime, Alberich, Siegfried, the Wood Bird

Act 3
80
Wild Region at the Foot of a Rocky Mountain, Brünnhilde's Rock
Scene i
The Wanderer, Erda
Scene ii
The Wanderer, Siegfried
Scene iii
Siegfried, Brünnhilde

The Voices

Mime, a Nibelung dwarf and smith, Alberich's brother and Siegfried's foster
father · Tenor
Siegfried, son of Siegmund and Sieglinde, Wotan's grandson · Tenor
The Wanderer, Wotan in disguise · Bass
Alberich, a Nibelung dwarf, Mime's brother · Bass
Fafner, a dragon, formerly a giant · Bass

The Wood Bird · Soprano
Erda, the Earth Mother · Contralto
Brünnhilde, a Valkyrie, daughter of Wotan and Erda · Soprano

Act 2, Scene ii

Act 1, Scene i

A rocky cavern in a forest. There is a naturally formed forge with a huge bellows.

Mime sits alone in front of an anvil, hammering at a sword. He throws down his hammer with disgust; Siegfried is always forcing him to make a sword, but the boy easily snaps into pieces even Mime's best effort. Mime ponders: there is a sword Siegfried could never shatter. With Notung, the fearless boy might kill Fafner the dragon and win the ring for Mime. But Mime is unable to reforge Notung's fragments. So he goes on as Siegfried insists, making swords the boy shatters.

Siegfried calls out from the woods, promptly entering in rough forester's dress, a silver horn on a chain at his waist. He is leading a bear on a rope and drives it toward Mime merrily. Siegfried laughs loudly as Mime runs behind the forge in terror. When Mime cries that the sword is finished, Siegfried releases the bear back into the forest. Safe, Mime comes out, but he complains about the bear.

Siegfried says the bear makes a better companion than Mime. He uses his horn in the forest to call for a friend; today the bear appeared, and though he prefers the bear to Mime, he'd like yet a better friend.

Siegfried roughly snatches the sword Mime has finished. Disgusted, he easily shatters it on the anvil, complaining that Mime talks of giants and brave battles and daring deeds but cannot make a decent sword. Siegfried petulantly throws himself down on a stone seat.

Mime reminds Siegfried to treat him with thanks and obedience, but the boy turns his back in ill humor. Mime brings him food; Siegfried knocks it to the ground.

Mime wails at the boy's ingratitude; he has raised him from a baby as though he were his own. He works while Siegfried roams. He has given him toys, a bed, even his wisdom. Siegfried tells Mime there is only one thing he has not taught him: "How to tolerate you . . . I long to seize you by your nodding neck and make an end of your obscene blinking!"

Siegfried tenderly describes watching the animals in the forest, how husband and wife nourish their children. He asks where Mime's wife is, so that he can call her mother. Mime says: "I am both your mother and your father."

But Siegfried has observed that children resemble their parents. Seeing his own reflection in a brook, he knows he bears no resemblance to Mime; they are as similar as a toad to a glittering fish. He seizes Mime by the throat and, just as he once had to force Mime to teach him to speak, threatens that Mime must now tell him: "Who are my father and mother?"

Mime finally reveals the truth: one day he found a woman lying whimpering in the field. He brought her into the cave, where she gave birth to Siegfried and then died. Siegfried slowly realizes he thus caused his mother's death. Mime reveals her name: Sieglinde. And his father? Sieglinde said only that he was killed, Mime says.

Siegfried demands proof, and Mime shows him the two pieces of a shattered sword. Sieglinde said the boy's father carried it in his fatal fight. With sudden excitement, Siegfried demands that Mime immediately reforge the fragments.

He rushes into the forest, rejoicing: Mime is not his father, and with the new sword he will be free to leave, "wending my way like the wind over the woods, nevermore, Mime to see you again!"

Mime looks after Siegfried with astonishment, then returns to his anvil dejectedly: how can he now lead Siegfried to Fafner, and how can he forge the sword? "Nibelung hatred, trouble and toil will not knit Notung together for me."

Act 1, Scene ii

As Mime sinks down in despair, the Wanderer enters from the door at the back of the cave. He wears a long, dark blue cloak; a wide-brimmed hat is pulled low over his eyes. He carries a spear as staff.

He greets Mime as a wise smith and asks for his hospitality. Mime starts in alarm, asking who has come. "The world calls me Wanderer." Mime asks him to wander away.

He chides Mime: the Wanderer has learned much and has given good counsel to many who needed it. Mime says that his own wits suffice and again asks the intruder to leave.

But the visitor comes closer and sits at the hearth. He proposes a war of wits; he will forfeit his head if he does not answer Mime's questions.

Mime cautions himself to be clever and tries to gather his courage. After some thought, Mime asks three questions, which the Wanderer answers without hesitation:

Which race dwells in the earth's depths?

The Nibelungs, once ruled by Alberich, whose magic ring and golden hoard might have won him the world.

Which race dwells on the earth's face?

The giants, who envied and won the gold. Fafner slew Fasolt and now guards the gold as a savage dragon.

Which race lives in the cloudy heights?

The gods, spirits of light, whom Wotan—here the Wanderer calls himself "Light-Alberich"—rules through his eternal spear. "Custody of the world lies in the hand that controls the spear."

As if by accident, the Wanderer strikes his spear on the ground, causing a roll of thunder; now recognizing his guest as Wotan, Mime is filled with terror. Mime tells the stranger he has redeemed his head; Mime tries to dismiss him, but the Wanderer says Mime should have asked what he needed to know. Now Mime's head is forfeit if he cannot answer the Wanderer's three questions. Mime again tries to compose himself. The Wanderer asks his questions.

Which is the race Wotan oppressed but still holds dear?

Revealing that he knows more than he has told Siegfried, Mime answers that the Volsungs, Siegmund and Sieglinde, "are the love-children that Wotan fathered and fondly cherished." From them came Siegfried.

A Nibelung watches over Siegfried, plotting to gain the ring from Fafner. What sword might Siegfried use to kill Fafner?

Mime rubs his hands in glee: Notung was placed in the ash tree by Wotan and withdrawn by Siegmund. It snapped on Wotan's spear, but Mime keeps the pieces, knowing that with that sword Siegfried can slay the dragon.

The Wanderer laughs and compliments the clever dwarf. Then he asks the final question:

"Who will forge the sword?"

Mime throws his tools about in terror and despair. Who will do it if he cannot?

The Wanderer rises slowly. He says that Mime asked about useless things; it did not occur to Mime to ask what he needed to know, so the Wanderer tells Mime the answer: "Only one who has never felt fear shall forge Notung anew."

The Wanderer starts to leave but turns back to Mime: "From today ward [guard] your wise head well: I leave it forfeit to him who has never learnt fear!" With a smile, he disappears into the forest.

Overwhelmed, Mime sinks back onto his chair.

Act 1, Scene iii

Mime stares before him into the sunlit forest. In his desperation he hallucinates violently that Fafner is crashing and roaring in the forest. He hides behind his anvil.

But it is Siegfried who breaks through the forest into the cave and demands the sword. Mime comes out from behind the anvil. He is still dazed and repeats the Wanderer's words to himself: his head is forfeit to one who has never learned fear.

Mime tells the boy that his mother made Mime promise to teach Siegfried fear before he goes into the world. Siegfried demands to know what fear means. Mime conjures a frightening picture of twilight in the gloomy forest, rustling and rumbling, flames flashing, grim horror, heart hammering: "If you've not yet felt that, fear is still a stranger to you!"

Siegfried responds that this must be a wonderful feeling. How can Mime teach it to him? Well, says Mime, he knows of an evil dragon who has killed many men. He lives at Neidhöhle, on the edge of the forest, not far from "the world." Siegfried responds excitedly: Mime must take him there. He'll learn fear and then be off into the world. Again he demands that Mime remake the sword.

Mime confesses he cannot forge it. Siegfried brushes him aside: he will do it himself. He starts flinging Mime's tools about impetuously. Mime chides him for not learning the smith's craft, but Siegfried asks, "how could the pupil perform what the master cannot manage?" He will forge the sword his own way.

Siegfried builds up a large fire. Mime advises him to weld the pieces, but Siegfried pushes the solder away. He will shred and melt the pieces and then reforge them. As the smith looks on in wonder, Siegfried files down the pieces of the sword.

As Siegfried works, Mime ponders and plots. He is now sure that Siegfried will slay Fafner and gain the ring. But how can Mime get it from him afterward?

At the bellows, Siegfried fans the fire and melts the filings in a crucible. He calls on Mime to tell him the name of the sword. Siegfried sings as he fans the flames: "Notung! Notung, trusty sword! . . . Blow, bellows! Blow on the blaze!"

Mime comes up with a plan: when Siegfried kills the dragon, he will be thirsty. Mime will offer a drugged drink to make Siegfried sleep, then kill him with the sword. Thus he will gain ring and treasure for himself.

Siegfried pours the melted filings into a mold and plunges it into cold water. He withdraws the mold and thrusts it back into the fire. He notices derisively that Mime is now preparing a stew—the former master, as cook, now serves the boy.

Siegfried draws the mold from the fire. He lays the glowing steel on the anvil and with a heavy hammer begins to shape the blade. He plunges it into the water and laughs as it steams and hisses. He fixes the blade into a hilt, finishing the sword with a small hammer.

Mime is filled with an increasing, crazed delight. He jumps onto a stool: he will gain the ring. The Nibelungs will be his slaves—even Alberich. His hordes will defeat gods and heroes. "Mime the bold, Mime is king, prince of the elves, ruler of all!"

Siegfried raises the finished sword. Though it splintered for his father, the son has fashioned it anew. With it, he will "smite the false, fell all knaves!"

Brandishing Notung, he turns to Mime: "See . . . how sharp is Siegfried's sword!" He swings the sword into the anvil, which splits in two and crashes with a loud noise. Mime falls to the ground in terror.

Siegfried swings the sword high in exultation.

Act 2, Scene i

Neidhöhle, deep in the forest. The ground rises from the front to a small knoll, which obscures the bottom part of a cave, seen at the back. Through the trees on the left: a fissured cliff. It is darkest night.

Alberich broodingly keeps watch under the rocky cliff.

A bluish stormy light shines in the trees on the right and Alberich wonders whether the dragon's destroyer is at hand. The wind dies; the light fades. A shadowy figure comes out of the wood. Alberich asks who approaches from the shadows.

The moonlight breaks through to reveal the Wanderer. Alarmed, Alberich recognizes Wotan in disguise and angrily demands to know how he dares show himself at Neidhöhle. The Wanderer assures the dwarf that he "came to watch, not to act."

Thinking of Wotan only as his rival for the ring, Alberich warns him: the contract with the giants, like all Wotan's pacts, remains inscribed on his spear. He therefore cannot snatch the ring back—a violation of the contract would shatter the spear. The Wanderer says no such treaty binds him with respect to Alberich, whom he has subdued once before.

Alberich says he knows that Wotan is consumed over who will inherit the ring from the doomed Fafner, and he hurls another threat at the god: "if I once get it again in my grasp, unlike the stupid giants I will use the power of the ring: . . . I will storm Valhalla's heights with Hella's hosts: then I shall rule the world!" But the Wanderer answers that Alberich's plans do not trouble him: "Let him who wins the ring be its master."

Alberich says he sees through this trick, knowing that Wotan depends on a hero descended from Wotan himself. The Wanderer advises Alberich rather to concern himself with Mime, who is using the hero to gain the ring for himself. Siegfried "knows nothing of me . . . knows nothing of the ring . . . I leave [him] to fend for himself; he stands or falls, but is his own master."

Alberich asks: Who will win the ring? The Wanderer will say only that a hero approaches the treasure, craved by the two Nibelungs, and that Fafner will fall. He jokes that Fafner, to save his life, might simply give the ring to Alberich, who wonders if he really would.

The Wanderer calls to Fafner to wake up. Alberich warns the dragon that a hero is coming to fight him to take the ring. Alberich proposes: "give me the ring as reward, and I will prevent the fight." Fafner can keep the rest of the treasure in peace. But Fafner responds: "Here I lie and here I hold; let me sleep!"

The Wanderer laughs but has a final word for Alberich: "Everything goes its own way: you can alter nothing. . . . Contend with your brother . . . . More than that you will soon learn too!" The Wanderer departs quickly in the bright glow of a storm, which quickly subsides.

Vowing once more to overthrow the "frivolous, pleasure-seeking crew of gods," Alberich slips into a cleft and resumes the watch.

Act 2, Scene ii

As morning breaks, Siegfried and Mime arrive at Neidhöhle. Siegfried wonders if this is where he will finally learn fear and be free of Mime at last.

Mime points to the cave where the savage dragon lives. He warns Siegfried about Fafner's huge jaws, poisonous spittle, and thrashing tail. Siegfried takes note and says he will strike Fafner in the heart but doubts this will teach him fear. Mime assures him it will.

Mime leaves Siegfried to wait back at the spring; when the sun is high, Fafner will come out to drink. Siegfried laughs that he will send Fafner to the spring and will kill him only after the dragon has eaten Mime. As he is driven away, the dwarf says he will bring Siegfried refreshment after the fight. Delighted that his plan is working, he disappears into the woods.

Siegfried stretches out under a lime tree. He enjoys the coolness and rejoices once more that Mime is not his real father.

Siegfried looks up through the branches. Listening to the gentle murmurs of the forest, he thinks tenderly of his mother. Why did she have to die at his birth? If only he could see her.

The murmurs grow stronger, and Siegfried listens to a bird singing in the branches above him. If he could understand its song, perhaps it would tell him about his mother. Mime has told Siegfried that some men can understand the birds; if he imitates bird sounds on a pipe, maybe he and the Wood Bird will understand each other.

Siegfried runs to the spring, cuts off a reed with his sword, and fashions a crude pipe out of it. The bird seems to listen, but Siegfried smiles at his own feeble effort to imitate the bird's song. He throws the pipe aside and takes his horn; now he will play the bird a cheerful woodland tune.

Siegfried blows gaily on the silver horn. This rouses Fafner, who comes out of the cave and yawns loudly. Siegfried looks at the dragon in astonishment, delighted at the fearsome sight.

Fafner demands to know who has come. Siegfried says he has come to learn fear. The dragon rebukes the insolent boy, but Siegfried says he'll cut him to shreds if he does not teach him fear. Fafner replies: "I wanted a drink: now I've also found food!"

Fafner opens his jaws menacingly; Siegfried draws his sword and with a laugh threatens to shut it. Fafner draws himself forward and spits a venomous steam, which Siegfried avoids. Fafner lashes his tail, but Siegfried jumps out of the way and stabs it. Fafner roars, rising to throw himself on Siegfried, but the boy plunges Notung into the exposed breast. As Fafner falls, Siegfried lets go of the sword and jumps aside.

Fafner, dying, asks who has wounded him and who put him up to it. Siegfried says Fafner himself put him up to it. Fafner tells Siegfried he has murdered the last of the race of giants. And then a warning: "Keep a sharp watch, jubilant boy; he who prompted you . . . is now, after your triumph, plotting your death."

Siegfried wants to learn more. "Tell me where I came from . . . You will know from my name . . . Siegfried." Fafner raises himself, uttering "Siegfried!" and dies.

As Siegfried pulls Notung from Fafner's breast, the dragon's blood sears his hand. Involuntarily Siegfried sucks the stinging blood from his hand, and to his delight discovers that he can now understand the birds.

The Wood Bird calls to him: the Nibelung treasure is now Siegfried's; it lies in the cave. The Tarnhelm can help him do great wondrous deeds, but the ring would make him the ruler of the world!

Siegfried thanks the bird and descends into the cave.

Act 2, Scene iii

Mime enters timidly, making sure Fafner is dead. He starts to go back to the cave, but Alberich rushes forward. Mime dreads the sight of his accursed brother.

Alberich accuses Mime of stealing his treasure, but Mime says that what he has won by hard work is now his. They quarrel, and Mime finally proposes that Alberich remain master of the ring if Mime can only keep the Tarnhelm.

Alberich says he would never sleep safely if Mime had the Tarnhelm and refuses to share anything with his brother. Mime threatens to call in Siegfried against Alberich and to keep the whole treasure for himself.

Siegfried appears in the background and, to the brothers' consternation, is carrying both the Tarnhelm and the ring. Mime and Alberich quickly resume their hiding places.

Siegfried walks slowly onto the knoll, contemplating the golden booty. He doesn't know what use they are, but he will keep them as trinkets that will remind him of the fight, though it did not teach him fear. He stuffs the Tarnhelm into his belt and slips the ring onto his finger.

Once more the Wood Bird sings to him: Siegfried must not trust the treacherous Mime! Because of the dragon's blood, Siegfried will now hear, in Mime's words, what Mime is thinking in his heart. Siegfried stands calmly as Mime creeps out of hiding.

Mime intends to fool the boy with flattery, but his intentions are revealed to Siegfried: he will close Siegfried's eyes and take the treasure. Siegfried calmly asks if Mime is planning to harm him.

"Did I say so?" Mime presses on in a flattering manner, but his heart says he has always hated Siegfried. He reared him not out of love but from desire for the gold. Siegfried must pay with his life. Siegfried again asks if Mime means to kill him.

"That's not what I said!" Offering the fatal drink, Mime becomes hysterically exuberant, and his heart reveals that he will hack off Siegfried's head with Notung and take the treasure: "Drink and choke yourself to death."

Filled with sudden loathing, Siegfried strikes Mime with the sword, and the dwarf falls dead. Alberich's mocking laughter is heard from the cleft.

Siegfried picks up Mime's body and throws it into the cave. With a great effort he pulls Fafner's body across the front of the cave to seal it. "Guard the glittering treasure, together with your booty-envying enemy: may you both find rest now!"

Siegfried, hot and weary, rests under the lime tree. He looks up into the branches and again sees the little bird happily twittering with its fellows. Siegfried reflects sorrowfully on how alone he is, without brothers or sisters. His mother is dead, his father slain. His only companion tried to kill him. He asks the bird to find him a good companion.

The Wood Bird answers that it knows of a wonderful wife for Siegfried, one who sleeps on a rocky height. Whoever can break through the fire and wake her would win Brünnhilde.

Siegfried jumps up excitedly. The bird's story fills him with a new and burning feeling that he does not understand. The Wood Bird tells him it is a song of love, but only one who does not know fear can win Brünnhilde.

Now he is shouting with joy: "the stupid boy who knows not fear . . . that is I! . . . I vainly strove to learn fear from Fafner: now I burn with longing to learn it from Brünnhilde!" The bird flutters up, as if to lead the way, and Siegfried says he will follow.

For a time, the bird teases, flitting here and there, and then flies off toward the back. Siegfried happily follows.

Act 3, Scene i

A wild spot at the foot of a mountain, which rises steeply at the back. It is night—lightning and violent thunder.

The Wanderer strides resolutely to a cavernous opening in the rocks to summon Erda from her sleep in the depths. She rises gradually in a bluish light, asking who has disturbed her sleep. He says he has wakened her in quest of knowledge.

The Norns do not sleep, she says; why not ask them? They cannot change the course of events; he wants "to learn how to hold back a rolling wheel."

Erda says she was once overcome by a conqueror and bore him a daughter, Brünnhilde. Why not seek her counsel? The Wanderer answers that she flouted him and has been punished.

Erda is confused: does the one who taught defiance now punish it? Does he who defends what is right now rule through lies? She asks him to let her sleep.

But he will not let her go. Once before she warned him of a shameful end. How can he now conquer his cares? But Erda, disoriented, says only that he is no longer who he once was.

It is you, the Wanderer says, who is no longer what she believes: "the earth-mother's wisdom is drawing to an end: your wisdom will wither before my will." Here is Wotan's will: he no longer fears the downfall of the gods; he now wishes it. No longer to the Nibelung, but to the brave Volsung will he leave his legacy. The Volsung has gained the ring. Innocent and noble, he will overcome Alberich's curse. Brünnhilde "will waken to the hero [and] will do the deed that will redeem the world."

He commands Erda back down to everlasting sleep. Whatever may happen, he happily yields his place to Siegfried and Brünnhilde. Erda, eyes closed, slowly descends to endless sleep.

Act 3, Scene ii

Dawn begins to break; the storm is over.

The Wanderer leans back against the rocks as Siegfried approaches. The little bird flutters into view but then flies off in alarm. Siegfried enters.

The Wanderer announces himself, asking where the youth is headed. Siegfried stops at the sound and asks who has called to him—perhaps he can show him the way. He tells the Wanderer he seeks a flaming rock where a woman sleeps that he would waken.

Asked who has sent him, Siegfried says it was a forest songbird. The Wanderer laughs that no man can understand a bird, and the boy tells him about the magic blood of the dragon. Who induced him to kill the dragon? Mime, a treacherous dwarf, led him to Fafner to learn fear. Who made the sword that killed the dragon? Siegfried answers that he forged it himself.

Now the Wanderer asks a question Siegfried cannot answer: "Who made the sturdy splinters from which you forged yourself the sword?" Siegfried only knows that the fragments would have been useless had he not reforged it. The Wanderer laughs good-naturedly and gazes on Siegfried with great pleasure.

But Siegfried is annoyed by the old man and his questions. He tells him to show him the way or be quiet. Still enjoying the encounter, the Wanderer advises the boy to respect his elder. Siegfried heatedly responds that all his life an old man has stood in his way; he warns the Wanderer not to end up like Mime.

Siegfried moves to take a closer look at the old fellow under the wide-brimmed hat. He is missing an eye! "Doubtless someone struck it out whose way you stubbornly barred? Now take yourself off, or you might easily lose the other one too."

The Wanderer is disappointed by Siegfried's brashness but is still solicitous. He says that Siegfried himself is using the missing eye to gaze on the Wanderer. Siegfried misses the reference to their blood relationship. He bursts out laughing and once more demands that the old man either show him the way or be chased away.

Gently, the Wanderer tries to warn Siegfried, whom he loves, not to rouse his anger today: "it would ruin both you and me!" Siegfried has no more time for chatter. He doesn't need help anyway; he'll just continue in the same direction the Wood Bird showed him. Again he orders the obstinate old man to clear off.

As the skies grow dark, the Wanderer at last breaks out in genuine anger. He tells Siegfried that the bird flew away in fear when it saw the Wanderer, who is also the lord of the ravens (see 102–Ravens in chapter 3): Siegfried, he says, will not pass.

The flames above grow in brightness. He warns the boy to fear the guardian of the rock. The maiden sleeps under his might, and whoever wakes her would deprive him of his power forever. He tries to frighten Siegfried: "Soon the raging fire will devour and consume you. Go back then, rash boy!" Siegfried starts to move past him toward the flames.

The Wanderer stretches out his spear: "If you do not fear the fire, then my spear must bar your way! . . . This shaft once shattered the sword you bear: once again then let it break on the eternal spear!"

Siegfried eagerly draws his sword—he has found his father's foe! With a single stroke he shatters the spear. Lightning flashes, and a single clap of thunder quickly dies away.

The Wanderer quietly stoops to pick up the pieces of the spear: "Forward then! I cannot stop you!" He disappears in the darkness.

Siegfried wonders if the coward has escaped. The glowing brightness continues to descend toward Siegfried. "Ah! Wondrous glow! Gleaming radiance! . . . I will bathe in the fire, in the fire find my bride!"

Calling out joyously on his horn, he plunges upward into the flames, which completely engulf the stage.

Act 3, Scene iii

The brightness of the flames gradually gives way to a cloud, glowing with a dawn-like redness. The cloud dissolves into a rosy mist which in turn gives way to a blue sky above and a rocky precipice below.

The scene is the same as at the end of The Valkyrie: *Brünnhilde, covered in shining armor, lies in deep sleep in the foreground under a fir tree.*

Siegfried, from the back, reaches the summit and for a long time gazes around in wonder. He looks into the woods at the side and sees a sleeping horse. Then he catches sight of glittering armor and assumes a man lies underneath.

He lifts the shield to reveal a figure, still concealed by helmet and breastplate.

He wishes to comfort the sleeper so he gently removes the helmet; he notes tenderly how fair the sleeper is. To ease the sleeper's breathing, Siegfried uses his sword to cut through the rings holding the breastplate. Brünnhilde lies before him, and he jumps back: "That's no man!"

Seized with terror, he cries out for help: "Mother, mother!" He sinks, as if fainting, onto Brünnhilde.

After a long moment he stands; he wants to wake the maid and wonders if he will be dazzled by her gaze. A painful yearning grips him. His hand and heart tremble; the sleeping woman has taught him to be afraid.

He approaches Brünnhilde again: he must wake her so that he himself may awake. When he bends over her, his fear is soothed by her quivering mouth and fragrant breath. He calls on her to awaken, but she does not. With great effort and even, he thinks, if he will die in doing so, he kisses her.

Brünnhilde opens her eyes and slowly rises to a sitting position. She greets the radiant sun, the light, and the day. She asks who has awakened her.

Entranced by her look, Siegfried tells her he forced his way through the fire: "I am Siegfried, and I woke you." The hero she had prophesied and Wotan had promised her has come! Brünnhilde thanks the gods: her sleep is over, and Siegfried has awakened her! In glowing ecstasy, they both extol Siegfried's mother for nourishing the hero that now looks on Brünnhilde.

If Siegfried only knew how long she had loved him! Her shield protected him even before he was born. She alone divined Wotan's thought, defied him, and was punished for her defiance and for her love for Siegfried.

Deeply agitated, Siegfried cannot grasp what she says—his senses are inflamed by her, and he would have her quench them.

Brünnhilde sees her awakening horse, her shield, and breastplate, and she suddenly feels sadness and shame for her lost godhood and her new mere humanity. She is confused and frightened by Siegfried's sexual passion.

Siegfried embraces her impetuously, but she pushes him away, terrified at the physical intimacy. Her virginity was sacrosanct in Valhalla, and this indignity disgraces her: "He who woke me has wounded me . . . I am Brünnhilde no more."

Siegfried urges her to awaken to him, but she is inconsolable. Siegfried gently removes her hands from her eyes; he urges her to emerge from the darkness: the day is bright.

But for her the sun only illuminates her shame. She has always thought of his welfare; she begs him to leave her, not to overcome her with his overwhelming strength and destroy her.

Siegfried presses forward: "I love you [and] am no more my own . . . Awaken, Brünnhilde! . . . Laugh and live, sweetest delight! Be mine!" With deep feeling she now freely admits she has always been his and will always be his.

He tells her to be his now. If they breathe each other's breath, embrace breast to breast, eye to eye, mouth to mouth, then there would be no doubt that Brünnhilde is his.

With increasing fervor, she relinquishes heaven's wisdom for the joy of love. She embraces him: is he not devoured by her ardor, does he not fear her? In joyful surprise, he says the raging fire between them has brought back his courage; "fear, I think, I have foolishly quite forgotten already!"

Wild with joy, she embraces her new life: laughing, she will love him. Laughing, they will perish together.

Together, they sing: Brünnhilde bids farewell to Valhalla and the "resplendent pomp of the gods"; now Siegfried is her "inheritance . . . my one and all: radiant love, laughing death!"

For Siegfried, "Brünnhilde lives, Brünnhilde laughs! . . . My one and all: radiant love, laughing death!"

She throws herself into Siegfried's arms.

TWILIGHT OF THE GODS

Prologue
87
The Valkyrie's Rock
The Three Norns, Brünnhilde, Siegfried

Act 1
89
The Gibichungs' Hall
Scene i
Gunther, Hagen, Gutrune
Scene ii
Gunther, Hagen, Gutrune, Siegfried
Scene iii
The Valkyrie's Rock
Brünnhilde, Waltraute, Siegfried

Act 2
93
In Front of the Gibichungs' Hall
Scene i
Alberich, Hagen
Scene ii
Hagen, Siegfried, Gutrune
Scene iii
Hagen, the Gibichung Men
Scene iv
Gunther, Brünnhilde, Siegfried, Gutrune, Hagen, Gibichung Men and Women
Scene v
Brünnhilde, Gunther, Hagen

Act 3
97
A Wooded Place on the Rhine
Scene i
The Three Rhine Daughters, Siegfried
Scene ii
Siegfried, Gunther, Hagen, Gibichung Men

Scene iii

The Gibichungs' Hall

Gutrune, Hagen, Gunther, Gibichung Men and Women, Brünnhilde,
the Rhine Daughters

The Voices

THE NORNS

First Norn, the oldest · Contralto

Second Norn · Mezzo-Soprano

Third Norn, the youngest · Soprano

Brünnhilde, Siegfried's wife, daughter of Wotan and Erda · Soprano

Siegfried, a Volsung, son of Siegmund and Sieglinde · Tenor

Gunther, son of King Gibich, leader of the Gibichungs · Baritone

Hagen, son of Alberich, half-brother of Gunther and Gutrune · Bass

Gutrune, Gunther's sister · Soprano

Waltraute, a Valkyrie · Mezzo-Soprano

Alberich, a Nibelung dwarf, Hagen's father · Baritone*

Gibichung Men · Basses and Tenors

Gibichung Women · Sopranos

THE RHINE DAUGHTERS

Woglinde · Soprano

Wellgunde · Mezzo-Soprano

Flosshilde · Contralto

*Note that in *Siegfried* (Schirmer), Alberich is listed as a bass.

Act 2, Scene iv

Prologue

The setting is the same as at the close of The Valkyrie *and* Siegfried: *the summit of a rocky mountain, a cave on the left, a copse of trees on the right. Firelight shines up from the valley to the back. A still and gloomy night.*

The oldest Norn lies under the fir tree on the right, the second is stretched on a rock in front of the cave, and the youngest sits on a rock at the back, under a precipice.

The Third Norn asks why they are not spinning and singing.

The First Norn unties a golden rope from around herself, fastening one end of it to a branch on the fir tree: she once spun and sang at the World Ash Tree. A spring whispered wisdom at its base. Wotan came to drink, and paying an eye as forfeit, cut a branch from the tree to fashion a mighty spear.

The ash tree withered, the spring waned. Today she spins at the fir tree, which must suffice. She throws the rope to the Second Norn, who wraps it around a rock in front of the cave and asks: "Do you know what happened?"

The Second Norn tells how Wotan carved treaties into the spearshaft, which was shattered by an audacious hero. Wotan then ordered his heroes from Valhalla to hack the ash tree to pieces. The spring dried up forever. She fastens the rope to the rock and, throwing the rest to the Third Norn, asks: "Do you know what will happen?"

The Third Norn says that gods and heroes sit with Wotan in Valhalla, where they have piled up the pieces of the ash tree. When the wood burns, it will bring their end. If they wish to know more, they must spin more rope. She tosses it back to the First.

The First Norn fastens the rope to another bough: she sees a light but cannot tell if it is the new dawn or Loge's flickering flame. Her eyes and memory fail. Do the others know what happened to Loge?

The Second wraps the rope around the rock again: Wotan tamed Loge and made him burn around Brünnhilde's rock. Do you know what will happen to him? The Third: one day Wotan will use Loge as fire to ignite the ash tree's logs.

The First says that the night is fading—she can see no more. She asks what happened to Alberich, who once stole the Rhinegold.

The Second says the rock is cutting into the rope. She sees the Nibelung's ring rise; its curse frays the rope. Do you know what will come of it?

The rope is thrown to the Third Norn, but it is too slack. She stretches it tighter: it snaps!

All three Norns gather at the center in great terror: "Our eternal knowledge is at an end!" Third: "Down!" Second: "To mother!" First: "Down!"

They vanish.

Dawn begins to break. Its glow intensifies as the light from the fire fades. The sun rises, bringing broad daylight.

Brünnhilde and Siegfried emerge from the cave. He is armed; she leads her horse, Grane.

Brünnhilde tells Siegfried that because she loves him, she must let him go to do great deeds. She has given him all the wisdom and strength she can. She hopes he will not despise her for having nothing more to give.

He tells her that she has given him more than he can understand. He knows only one thing: to remember Brünnhilde. He will leave her on the mountaintop, protected by the fire. He takes Alberich's ring from his finger and hands it to her: "I give you this ring. Within it resides the virtue of whatever deeds I wrought. . . . Take its power into your keeping as the pledge of my troth!"

Rapturously placing the ring on her finger, she pledges to prize it as her greatest wealth. In return she gives him Grane, her noble horse.

With Brünnhilde's horse and shield, Siegfried is no longer himself alone; he is part of her. "Wherever I am shall we both be found . . . [and wherever she is] will hold us both, since we are one."

In highest excitement she says: "O sacred gods! Supreme beings! Feast your eyes on this dedicated pair! Apart, who shall separate us? Separate, we shall never part!"

"Hail, Brünnhilde, radiant star! Hail, resplendent love!"

"Hail, Siegfried, victorious light! Hail, resplendent life!"

Leading Grane, Siegfried disappears down the slope at the back. Brünnhilde watches for a time. Siegfried's horn call is heard from the valley. She catches a last glimpse of him and waves with delight.

Act 1, Scene i

The Hall of the Gibichungs. At the back, the shore of the Rhine, enclosed in rocky heights.

Gunther and Gutrune are enthroned on the right. Hagen sits at a table before them. Gunther calls on Hagen to tell him if he can hold his head high on the Rhine for maintaining Gibich's glory.

Hagen replies that their mother, Grimhilde, made him promise to respect Gunther's legitimacy and title. Gunther says he envies Hagen for his wisdom, which went to Hagen alone and which Gunther seeks; Hagen responds that Gunther's reputation is not secure as long as he and his sister Gutrune are unmarried.

Gunther asks whom he would marry. Hagen knows that the finest woman in the world will be won only by someone who can break through the fire that protects her, and Gunther is not strong enough to do this. Only Siegfried, the Volsung, son of Siegmund and Sieglinde, who killed the dragon and won the Nibelung hoard, can win Brünnhilde.

Gunther rises angrily: why does Hagen make him want what he cannot have? Hagen asks whether Siegfried would willingly bring Brünnhilde to Gunther if Gutrune were to capture Siegfried's heart.

Gutrune now rises. "Mocking, hateful Hagen! How could I capture Siegfried? If he is the world's mightiest hero, the loveliest women on earth have long since rejoiced him."

Hagen speaks secretively: the potion in the chest, which Hagen has brought, would make Siegfried forget Brünnhilde and bind him to Gutrune. Gunther and Gutrune approve the plan.

A horn call is heard down the river. Hagen observes that Siegfried, joyously roaming the world for adventures, has come to the Gibichungs. As Siegfried's boat passes, Hagen calls to him. Siegfried calls back that he seeks "Gibich's stalwart son." Hagen: "To his hall I invite you. This way! Lay to!"

Act 1, Scene ii

Siegfried brings the boat to the riverbank. Hagen secures it with a chain, and Siegfried, leading Grane, jumps on shore. Hagen greets Siegfried by name.

Siegfried asks which is Gibich's son. "Far along the Rhine I have heard of your fame: now fight with me or be my friend!" Gunther steps forward and warmly greets Siegfried.

Siegfried turns to Hagen and asks how he knew his name. Hagen: "I knew you by your strength alone."

Siegfried hands Grane over to Hagen, asking him to tend the horse well. Hagen leads Grane away, gesturing to Gutrune, who retires to her room.

Gunther welcomes his guest, saying all that he owns is Siegfried's. Siegfried responds that all he has to offer, his sword, is Gunther's.

Hagen returns, saying he has heard Siegfried has also won the Nibelung treasure. Siegfried says he almost forgot about it, so little does he value it. He left it in a dragon's cave. Hagen asks if he took nothing. Siegfried shows them the Tarnhelm, though he does not know its purpose. Hagen tells him: "it enables you to take any shape; if you long for some distant place, it takes you there in a trice."

Hagen asks if Siegfried took anything else. A ring. Is it kept safe? "A wondrous woman keeps it." Hagen knows this is Brünnhilde.

Gunther says that Siegfried need give him nothing; he would gladly serve with Siegfried without reward.

Gutrune enters carrying a drinking horn. Greeting Siegfried, she offers the horn. Siegfried courteously takes it and says to himself with great feeling: "Brünnhilde, to you I offer this first drink to faithful love!" He takes a long drink—and loses all memory of Brünnhilde.

As he returns the horn to Gutrune, he fixes his eyes on her with sudden passion: her glance sears his sight. He asks her name, grabs her hand impetuously and ardently offers himself to her. Gutrune involuntarily glances at Hagen, bows her head in a feeling of unworthiness, and leaves on faltering steps. Siegfried gazes after her.

Siegfried asks Gunther if he is married, and Gunther says he has set his sights on someone he'll never have, a woman who lives on a mountaintop surrounded by fire; only one who braves the fire can win Brünnhilde. Siegfried repeats Gunther's words as if making an intense effort to remember, but to no avail.

Coming out of this dreamy state, Siegfried says he has no fear of the fire and will win the woman for Gunther if he is given Gutrune as bride. Gunther is quick to agree, but how would Siegfried do this? By the trickery of the Tarnhelm, says Siegfried: "I will change my shape to yours."

To seal their friendship and commitment, they swear an oath of blood-brotherhood. Hagen begins by filling the drinking horn with wine and holding it out. Gunther and Siegfried cut an arm with their swords, drip blood into the horn, and place two fingers on the rim: "I pledge faith to my friend . . . If a friend betrays his trust [blood] shall flow in torrents in full atonement."

They drink from the horn until it is empty, and Hagen breaks it in two. Siegfried asks Hagen why he did not drink. Hagen answers that his blood is not so pure and noble as others'; he abstains from oaths of honor and glory. Gunther advises Siegfried to pay no attention to the unhappy man.

Not wanting to delay for even a moment, Siegfried tells Gunther they should leave at once. Gunther will wait in the boat for the night while Hagen guards the hall. They board the boat and put up the sail. Gutrune comes into the hall again, but Siegfried has already pushed the boat into the middle of the stream.

Hagen tells Gutrune that Siegfried rushes to woo Brünnhilde in order to win Gutrune as bride. She cries: "Siegfried—mine!" and returns to her chamber to await the hero's return.

With strong strokes, Siegfried has steered the boat from view.

Hagen is alone. He leans back against a post at the hall's entrance and watches Gunther and Siegfried sail away: Siegfried will return, bringing his own wife to Gunther, "but to me he brings—the ring! . . . You sons of freedom, . . . you will yet serve the Nibelung's son."

Act 1, Scene iii

The rocky height, as in the Prologue.

Brünnhilde sits in front of the cave contemplating Siegfried's ring. She looks up when she hears the rumble of distant thunder. A flash of lightning—a dark thundercloud approaches. From a distance, there is a call: "Brünnhilde! Sister!" She recognizes Waltraute and welcomes her delightedly, not noticing the anxious Valkyrie's fear.

Brünnhilde wonders with excitement if Wotan has forgiven her. Wotan's punishment has brought her the highest happiness, the greatest of heroes as husband.

Waltraute finally makes her sister understand that she has come out of dire need. Frightened, Brünnhilde asks if some harm has befallen the gods.

Waltraute tells her story: since punishing Brünnhilde, Wotan no longer sends the Valkyries to harvest fallen heroes. He roamed the world as the Wanderer, and a hero splintered his spear. He then sent his own heroes to chop up the World Ash Tree and pile up the logs around the sacred hall at Valhalla. He ordered the other gods, Valkyries, and heroes to sit with him in the hall. He does not speak, holding the spear's splinters, and refuses Freia's apples.

Wotan has now dispatched two ravens; if they return with good news, then the god might smile again. If Brünnhilde would return the ring to the Rhine's daughters, the gods would be freed. So Waltraute stole away from Valhalla to ask Brünnhilde to end the gods' torment. She throws herself down before her sister.

Brünnhilde does not understand Waltraute's story. What does she want? Waltraute asks Brünnhilde to throw the accursed ring away, back to the Rhine's daughters. Brünnhilde: "Siegfried's pledge of love? Are you out of your mind?"

Waltraute asks again, but Brünnhilde is adamant: "More than the glory of the gods is this ring to me . . . For from it shines Siegfried's love on me like a blessing . . . Go back to the gods' holy council. Tell them this about my ring: I will never renounce Siegfried's love . . . though Valhalla's sublime splendor collapse in ruins!"

Waltraute rushes away in a storm cloud of despair. Evening has fallen. From below, the light of the fire glows more brightly. The flames gradually build up, licking the rocky ridge.

Siegfried's horn call is heard. Brünnhilde starts up with joy and hurries in rapture to the edge of the rocks. Siegfried, wearing the Tarnhelm and appearing in Gunther's shape, leaps into view. Brünnhilde shrinks back in horror: "Betrayed! Who has forced a way to me?"

Siegfried gazes motionlessly at Brünnhilde for some time. Then, disguising his voice, he tells her a suitor has come whom she must follow. Brünnhilde demands to know what monster has climbed up to her. Siegfried identifies himself as Gunther, a Gibichung.

In an outburst of despair, Brünnhilde rails at Wotan: "Wrathful, ruthless god! Alas! Now I see the meaning of my sentence! You doom me to derision and distress!"

As Siegfried approaches her, Brünnhilde holds up the ring: "Stand back! Fear this token! You cannot compel me into shame so long as this ring shields me."

But Siegfried says the ring is Gunther's by husband's right, and with it she will be married to him. He moves forward and seizes her. Twice she escapes. The third time he wrenches the ring from her finger. She screams—broken and faint, she falls into his arms.

He commands her to lead them to the cave. Exhausted and trembling with unsteady steps, she enters the cave.

Alone, Siegfried draws his sword and in his natural voice pledges: "Now, Notung, be witness that my wooing was chaste. Keeping faith with my brother, separate me from my bride!" He follows Brünnhilde into the cave.

Act 2, Scene i

On the shore of the Rhine before the Gibichung hall, which is entered on the right. The river is on the left. At the bank, a rocky height with mountain paths leading to altar stones dedicated to Wotan, Fricka, and Donner. It is night.

Hagen sleeps, leaning against a pillar of the hall. The moon suddenly shines out to reveal Alberich crouching before Hagen, his arms on Hagen's knees.

Alberich calls softly: "Are you asleep, Hagen, my son?" Hagen appears to sleep but says "I hear you, hateful gnome" and asks what Alberich has come to tell him.

Alberich encourages Hagen to be as strong as the mother who bore him. Hagen has no reason to thank the woman who fell victim to Alberich's guile and gave him life. "Prematurely old, pale and wan, I hate the happy and am never glad!"

Yes, says Alberich, he must hate their happy enemies. He tells Hagen that Wotan has fallen to the Volsung and is no longer to be feared. He and Hagen will inherit the world if Hagen will loyally serve Alberich's hatred.

Alberich says that Siegfried has killed the dragon and gained the ring, but the curse will not work against him because he does not know the ring's value nor how to use its power. "Our one end now is to destroy him!"

Hagen says that Siegfried is already helping him toward his own ruin. Alberich urges Hagen to hurry; if Brünnhilde ever advised Siegfried to return the ring to the Rhine Daughters, no ruse could ever retrieve it. Hagen, bred in hatred, must swear to avenge his father.

As the day begins to dawn, Alberich is increasingly enveloped in dark shadow. Hagen says: "I will have the ring . . . I have sworn it to myself." As he disappears, Alberich urges: "Be loyal! Keep faith! Faith!"

Hagen, alone, looks with fixed eyes over the Rhine. The glow of dawn now colors the river red.

Act 2, Scene ii

Siegfried suddenly appears, in his own form, from behind a bush at the shore. He greets Hagen and says he has returned by the Tarnhelm's magic from Brünnhilde's rock; Gunther and Brünnhilde follow in the boat.

Siegfried wants to know if Gutrune is awake yet. Hagen calls, and she enters the hall: "May Freia welcome you in the name of all women!" Siegfried exults: "Today I have won you as wife."

Answering Gutrune's questions, Siegfried says he walked safely through the fire in Gunther's shape. Brünnhilde took him for Gunther. He overcame her, and though he claimed her as wife, Notung kept them apart during the night in the cave. In the morning she followed him down to the river but did not see him change places with Gunther.

The boat approaches; Hagen can see the sail in the distance. Gutrune urges a gracious welcome for Brünnhilde. She asks Hagen to assemble the vassals; she will call the women. Gutrune takes Siegfried's hand, and they enter the hall together.

Act 2, Scene iii

Hagen ascends a rock at the back. Blowing loudly on a cow horn, he calls the vassals to arms. Other horns are heard in reply. The vassals rush onto the stage, ready to fight. They ask Hagen what has happened.

Hagen orders them to greet Gunther, who is returning with his bride. They must sacrifice animals to Wotan, Froh, Donner, and Fricka. They must celebrate with the women until they are drunk. Laughing, the vassals marvel at Hagen's high spirits.

Enough laughter, says Hagen—Brünnhilde approaches with Gunther. As the vassals look up the river to see, Hagen adds: "Serve [your lady] loyally: if she is ever wronged, be swift to avenge her!"

The boat with Gunther and Brünnhilde comes into view. The vassals press close to the riverbank, some jumping into the water to pull the boat ashore: "Hail! Welcome! Welcome Gunther! Hail!"

Act 2, Scene iv

Gunther steps ashore, leading Brünnhilde ceremoniously. The vassals arrange themselves and greet Gunther and his bride. They bang their weapons together noisily.

Brünnhilde follows Gunther with pale face and downcast eyes. Gunther presents her with great praise and pride. The vassals again clash their weapons: "Hail to you, fortunate Gibichung!"

Brünnhilde is led by Gunther to the front of the hall, from which Siegfried and Gutrune emerge with the Gibichung women. Gunther greets hero and sister: "Two happy couples I see here . . . Brünnhilde and Gunther, Gutrune and Siegfried!"

At this, Brünnhilde raises her eyes; her gaze remains fixed on Siegfried in astonishment. All are perplexed by her reaction. Gunther releases her hand, which shakes violently. She begins to tremble, and the vassals ask what ails her.

Siegfried comes forward: "What troubles Brünnhilde's brow?" Brünnhilde can scarcely control herself. Siegfried confirms that Gunther's gentle sister will be married to him, as she to Gunther.

Brünnhilde: "I . . . to Gunther . . . ? You lie!" She staggers in a faint; Siegfried supports her. She looks up into his face: "Does Siegfried not know me?" He calls Gunther forward to care for his wife.

Brünnhilde spots the ring on Siegfried's finger and cries with terrible vehemence: "Ah! The ring . . . on his hand!"

Amidst the general confusion, Hagen moves among the vassals, telling them to mark her words carefully.

Brünnhilde makes a great effort to gain control of herself. She says the ring on Siegfried's hand does not belong to him but to Gunther who took it from her. Siegfried says he did not get the ring from Gunther. She tells Gunther to claim the ring, but Gunther, confused, says he knows nothing of the ring.

Suddenly Brünnhilde rages at Siegfried: "Ah! He it was who tore the ring from me: Siegfried, the thieving deceiver!" Siegfried seems absorbed in distant thoughts as he contemplates the ring; he says he neither gave nor received the ring from a woman: he won it from a fierce dragon at Neidhöhle.

Hagen steps forward; he says that if Brünnhilde gave the ring to Gunther, then Siegfried obtained it by a trick, "for which the traitor must atone!" Brünnhilde shrieks: "Treachery, to be revenged as never before!"

Gutrune and the other Gibichungs cannot understand the accusation.

Brünnhilde appeals to the gods to assist her revenge against Siegfried. Then, pointing to Siegfried, she announces: "Know you all: not to [Gunther], but to that man there am I married . . . He wrung from me gratification and love."

Amidst general consternation, Siegfried denies this: Notung separated him from the unhappy woman. Brünnhilde responds that sword and scabbard hung from the wall of the cave "when its lord wed his beloved."

The vassals surround Siegfried indignantly; they demand to know if he has tarnished Gunther's honor. Gunther, Gutrune, and the vassals call on Siegfried to clear himself and deny the accusation. Siegfried says he will so swear. Hagen holds out his spear point, which Siegfried grabs: may the spear pierce him if Brünnhilde's accusation is true.

Brünnhilde furiously strides into the circle and tears Siegfried's hand from the spear point, replacing it with her own: may the spear then fell him, "for this man has broken his entire oath and now has perjured himself!"

In an uproar, the vassals call for Donner's thunder to silence the disgraceful tumult. Siegfried appeals to Gunther to control the wild woman. He comes close to Gunther: perhaps the Tarnhelm only half concealed him. But never mind! "Women's anger is soon appeased."

Siegfried turns gaily to the vassals and women, and bids them follow him to prepare the wedding feast. He throws his arm around Gutrune and leads her back into the hall. Vassals and women follow in the same high spirits.

Brünnhilde, Gunther, and Hagen remain behind.

Act 2, Scene v

Gunther sits to one side, hands covering his face, deep in shame and dejection. For some time, Brünnhilde gazes sadly after Siegfried and Gutrune, then drops her head in thought.

She wonders by what magic this catastrophe has come to pass. She has no wisdom to deal with it; she gave her wisdom to Siegfried and is now in his clutches. She asks who will be the sword to cut her bonds. Hagen comes close: "Trust me . . . I will take revenge on your betrayer." She laughs bitterly; a single flicker from Siegfried's eyes would melt Hagen's courage.

Then whisper to me, Hagen says: is Siegfried not vulnerable in any way? Brünnhilde answers that without Siegfried's knowing, she has protected him with her magic, except that she knew he would never turn his back on a foe and therefore did not protect him there. Hagen exults: "There my spear shall strike!"

Gunther wails in his disgrace. Hagen assures him he is indeed dishonored. Brünnhilde turns on Gunther, who had hidden behind Siegfried like a coward.

Gunther appeals to Hagen, but his half-brother says: "Naught can help you . . . save Siegfried's death!" Gunther is horrified; he and Siegfried have sworn an oath of blood-brotherhood. Hagen insists that blood alone can atone for the broken bond.

Brünnhilde adds that she has been betrayed by them all, but one death will satisfy her: "Siegfried shall die to redeem himself and you!"

Out of Brünnhilde's hearing, Hagen assures Gunther he will profit from Siegfried's death—the immense power of the ring will be his! "Brünnhilde's ring?" asks Gunther. "The Nibelung's ring," Hagen answers.

Gunther wonders how they will justify themselves to Gutrune. Brünnhilde rises furiously; it now comes to her that it is Gutrune's sorcery that has lured Siegfried from her. "May anguish overcome her!"

Hagen assures Gunther they will hide the deed from Gutrune. Tomorrow they will go hunting, and "a boar will bring him down."

The three come together in a fearsome oath. Brünnhilde and Gunther appeal to Wotan to guard their vow of vengeance. Hagen invokes his father: "Fallen prince! Guardian of night! Lord of the Nibelungs! Alberich, hear me! Bid the Nibelung host once more obey you, Lord of the ring!"

The bridal procession emerges from the hall. Boys and girls wave flowers joyously. Siegfried and Gutrune are carried aloft. Servants move up the mountain paths, carrying flowers to adorn the altars and leading animals to sacrifice. Siegfried and the vassals sound the wedding call on their horns.

Gutrune beckons Brünnhilde with a friendly smile, and the women invite her to join Gutrune. Brünnhilde at first recoils from Gutrune, but Hagen steps forward and forces her toward Gunther, who takes her hand.

Gunther, too, is raised up on a shield, and the procession makes its way up toward the altars.

Act 3, Scene i

On the banks of the Rhine—a wild valley, rocks and woods, a steep cliff in the background.

Hunting horns are heard at different distances, one seeming to answer another.

The three Rhine Daughters rise to the surface of the water and circle about as if dancing. They sing once more of the rays of light the sun sends down into the water. This time the depths remain dark; once they shone with the lustrous gold.

Hearing a distant horn call, they splash joyfully and ask the sun to send them the hero who will give back the gold. They dive back down to decide what to do.

Siegfried appears on the cliff, fully armed. He has lost his way while tracking a bear.

The maidens return to the surface. They call Siegfried by name and playfully ask what he is grumbling about. He smiles, asking if they have lured the beast he lost. Woglinde asks what he would give if they returned his quarry. When he asks what they would want, Wellgunde answers: the gold ring on his finger; they all cry: "Give it to us!"

He says he slew a dragon for it, and it is worth more than a bearskin. They chide him for being miserly. Siegfried says his wife would scold him. Wellgunde asks if she beats him, and they laugh again. Siegfried good-naturedly tells them to laugh if they like, but he will never give them the ring. They dive out of sight.

Siegfried climbs down to the water's edge. Responding to their jibes, he takes the ring from his finger and calls loudly after them: "You merry water-maidens! Come quickly! I'll give you the ring!"

They return to the surface, but this time are solemn. They tell him he will soon learn the calamity that attends the ring. He quietly puts the ring back on his finger and asks them to tell him more.

They sing of the evil in store for him: the ring was wrought from the stolen Rhinegold; he who fashioned it lost it but put on it "a curse into all eternity to doom to death whoever wears it."

Just as he once killed a dragon, so will he be slain this very day if he does not restore the ring to them. Only the waters of the Rhine can wash away the curse. Siegfried laughs that since their wit did not convince him, far less can they frighten him.

They solemnly warn him again to avoid the curse. "Nightly the weaving Norns twisted it into the rope of primeval law." Even so, he boasts, he would sever the Norns' rope as he once shattered a spear. The dragon warned him of the curse but did not teach him to fear it.

He gazes at the ring. Though it could win the world's wealth, he would happily give it up for love, but threats to his life will not work—for life and limb he cares no more than for a clod of dirt.

The maidens, wildly excited, determine to leave the madman: "A glorious gift was granted him. He does not realize that he renounced it. Only the ring which dooms him to death . . . the ring alone he seeks to retain!"

They leave Siegfried with a final prophecy: "Stubborn man, a proud woman today will inherit your treasure: she will give us a better hearing. To her! To her!" They resume their dance and swim away, to the back.

Siegfried smiles after them and ponders the ways of women: "If their cajolery does not convince, they scare with threats; and if one dares to defy these, they start to scold. And yet, had I not given Gutrune my word, I would cheerfully have chosen for myself one of these pretty women!"

He gazes after them without moving.

Act 3, Scene ii

Far away, horns are heard and Hagen's voice, calling.

Siegfried comes out of his reverie to answer the call on his own horn. Groups of vassals answer. More horns. Hagen appears on the rocky height and sees Siegfried, who invites him to come down to him where it is cool.

The vassals and Gunther arrive at the cliff and descend to the riverbank. The game they have killed is piled up. Hagen orders a meal prepared and the wine-skins brought out. All lie down to rest.

Siegfried laughs that he has caught nothing: "Only waterfowl showed itself . . . three wild water-birds who sang to me there on the Rhine that this very day I should be slain." Startled, Gunther looks at Hagen gloomily.

Hagen hands Siegfried a drinking horn. He has heard that Siegfried can understand the birds, but Siegfried says he has paid no attention to their chirping for some time.

Siegfried offers his horn to Gunther, who looks into it with horror: he sees only Siegfried's blood in it. Siegfried laughs and mixes his drink with Gunther's, which overflows onto the ground: "let it be a refreshment for Mother Earth!" With a deep sigh, Gunther murmurs: "You are too happy, my hero."

Siegfried turns to Hagen and quietly asks if Gunther is concerned about

Brünnhilde. Hagen wishes that Gunther understood Brünnhilde as well as Siegfried does the birds' songs. Finally taking up Hagen's suggestion, Siegfried turns to Gunther and says he will sing of his boyhood exploits to cheer him up.

All lie down while Siegfried sings. He tells the story of Mime, who out of envy for a dragon's treasure plotted his death. Siegfried reforged his father's sword and killed the dragon. Its blood let him understand a bird, who told him about the Nibelung treasure, especially the Tarnhelm and the ring, which he took.

The bird then told him that Mime would kill him—but Notung felled the dwarf. Hagen laughs harshly: "What he could not forge he could still feel!"

Hagen fills another horn for Siegfried and drops the juice of an herb into it. He gives it to Siegfried saying it will waken his memory. Siegfried looks thoughtfully into the horn and drinks slowly. The drink restores his memory, and he resumes his story: the bird told him about a wonderful wife sleeping on a rocky height. If he would break through the fire, the bird said, "Brünnhilde would be his."

Gunther listens with increasing astonishment as Siegfried continues in a state of growing ecstasy: he made his way through the flames and found the wondrous woman. "My bold kiss awakened her: oh, how ardently I was enfolded in fair Brünnhilde's arms!"

Gunther springs up in horror: "What do I hear?"

Two ravens fly up out of a bush, circle over Siegfried, and fly off toward the Rhine. Hagen asks if Siegfried can understand the ravens' cry, and Siegfried rises, turning his back to Hagen to follow their flight. Hagen drives his spear into Siegfried's back: "To me they cry revenge!"

Siegfried raises his shield and turns as if to crush Hagen. His strength fails; he drops the shield behind him and falls back on it.

The vassals and Gunther turn on Hagen: "What have you done?" He points at Siegfried: "I have avenged perjury!" Calmly, Hagen turns away and strides over the height.

Twilight has fallen. Gunther, grief-stricken, bends over Siegfried. The vassals stand around him sympathetically.

Siegfried is helped to a sitting position and opens his eyes: "Brünnhilde! Awake! Open your eyes! Who sank you again in sleep? . . . Your wakener came and kissed you awake . . . Brünnhilde laughed in delight at him! Ah, her eyes, forever open! . . . Sweet passing, blessed terror: Brünnhilde bids me welcome!"

He sinks back and dies.

Night has come. Gunther mutely commands the vassals to raise the body on the shield. As they reach the rocky height, the moon breaks through and shines on the procession. Mist gradually fills the stage, obscuring all.

Act 3, Scene iii

The mists part to reveal the inside of the Gibichung hall, as in Act 1. Moonlight is reflected on the Rhine.

Gutrune comes out of her room into the hall. She thinks she has heard Siegfried's horn, but no, he does not come.

Bad dreams have disturbed her sleep—wild horses, Brünnhilde laughing. She wonders whom she has seen walking down to the riverbank. Brünnhilde frightens her. She calls timidly at Brünnhilde's door and looks inside to find the room empty: "Then it was she I saw going to the Rhine!"

A horn in the distance. She listens, longing to see Siegfried again. Transfixed with fear, she hears Hagen approaching: "Hoiho! Awake! . . . We are bringing home the spoils of the hunt."

The glow of torches appears outside. Hagen enters the hall: "Up, Gutrune! Greet Siegfried! The mighty hero is coming home . . . No more will he go off hunting or into battle, nor woo lovely women."

Men and women join the funeral procession, which comes into the hall. The body is set down. Hagen continues: "A wild boar's prey, Siegfried, your dead husband." Gutrune shrieks and falls upon the corpse amid general horror and mourning.

Gunther tends to his sister, but she pushes him away, accusing him of murder. Gunther cries that Hagen is "the accursed boar who savaged this noble hero."

Hagen steps forward defiantly: "I, Hagen, struck him dead. He was forfeit to my spear, on which he swore falsely. I have now exacted the sacred right of reparation, for which I now demand this ring."

Gunther tells him to stand back—the ring is his. Hagen appeals to the vassals, but Gunther defies "the shameless son of a gnome" to lay hands on Gutrune's inheritance.

Hagen draws his sword and falls on Gunther: "Thus does his son demand the gnome's inheritance!" The vassals try to part them, but Hagen strikes Gunther, who falls dead.

Hagen grasps at the ring on Siegfried's finger, but the hero's hand rises threateningly. All are motionless with terror.

From the back, Brünnhilde advances solemnly and firmly: "Silence the shrill clamor of your grief! All of you betrayed his wife, who now comes for vengeance."

Gutrune rises from the ground and attacks Brünnhilde for bringing the catastrophe upon them: in her jealousy Brünnhilde turned the men against Siegfried. Brünnhilde stops her: "Silence, poor wretch! You were never his true wife . . . Siegfried swore eternal vows [to me] before he ever set eyes on you."

Gutrune now understands that Brünnhilde was Siegfried's true love driven from his mind by the potion. In violent despair, Gutrune curses Hagen for the plot that stole Brünnhilde's husband from her. Full of shame and grief, she turns away from Siegfried and bends over Gunther's body. Across the room, Hagen leans defiantly on his spear and shield.

Brünnhilde looks on Siegfried's face in shock and is overcome with grief. She turns to the vassals, commanding them to stack logs high by the shore; a mighty blaze will consume the noble body. With Grane she will follow, for she longs to share the hero's final honor.

Young men raise up a huge funeral pyre. The women throw flowers on it.

Absorbed in contemplation of Siegfried's face, Brünnhilde now says tenderly: "deceiving his wife, loyal to his friend, with his sword he separated himself from his own true love, alone dear to him." No man was ever so honest, true and pure, yet he betrayed all oaths, treaties, and truest love. Do you know why this was?

She looks upward, toward Wotan: "O you, heavenly custodian of oaths! Turn your gaze on my great grief, see your everlasting guilt!" So that Siegfried could recover the ring, Wotan sacrificed him to the curse that had fallen on him. "All is now clear to me! . . . With dreaded desired tidings I now send [your ravens] home. Rest, rest now, o god!"

She signals to the vassals to lift the body onto the pyre. She slips the ring from Siegfried's finger and looks at it thoughtfully. "Now I take my inheritance. Accursed ring, terrible ring, I take your gold and now I give it away."

She thanks the Rhine Daughters for their wise counsel. She will give them what they crave; they will take the ring from her ashes. The fire which consumes her will cleanse the curse from it, and they will keep the gold so disastrously stolen from them.

She puts the ring on her own finger, and taking a fire brand from one of the men, turns to the funeral pyre. She waves the torch and points to the back: "Fly home, you ravens! Recount to your master what you have heard here by the Rhine! Pass by Brünnhilde's rock: direct Loge, who still blazes there, to Valhalla; for the end of the gods is nigh. Thus do I throw this torch at Valhalla's vaulting towers."

She throws the brand onto the pyre, which quickly bursts into flame.

Two ravens fly up from a rock by the shore and disappear toward the back.

Two young men lead Grane into the hall. Brünnhilde runs to the horse and leans toward it affectionately:

Do you too know, my friend, where I am leading you? Radiant in the fire, there lies your lord, Siegfried, my blessed hero. Are you neighing for joy to follow your friend? Do the laughing flames lure you to him? Feel my bosom, too, how it burns; a bright fire fastens on my heart to embrace him, enfolded in his arms, to be one with him in the intensity of love! Heiajoho! Grane! Greet your master! Siegfried! See! Your wife joyfully greets you!

She swings up onto Grane and makes him leap into the fire.

The flames immediately blaze up, filling the space in front of the hall and seizing on the building itself. The Gibichungs press to the front in terror. The whole space of the stage seems filled with fire.

The Rhine overflows its banks in a mighty flood, rolling over the fire. The glow suddenly subsides, replaced by a cloud of smoke, which is drawn to the back.

The three Rhine Daughters swim on the waves. Hagen is filled with terror at the sight of them. He flings away his spear, shield, and helmet, rushing into the flood as if mad: "Keep away from the ring!"

Woglinde and Wellgunde entwine their arms about his neck and drag him backward into the depths. Flosshilde, swimming in front of the others as they withdraw, holds up the recovered ring exultantly.

A red glow breaks through the bank of clouds at the back, illuminating the Rhine Daughters: they swim in circles, joyfully playing with the ring in the calmer waters of the Rhine, which is gradually subsiding into its banks.

From the ruined hall, the men and women look in greatest apprehension at a growing firelight in the sky. At the light's brightest point, the interior of Valhalla appears. Gods and heroes sit just as Waltraute described them, with bright flames seeming to ignite the hall of the gods.

When the flames have completely hidden the gods from view, the curtain falls.

CHAPTER THREE

THE MUSIC

To EXPLORE the *Ring* story through its music, we turn to the most palpable and perhaps the most misrepresented of Wagner's musical innovations—the leitmotifs, or motives. These lie near the heart of Wagner's musical greatness, but they have given rise to much confusion and misjudgment.

We will look at the way the motives help tell the *Ring* story, recognizing nonetheless that narration is but one of their roles—motives are complex musical events. Detailed musicological analysis of Wagner's fantastic achievement in harmony, tonality, orchestration, and dynamics lies outside the scope of this book. The good news here is that the engaged listener does not need analytical expertise to enjoy the musical pleasures and rewards of *The Ring*. No technical knowledge of music is required, for example, for us to be deeply moved by the evolving confrontation between Brünnhilde and Siegmund in V-2-iv, which has at its center a musical phrase commonly but inadequately called Annunciation of Death.

Bryan Magee has remarked that an inordinate amount of the Wagner literature is not about Wagner's music.[1] Although music scholars have not ignored Wagner as composer, hundreds, perhaps thousands, of works have focused instead on his life, personality, politics, theories, and influence. Here we will start from Newman's perspective, that "It is only as a musician that Wagner will live." Newman continues:

> There is no need, no reason, to discuss the "philosophy" of [his] mind. He is not a philosopher: he is simply a perplexed and tortured human soul and

103

magnificent musical instrument. All that concerns us today is the quality of the music which was wrung from the instrument under the torture.[2]

By any measure, that music is characterized by its technical integrity and unceasing innovation. The motives are a striking aspect of Wagner's achievement, not the starting point. Wagner's mature works are among tonal harmony's finest and final hours: every page of the *Ring* score resounds, above all, with innovative and brilliant harmonic language. As dramatist, Wagner adapted that language to the stage and gave it shape as the thoughts, statements, actions, and symbols of his many characters.

Wagner's skills at orchestration also help create the context within which the motives operate. Pierre Boulez, who conducted the controversial Chéreau *Ring* at Bayreuth in the late 1970s (see "Staging *The Ring*" in the Appendix), insists on the brilliance of Wagner's orchestration. The cerebral Boulez has been called a modernist, an antiromantic, and by fallacious extension, an anti-Wagnerian. Yet he has written:

> In the whole of the nineteenth century—and this bears repetition, because there is often still a hackneyed notion about a massive, undiscriminating, unsubtle sound [in Wagner]—there is no orchestral score more brilliant and intricate, founded in the text and the acoustic at the same time and bringing together the properties of both in an admirably rich mixture.[3]

Wagner's harmonic ideas, polyphonic constructions, and orchestral sounds are packaged in a motivic system of musical speech. Taken together, these elements project a musical language of unprecedented immediacy and communicativeness. The words can be seen as secondary. As Newman wrote, "Wagner did not set words to music: the words were merely the projection of an already conceived musical emotion into the sphere of speech."[4]

Thus the motives are more than narrative equivalents; they cannot be labeled like so many calling cards. Wagner himself was the first to discourage what has been called motive hunting. The word *leitmotif*, or literally leading motive or guide motive, was used not by Wagner but by his friend and disciple Hans von Wolzogen. Von Wolzogen edited a pro-Wagner journal founded by the composer, *Bayreuther Blätter*, and developed the first set of motive labels.[5]

Wagner himself never articulated in writing a clear or wholly convincing account of his own motivic style. Although he wrote prolifically about his aesthetic theories and intentions, he left behind no catalogue of motives or other record of any overtly systematic approach to the subject. To the contrary, the preponderant evidence, both in Wagner's writings and in analyses of his creative process, suggests that the astounding coherency of the *Ring* music was woven from an intuitive sensibility, disciplined by scarcely imaginable powers of recall and invention.

Moreover, the artist in theory is clearly at odds with his practice, especially regarding the primacy of music over words. According to Robert Gutman, perhaps the most insightful of Wagner biographers in English, Wagner insisted that "motifs of remembrance derived from the vocal line; when later reiterated by voice or instrument, they were to represent ideas germane to the words originally sung."[6]

We know, however, that a great deal of seminal music is heard before it is ever attached to voice or text. As Gutman writes, Wagner must also have "sensed that themes of orchestral origin upset his theory of deriving music from verse. Defensively and obscurely he explained their function as that of kindling presentiments or preparing for what was yet to materialize."[7] In fact, emphasis ultimately shifts from singer to orchestra.

In his mature masterpieces (after *Lohengrin*), Wagner's motives are no longer melodies but rather are fragments or phrases—generally short, compressed, incomplete, and interdependent. Gutman explains that, obliterating the "boundaries between aria and recitative, [they] abandoned their former Berlioz-like length and lyricism. Becoming trenchant, they took the form of a harmonic complex, a rhythmic configuration, a melodic outline, or any combination of these."[8]

In a measure or two these musical fragments convey a thought, action, or underlying motivation, and immediately give way to the next musical and dramatic moment. Thus the important distinction between length and pace in Wagner's operas: they may be long, but the dramatic action, expressed in the music, never stops moving forward.

Through the course of *The Ring*, compression, fragmentation, and mingling of motivic phrases accelerate. Plasticity is everywhere; the motives evolve musically and conceptually, appearing in foreshadowed, incipient, definitive, and mutated forms. They contract, expand, merge, invert, and reverse. They evolve in meaning through change in harmony above all, but also through changes in orchestral color, dynamics, cadence, and tempo—and always as these relate to characters, dramatic situations, and text. They suggest, remind, characterize, declaim, announce, belie, contradict, and reveal. They are never just repeated but convey at each occurrence a new form and meaning. They refer as often to what is unseen as seen.

The listener's encounter with these musical ideas can hold the keenest pleasures—thousands of moments of illumination, evoking the memory of things heard before, carrying us toward things yet to come. Truly hearing *The Ring* is a process; revelations always lie ahead. While writing *Wagner's "Ring" and Its Symbols*, Donington observed that "up to the moment of going to press, I was still noticing new [underlying similarities] . . . . There . . . seems no reason why this discovery of hitherto unnoticed subtleties should ever stop."[9]

Wagner did not want his audience to be objective or analytical but rather to experience the music intuitively and emotionally. He projected, in his own words, "motives of reminiscence and presentiment," motives that looked backward and forward, conveying emotional experience at a depth only music, not words, can reach, and no matter how technically sophisticated the musicological intelligence underlying them. In this regard, Wagner's aim to "emotionalize the intellect" remains an apt characterization of his art.

THE 145 music examples in this chapter offer a reasonably comprehensive overview of the music of *The Ring*. Although most commentaries include fewer examples, there could have been hundreds more. The examples are listed here in the order in which they occur in the tetralogy. (In chapter 4 we will revisit motives in the context of each character or character group.)

Each motive is identified by both a number and a name, and by the opera, act, and scene in which it is first heard or in which it occurs most definitively. I have also cited the relevant location in the G. Schirmer Vocal Scores, which should help readers who wish to follow both text and music. Page and staff numbers are consistent in all editions of the Schirmer scores.

The motive names or descriptions used here are simply a useful shorthand. There is certainly no single correct name for any *Ring* motive, but there is much consistency among the major analyses, and I have not often drifted far from these. Occasionally analysts have eschewed names altogether in favor of numbers. While this practice avoids the problem of labeling, I doubt that identifying a certain musical phrase only as 13 is really more helpful than calling it Renunciation of Love. This chapter offers both names and numbers.

The music notation for each example is taken from the G. Schirmer Vocal Scores. The words sung at each occurrence of the motive, the actions undertaken, and/or the stage directions appear in italics directly below the music notation. Characters' words are taken from the Salter and Mann translations. Stage directions are from the Schirmer Vocal Scores.

Each example includes a brief commentary on the narrative use of the musical fragment. My comments are sometimes at odds with the conventional wisdom, but interpretation is appropriate in these matters. I have also frequently quoted names or descriptions given to motives by four prominent *Ring* analysts, all of whose works are highly recommended. Points of concurrence and divergence illustrate a key aspect of Wagner's motives: they are systemic but cannot be considered part of a rigid system. The works referred to here are:

Ernest Newman, *The Wagner Operas,* 1963

Robert Donington, *Wagner's "Ring" and Its Symbols,* 1963

Deryck Cooke, *An Introduction to Wagner's "Der Ring des Nibelungen,"* 1972

Owen M. Lee, *Wagner's "Ring": Turning the Sky Round,* 1990.

MOTIVES
(in order of appearance)

The Rhinegold

1–Beginning

2–Nature

3–Rhine

4–Rhine Daughters

5–Warning

6–Alberich

7–Woe

8–Water Murmurs

9–Gold

10–Rhine Daughters' Joy in the Gold

11–Rhinegold

12–The Ring

13–Renunciation of Love

14–Valhalla

15–Love's Enchantment

16–Love

17–Giants

18–Power of the Gods

19–Treaty

20–Love (Fasolt)

21–Holda's Golden Apples

22–Withering of Life

23–Froh

24–Spear

25–Loge

26–Loge's Craft

27–Woman's Worth

28–Nibelungs

29–Tarnhelm

30–Servitude

31–Power of the Ring

32–Serpent

33–Hoard

34–Hatred

35–Curse

36–Erda

37–Downfall

38–Donner's Call

39–Rainbow Bridge

40–Sword

41–Rhine Daughters' Lament

42–Rhinegold Conclusion

The Valkyrie

43–Storm
44–Siegmund
45–Sieglinde
46–Dawning Love
47–Volsungs' Woe
48–Hunding
49–Rights
50–Bride's Lament
51–Volsung Race
52–Crisis
53–Purpose of the Sword
54–Volse
55–The Sword's Chosen
56–Spring Song
57–Love (Sieglinde)
58–Bliss
59–Love's Deepest Distress
60–Notung

61–Valkyries
62–Hojotoho!
63–Fricka
64–Withered Love
65–Frustration
66–Struggling against Fate
67–Rage
68–Hunding's Pursuit
69–Fate
70–Annunciation of Death
71–Brünnhilde's Defiance
72–The Heroic in Siegfried
73–Redemption
74–Brünnhilde's Reproach
75–Brünnhilde's Love for Wotan
76–Sleep
77–Brünnhilde in Sleep
78–Wotan's Love for Brünnhilde

Siegfried

79–Brooding
80–Siegfried's Horn Call
81–Youthful Energy
82–Mime's Mission
83–Yearning for Knowledge
84–Yearning for Love
85–Joy of Freedom
86–Mission
87–Mime's Frustration
88–Wanderer
89–World Ash Tree
90–Blow, Bellows!
91–Hammering
92–Fafner as Dragon
93–Mission (Mutation)
94–Forest Murmurs

95–Wood Bird
96–False Flattery
97–Siegfried's Horn Call (Mutation)
98–Yearning for Love/Mission
99–Act 3 Prelude
100–Wala! Awake!
101–World's Inheritance
102–Ravens
103–Resistance
104–Awakening
105–Love's Greeting
106–Love's Ecstasy
107–Immortal Beloved
108–World's Treasure
109–Laughing at Death

Twilight of the Gods

110–Prelude
111–Rope of Fate
112–Siegfried (Definitive)
113–The Woman Brünnhilde
114–Giving in Love
115–Mission (Definitive)
116–Radiant Star, Victorious Light
117–Treachery
118–Hagen
119–Gunther
120–Gutrune
121–Potion
122–Plotting
123–Rowing
124–Friendship
125–Gutrune's Deception
126–Mission (as Blood-Brotherhood)
127–Blood-Brotherhood

128–Vow of Atonement
129–Hagen Ascendant
130–Escape
131–Betrayal
132–Honor
133–Murder
134–Dawn
135–Grim Hagen
136–Gutrune's Greeting
137–Hoiho!
138–Gibichungs' Horn Call
139–Vassals' Song
140–Vassals' Greeting
141–Oath
142–Brünnhilde's Betrayal
143–Rhine Daughters (Continued)
144–Death
145–Rest

THE RHINEGOLD

1–Beginning

R-Prelude; Schirmer Vocal Score page 1 staff 1

The curtain is down.

The revolutionary opening of *The Ring* constitutes the perfect beginning to the monumental work: two notes in sixteen measures that last, in the Solti recording, a full thirty-four seconds. Not a motive in the sense of a recognizable phrase that is repeated and changed, these notes instead stand as poles between which all that follows makes its way.

The deep E-flat, played on the double basses and barely heard, takes us at a single stroke to the beginning of the natural world. The second note is B-flat, establishing a perfect fifth, which embraces harmonically both the tonic and dominant, stability and change. At his first two tones, Wagner has framed a universal musical context for a *Ring* story that will span the broadest range of human experience.

2–Nature

R-Prelude; Schirmer 1 staff 2

The curtain is down.

The opening notes evolve into a triad, a major chord, which is as fundamental to music as the world of nature is to *The Ring*. Rising arpeggios often articulate aspects of the natural world, just as rising musical figures can often be associated with positive aspects of growth and falling figures with corruption or decline.

Newman: "Primal substance."
Donington: "The depths of the Rhine as undifferentiated nature."
Cooke: "Nature (Incipient)."
Lee: "The primal element."

3–Rhine

R-Prelude; Schirmer 2 staff 3

The curtain is down.

While all four commentators note the symbolic importance of the river and water in nature, the obvious should not be overlooked: that Wagner chose a real place as the geographical center of the world of *The Ring*. The Rhine Valley was the historical homeland of the Gibichungs, from whom much of the German mythology evolved (see "Gunther," pages 231–232). The music is an undulating extension of 2–Nature.

Newman: "The river or the primal element."
Donington: "First stirring under the Rhine as a premonition of consciousness."
Cooke: "The 'definitive' Nature motive. At twice the speed, becomes Rhine motive."
Lee: "Water (from the primal element)."

4–Rhine Daughters

R-i; Schirmer 5 staffs 4–5

Woglinde circles with graceful swimming motions: "Weia! Waga! Waft your waves,
ye waters! Carry your crests to the cradle! Wagalaweia! Wallala weiala weia!"

The first two notes of this passage, and the last two, are sung to the onomatopoeic
"Weia!" This musical figure is a falling step that will appear frequently; for example, in 7–Woe, 11–Rhinegold, 30–Servitude, 31–Power of the Ring, 100–Wala!
Awake!, 102–Ravens, and 137–Hoiho! It is a striking demonstration of Wagner's
ability to create so much out of very little.

Donington: "The song of the Rhinemaidens as tempters back to immature
　　innocence."
Cooke: "The Rhinemaidens."
Lee: "Song of the water maidens."

5–Warning

R-i; Schirmer 7 staff 1

Flosshilde: "Badly you guard the sleeping gold."

Flosshilde interrupts the carefree play of her sisters to introduce a central danger:
desire for the gold. This brief phrase, the first significant passage in *The Ring* in a
minor key, foreshadows 95B–Wood Bird; the Wood Bird warns Siegfried about
Mime in S-2-iii.

6–Alberich

R-i; Schirmer 12 staff 2

Alberich climbs with implike agility to the top of the rock.

This music depicts Alberich clambering over the rocks; it does not fully describe
the dwarf and is hardly developed later. For Alberich's more substantial musical
contributions, see "Alberich," page 179.

Cooke: "Alberich."

7–Woe

R-i; Schirmer 24 staff 1

Alberich is rejected by the Rhine Daughters.

This is the first mutation of the falling-step phrase first heard at "Weia!" in 4–Rhine Daughters, now used to convey the dwarf's grief, which is caused by the nymphs' rejection of him.

Donington: "Woe or grief, whether accepted or not."
Cooke: "Alberich's Lament."

8–Water Murmurs

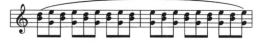

R-i; Schirmer 31 staff 1 and following

The rays of the sun penetrate the waters.

Wagner's depiction of murmurs inherent in nature is among his most charming conceptions. Here under the Rhine and later in the forest murmurs of Neidhöhle in S-2, one senses an eternal, pervasive life force.

Donington: "The glitter of the sun's light playing with the gold under the water, as childhood's innocent delight."
Lee: "Water murmurs."

9–Gold

R-i; Schirmer 31 staffs 1–2

The rays of the sun illuminate the gold.

An important motive, 9–Gold here conveys the shining, innocent beauty of the Rhinegold in its unfashioned state. Wagner continually reworks motivic fragments to convey the changing dramatic meaning of the moment. For example, a particularly chilling mutation of 9–Gold forms a bridge between the end of Siegfried's Rhine Journey in T-Prologue and the terrible conspiracy of T-1-i.

Newman: "The Gold."
Donington: "The gold as true worth."
Cooke: "The Gold."
Lee: "The Rhine gold."

10–Rhine Daughters' Joy in the Gold

R-i; Schirmer 33 staff 1

The maidens rejoice as the sun wakes the gold.

This music is a swirling relative of 3–Rhine and 4–Rhine Daughters. The phrase is built around a fragment consisting of four notes: a falling third followed by two rising whole steps returning to the first note. This figure will appear in many other motives, including 28–Nibelungs, 31–Power of the Ring, 117–Treachery, 125–Gutrune's Treachery, and 127–Blood-Brotherhood.

Cooke: "The Rhinemaidens' Joy in the Gold."

11–Rhinegold

R-i; Schirmer 33 staff 2

Rhine Daughters: "Rhinegold! Rhinegold! Dazzling delight, how brightly and bravely you laugh!"

The motive here is an assertive statement based on a falling step, as in 7–Woe. The Rhine Daughters' joy is now focused on the gold it is their duty to guard. The phrase will be converted into a haunting lament for the Rhinegold at the end of R-iv.

Donington: "Rhinegold! Rhinegold!"
Cooke: "Rheingold!"
Lee: "Water cries."

12–The Ring

R-i; Schirmer 41 staff 3 and following

Wellgunde: "He who from the Rhinegold fashioned the ring that would confer on him immeasurable might could win the world's wealth for his own."

This key musical phrase displays an important aspect of Wagner's mature motivic expression. As a musical fragment, it can hardly stand alone. Its structure is round, without a specific point of reference, like the ring itself. Its focus and tonality are elusive. Yet it is a figure of profound adaptability, used to convey a broad range of shadings and feelings. The ring does not exist in nature but is a fashioned object with specific aspects, and the complex tonality of its music carries us into an inner and more complex level of emotional expression.

Newman: "The Ring."

Donington: "The ring as underlying purpose." Further, "An eerily cornerless motive: rings have no corners. . . . No other motive in the Ring is quite so musically ambivalent, nor more readily combined with other motives."[10]

Cooke: "The Ring."

Lee: "The Ring."

13–Renunciation of Love

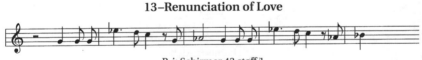

R-i; Schirmer 43 staff 1

Woglinde: "Only he who forswears love's power, only he who forfeits love's delight, only he can attain the magic to fashion the gold into a ring."

This passage defines a recurring problem in *The Ring*, the consequences of lovelessness. It is the last key motive introduced in R-i. It has also attracted substantial controversy, principally because Siegmund sings it in V-1-iii (as does Brünnhilde in T-1-iii) as an affirmation, rather than as a rejection, of love.[11]

The phrase may have some relationship to 16B–Love and 21–Holda's Golden Apples. Yet *The Ring* is filled with hundreds of musical fragments that may (or may not) relate to one another. Drawing such connections can be highly speculative; it can lead both to extraordinary insights and to the worst excesses of motive hunting.

Newman: "Renunciation of Love."

Donington: "Renunciation; often amounting to acceptance of destiny." It is "a
motive not harsh and forbidding, as might on the face of it be expected, but
of a singularly sad, moving and resigned nobility."[12]

Cooke: "Renunciation of Love."

Lee: "The moment of choice."

14–Valhalla

R-ii; Schirmer 55 staff 1 and following

Wotan: "'Tis completed, the everlasting work: on the mountain peak stands the
gods' stronghold, superbly soars the resplendent building!"

This famous music has four segments which sometimes appear separately. The
first carries the strongest associations with Valhalla. A direct transformation of
12–Ring, it marks the first time in *The Ring* that Wagner changes the harmony and
color of one phrase to turn it into something quite different. Falling and then rising over an arpeggiated chord, the motive projects stately nobility, a relatively
positive side of the absolute power sought by Wotan.

The second segment resembles the rising three notes heard in 10–Rhine Daughters' Joy in the Gold. It will provide a pulsing, insistent undercurrent as the gods
enter Valhalla at the close of R-iv.

The third segment consists of two alternating notes reminiscent of the murmurs element and sometimes heard when the power of the gods takes on an
impotent or passive aspect. It reaches its most moving expression in 145–Rest in
T-3-iii.

Cooke describes the fourth segment as a kind of cadence, attaching itself here and there to finish other musical phrases.[13] In structure, however, it is identical to 16B–Love. With an emphatic gesture in R-ii, Wotan shows that he will not renounce love or Freia to gain the treasure. As he tells Brünnhilde in V-2-ii, young love once waned in him, and he sought worldly power, but "I could not let go from love."

Newman: "Valhalla."

Donington: "Valhalla as genuine achievement; also as Wotan's genuinely
     creative thoughts."

Cooke: "Valhalla."

Lee: "Valhalla."

15–Love's Enchantment

R-ii; Schirmer 61 staffs 1–2

Fricka: "A stately dwelling, splendidly appointed, might tempt [Wotan] to tarry here and rest."

The passage is commonly associated with Fricka's nagging desire to keep Wotan at home; Cooke refers to it as Domestic Bliss. However, Wotan immediately repeats the phrase while defending his love of roaming. Near the end of S-3-ii, the motive is substantially transformed into 103–Resistance when Wotan tries to bar Siegfried from reaching Brünnhilde. It is heard again as Siegfried reaches Brünnhilde's rock in S-3-iii. This extended, lovely phrase conveys more than the mere domestic tranquility sought by Fricka.

Newman: "Love's Enchantment."

Cooke: "Domestic Bliss."

16–Love

A.

B.

R-ii; Schirmer 64 staff 1

Freia enters in hasty flight.

This rapid segment contains the seeds of two principal love motives in *The Ring*. The first is a steeply rising chromatic phrase, restated, for example, in Loge's R-ii narration, the annunciation scene in V-2-iv, when Siegfried reaches Brünnhilde's rock in S-3-iii, and elsewhere.

The second segment is reminiscent of both 13–Renunciation of Love and 14D–Valhalla. It will dominate the love music of V-1, especially at Sieglinde's definitive statement to Siegmund: "You are the spring." The phrase will take on the full force of love denied in much of the music of V-2.

Newman: "Freia or Flight."

Donington: "Freia as young love; also Agitation, but including both passion and compassion."

Cooke: "Love."[14]

17–Giants

R-ii; Schirmer 68 staff 1

The giants, Fasolt and Fafner, enter armed with strong clubs.

The music, like the giants, is simple, rough, and insistent.

Newman: "The giants."

Donington: "The giants as brute strength; the brutal aspect of parental authority."

Cooke: "The Giants."

18–Power of the Gods

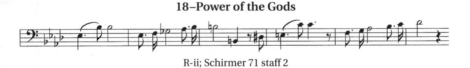

R-ii; Schirmer 71 staff 2

Fasolt: "What you [gods] are, you are only by contracts: limited and well defined is your power."

The rising scale sounds like an inversion of 24–Spear, the genuine if compromised symbol of Wotan's political authority. Also noteworthy are the repeated, pulsating chords underneath, which lend additional urgency to the passage. In T-3-iii, at the beginning of the immolation scene, the motive will reach a point of stately resolution.

Cooke: "The Power of the Gods."

19-Treaty

R-ii; Schirmer 72 staff 1

Fasolt: "I will ... flee from your peace if openly, honorably and freely you do not know to keep faith in your bond."

The motive begins with a rising arpeggiated chord and then descends in an apparent reference to 24–Spear. As Loge and Froh pile up the hoard in R-iv, it is combined with 28–Nibelungs to great effect.

20–Love (Fasolt)

R-ii; Schirmer 73 staff 3

Fasolt: "To win a woman who, winsome and gentle, will live with us poor creatures."

Both parts of 16–Love are slowed in this remarkable passage. The sense of agitation is gone. Here, as always, Wagner eschews the facile and one-dimensional to give us credible characters of surprising complexity and interest. Newman: "Wagner here lays the gentlest of hands on the uncouth Giant who has a strain of tenderness in him."[15]

21–Holda's Golden Apples

R-ii; Schirmer 74 staff 2

Fafner: "Golden apples grow in [Freia's] garden; only she knows how to tend them."

The music glows with the affirmation of Freia's life-giving fruit. The gods need the apples to maintain their eternal youth.

Newman: "Golden apples."
Donington: "Freia's golden apples as the joy of life."
Cooke: "Golden Apples."

22–Withering of Life

R-ii; Schirmer 74 staff 4

Fafner: "Sick and wan, [the gods'] bloom will wane."

This fragment illustrates the immense motivic flexibility at Wagner's disposal. It is a brief figure but creates an immediate impression. Borrowed from the first segment of 21–Holda's Golden Apples, it falls but does not rise, as though cut off from the life-giving apples themselves; it is literally a musical withering of their powers.

23–Froh

R-ii; Schirmer 75 staff 4

Froh: "To me, Freia! Let her be, rascal! Froh will protect the fair one."

A rhythmic transformation of 21–Holda's Golden Apples; Freia's welfare is always Froh's overriding concern.

24–Spear

R-ii; Schirmer 77 staff 1

Wotan stretches his spear between Froh and Donner and the giants to prevent violence to the spear's contracts.

The descending scale of 24–Spear symbolizes Wotan's temporal authority and its limitations. The motive was foreshadowed by both Fricka and Fasolt in earlier references to the contract with the giants. The treaties and contracts Wotan has made over time to subdue other races are inscribed on the spearshaft.

Cooke, who sees the motives as highly systemic, believes 24–Spear generates a family of motives, related both to Wotan's power and to his will.[16]

Newman: "Wotan's Treaty with the Giants."

Donington: "The spear as Wotan's willful authority, but also with entanglements and inhibitions."

Cooke: "The Spear."

Lee: "The spear."

25–Loge

A.

R-ii; Schirmer 77 staff 4

B.

Schirmer 78 staff 1

C.

Schirmer 78 staffs 1–2

Wotan turns and sees Loge coming: "Loge at last! Is this how you hasten to right the evil bargain that you concluded?"

Loge, both as character and as music, is an intermediary between the worlds of nature and the conscious ambitions of the *Ring* characters. Loge's music consists of three basic segments. The first, associated with a flickering fire, recurs frequently, even if Loge is not present or mentioned, as a reference to intelligence or quick-witted scheming (as opposed to ominous and dark 79–Brooding).

The second segment reinforces the alignment of Loge's fire as an active force of nature. It is a roiling form of the murmurs figure that evokes nature's inherent but undirected energy.

The third segment, representing the power of fire, consists of a falling step, like 7–Woe and 11–Rhinegold. It reaches its fullest expression in the magic fire of V-3-iii and the immolation scene of T-3-iii, when Loge as fire dominates both stage and music.

Newman: "The God of Craft."
Donington: "Loge the god of fire as primal energy and its ambivalence."
Cooke: Loge as "the sense of the mysterious and inscrutable that surrounds human life."[17]

26–Loge's Craft

R-ii; Schirmer 84 staff 2

Wotan: "Loge's . . . counsel is of richer weight when he delays in giving it."

Wotan has staked his future on Loge's wit. The deeply falling and rising figure swings back and forth, perhaps suggesting that such reliance is ill-founded. Similarly plunging music, especially in *Twilight,* will be associated with treachery and deceit; for example, in 118–Hagen and 122–Plotting.

27–Woman's Worth

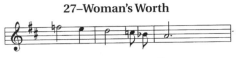

R-ii; Schirmer 85 staff 4

Loge: "In the whole wide world nothing is so rich that a man will accept it in lieu of woman's beauty and delight."

At this point in R-ii, Loge explores a central theme in *The Ring,* the supreme value of love, as represented by man's love for woman. In fact, this phrase is one of the drama's most pervasive musical ideas. The falling scale of six notes, which recurs more than forty times in the course of the tetralogy, is always readily identifiable. It is also among the most plastic, formless, and intriguing phrases in *The Ring.* We often hear it as a cadence, a kind of closing attached to quite different ideas or music.

The phrase suggests something beyond the value of woman and love. To Cooke, it is a second form of 13–Renunciation of Love "which often occurs as a mournful cadence, expressing futility."[18] For Donington, the phrase "conveys a mood not unlike that of the 'renunciation' motive: it speaks of grief and destiny; it also speaks, not in all but in some of its harmonic and dramatic contexts, of acceptance and resignation."[19]

Most *Ring* characters either sing the phrase or are described by the orchestra's playing it: Loge, Froh, Wotan, Alberich, Fasolt, Erda, Siegfried, the Norns, Hagen, Brünnhilde, Gunther, and the Rhine Daughters come to mind. Moreover, the words spoken and the emotions expressed are widely varied and generally of high importance. (For a more detailed account of the key occurrences, see "A Core Motive: Woman's Worth" in the Appendix.)

Donington: "Destiny accepted."

Cooke: "Renunciation of Love (Second Form)."

28–Nibelungs

R-ii; Schirmer 113 staff 1

As Wotan and Loge descend to Nibelheim, an increasing clamor of hammering is heard.

The famous 28–Nibelungs motive, foreshadowed in Loge's narration in R-ii, is built around the rising three-note figure also heard in 10–Rhine Daughters' Joy in the Gold. The music no longer reflects the joy of the Rhine Daughters which, like the happiness of the Nibelungs, has been compromised by the theft of the gold and the power of the ring.

Newman: "The toiling dwarfs, slaves to the power of the Ring, who are smithing the gold for Alberich."
Donington: "Mime as smith; forging generally."
Cooke: "The Nibelungs."

29–Tarnhelm

R-iii; Schirmer 117 staffs 2–3

Alberich picks up the Tarnhelm, which Mime has dropped, and examines it carefully.

A slow and mysterious figure, 29–Tarnhelm also centers on a rising three-note fragment. The phrase rises to a harmonic resolution, as it does in 31–Power of the Ring on the two occasions in R-iii and R-iv when Alberich actually wields the ring to command the Nibelungs. The Tarnhelm always does what its master commands.

Newman: "Tarnhelm."
Donington: "Tarnhelm as unconscious fantasy."
Cooke: "The Tarnhelm."

30–Servitude

R-iii; Schirmer 121 staff 5

Alberich has gained the Tarnhelm, which completes his enslavement of the Nibelungs.

As we descend to Nibelheim, we hear 28–Nibelungs beneath the falling half-steps of 30–Servitude, assuring us that the Nibelungs now serve Alberich, the lord of the ring. Wagner frequently projects two or more motivic references at the same time, building a masterful polyphony that enriches the dramatic possibilities of the music.

Newman: "Servitude."

Cooke: "Servitude."

Lee: "World enslavement."

31–Power of the Ring

R-iii; Schirmer 133 staffs 3–4

Alberich (to the Nibelungs): "Tremble with terror, abject throng: at once obey the master of the ring!"

This music accompanies the two moments in *The Ring* when the ring's power is actually seen to work (as the Nibelungs pile up the hoard at Alberich's command in R-iii and again in R-iv): it reaches a harmonic resolution in a major key. This is a composite motive, combining 30–Servitude with the now-familiar rising three-note figure from 10–Rhine Daughters' Joy in the Gold.

Cooke: "The Power of the Ring."

32–Serpent

R-iii; Schirmer 150 staff 3

Alberich uses the Tarnhelm to take the shape of a huge serpent.

The passage readily suggests the slow, ominous movements of Alberich as serpent in R-iii. It is also echoed in V-3-i as Siegrune and Schwertleite urge Sieglinde to hide in Neidhöhle where Fafner has assumed the form of a dragon, and it evolves into the definitive 92–Fafner as Dragon in S-2.

Newman: "Serpent."

Donington: "Fafner as the enormous backward pull (or inertia or resistance to change) of the unconscious."

33–Hoard

R-iv; Schirmer 166 staff 1

Alberich (to the Nibelungs): "Bring it in there as I command! Pile the hoard into a heap!"

The phrase is another rising three-note figure; like all motivic elements in *The Ring,* however, it has its own distinctive flavor and feeling. In *The Rhinegold* the development of these three-note phrases traces the transformations of 10–Rhine Daughters' Joy in the Gold, 28–Nibelungs, 29–Tarnhelm, 30–Servitude, and 31–Power of the Ring. The golden hoard has been mined by the slave Nibelungs under the power of the ring.

Newman: "The Hoard."

Cooke: "The Hoard."

34–Hatred

R-iv; Schirmer 174 staff 4 and following

Alberich, untied by Loge: "Am I now free? Truly free? Then thus I give you my free-dom's first greeting!"

A chilling treatment of Alberich's consuming hatred, which continues as an active force through *Twilight*, reappears with Alberich in S-2-i and T-2-i. The motive combines the rapid rising scale (similar to 43–Storm at the beginning of V-1) with an arrhythmic, repeated triad.

Newman: "Annihilation."
Donington: "Alberich's obsessive will as a force of destiny."
Cooke: "Resentment."

35–Curse

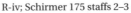

R-iv; Schirmer 175 staffs 2–3

Alberich: "Since by curse it came to me, accursed be this ring!"

This motive will be repeated as Alberich's curse works its way through the drama. Both Cooke and Donington consider the motive, as it rises and then falls, to be an inversion of 12–The Ring.

Newman: "The Curse on the Ring."
Donington: "Alberich's curse as an expression of destiny."
Cooke: "The Curse."

36–Erda

R-iv; Schirmer 192 staff 3

From a rocky cleft on one side breaks a bluish light in which Erda becomes sud-denly visible, rising from below to half her height.

Erda's music is among the most pointed and evocative in *The Ring*. It grows directly out of 2–Nature and 3–Rhine transposed to a minor key. Erda is a transitional force between nature and the conscious struggles of the principal characters.

Newman: "Erda."
Donington: "Erda, the Earth Mother, as ancestral wisdom."
Cooke: "Erda, the earth goddess."
Lee: "Earth (from the primal element)."

37–Downfall

R-iv; Schirmer 194 staff 2

Erda: "A dark day dawns for the gods."

The music of 37–Downfall is among the most sweeping statements in *The Ring*. Here it foreshadows the end of the world of the gods, which it ultimately accompanies in T-3-iii. It is an inversion of 36–Erda, and the two figures are frequently coupled. The downward motion conveys the decline of the old order: 37–Downfall bears a resemblance to another important falling scale, 27–Woman's Worth. Both reflect on the most poignant issues—the passing of time and life, engagement with fate, and inevitable relinquishment.

Newman: "Twilight of the Gods."
Donington: "The downfall of the gods."
Cooke: "Twilight of the Gods."
Lee: "Reversion to the primal element."

38–Donner's Call

R-iv; Schirmer 204 staffs 1–2

Donner: "Heda! Heda! Hedo! Come to me, mists! Vapors, to me! Donner your master summons you to his host."

Donner is Storm God, a vital force of nature rendered in dynamic, conscious form. Summoning the mists is the only effective action he takes in *The Ring*. The music's heroic quality may be ironic, given the compromising behavior of the gods in general and Donner's raging impotence in particular. We hear a reminiscence of the motive in V-1-Prelude.

Newman: "Donner's horn call."

Donington: "The thunder as masculine spirit."

Cooke: "Donner."

39–Rainbow Bridge

R-iv; Schirmer 208 staffs 3-4

Froh: "The bridge leads to the fortress, light but firm beneath your feet: boldly tread its terrorless path!"

Froh's only real contribution to the *Rhinegold* story is his conjuring of the rainbow bridge which the gods cross to the apparent shelter of Valhalla. In its shimmering beauty, 39–Rainbow Bridge grows directly out of 2–Nature and 3–Rhine to close the first Ring opera.

Newman: "Rainbow."

Donington: "The rainbow bridge to Valhalla."

Cooke: "The Rainbow Bridge."

40–Sword

R-iv; Schirmer 213 staff 1

Wotan, as if seized by a great thought, very firmly: "Thus I salute the fortress, safe from terror and dread."

We will hear 40–Sword on many occasions through the remainder of *The Ring*. In R-iv the motive represents Wotan's plan to escape from his dilemma, which is to regain the ring from Fafner without violating his bargain with the giant. At this point the sword is pure concept, articulated only in the music, not in words. In V-1 and after, the sword is a significant physical object and symbol, and its music undergoes a wide range of treatments and associations. This continuity and transition, in 40–Sword and throughout the musical fabric of *The Ring*, are fundamental to its astonishing coherency.

Newman: "The Sword."

Donington: "The sword as true manhood."

Cooke: "The Sword."

Lee: "The sword."

41–Rhine Daughters' Lament

R-iv; Schirmer 216 staffs 2–3

The Rhinemaidens' voices float up from the valley: "Rhinegold! Rhinegold! Purest gold! How clear and bright you once shone on us!"

This extended motive, which moves *The Rhinegold* to a close, is another composite passage, beginning with a restatement of 11–Rhinegold. It hauntingly recalls, in inverted form, 10–Rhine Daughters' Joy in the Gold. Their joy now lies far behind.

42–Rhinegold Conclusion
R-iv; Schirmer 216 staff 2 and following

As much as anything, Wagner knew how to close a piece. The final bars of *The Rhinegold* contain an elaborate recapitulation of music heard before. These musical reminiscences of momentous stage events pull us in several emotional directions at once. Donington has described 41–Rhine Daughters' Lament as a "poignant inspiration . . . piercing our hearts with sudden longing, melting our bones with nostalgic desire."[20]

This is not the whole story. In the last nineteen staffs of the opera, we hear references to the following: 14B–Valhalla, 41–Rhine Daughters' Lament (three segments), 14A–Valhalla (especially the latter half, which pulses like a heartbeat underneath the other music), 25A–Loge, 40–Sword, 39–Rainbow Bridge, and 14C–Valhalla. At this point motivic labels are only a nuisance; the motives flood over us with their own inherent logic and urgency. They elevate *The Ring* to wordless poetry. This is precisely what Wagner meant by "emotionalizing the intellect."

THE VALKYRIE

43–Storm

V-1-Prelude ; Schirmer 1 staff 1

The curtain is down.

The Storm Prelude anticipates our first encounter with Siegmund, whose life has been especially stormy and who is now in full flight from his enemies. As usual, Wagner plunges us immediately into the action of the moment.

Newman: "Storm wind."
Donington: "The storm . . . as Wotan's resistance to destiny."
Cooke: "The Storm."

44–Siegmund

V-1-i; Schirmer 5 staffs 4–5

Siegmund appears, entering Hunding's house.

The falling movement of 24–Spear is "contradicted by a rising motion," as Cooke notes.[21] Siegmund will oppose Wotan's will.

Newman: "Siegmund."
Donington: "Siegmund as hero schooled in misfortune."
Cooke: "Siegmund."

45–Sieglinde

V-1-i; Schirmer 7 staff 3

Sieglinde enters and finds Siegmund exhausted on her hearth. She bends over him, listening to his breathing.

Wagner's musical phraseology is highly compressed; it derives much power by communicating so much in a short time. Within a few seconds of the curtain's rise, we have been introduced to the personal music of both principal characters, music as intertwined as their lives will be. For Sieglinde, the strings sweetly rise and then fall in an inverted, complementary response to 44–Siegmund. The motive conveys at once Sieglinde's inner beauty and her misfortune.

Newman: "Sieglinde's pity."
Donington: "Sieglinde as heroine schooled in misfortune."
Cooke: "Sieglinde."

46–Dawning Love

V-1-i; Schirmer 9 staff 2

Siegmund and Sieglinde gaze upon each other with growing interest.

The 16B–Love motive first introduced by Freia in R-ii dominates the first two acts of *The Valkyrie,* as Siegmund and Sieglinde's love blossoms in V-1 and is threatened in V-2. Here the motive is extended to unusual length.

Newman: "Dawning love."

47–Volsungs' Woe

V-1-i; Schirmer 15 staffs 1–2

Siegmund determines to leave Sieglinde to spare her the ill fate that pursues him. She responds that ill fate already lives in her home. He gazes at her, deeply moved, and she drops her eyes in shame and sadness.

The motive struggles to rise and then falls in a way that is reminiscent of both 44–Siegmund and 45–Sieglinde.

Newman: "Volsung's Woe."
Donington: "The Volsungs as instruments of destiny."
Cooke: "The Volsungs' Bond of Sympathy."

48–Hunding

V-1-ii; Schirmer 16 staff 2

With spear and shield, Hunding crosses the threshold.

Hunding's aggressive music is introduced by a repeated triad, followed by a sharply punctuated segment. It is a passage that will recall Hunding at once when it appears later in *The Ring.* A figure resembling 43–Storm is heard underneath.

Newman: "Hunding."

Donington: "Hunding as Siegmund's dark shadow."
Cooke: "Hunding."

49–Rights

V-1-ii; Schirmer 17 staff 2

Hunding (to Siegmund): "My house is holy. Treat my house as holy too."

There is a sense here of hypocritical values nevertheless rigidly held, a pushy insistence on legal rights without moral content. The figure falls, as does 24–Spear.

Donington: "Obligation as an expression of destiny."
Cooke: "Hunding's Rights."

50–Bride's Lament

V-1-ii; Schirmer 30 staff 1

Siegmund tells of striking down the bride's brothers: "In a flood of wild tears she gazed weeping at the carnage."

Foreshadowed in V-1-Prelude and heard amidst the dawning love between the twins in V-1-i, this falling figure evokes both the desperate distress and the hope in the lives of Siegmund and Sieglinde. The fragment is given a more pointed treatment in V-2-i when Fricka accuses Wotan of abandoning the race of gods. Descending musical figures in *The Ring* are often associated with distress or decline.

Newman: "The maiden's grief."

51–Volsung Race

V-1-ii; Schirmer 32 staffs 2–3

Siegmund: "Now you know why I am not called 'Peaceful.'"

Wotan has fostered the Volsung race, whose noble music recalls 14A–Valhalla.

The treatment here reflects the distress of the Volsungs. The first segment will subsequently evolve into the aggressive, optimistic statement of 55–The Sword's Chosen; it also foreshadows the opening of the lyrical love statement, 56–Spring Song.

Newman: "The Volsungs, the tragic race doomed to suffering."
Donington: "The tragic but heroic destiny of the entire Volsung race."
Cooke: "The Volsung Race."

52–Crisis

V-1-ii; Schirmer 34 staff 2

With anxious gestures, Sieglinde steps between the two men.

A fragment expressing a pure state of heightened emotion. Newman's description of 132–Honor is applicable here: "An epigrammatic condensation of rhythm . . . which only Wagner could have invented, and which no other composer but Beethoven would have dared to use if it had been offered to him."[22] In V-2-iii, 52–Crisis will be restated when Brünnhilde commits herself to defy Wotan and help Siegmund against Hunding.

53–Purpose of the Sword

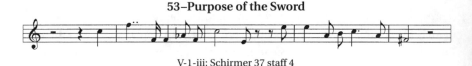

V-1-iii; Schirmer 37 staff 4

Siegmund: "My father promised me a sword: I would find it in deepest distress."

Siegmund calls out for the promised weapon. The phrase begins as 40–Sword, but both the change in harmony and the falling motion at the end reflect Siegmund's frustration at this moment.

Cooke: "The Purpose of the Sword."

54–Volse

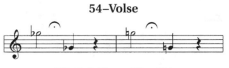

V-1-iii; Schirmer 38 staff 4

Siegmund: "Volse, Volse, where is your sword?"

These high notes, sustained over a thundering orchestra, are an obvious challenge to the tenor. The falling octave underlines the urgency of Siegmund's impassioned call, as in 60–Notung.

Newman: "Volse! Volse!"
Cooke: "Volse!"

55–The Sword's Chosen

V-1-iii; Schirmer 47 staff 3

Sieglinde: "Oh! could I find him here and now, that friend."

Sieglinde now knows it is Siegmund who is destined to retrieve the sword from the ash tree. The phrase recalls 51–Volsung Race and builds directly on 45–Sieglinde; she has led Siegmund to the weapon.

56–Spring Song

V-i-iii; Schirmer 53 staff 3

Siegmund: "Wintry storms have vanished before Maytime."

This passage, among the most loved by *Ring* audiences and one bearing the closest resemblance to a conventional aria, grows out of 51–Volsung Race. It does not develop additional motives and is repeated only once more, when Wotan appeals to Fricka to bless the twins' love in V-2-i.

Newman: "Spring Song."
Donington: "Siegmund's love song of the coming of spring, as his experience of fulfillment with Sieglinde."
Cooke: *"Winterstürme."*

57–Love (Sieglinde)

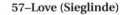

V-1-iii; Schirmer 58 staff 1

Sieglinde: "You are the spring for which I longed in the frosty winter time."

Sieglinde's response to Siegmund's love statement is her own version of 16B–Love; hers is a definitive statement of this principal love motive.

58–Bliss

A.

V-1-iii; Schirmer 62 staff 2

B.

Schirmer 61 staff 3

Siegmund: "O sweetest bliss!"

These fragments offer a further demonstration of the compelling logic at the heart of Wagner's music. The first example consists of three notes, an unresolved phrase conveying a yearning for bliss. In the second example, two notes are added, completing the phrase both musically and emotionally into a fulfillment of that longing.

Newman: "Bliss."
Donington: "Bliss and the longing for bliss."

59–Love's Deepest Distress

V-1-iii; Schirmer 71 staff 3

Siegmund: "Holiest love's deepest distress, yearning love's scorching desire, burn bright in my breast."

Siegmund very clearly makes this statement to 13–Renunciation of Love, but his action affirms love. This apparent contradiction has been the subject of much interpretive discussion. The phrase is heard as Wotan turns away from Brünnhilde in V-3-iii, but Brünnhilde also sings it in T-1-iii when she tells Waltraute she will never renounce love. Perhaps the phrase reflects the making of a decision for or against love, a critical choice. The controversy amply demonstrates the dangers of rigid motive labeling.[23]

60–Notung

V-1-iii; Schirmer 72 staff 1

Siegmund: "Needy, Needy, I name you sword."

The sword was promised to Siegmund in his hour of greatest need, and Mann awkwardly but correctly translates "Notung" as "Needy." The falling octave used as an invocation is similar to 54–Volse. Siegmund's son Siegfried will sing 60–Notung while he reforges the sword in S-1-iii.

Newman: "Notung."
Donington: "Notung as the promised or longed-for sword."
Cooke: "Notung."

61–Valkyries

V-2-Prelude; Schirmer 80 staff 6

The curtain rises during this passage to reveal Wotan and, for the first time, Brünnhilde.

The initial appearance of this famous music here in the V-2-Prelude foreshadows its full statement at the beginning of V-3. The Valkyries have been fostered by Wotan to bring fallen heroes to Valhalla in order to create an army to defend the gods against attack by Alberich's Nibelung hordes.

Newman points out that this much-maligned music suffers from two common recital hall errors: the short note of each measure tends to be dropped and the fourth note of the measure emphasized rather than the first, contrary to Wagner's directions.[24] Wagner used the title "Ride of the Valkyries" only in connection with the concert version of this music.

Newman: "Valkyries and Brünnhilde."
Donington: "The Valkyries as the masculine element in women."
Cooke: "Riding."

62–Hojotoho!

V-2-i; Schirmer 82 staff 2

Spurred by Wotan to help Siegmund in the coming fight, Brünnhilde springs from rock to rock, shouting: "Hojotoho! Hojotoho! Heiaha!"

Employing the same energetic syncopation as 61–Valkyries, the music expresses Brünnhilde's manly enthusiasm for her mission, as Wotan's favorite, to help Siegmund against Hunding; at her first appearance she is very much a Valkyrie whose purpose is to serve Wotan by bringing fallen heroes to Valhalla.

Newman: "Hojotoho!"

63–Fricka

V-2-i; Schirmer 86 staffs 1–2

Wotan, as Fricka strides impetuously toward him: "The old storm, the old trouble!"

The motive is one of the most descriptive in *The Ring*. It reverberates with Fricka's relentless opposition to Wotan's plan. The phrase recalls the frustration expressed in the second segment of 53–Purpose of the Sword, but here conveys Fricka's standing in the way of Wotan's sword and purpose.

Newman: "Wrath."

Cooke: "Fricka in *Die Walküre*."

64–Withered Love

V-2-i; Schirmer 92 staff 2

Fricka: "Why do I protest about marriage and its vows since you were the first to break them?"

The passage is commonly associated with Fricka's persistent nagging. In fact, it is a twisted, chromatic mutation of 16B–Love, illuminating the unhappy state of Fricka's marriage.

Newman: "Fricka's reproach."

65–Frustration

V-2-i; Schirmer 99 staff 2

From here, Wotan's whole demeanor expresses uneasiness and gloom, as Fricka undermines his argument.

This remarkable passage conveys a key development in the *Ring* drama—the frustration of Wotan's will and plans when Fricka exposes their underlying fallacy: that Wotan cannot create and manipulate a free will in others. The motive occurs frequently from this point to color that frustration and its consequences.

Like 24-Spear, the fragment is shaped around a falling scale, a symbol of Wotan's compromised authority, but its twisting chromaticism gives it a flavor all its own.

Newman: "Dejection."
Donington: "Wotan's will frustrated."
Cooke: "Wotan's Frustration."

66–Struggling Against Fate

V-2-ii; Schirmer 120 staff 4

Wotan: "Only one person could do what I may not: a hero whom I have never stooped to help."

Wotan's efforts to escape or otherwise come to grips with his fate are accompanied by urgent echoes of 36–Erda, 37–Downfall, and 65–Frustration. These elements inform the explosive Prelude to S-3, before Wotan's final confrontations with Erda and Siegfried. Wotan's struggles and 66–Struggling Against Fate are quietly laid to rest in the incomparable music of T-3-iii, the immolation scene, when Brünnhilde says: "Rest, rest now, o god!" (see 145–Rest).

Newman: "Need of the Gods."
Cooke: "The Need of the Gods."

67–Rage

V-2-ii; Schirmer 136 staff 4

Wotan (storms always having warned Brünnhilde): "Your courage would fail you, if ever a crushing spark of my rage burst upon you."

Wotan's warning to Brünnhilde falls like hammer blows. The earthshaking wrath of the god builds as Wotan determines to wreck his own plans and to murder his own son. It is this fragment that closes the monumental V-2 when Wotan rides off to find and punish Brünnhilde.

68–Hunding's Pursuit

V-2-iii; Schirmer 150 staff 1

Sieglinde: "[Hunding's] gangs are coming fully armed. No sword will serve when their dogs attack."

An ominous, challenging phrase that rolls beneath Sieglinde's fears like an approaching storm. Like 24–Spear, the figure builds around a descending scale, but its sinuous chromaticism is reminiscent of 65–Frustration.

69–Fate

V-2-iv; Schirmer 152 staff 4

Brünnhilde comes out of the cave and advances toward Siegmund.

Brünnhilde approaches Siegmund to take him away in death to the glory of Valhalla. Destiny and its mysterious power are the core truths here, and the treatment is ominous: fate will carry most of the *Ring* characters toward destruction and doom.

Donington: "Destiny as the power to which all must in the end surrender."
Cooke: "Fate."

70–Annunciation of Death

V-2-iv; Schirmer 152 staff 5

As she approaches, Brünnhilde pauses and observes Siegmund from a distance.

This passage represents the imaginative power of Wagner's music as well as any. Like many motives, it grows dramatically and musically from what has come before; thus we hear 69–Fate at the end of the phrase. The tonality is subtle and infinitely flexible—the passage will subsequently take on a wealth of different emotional implications. In fact, in the extraordinary conversation between Brünnhilde and Siegmund, the musical evolution of the phrase parallels their thoughts and feelings so precisely that the words merely confirm the music's meaning.

Ernest Newman wrote about this motive: "The mere announcement of [Siegmund's death] is next to nothing; the infinities and the solemn silences only gather about it when the orchestra gives out [this] wonderful theme."[25]

Newman: "Death."

Donington: "Relinquishment."

Cooke: "The Annunciation of Death."

71–Brünnhilde's Defiance

V-2-iv; Schirmer 171 staff 4

Brünnhilde promises to help Siegmund. She rushes away exultantly. Storm clouds sink down.

Against all that her Valkyriehood stands for and disobeying her father's explicit command, Brünnhilde commits herself to the human love between Siegmund and Sieglinde. Wagner sometimes uses mere nonmelodic fragments like this agitated ascent to underscore great emotional, even ecstatic, intensity.

In contrast to such states of pure emotion, *The Ring*'s brief passages that describe overtly physical activity are perhaps its weakest and most melodramatic music. Siegmund's fight with Fafner in S-2-ii and his struggle with Brünnhilde for the ring in T-1-iii are examples.

72–The Heroic in Siegfried

V-3-i; Schirmer 226 staffs 3–4

Brünnhilde: "The noblest hero in the world, woman, you are carrying in the shelter of your womb."

This is the first of the motives to characterize the nascent hero, Siegfried—in this case, the heroic aspects of his nature and purpose. The triad may derive, as Cooke suggests, from 36–Erda,[26] but the passage also seems to vault over 70–Annunciation of Death; Brünnhilde is here announcing a new life filled with potential.

Newman: "Siegfried."

Donington: "Siegfried's heroism as acceptance of his destiny."

Cooke: "Siegfried."

73–Redemption

V-3-i; Schirmer 228 staffs 1–2

Sieglinde: "Oh, mightiest of miracles, most glorious of women."

With a gleaming promise of hope for the future, this passage emerges suddenly from Sieglinde's distress and Brünnhilde's doom. The motive will not be heard again until T-3-iii, when it will have the honor of concluding the *Ring* cycle. It has often been regarded as a reference to unborn Siegfried, but as Owen Lee points out, Sieglinde praises Brünnhilde here, and it is Brünnhilde who will do the redeeming deed at the end.

Newman: "Redemption by Love."
Donington: "Transformation."
Cooke: "Redemption."
Lee: "Brünnhilde."

74–Brünnhilde's Reproach

V-3-iii; Schirmer 265 staff 4

Brünnhilde: "Was it so shameful what I did that you punish my misdeed so shamefully?"

With increasing firmness Brünnhilde challenges Wotan's anger and punishment as misguided and severe. At first the phrase makes a dry and mournful broken reference to 24–Spear as Wotan's authority again is used wrongfully. But soon it will be transformed into a passage of regal beauty in 75–Brünnhilde's Love for Wotan.

Cooke: "Brünnhilde's Reproach."
Lee: "Brünnhilde's plea (the spear)."

75–Brünnhilde's Love for Wotan

V-3-ii; Schirmer 274 staff 1

Brünnhilde: "[Wotan's] love breathed this into my heart; [Wotan's] will it was that allied me with the Volsung: and faithful to you inwardly I disobeyed your command."

The music of 74–Brünnhilde's Reproach magically blossoms to express her loyal love and compassion, for the son Wotan truly loved, Siegmund, but most of all for her father, whose inner wishes she feels she has obeyed. There is no better example in *The Ring* of musical transformation—the same notes communicate two entirely different emotions (in 74–Brünnhilde's Reproach and 75–Brünnhilde's Love for Wotan) through differences in harmony, instrumentation, dynamics, and key.

Donington: "Love as fulfillment."
Cooke: "Brünnhilde's Compassionate Love."
Lee: "Wotan's response (the spear)."

76–Sleep

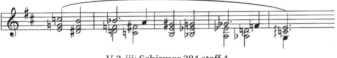

V-3-iii; Schirmer 284 staff 4

Wotan: "In deep sleep I shall enclose you. Whoever wakes you defenseless, has you as wife when you wake."

Brünnhilde sinks away from her relationship with Wotan and from her godhood. The very picture of descent into sleep, this is among the most literal or programmatic passages in *The Ring*. Its measured, mysterious quality resembles 29–Tarnhelm and 121–Potion. The segment falls, as does 37–Downfall. At the same time, it provides an effective transition between 75–Brünnhilde's Love for Wotan and 77–Brünnhilde in Sleep.

Newman: "Magic Slumber."
Donington: "Magic sleep as regression to the unconscious."
Cooke: "The Magic Sleep."

77–Brünnhilde in Sleep

V-3-iii; Schirmer 285 staff 4

Brünnhilde: "If enchaining sleep is to bind me fast, the feeblest man's easy acquisition: one thing you must grant."

This music was foreshadowed at the beginning of V-2-ii when Brünnhilde lay her head and hands on Wotan's knees with loving concern. The falling motion of both 75–Brünnhilde's Love for Wotan and 76–Sleep recurs here, but there are other associations. In S-2-iii, after Siegfried has killed Fafner, we hear this motive when Siegfried says he still has not learned fear; he will learn fear when he wakes the sleeping Valkyrie.

Newman: "Slumber."

Donington: "Brünnhilde sinking into the innocent sleep from which she will be woken into womanhood."

Cooke: "The Sleeping Brünnhilde."

Lee: "Slumber."

78–Wotan's Love for Brünnhilde

V-3-iii; Schirmer 296 staff 4 and following

Wotan: "For the last time let [your radiant eyes] delight me with farewell's last kiss!"

Wagner is at his incomparable best reflecting emotions, rather than physical actions, and nowhere else in *The Ring* is this more broadly evident. Wotan's music universalizes any father's regretted separation from a beloved daughter. It also exposes the side of Wotan that does not hunger for power. For many listeners, Wotan's farewell from Brünnhilde, his final glance upon the maiden who sleeps surrounded by the forbidding fire, is the musical and emotional summit of *The Ring.*

Newman: "Last Greeting."

Donington: "Wotan's grief at parting from Brünnhilde."

Cooke: "Wotan's Affection for Brünnhilde."

SIEGFRIED

79–Brooding

S-1-Prelude ; Schirmer 1 staff 1

The curtain is down.

Siegfried carries us into a new time and place: the dark forest of Neidhöhle a generation after *The Valkyrie*. The *Siegfried* Prelude ominously announces that dangers lie ahead. Most immediate is Mime's plot against Siegfried, but Alberich will also reappear, and Mime himself is tested by Wotan. As a psychological tone poem, the S-1 Prelude is another *tour de force:* 79–Brooding was foreshadowed by Mime in R-iii; in T-1-i it will evolve into the more purposeful 122–Plotting. The fragment encapsulates the elusive harmony of 12–The Ring. An ominous, deeply plunging interval is also heard in 118–Hagen and 122–Plotting.

Newman: "Reflection."

Donington: "Purposeful brooding."

80–Siegfried's Horn Call

S-1-i; Schirmer 11 staff 1

Siegfried boisterously enters Mime's hut, leading a large bear on a rope.

This motive will be stated definitively in S-2-ii when Siegfried plays his silver horn and wakens Fafner. It will evolve over the course of Siegfried's life and at his death. Here at its first appearance, the motive is as exuberant and undisciplined as the youth himself.

Newman: "Siegfried."

Donington: "Siegfried's horn call expressing his free spirit."

Cooke: "Siegfried's Horn Call."

81–Youthful Energy

S-1-i; Schirmer 16 staff 2

Siegfried, smashing a sword Mime has made him: "There are the bits for you, base bungler."

This music expresses all the animated but unshaped energy of the youthful Siegfried. It will take on different forms as he reforges the sword and falls in love. For example, 109–Laughing at Death is basically a mutation of this phrase. The figure is built around four descending notes which will take many forms as an expression of Siegfried's heroic mission and Mime's scheming one.

Newman: "Siegfried's youthful impetuosity."

Donington: "Siegfried's youthful strength."

Cooke: "Siegfried's anger."

82–Mime's Mission

S-1-i; Schirmer 21 staff 3

Mime: "I brought you up, a puling babe, gave the little mite warm clothes."

During *Siegfried*, both Mime and Siegfried struggle with questions about their purpose in life. For both, a falling four-note phrase frequently conveys their parallel but opposing paths and destinies. The development of this figure is one way Wagner tells the story of *Siegfried*.

Mime already sang a form of this phrase when he recalled the Nibelungs' happy past in R-iii. In the present example, Mime's words, designed to elicit sympathy and obedience from Siegfried, instead remind us that the dwarf has abused the boy by falsehood and deprivation—with respect to parents, knowledge, the sword, and genuine affection.

Donington: "Mime's complaint."

Cooke: "Mime's 'Starling Song.'"

83–Yearning for Knowledge

S-1-i; Schirmer 27 staff 1

Siegfried (to Mime):"The trees and birds, the fish in the stream, are more welcome to me than you."

Siegfried is very much about longing and learning, about finding the path to knowledge and to love. Audiences and critics sometimes underestimate the strength of Siegfried's drive for knowledge and for the truth about his life and the world.

Siegfried intuitively knows that Mime is lying when he claims to be Siegfried's father (and mother), and Mime's frustration of Siegfried's quest for knowledge makes him treat the smith harshly. Here the falling four-note fragment begins to evolve as Siegfried struggles to articulate the need to know his origins.

84–Yearning for Love

S-1-i; Schirmer 27 staff 3

Siegfried (to Mime): "How comes it that I return? If you're clever, tell me that."

Siegfried's longing for physical and emotional comfort is painfully evident in this extended passage. The struggling, rising figure bears a resemblance to 16A–Love, first associated with Freia in R-ii.

Newman: "Love."
Donington: "Bliss, and the longing for bliss."
Cooke: "Siegfried's Longing for Love."

85–Joy of Freedom

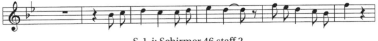

S-1-i; Schirmer 46 staff 2

Siegfried has learned the truth about his mother and the sword fragments: "To go forth from the forest into the world, nevermore to return! How glad I am to be free."

The knowledge that Siegfried has at last extracted from Mime—about his parents and the sword's fragments–is the key to his liberation, and he gaily prepares for a new world and new possibilities. This arietta-like passage expresses an unrestrained joy; it plays on a rising three-note figure as in 10–Rhine Daughters' Joy in the Gold.

86–Mission

S-1-i; Schirmer 47 staffs 1–2

Siegfried: "I flee from here, flowing forth, wending my way like the wind over the woods."

Near the end of the 85–Joy of Freedom passage, we hear the first full articulation of Siegfried's 86–Mission, an exuberant but heroic treatment of the falling four-note fragment. Now Siegfried has found the means of leaving Mime and the forest for "the world" where, armed with the sword, he can "smite the false, fell all knaves!" There is no hint at irony here, even though Siegmund, too, left the forest for the world, which will treat Siegfried as badly as it did his father.

Newman: "Siegfried's Mission."

Donington: "Siegfried's heroic freedom from entanglements."

87–Mime's Frustration

S-1-i; Schirmer 50 staff 2

Mime: "Nibelung hatred, trouble and toil will not knit Notung together for me."

Mime, too, craves knowledge: how to murder Siegfried and gain the treasure. But his immediate task is to reforge Notung, which he lacks the knowledge to do and fails to learn in his test of wits with the Wanderer. His yearning is as frustrated as his purpose is corrupt, aptly reflected in this falling phrase.

88–Wanderer

S-1-ii; Schirmer 50 staff 3

Wotan, entering Mime's hut: "Greeting, wise smith! To a way-worn guest grant the hospitality of your house and hearth."

A transformed Wotan is revealed in 88–Wanderer. He is older now, more observer than active player—at least he thinks he is. The motive conveys a sense of dignity that comes from mature wisdom. The pace is slow and deliberate, as is 76–Sleep, which is also associated with relinquishment.

Newman: "Wotan, the unhurrying tread of a God."

Donington: "Wotan the Wanderer as the wise old man in touch with the unconscious."

Cooke: "The Wanderer."

89–World Ash Tree

S-1-ii; Schirmer 62 staffs 2–3

Wotan (to Mime): "From the holiest branch of the primeval ash [Wotan] cut himself a shaft."

The ash tree, like the gold, is intermediate: just as the ring was fashioned from the gold, Wotan's spear was hewn from the World Ash Tree. The passage bears a strong resemblance to 36–Erda; also an intermediary, Erda has been part of Wotan's search for knowledge and power.

Cooke: "World Ash Tree."

90–Blow, Bellows!

S-1-iii; Schirmer 107 staff 2

Siegfried starts to work the bellows.

In the forging scene, Siegfried explodes with newly liberated energy now focused on a specific mission, one that will lead to a wider purpose in "the world." The sword is the central symbol of that liberation, and the bellows, forging, and hammering graphically convey the process of empowerment.

   The scene introduces many new motives and mutations of other motives around these themes of physical strength and growth. Yet another variation on the four-note fragment recurs in 90–Blow, Bellows! Its insistent downward movement projects the raw power that Siegfried now wields.

91–Hammering

S-1-iii; Schirmer 119 staff 4

Siegfried begins to hammer the newly forged sword.

Siegfried's dynamic pounding and the orchestra's exuberant accompaniment based on 81–Youthful Energy provide a vivid contrast to Mime's ineffectual tapping in his version of 28–Nibelungs at the beginning of S-1-i.

92–Fafner as Dragon

S-2-Prelude; Schirmer 136 staffs 2–3

The curtain is down.

Siegfried's confrontation with Fafner, the savage dragon, will come in S-2. Opening in stunning contrast to the triumphant conclusion of S-1-iii, the Prelude paints a vivid picture of the gloomy and dangerous forest at Neidhöhle. Here 92–Fafner as Dragon is interwoven with 17–Giants, 79–Brooding, 12–The Ring, 35–Curse, 34–Hatred, 30–Servitude, and 37–Downfall.

92–Fafner as Dragon, first heard in Siegrune's and Schwertleite's description in S-3-i, is a transformation of 32–Serpent, which described Alberich's taking that form in R-iii. In this example, the bass drum's playing of 17–Giants evokes the memory of Fafner's former life.

93–Mission (Mutation)

S-2-i; Schirmer 151 staff 4

Wotan (to Alberich): Siegfried "stands or falls, but is his own master."

The Wanderer's announcement is momentous: Siegfried will be allowed the free agency that Wotan denied Siegmund in V-2. The music is a mutation of Siegfried's heroic 86–Mission, resonant with the nobility of Wotan's relinquishment and self-restraint. The phrase begins in the vocal line but is promptly given over to the orchestra.

94–Forest Murmurs

S-2-ii; Schirmer 171 staff 1 and following

As Mime disappears, Siegfried stretches comfortably under the lime tree to await the dragon.

Thinking himself free of Mime, Siegfried reclines as his senses and ours are filled with nature's eternal undercurrent. This passage is the arboreal equivalent of 8–Water Murmurs. As Wagner has treated some other aspects of the natural world, the music here is passive, lyrical, and seemingly without overt purpose.

Newman: "Forest Murmurs."

Donington: "The forest murmurs as Siegfried's childlike innocence and playful thoughts."

Cooke: "Forest Murmurs."

Lee: "Forest murmurs."

95–Wood Bird

A.

S-2-ii; Schirmer 177 staff 5

B.

Schirmer 177 staff 2

Amidst the gentle forest murmurs, Siegfried's attention is drawn to a Wood Bird singing in the branches above him.

The Wood Bird and the Rhine Daughters might be seen as intermediaries between the unintentional ways of the natural world and the pointed strivings of man. Both become engaged in the affairs of the world but without ambitions of their own for control and power: 95–Wood Bird closely quotes 4–Rhine Daughters.

In R-i, Flosshilde's 5–Warning in a minor key foreshadowed 95B–Wood Bird; the bird will warn Siegfried about Mime.

Donington: "The song of the forest bird as initiator out of immature innocence."

Cooke: "The Woodbird."

Lee: "Song of the forest bird."

96–False Flattery

S-2-iii; Schirmer 210 staff 3

Mime approaches Siegfried with flattering gestures.

Mime's doomed mission—to murder Siegfried, capture the ring, and enslave others—is cloaked in transparent lies. Wagner sometimes applies grace notes to Mime's music to suggest his insubstantial nature.

97–Siegfried's Horn Call (Mutation)

S-2-iii; Schirmer 225 staff 3

Siegfried has thrown Mime's body into the cave and blocked the entrance with Fafner's body: "I am hot from my heavy task."

As Siegfried thirsts for self-knowledge, searing introspection replaces youthful, naive confidence. Fafner's blood has given him coldblooded insight into Mime's treachery; the adolescent rages with incipient manhood as he carries out the rites of passage common to many cultures and their mythologies.

The harmonic and dynamic transformation that conveys Siegfried's turbulent feelings here is among the most brilliant in *The Ring*. The initial element of 80–Siegfried's Horn Call, already mutated as part of the boy's forging in S-3-iii (at Schirmer 98 staff 4), is transformed here almost beyond recognition.

98–Yearning for Love/Mission

S-2-iii; Schirmer 227 staff 1

Siegfried calls to the Wood Bird, blithely swaying in the branches with its brothers and sisters. Can the bird lead him to a friend?

Wagner combines two motives into a unified phrase as Siegfried's mission in life focuses on finding a "good companion." Here 84–Yearning for Love is linked to 86–Mission, which becomes urgent and probing; it aches with unresolved longing, completely unlike the emotion of the motive's earlier energetic form or its later, heroic resolution. At no other point is Siegfried so compelling a figure as in this expression of self-examination and vulnerability.

99–Act 3 Prelude

The Prelude to Act 3 of *Siegfried* marks Wagner's resumption of the musical composition of *The Ring* after a break of nearly twelve years. His renewed energy and even richer compositional powers are not difficult to detect. The Prelude weaves together 36–Erda, 61–Valkyries, 65–Frustration, 24–Spear, 37–Downfall, 88–Wanderer, 76–Sleep, 31–Power of the Ring, and 69–Fate. This is no list of musical calling cards. Individual elements are integrated into a compelling whole, rich in associations with the past and implications for future events.

100–Wala! Awake!

S-3-i; Schirmer 242 staff 3

Wotan summons Erda from sleep.

The simple passage is charged with reminiscent meaning. The first segment is a falling step, first heard at the beginning of R-i (Woglinde's "Weia!") and the basis of so many other motives. The full phrase also recalls both 14D–Valhalla, whose purpose Wotan is now prepared to relinquish, and 16B–Love, as Wotan prepares to abdicate the pursuit of power in favor of the redeeming love between Siegfried and Brünnhilde.

101–World's Inheritance

S-3-i; Schirmer 257 staffs 3–4

Wotan tells Erda: "What once I resolved in despair . . . now I freely perform, gladly and gaily . . . Now to the valiant Volsung I leave my heritage."

Wotan's acceptance of his fate, to step aside in favor of Siegfried and Brünnhilde, reflects his noble and wise aspects, and the music soars radiantly. This is another pivotal moment in *The Ring:* the music looks both to the past and future, or, to paraphrase Wagner, it conveys both reminiscence and presentiment. It is as though we have heard the passage before. It also leads directly to 107–Immortal Beloved, the music of Siegfried and Brünnhilde who are the intended heirs of Wotan's legacy.

Newman: "World inheritance."

Cooke: "The World's Inheritance, a heroic motive generated by the motive of The Sword."

102–Ravens

fp

S-3-ii; Schirmer 274 staff 1

Provoked by Siegfried, the Wanderer threatens to bar his path, vowing that the Wood Bird "flew from you to save itself! The lord of the ravens it learnt was here . . . You shall not take the way it showed!"

In *Twilight*, Wotan's ravens will fly up at two fateful moments. In T-3-ii, they rise when Siegfried reveals he is the true husband of Brünnhilde. He turns his unprotected back on Hagen to watch them and is killed. Near the end of T-3-iii, Brünnhilde instructs the ravens to tell Wotan what has happened there on the Rhine. They will pass by her rock and carry Loge's flames with them to burn down Valhalla.

This is another figure consisting of a simple falling step, yet it unmistakably belongs to these birds of fate, again an indelible marking. As Newman writes, "every motive has a physiognomy as distinct from all others as the face of any human being is distinct from all other faces. The motives are unforgettable once we have heard them. They depict their subject once and for all."[27]

103–Resistance

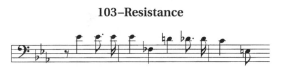

S-3-ii; Schirmer 275 staff 2

The Wanderer, resisting Siegfried's advance: "He who wakes [Brünnhilde], he who wins her, deprives me of my power forever!"

This passage, defining Wotan's final grasp at survival in spite of himself, illuminates the depth of *The Ring*'s motivic fabric. It is a harsh mutation of 15–Love's Enchantment, one of the loveliest phrases in *The Rhinegold*, written fifteen years before. Although Wotan has just nobly announced his own passing, Siegfried's impudence has prompted an irrational, very human resistance in the great god. And it is the lure of love's enchantment, which Siegfried is about to discover in Brünnhilde, that drives the young hero past his grandfather.

104–Awakening

S-3-iii; Schirmer 296 staff 4

Brünnhilde opens her eyes at Siegfried's kiss and greets the sun, the light, and the radiant day.

The simple figure, which will open both *Twilight of the Gods* and the dying Siegfried's final reminiscence in T-3-ii, conveys Brünnhilde's glorious awakening to life's potential. It is a dramatic reversal of the basic falling whole-step fragment, which has been heard so often before.

Newman: "Greeting to the world."
Donington: "Sunlight representing returning consciousness."
Cooke: "Brünnhilde Awakes."

105–Love's Greeting

S-3-iii; Schirmer 300 staffs 2–3

Siegfried, as Brünnhilde has awakened: "Hail to my mother that bore me, hail to the earth that nourished me."

This new music defines the heroic aspect of the love to come between Brünnhilde and Siegfried. It may contain a suggestion of 16B–Love, and possibly at the end, the falling four-note fragment of 86–Mission. A speculative motivic connection is hardly necessary to bask in the lovers' exultation.

Donington: "Love as fulfillment."
Cooke: "Love's Greeting."

106–Love's Ecstasy

S-3-iii; Schirmer 301 staff 3

Siegfried and Brünnhilde gaze on each other in glowing ecstasy.

The S-3-iii encounter between Brünnhilde and Siegfried, the second of only two love duets in *The Ring*, introduces a great deal of new music associated with passionate love. The scene contrasts with the more popular V-1-iii scene between Siegmund and Sieglinde in its statuesque, nearly manic intensity.

Newman: "Rapture of Love."
Donington: "Truly innocent delight."
Cooke: "Love's Ecstasy."

107–Immortal Beloved

S-3-iii; Schirmer 318 staff 4

Brünnhilde: A pleasing picture has come to her mind, and she turns again to Siegfried with tenderness.

A restrained mutation of 101–World's Inheritance, 107–Immortal Beloved is especially well known to concert audiences for its place in Wagner's instrumental work of 1870, the *Siegfried Idyll* (as is 108–World's Treasure). Perhaps as a result, the passage strikes us as relatively formal in presentation despite its beauty. For once, Wagner's continuous music slows. The phrase does not appear in *The Ring* again.

Donington: "Siegfried's tender love for Brünnhilde and hers for him."
Cooke: "Immortal Beloved."

108–World's Treasure

S-3-iii; Schirmer 319 staff 3

Brünnhilde: "O Siegfried! Glorious being! Wealth of the world!"

This figure also is heard in the *Siegfried Idyll.*

Donington: "Brünnhilde's holy love."

Cooke: "The World's Treasure."

109–Laughing at Death

S-3-iii; Schirmer 333 staff 4

Brünnhilde: "Laughing I must love you . . . Laughing let us perish." Siegfried: "Laughing, you awake in rapture to me: Brünnhilde lives."

The phrase, which initiates the concluding passage of *Siegfried*, is a definitive transformation of 81–Youthful Energy. It is a motive of energy and passion but also of resolution, as Siegfried and Brünnhilde, having confronted great emotional changes in just a few minutes, are united in love and purpose.

Both characters are transformed. She has completed the journey from godhood and the glittering illusions of Valhalla, and now accepts her destiny as a mortal woman fulfilled in love. Siegfried has grown from boy to man, gaining self-knowledge and defining his sense of purpose (heard as 86–Mission). Youth laughs not so much at death but at whatever fate and life will hold in their future, which is related in *Twilight of the Gods.*

Newman: "Love's Resolution."

Donington: "Siegfried's infectious impetuosity in love."

Cooke: "Love's Resolution."

TWILIGHT OF THE GODS

110–Prelude
Schirmer 1 staffs 1–4 to Schirmer 2 staffs 1–2

In *Twilight*, the long Prologue consists of an orchestral prelude, the Norn scene, transitional music, a scene with Siegfried and Brünnhilde, and the transitional music known as Siegfried's Rhine Journey. The orchestral prelude, consisting of twenty-six measures, includes (in order) 104–Awakening, 2–Nature, 3–Rhine, 69–Fate, 12–The Ring, and 89–World Ash Tree.

In the Norn scene the music assumes a sinuous, ambiguous, mysterious quality. While there are few new motives in the scene, it is a seamless recapitulation of many motives heard before, including (again, in order of appearance) 8–Water Murmurs, 31–Power of the Ring (including the second segment), 69–Fate, 14A–Valhalla, 40–Sword, 70–Annunciation of Death, 18–Power of the Gods, 24–Spear, 37–Downfall, 25A–Loge, 76–Sleep, 12–The Ring, 9–Gold, 11–Rhinegold, 80–Siegfried's Horn Call, and 35–Curse.

These musical themes ably fulfill the dramatic purpose of the scene: to recall past events and to depict the Norns' loosened grasp on fate as the old order passes. The world nears a historic dislocation, and the future cannot be seen.

At no other point in *The Ring* does Wagner so effectively engage us in reminiscence. Motives are not merely restated to describe past events; they are woven into *The Ring's* lushest fabric, piled atop one another, swept along like leaves in the wind. Partly because there is so little action in the scene, it is a huge musical achievement, perhaps the most purely musical scene in *The Ring*.

111–Rope of Fate

T-Prologue; Schirmer 3 staff 2

The First Norn unwinds the golden rope.

The music of 111–Rope of Fate seems directly related to 12–The Ring. Both fall and rise ambiguously, and both are objects with definable powers and purposes, which sets them apart from the primal but undifferentiated forces of nature.

Newman: "Weaving of the Norns."
Donington: "The Norns' rope of destiny."

112–Siegfried (Definitive)

T-Prologue; Schirmer 21 staff 1

Siegfried and Brünnhilde emerge from the cave. He is fully armed.

Throughout *Siegfried*, we watched the young man grow, both in his sense of life's purpose and in his capacity for love. The impetuous music of the horn call heard in S-1-i and even when Fafner wakes in S-2-ii now gives way to a majestic announcement of the hero in all his manifest potential—armed with wisdom and weapon, basking in blissful knowledge of love.

Newman: "New Siegfried."

Donington: "Siegfried's heroic deeds as the ever-reborn spirit of youth."

113–The Woman Brünnhilde

T-Prologue; Schirmer 21 staff 2

Brünnhilde: I must "let you go forth to new deeds, dear hero."

Brünnhilde, too, is fully transformed, from virginal warrior maiden of the gods into mortal woman, ordinary in wisdom, disarmed, rich in love and generosity. The first segment of this passage brilliantly transforms 47–Volsungs' Woe into the joy she now shares with the Volsung, Siegfried.

Newman: "New Brünnhilde."

Donington: "Brünnhilde as loving woman."

Cooke: "Brünnhilde as Mortal Woman."

114–Giving in Love

T-Prologue; Schirmer 23 staffs 3–4

Gladly out of love, Brünnhilde has given Siegfried all her wisdom and strength.

This is the last of the new love music to emerge between Brünnhilde and Siegfried. It is heroic and unabashed; the end of the phrase is a confident restatement of 16B–Love.

There is also significant irony at work. Brünnhilde gives to Siegfried, gladly out of love, what superhuman wisdom and strength she has left. She will pay dearly for her gift. When Siegfried's betrayal leaves her bereft of the insight to deal with the crisis in T-2, she will turn, like Alberich, to hatred and revenge.

Newman: "Heroic Love."

Cooke: "Heroic Love."

115–Mission (Definitive)

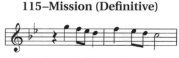

T-Prologue; Schirmer 33 staff 3

Siegfried: "I can no longer count myself Siegfried, I am but Brünnhilde's arm."

At the beginning of this scene, we heard the completed musical expression of Siegfried's heroic nature in 112–Siegfried (Definitive). Siegfried's development as a person has been completed by Brünnhilde's love, including their sexual love.

We have also heard since S-1-i the continuing evolution of Siegfried's mission or purpose, which has frequently been associated musically with a falling four-note phrase. Here Siegfried's mission is majestically articulated, perfected by Brünnhilde's additional gifts of wisdom, shield, and horse.

Newman: "Freedom."

Donington: "Siegfried's heroic freedom from entanglements."

116–Radiant Star, Victorious Light

T-Prologue; Schirmer 36 staffs 1–2

Siegfried: "Hail, Brünnhilde, radiant star!"
Brünnhilde: "Hail, Siegfried, victorious light!"

This is a resplendent musical moment in *The Ring;* when even newcomers struggling with the moving target of continuous music sit bolt upright with pleasure. A passage of soaring lyricism, it sets a cap on our sympathy for the ecstatic couple.

117–Treachery

T-Prologue; Schirmer 44 staff 5

The curtain is down.

At the end of the transitional music known as Siegfried's Rhine Journey, an ominous variation on 31–Power of the Ring intrudes, leaving no doubt that Siegfried has left the perfect world atop Brünnhilde's rock.

This bears a powerful resemblance to the rising three-note figure, first heard in 10–Rhine Daughters' Joy in the Gold and especially as heard in 28–Nibelungs.

It sets the stage for the plot against Siegfried (and Brünnhilde) in T-1-i. It will also appear in the middle of 125–Gutrune's Treachery, when she offers the magic potion to Siegfried, and in other motives associated with the Gibichungs.

118–Hagen

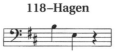

T-1-i; Schirmer 45 staff 1

Gunther: "Now hark, Hagen."

Hagen's character is not yet clear to us when Gunther first addresses his half-brother. Later on, the motive will convey his driven, malevolent energy during the short scene known as Hagen's Watch at the end of T-1-ii. The plunging interval will attach itself to much of what goes wrong in *Twilight*.

Newman: "Hagen."

Donington: "Hagen as Siegfried's dark shadow, and the Gibichung race generally in this negative aspect."

Cooke: "Hagen."

119–Gunther

T-1-i; Schirmer 45 staff 2

Gunther (to Hagen): "Can I hold my head high on the Rhine?"

A manly, heroic passage. We will learn that these aspects are false in Gunther.

Newman: "Gibichung Race."

Donington: "Gunther's illusory appearance of heroism, hinting at the weakness in the shadow aspect of the Volsung race itself, especially Siegfried, since Gunther stands for part of Siegfried's shadow."

Cooke: "Gunther."

120–Gutrune

T-1-i; Schirmer 49 staff 4 and following

Gutrune's first words are to Hagen: "What doughty deed did [Siegfried] do to be deemed the most splendid of heroes?"

This lovely music establishes Gutrune's modest but vulnerable nature. We are given this insight into her character before she participates in the conspiracy against Siegfried.

121–Potion

T-1-i; Schirmer 52 staff 3

Hagen, in a gesture full of hidden meaning, draws Gunther to him.

The motive is an extended version of 29–Tarnhelm and evokes the same feelings of unseen power and mystery. Subsequently, 121–Potion is shortened to just its last two notes, which nevertheless unmistakably identify the drugged drink and its effect.

Newman: "Magic Deceit."
Donington: "The magic potion as unconscious repression."
Cooke: "The Potion."

122–Plotting

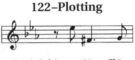

T-1-i; Schirmer 53 staff 2

Gutrune: "You mocking, hateful Hagen! How could I capture Siegfried?"

Deeply plunging intervals, first heard in 118–Hagen, play a prominent role in this scene. Here the interval is completed by the addition of a third note rising one step, the new phrase suggesting evil plotting at work. This is the same technique of transformation that Wagner used in V-2, where he deleted the third note from 58–Bliss to create the feeling of incompleteness that Donington has called "longing for bliss."

Newman: "Enticement."
Cooke: "Seduction."

123–Rowing

T-1-i; Schirmer 58 staff 3

Siegfried is rowing up the Rhine to the Gibichungs.

This is not a new motive but rather a combination of motives that illustrates how Wagner transforms otherwise unremarkable moments into passages full of descriptive power. From the merging of 11–Rhinegold and 80–Siegfried's Horn Call comes a palpable sense of Siegfried's powerful but easy stroke, which carries him toward those who will deceive and destroy him. As the scene builds to Siegfried's arrival at the hall, the music rises with majestic irony to incorporate 122–Plotting juxtaposed with 80–Siegfried's Horn Call; finally 11–Rhinegold twists its way into a restatement of 31–Power of the Ring.

124–Friendship

T-1-ii; Schirmer 63 staff 4 and following

Gunther comes forward to greet Siegfried.

This is a phrase of masculine warmth and dignity. Yet the plunging interval from 118–Hagen, which pervades dealings with the Gibichungs, lets us know that Gunther's friendship with Siegfried is based on deceit.

Newman: "Friendship."

Donington: "Honorable intentions; the appearance of honor and good faith; the longing for normality."

Cooke: "Friendship."

125–Gutrune's Deception

T-1-ii; Schirmer 68 staff 2

Gutrune approaches Siegfried carrying the drinking horn.

The motive, commonly considered Gutrune's personal music, reflects a patent artlessness that betrays her uneasy but willing part in the deception. It is a brilliant mutation of 122–Plotting. Especially in T-2, it is restated aggressively as 138–Gibichungs' Horn Call.

Newman: "Gutrune."
Donington: "Gutrune as foredoomed heroine."
Cooke: "Gutrune."

126–Mission (as Blood-Brotherhood)

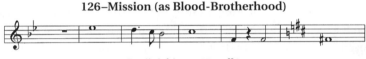

T-1-ii; Schirmer 75 staff 3

Siegfried: "Let the oath be of blood-brotherhood!"

The music seems straightforward and handsome: Siegfried has no sense of the underlying deception now at work against him. The phrase stands effectively alone but is in fact the coupling of two earlier motives, 86–Mission and 122–Plotting. In another perfect fusion of music and drama, Siegfried's mission here becomes fatally enmeshed in the plot against him. The phrase is immediately followed by 35–Curse.

127–Blood-Brotherhood

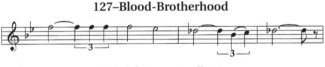

T-1-ii; Schirmer 76 staffs 2–3

Siegfried lays two fingers on the drinking horn: "Flourishing life's refreshing blood have I dropped into the cup."

This is a heroic, affirmative statement of loyalty, which will be treated with heartbreaking poignancy as Gunther commits himself to Siegfried's death in T-2-v. The rising three-note figure, also heard in 117–Treachery, occurs in the middle of the phrase.

Cooke: "Blood Brotherhood."

128–Vow of Atonement

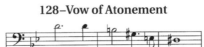

T-1-ii; Schirmer 77 staff 3

Gunther: "If a brother breaks a bond . . . ." Together with Siegfried: "What we have solemnly drunk in drops today shall flow in torrents in full atonement to a friend!"

By the pledge of loyalty here and the consequences of breaking his oath in T-2, Siegfried is further ensnared in Hagen's plot, with fatal results. The music is drawn directly from 49–Rights, first sung by Hunding in V-1-ii.

Donington: "Atonement as a force of destiny."
Cooke: "Vow of Atonement."

129–Hagen Ascending

T-1-ii; Schirmer 86 staff 3

Hagen: "You sons of freedom, cheerful companions, gaily sail away!"

Hagen's Watch is a chilling coda to T-1-ii and also sets the stage for his confrontation with Alberich in T-2-i. This deliberate, rising scale is filled with menace. The phrase inches its way up, as Hagen's plan is now fully at work. The phrase may have an ironic relationship to the similarly rising figure of 101–World's Inheritance, as Hagen seeks to recover the ring, the "gnome's inheritance."

130–Escape

T-1-iii; Schirmer 107 staff 3

Brünnhilde: "From the gods' holy heaven in the clouds I was banished, in my folly: I do not grasp what I am told."

Brünnhilde is now a mortal woman, without a Valkyrie's wisdom. She cannot comprehend Waltraute's desperate plea to relinquish the ring to save the gods. This disconnection with her past in fact liberates her from further entanglements with the hopeless position of the gods. The fragment is of particular musical interest because of its striking resemblance to the innocent fool music from *Parsifal*.

131–Betrayal

T-1-iii; Schirmer 122 staff 1

Brünnhilde: "Wotan! . . . Now I see the meaning of my sentence!"

Brünnhilde, believing herself betrayed, will side with the Gibichungs against Siegfried. The phrase is expressed with shattering finality in T-3-v when Hagen declares that only Siegfried's death can atone for his betrayal of Gunther. The falling phrase is interrupted by a plunging interval, also heard in 118–Hagen and 122–Plotting.

Newman: "Brünnhilde's Calamity."

132–Honor

T-1-iii; Schirmer 127 staff 2

Siegfried, in Gunther's form, has driven Brünnhilde into the cave: "Notung, be witness that my wooing was chaste. Keeping faith with my brother, separate me from his bride!"

We know that Siegfried will treat Brünnhilde honorably this night, even though his overcoming her by force is wildly misguided. Falling octaves also define 54–Volse and 60–Notung.

Donington: "Honorable intentions; the appearance of honor and good faith."
Cooke: "Honor."

133–Murder

T-2-i; Schirmer 137 staff 3

Alberich (to Hagen): "The golden ring, that is what we must obtain!"

Alberich incites his son to be steadfast in the plot against Siegfried, and it is now clear that the Nibelungs' plan to recover the ring includes Siegfried's murder. The fragment twists and turns much like 65–Frustration, but with savage aggression.

Cooke finds its harmonic basis in 12–The Ring: "so this dissonance permeates *Götterdämmerung,* creating an atmosphere of progressive dissolution. Wagner made the sinister harmony of the Ring Motive eat its way more and more into the fabric of the score, to reflect the fact that the sinister symbol of the ring itself eats its way more and more into the drama."[28]

Cooke: "Murder."

134–Dawn

T-2-ii; Schirmer 141 staffs 2–3

The light of dawn spreads, and the Rhine is reddened by its glow.

Coming at the end of Hagen's dreadful confrontation with Alberich, the serene music evokes the positive qualities inherent in 3–Rhine. However, it evolves into something completely different, the convulsive 135–Grim Hagen: it is the day of the Nibelungs' revenge that is dawning. The phrase will be repeated with boisterous energy in 139–Vassals' Song.

Donington: "The dawn of Hagen's day."
Cooke: "Dawn."

135–Grim Hagen

T-2-ii; Schirmer 141 staff 5

As the light of dawn grows, Hagen makes a compulsive movement.

Hagen's plan is working. The pivotal events will take place this new day: 134–Dawn rises only to reach a climax in a savage, falling figure.

136–Gutrune's Greeting

T-2-ii; Schirmer 144 staff 1

Gutrune (to Siegfried): "May Freia welcome you in the name of all women!"

Gutrune's spirits soar as the famous hero returns to her. Against all logic or hope, she sees that Hagen's plan is working and Siegfried might indeed be hers. Gutrune is as deluded as Siegfried, and the reference to Freia, the symbol of love, underlies both the pathos and irony at work here.

137–Hoiho!

T-2-iii; Schirmer 150 staff 4

Hagen has climbed a rock; he blows on a cow horn and summons the vassals.

The simple falling figure, which Woglinde sang at the opening of R-i ("Weia!"), has now become a brutal expression of raw power. It will be heard again in T-2-v when Hagen convinces Gunther that Siegfried has betrayed the oath of blood-brotherhood and must die.

Cooke: "Hoi-Ho!"

138–Gibichungs' Horn Call

T-2-iii; Schirmer 151 staff 2

Hagen calls on the vassals to arm themselves.

This is a definitive statement associated with all the Gibichungs, and it encapsulates both 117–Treachery and 125–Gutrune's Deception. It also echoes the boisterous masculinity of 80–Siegfried's Horn Call, and both ring out to one another in T-3-ii.

139–Vassals' Song

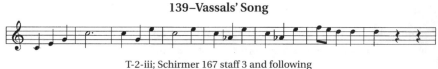

T-2-iii; Schirmer 167 staff 3 and following

Vassals: "Good fortune and prosperity now smile on the Rhine if grim Hagen can be so merry!"

Astonished by Hagen's rare good humor, the vassals sing *The Ring's* only chorus. The passage combines 134–Dawn, 135–Grim Hagen, and 138–Gibichungs' Horn Call. Wagner's use of a traditional operatic chorus at this point has been seen as an example of his rejection, especially in *Twilight*, of his own principles of music drama.[29] Whether or not this is true, the chorus may have merely survived from the first libretto for *Twilight* that Wagner wrote in 1848, before he wrote the other

Ring librettos or any of the *Ring* music that is so radically different from his earlier work.

In any case, the chorus makes several contributions. It breaks the extreme tension between the gloomy Hagen–Alberich scene in T-2-i and the confrontation between Siegfried and Brünnhilde which follows in T-2-iii. The brief chorus scene also establishes the Gibichungs as an active element in the drama, as they will hereafter react to and comment on the action, very much like a Greek chorus (see "Gibichungs," page 241).

140–Vassals' Greeting

T-2-iv; Schirmer 175 staff 3 and following

Vassals: "Greetings, Gunther! Hail to you and your bride! Welcome!"

The simplicity of this passage highlights the irony of the moment. The Gibichungs celebrate the glorious betrothals of both Gunther and Gutrune. They are as unaware as Brünnhilde of the treachery at work.

141–Oath

T-2-iv; Schirmer 199 staffs 2–3

Siegfried: "Shining spear, hallowed weapon, aid my eternal oath!"

The motivic texture of *The Ring*, especially in *Twilight*, is dense. On its surface, 141–Oath is strong and affirming as Siegfried and Brünnhilde make their pledges in good faith, but it also reworks 131–Betrayal. As in that motive, the falling four-note fragment from 86–Mission is broken up by a plunging interval, suggesting the further corruption of Siegfried's intended heroic works. Above all, the passage demonstrates how Wagner projects his true dramatic meaning in the music, which belies the surface expression of the characters' words and gestures.

Cooke: "The Swearing of the Oath."

142–Brünnhilde's Betrayal

T-2-v; Schirmer 215 staff 4

Brünnhilde reveals to Hagen that Siegfried's back is unprotected by her magic.

Feeling betrayed and bewildered, Brünnhilde is here at her most unworthy as she seeks revenge by providing Hagen with information that will be fatal to Siegfried. The motive is all the more striking because its quiet, sinewy, sensual treatment highlights the horror of its terrible consequence and surprising source: it is a twisted form of 106–Love's Ecstasy.

143–Rhine Daughters (Continued)

A.

T-3-i; Schirmer 232 staff 6

B.

Schirmer 233 staff 3

C.

Schirmer 233 staff 4

As the curtain rises on the final act, the Rhine Daughters rise to the surface of the water and swim about.

Three new elements describe the water nymphs in T-3-i, alongside other motives from The Rhinegold (2–Nature, 4–Rhine Daughters, 9–Gold, and 41–Rhine Daughters' Lament).

The first projects their seductive nature, as they try to lure the ring from Siegfried. The broad sweeping movement of the second is suggestive of the high consequences involved in the ring's final disposition. The third element is a kind of farewell to Siegfried, who has refused to give up the ring. Brünnhilde will give the Rhine Daughters a more positive response.

Donington: "Rhine Daughters' deceptive delight."

144–Death

T-3-ii; Schirmer 296 staff 4

Vassals: "Hagen what have you done?"

The heroic life of Siegfried, which held such promise at the beginning of *Twilight*, is now over. The brutal repeated triad that opens the phrase strikes at us as much as Hagen has struck Siegfried. It recalls a similar figure at the beginning of 48–Hunding: it was Hunding who felled Siegmund. The second segment struggles to rise in a gloomy, chromatic fashion but is turned back into a falling figure at the end.

Donington: "The darkness of death itself."

145–Rest

T-3-iii; Schirmer 326 staff 3

Brünnhilde (to Wotan): "Rest, rest now, o god!"

Moments before her self-immolation, Wotan's favorite daughter understands, forgives, and puts to rest the cosmic struggles of the great god. This passage reverberates with the most poignant of human feelings, those that come when grown children can accept and forgive the failures of their own parents who were once children themselves. Compressed and integrated here are 11–Rhinegold, 14C–Valhalla, 66–Struggling Against Fate, 37–Downfall, and 14D–Valhalla: no other passage in *The Ring* evokes a more moving flood of piercing reminiscence.

Lee: "World release."

CHAPTER FOUR

THE CHARACTERS

THE *Ring* story is played out by thirty-four characters. There are five gods, one demigod, two dwarfs, two giants, nine warrior maidens or Valkyries, three water nymphs, four fates, seven mortal humans (some of whom are related to gods or dwarfs), and a Wood Bird. As many as twenty of these can be considered major characters. There are also two large groups—Nibelungs and Gibichungs.

The dramatis personae of *The Ring* operate on three fundamental, interconnected levels: the mythological, the psychological, and the individual. Wagner developed these characters from hundreds of figures in the myths and sagas, and they never lose touch with their roots. Secondly, as psychological archetypes and as symbols of our own inner drives and conflicts, they can move as powerfully.

Yet it is on a third level, as individuals—greatly enhanced by both the mythological and psychological dimensions—that the *Ring* characters capture our most immediate attention. This huge roster of major characters is as remarkable for its depth as for its breadth: each is vividly drawn by his or her own thoughts, gestures, words, deeds, and music. No one of them is like another. Each is consistent and convincing, thinking and acting in a way that is shaped by individual motivations and the stamp of personality.

While the story and music of *The Ring* are described in chapters 2 and 3 respectively, this chapter focuses on each remarkable character or group in twenty-five sections, in order of appearance in the drama. Each section includes:

SOURCES

Every character in *The Ring* can be traced to the source materials, both primary and secondary, that Wagner researched so prodigiously. No matter how much he compressed, conjoined, deleted, or even invented, *The Ring* takes place on an overtly mythological stage, and the characters' antecedents loom over them like a memory of the past and a window into their inner worlds.

RELATIONSHIPS

Each character's most significant relationships to other characters are noted. These relationships can be confusing, but while it is essential to know that Wotan was the father of Brünnhilde, the other Valkyries, and the Volsung twins, it is not critical that Froh, as brother-in-law to Wotan and through Siegfried's marriage with Gutrune, could have had some sort of legal relationship with Alberich, since the dwarf was the father of Gutrune's half-brother.

APPEARANCES

Each character's initial and subsequent appearances in the story on a scene-by-scene basis are briefly summarized. A full description of the story comprises chapter 2, and a concordance, citing occurrences of each character's name as well as other references, is provided in chapter 5.

COMMENTS

These sections contain my observations on each character's place in the story. I have focused on the characters' behavior as individuals more than on their mythological or psychological aspects and have also addressed some question-able interpretations that have gained currency in contemporary productions. Unless otherwise noted, these observations are wholly my own.

MUSIC

It is through the music, more than the texts, that the characters of *The Ring* come most vibrantly alive. This chapter describes the music specifically associated with each character. (See chapter 3 for a more comprehensive review and music examples.)

The costume designs are by Rolf Langenfass for the Metropolitan Opera's *Ring* production of the late 1980s and early 1990s.

CHARACTERS
(in order of appearance)

The Rhine Daughters Woglinde, Wellgunde, Flosshilde	Siegmund
	Sieglinde
Alberich	Hunding
Wotan	Brünnhilde
Fricka	The Valkyries
Freia	Gerhilde, Helmwige, Waltraute, Schwertleite, Ortlinde, Siegrune,
Fasolt	Grimgerde, Rossweisse
Fafner	Siegfried
Donner	The Wood Bird
Froh	The Three Norns
Loge	Gunther
Mime	Hagen
The Nibelungs	Gutrune
Erda	The Gibichungs

THE RHINE DAUGHTERS
Woglinde, Wellgunde, Flosshilde
Cruel Innocents—The Problem and the Solution

SOURCES

The Rhine Daughters are the only characters in *The Ring* who do not appear in any of the Scandinavian Eddas.[1] In the German *Nibelungenlied*, however, two or three mermaids or swan maidens in the Danube warn Gunther and Hagen that they will die in the land to which they are headed. These are also mentioned in Jacob Grimm's *Mythologie*. *Thidriks Saga* includes three mermaids in the Danube who originally came from the Rhine. Woodcuts of the mermaids in a contemporary edition of the *Nibelungenlied* appealed to Wagner.[2]

While these sources provided some basis for Wagner's characters, he greatly altered and expanded their story to meet his own purposes. He invented their crucial linkage to the gold and their appearances at both the beginning and ending of the story. In *The Ring*, the Rhine Daughters' moral innocence at the beginning and ability to lift the curse on the ring at the end enhance the thematic consistency of Wagner's story. By breathing life into these provocative creatures, the dramatist builds up what were originally minor, ambiguous figures to render the new tale more graphically. The Rhine Daughters offer a prime example of this Wagnerian technique.

Wagner always referred to the nymphs as Rheintöchter or Rhine Daughters, commonly treated as Rhinemaidens in English. It was their lament from the conclusion of R-iv that he played at his piano in Venice the night before he died.[3]

RELATIONSHIPS

The Rhine Daughters have no known relationships to other characters. They make several references to their father, who has warned them to guard the gold, but he is not identified. On the basis of the mythologies, we might speculate that he was the Supreme Being, father of Wotan and the rest of the physical world. There is no reference to their mother.

APPEARANCES

R-i

Swim playfully in the Rhine.

Tease and reject Alberich.

Greet the "waking" Rhinegold and reveal its secrets to Alberich.

Watch in horror as Alberich renounces love and steals the gold.

R-iv

Heard from offstage.

Lament the loss of the gold and ask the gods for its return.

Their plea is rejected; they censure the "false and faint-hearted" gods, concluding *The Rhinegold*.

T-3-i

Playfully call on Siegfried to give back the ring.

Warn Siegfried of the ring's curse, that it will claim his life that very day.

Prophesy to Siegfried that "a proud woman today will inherit your treasure: she will give us a better hearing."

T-3-iii

Reappear after the Rhine floods the Gibichung hall. Woglinde and Wellgunde drag Hagen to the depths as Flosshilde joyfully displays the recovered ring.

COMMENTS

True to their nature as water sprites, the Rhine Daughters are *The Ring*'s most seductive but elusive characters. They are hardly characters at all—except for Flosshilde's apparent seniority, they are undifferentiated. They display sophisticated human emotions and behavior: they show uninhibited joy over possessing the gold, they play sarcastic and cruel love games with Alberich, they genuinely lament losing the gold, and they provoke Siegfried good-naturedly. Yet, like Erda, they function more as archetypes than as individuals.

They are the first characters we see; their actions set the drama into motion. They are also the last characters seen, except for the gods glimpsed at their immolation and the Gibichungs who are on stage at the end. In between, we hear them at the end of R-iv and see them only in T-3-i. Their most decisive action after R-i, the good counsel they give Brünnhilde between T-3-i and T-3-iii, occurs outside the drama.

Even when they are on stage, their passivity is striking. Their job is to guard the gold in its unexploited, purposeless state. Their joy seems to come only from its beauty and the light it sheds. They are thus strongly aligned with the natural world, as is their music, rather than with the ring of power Alberich fashions from the precious metal.

It is tempting to associate the Rhine Daughters with original innocence and to equate their loss with the danger of losing contact with nature. This view is oversimple. In Jungian terms, the Rhine Daughters and their dark, watery abode are associated with the womblike unconscious, the mother/feminine intuitive, a natural state without responsibilities—in short, the infantile longings with which we all start life but which we must substantially abandon to reach adulthood.

We hardly need Jung to be able to see the shortcomings of the Rhine Daughters. The loss of the gold and the events that follow may be predestined, but no audience can escape the feeling that the Rhine Daughters' distress is a direct result of their own deliberate cruelty—their humiliation of Alberich and his violent reaction. Later, in T-3-i, they virtually provoke Siegfried into keeping the ring when he might just as well have given it away, so little does it mean to him.

At the end of the drama, the Rhine Daughters play happily once more as they display the recovered trinket. Mesmerized by the lure of the mermaids or by the shape of the ring itself, we might think that the story has come full circle. Yet *The Ring* has moved as a spiral, not a circle, for much has changed since R-i. The race of gods has perished in the flames of the castle so expensively built to protect them. A new race of heroes has lived and died. The final moment of *Twilight* soars and subsides in the ringing music of redemption, Brünnhilde's act of self-sacrifice and cleansing.

The Rhine Daughters are among the few survivors. At their appearance with Siegfried in T-3-i, we see in them a new seriousness, a genuine regard for the power of fate and for the future, a kind of wisdom. The ring, cleansed of Alberich's curse, is once more in their safekeeping. Will they do better next time?

MUSIC

The Rhine Daughters introduce some of the seminal music in *The Ring*. The first passage we hear, immediately as the curtain rises in R-i, is the Rhine Daughters' own music, 4–Rhine Daughters. Aligned with the more elemental motives, 2–Nature and 3–Rhine just heard in the Prelude, it strongly evokes the rolling waves of the river and the playful exuberance of the nymphs.

Sung by Woglinde to the onomatopoeic "Weia!," the first two notes of 4–Rhine Daughters form a falling step. This figure occurs in many motives throughout *The Ring*, including the glorious 11–Rhinegold itself, sung by the nymphs in R-i. The music of 11–Rhinegold, in turn, is also the first part of a longer motive, 10–Rhine Daughters' Joy in the Gold.

As the Rhine Daughters encounter Siegfried at the riverbank in T-3-i, they introduce several new musical elements, collectively identified as 143–Rhine Daughters (Continued). The first, 143A, alludes to their seductive nature, as they try to lure the ring away from Siegfried. The second, 143B, somehow suggests the broad sweep of events the nymphs helped set in motion so long ago. The third, 143C, conveys a sense of both nostalgia and detachment; the maidens will give up on Siegfried and try their luck with Brünnhilde, who "will give us a better hearing."

ALBERICH
Lord of the Nibelungs and the Ring

SOURCES

Wagner's Alberich has many ancestors. In the *Nibelungenlied*, Alberich, who is probably not a dwarf, is steward to two princes whom Siegfried slays in order to win a golden hoard. To avenge his masters, Alberich heads the Nibelung army against Siegfried. In the Scandinavian sagas, the dwarf Andvari is tricked out of his gold and ring by Odin and Loki. Eugel is the hoard-owning dwarf king of *Das Lied vom hürnen Seyfrid* and the son of King Nibelung.

Scholars of the myths, including Jacob Grimm, tend to characterize dwarfs as underground miners and cunning thieves. Elizabeth Magee describes Alfrik or Alpris in *Thidriks Saga* as "the notorious thief and most cunning of all the dwarfs mentioned in the ancient sagas."[4]

As much as any other character in *The Ring*, Alberich is a testament to Wagner's extensive reading of the sources and his ability to consolidate selected aspects from diverse stories to create a vivid, consistent, and psychologically compelling portrait.

RELATIONSHIPS

Brother of Mime; lord of the Nibelungs; lover of Grimhild who is wife of King Gibich and mother of Gunther and Gutrune; father of Hagen (with Grimhild).

APPEARANCES

R-i

Is smitten and rejected by the Rhine Daughters.

Learns of the gold and its potential power.

Curses love and steals the gold.

R-iii

Has fashioned the ring and enslaved the Nibelungs.

Seizes the Tarnhelm he has instructed Mime to fashion, completing his power
   over the Nibelungs.

Is tricked by Loge and Wotan, becoming their prisoner.

R-iv

Surrenders the gold and Tarnhelm; Wotan wrenches the ring from him.

Places his curse on the ring and whoever owns it.

S-2-i

Watching Fafner's cave, confronts and threatens Wotan.

Asks Fafner to give him the ring; Fafner refuses.

S-2-iii

Confronts Mime after Siegfried kills Fafner and claims all the treasure for himself.

His laughter is heard when Siegfried kills Mime.

T-2-i

Appears before sleeping Hagen and urges him to win back the ring.

COMMENTS

By any measure, Alberich is a central character in *The Ring*. He initiates the *Ring* drama by stealing the gold. Together with Wotan and Loge, he dominates the action of *The Rhinegold*. He does not appear in *The Valkyrie* and enters only briefly in *Siegfried* and *Twilight of the Gods*, yet his presence looms over the later operas. At the end, Alberich is the only major character left standing—every other protagonist has perished.

Current sensibilities, perhaps more conditioned by concepts of nonjudgmentalism and victimization than by guilt and responsibility, apportion to other *Ring* characters much of the blame for the greed, hatred, violence, and general unpleasantness related to Alberich's theft of the gold, renunciation of love, enslave-

ment of the Nibelungs, and curse on the ring. Certainly Alberich's original intention includes none of these things; he seeks only the physical love of one of the
nymphs. Their responses are so cruel and provide him such a blueprint for
revenge that we feel he is driven toward the dark course he subsequently takes.
Alberich becomes so believable that we ache for him and the meanness done to
him, not just by the Rhine Daughters but by Wotan in R-iv as well.

Parallels between Alberich and Wotan, who calls himself Light-Alberich in
S-1-ii, are especially striking. Both are leaders of their races and renounce love to
pursue power and wealth. Both gain and lose the ring; both mate with mortal
women to produce sons, as extensions of their wills, to recover it. In some *Ring*
productions, Alberich and Wotan are portrayed as moral equivalents.

This interpretation ignores the clear distinctions with which Wagner confronts us. In addition to the dissimilar cosmological positions they occupy in the
mythologies, Wotan and Alberich behave quite differently as individuals. For
instance, Alberich approaches the whole question of love in terms of immediate
physical gratification and he values love little more than lust: "If I cannot extort
love, then by cunning can I attain pleasure?"

Alberich is the only character in *The Ring* who succeeds in using the ring
because he is the only one who explicitly renounces love to gain its power. (Fafner
does this implicitly, by choosing gold over Freia.) Once it is his, Alberich opts for
tyranny and the enslavement of his own race. On two occasions he openly threatens Wotan with the destruction of the gods and the rape of their women. It is
Alberich above all who cannot give up the desire for the ring; he becomes the
greatest casualty of his own curse, living only for hatred and revenge.

Even the most ungenerous approach to Wotan does not ascribe such a nature
to him. His intentions and actions differ from Alberich's on every point. *Ring*
audiences identify with Wotan, whatever his faults, and the human problems—
love and power, control and freedom, ambition and withdrawal—with which he
futilely struggles. Alberich, rather, is a warning, the evil in us to be acknowledged
but resisted.

The *Ring* text sometimes offers glimpses of events that have occurred before
the opening of *The Rhinegold*. When the giants learn that Alberich has gained the
power of the ring, Fasolt says: "I grudge the gnome this gold; much harm the
Nibelung has already done us, yet the dwarf has always slyly slipped from out of
our clutches." Fafner: "New mischief will the Nibelung plot against us if the gold
gives him power."

Alberich also carries a grudge against the gods from the beginning. Strangest
of all, Loge and Alberich were once friends, Loge providing fire for Alberich's
forges, but in R-iii Alberich says: "If, false one, you're [now the gods'] friend as

once you were friend to me, ha ha! . . . I have faith in your faithlessness, not in your fidelity!"

We sometimes leave the theater after *Twilight of the Gods* wondering if the story continues, and we remember that only Alberich is unaccounted for. The ring itself seems safe; Alberich himself has told us, in T-2-i, "if ever [Brünnhilde] advised [Siegfried] to return the ring to the Rhinemaidens . . . then my gold would be lost and no ruse could ever retrieve it."

Yet we can have no doubt that his destructive lusts are as great as ever. The ring still exists, the object, perhaps, of another assault. Alberich and the evils he represents are still at large in the world.

MUSIC

Alberich's personal music is heard at his first appearance in R-i; 6–Alberich suggests his clambering about on the slippery rocks at the bottom of the Rhine. As a personal statement, it does not often reappear in the course of the tetralogy; compared to other musical and thematic elements associated directly with his actions, it is of limited impact.

Alberich also transforms the falling step "Weia!" from 4–Rhine Daughters into half-steps in an expression of grief or 7–Woe, as he is unable to secure one of the nymphs.

Humiliated by the Rhine Daughters, Alberich loses little time in rejecting love and stealing the gold. The music of 13–Renunciation of Love, discussed more fully in chapter 3, is among the best known of the *Ring* motives and the subject of substantial controversy.

When the ring is wrenched from him in R-iv, Alberich is filled with hatred, which we hear as the chilling, venomous fragment, 34–Hatred. Immediately after the first iteration of this motive, Alberich places a curse on the ring and on those who would possess it, heard as 35–Curse.

WOTAN
The Wanderer, Volse, and Wolf: Lord of the Spear

SOURCES

Wotan, known by many other names throughout the mythologies, was originally the early Teutons' god of battle. He emerged in the northern mythologies as god of all living creatures, as god of battle and those slain in battle, and as the Wanderer.[5]

The *Volsunga Saga* establishes Wotan's relationship to Siegmund and Sieglinde, although in the saga Odin and Volse are different individuals separated by several generations.

The *Prose Edda*, according to Deryck Cooke "the only coherent and comprehensive account of the Scandinavian gods in existence,"[6] contains two additional features carried into *The Ring* concerning Wotan: the promise of Freyja as wage and the loss of the golden apples.

The *Poetic Edda* and other sources contain a ballad in which Odin (Wotan) and Loki rob the dwarf Andvari of his gold, including a ring, to pay off a debt to two brothers. One of these, Fafnir, kills the other brother and turns himself into a dragon to safeguard the treasure. In these stories, Wotan is no more omnipotent than in *The Ring*. Another of the Eddic poems describes a prophetess like Erda, raised from the dead by Odin to tell him about the end of the gods.

RELATIONSHIPS

Husband of Fricka; lover of Erda; father (with Erda) of Brünnhilde; father (with Erda or an unknown mother) of the other Valkyries; father (with an unnamed Volsung woman) of Siegmund and Sieglinde; grandfather of Siegfried; brother-in-law of Freia, Froh, and Donner.

APPEARANCES

R-ii

Wakes to find Valhalla completed.

Tries to negate the contract with the giants, whereby Freia will be paid over as wage.

Prohibits violence against the giants by Froh and Donner.

Learns from Loge that Alberich has stolen the gold and forged the ring of power; says he must possess it.

As the gods fade, determines to descend to Nibelheim and secure the gold to free Freia.

R-iii

In Nibelheim, Loge tricks Alberich, and Wotan captures him.

R-iv

Takes the gold, Tarnhelm, and ring from Alberich by force; Alberich places a curse on the ring.

Relinquishes the gold and Tarnhelm to the giants but refuses to give up the ring until Erda persuades him. Freia is freed.

Determines to learn more of Erda's wisdom.

Watches as Fafner murders Fasolt and rues paying for Valhalla with unclean wages.

Is seized by a great thought (a plan to regain the ring without violating his contract with the giants).

Rebuffs the Rhine Daughters' plea for help and leads the gods into Valhalla.

V-2-i

After Fricka exposes the contradiction in his plan, pledges to support Hunding against Siegmund.

V-2-ii

In a long narration, describes his predicament, his plan, and its frustration.
    Reveals that Alberich has conceived an avenging son.

Orders Brünnhilde to ensure Siegmund's defeat.

V-2-v

Appears during Siegmund's fight with Hunding and shatters the sword so that Hunding can prevail.

Dismisses Hunding to death and Fricka.

Vows to punish disobedient Brünnhilde.

V-3-ii

Finds Brünnhilde among the Valkyries. Tells her she will be separated from the gods in sleep and will belong to the first man who wakes her.

Chases the Valkyries away.

V-3-iii

Explains to Brünnhilde that she has separated herself from him by opting for the mortal, Siegmund.

Yields to her plea for protection. Puts her to sleep and creates a ring of fire around her through which only a fearless hero may pass.

S-1-ii

Appearing as the Wanderer, outwits Mime, telling him his head is forfeit to one who does not know fear.

S-2-i

Joining Alberich in front of Fafner's cave, advises him that a hero is coming who stands on his own.

S-3-i

Summons Erda to test her wisdom for the last time. Tells her he bequeaths his inheritance to Siegfried and Brünnhilde, and sends Erda to eternal sleep.

S-3-ii

Though he does not intend to bar Siegfried's passing, is goaded by the boy into a final effort to resist his fate. His spear shattered, he watches Siegfried pass and then disappears.

COMMENTS

Wotan is rooted in pre-Christian, northern European religions and traditions. Sometimes addressed as Warfather or Battlefather, he is both the god of battle and the archetypal father who generates races of men and warrior maidens. He is first among the gods, and his relationship to political power and the law reverberates in every scene of *The Ring*.

Wotan stands as a key to both the mythological and psychological levels of meaning in *The Ring*, but it is Wotan's human qualities that elevate him to a central position in modern western art. He strives and quests, struggles against fate, and believes that the will of the individual can alter and overcome circumstance. He acts to create a world governed by law, not violence, but incites violence to protect himself from his enemies.

At times hugely self-confident, he is also a thinking, introspective man so racked by self-doubt as to risk self-defeat. He is passionate, loving women too well and given to roaming to escape the dry responsibilities of legal obligations and political power. He stands for order and the sanctity of contracts but becomes the victim of his own vanity and blind anger.

Another of Wotan's fundamental drives, often overlooked, is the quest for knowledge: he goes literally to the end of the world to attain it. In this he shows that he believes in a cosmos and an eternal body of truth that is greater than his own desires, laws, and godhood. In R-iv he acknowledges the high moral authority of Erda's wisdom and yields, in V-2-i, to the more prosaic intellectual truth of his wife's argument, even when this becomes his undoing.

Thus Wotan joins other imposing figures of western art—Lear, Faust, and Quixote, for example: dynamic and expansive, curious and creative, aggressive and moralistic, introspective and self-critical, destructive and self-destructive.

The story of *The Ring* seems to begin in R-i, with the renunciation of love and the theft of the gold. However, we learn at the beginning of R-ii that fundamental events have already occurred: Wotan has made a lawful treaty with the giants which he cannot honor, for giving up Freia would destroy the gods.

R-ii reveals an enormous amount about Wotan: his love of women and his obvious problems with his wife; his quest for power, which has led him to subdue other races and which leads to his own desire for the ring. He trusts Loge—his craft and cunning—when his own "simple courage" does not suffice. He will not permit Donner and Froh to effect a violent solution with the giants because that would subvert the law upon which his legitimacy is based. He is willing to act when circumstances are dire, which leads him directly to Alberich.

More than any other character, Wotan will infuse the purpose of the following two-and-a-half operas. He appears in every act of *The Ring* from R-ii to S-3, except for V-1 (over which he looms as the twins' father, whom Siegmund invokes, and as the strange visitor who placed the sword in the tree trunk; Wagner's original sketch placed him in this scene, too). With each passing scene, the character reveals himself more fully, acting on his own initiative but also reacting to changing events.

In R-iii he encourages Loge to trick Alberich. In R-iv, we are shocked when he resorts to brute force to secure the ring. He nevertheless is able to yield to the overriding wisdom of Erda. He conceives a plan (unrevealed until V-2-ii) to extricate the gods from danger, yet cruelly rebuffs the melancholy appeal of the Rhine Daughters.

In V-2-ii Wotan has the stage to himself for a long narration (it is as if Brünnhilde is not there). This recapitulation, a device common in myth-telling, does not cause the action of *The Ring* to stop but masterfully adds information we have not known before. More important, Wotan explores with disgust the trap he has set for himself: the contradiction inherent in creating and manipulating a free will. This is a moment of searing introspection in which the "play of ideas" has been compared to that found in Ibsen or Shaw.[7]

In V-3-ii and V-3-iii Wotan is virtually out of control, in the grip of his own frustration and rage, which he unfairly projects onto Brünnhilde. Still, his elaborate condemnation of his daughter persuades us how devastating her defiance has been to him: she has not simply disobeyed but has negated her very self which was also part of Wotan. In opting for love—mortal love—she has done the deed he so much desired to do but would not let himself. Typical of the *Ring* text, both Wotan's and Brünnhilde's arguments marshal real intellectual force; they are persuasive even on opposing sides of the same issue.

In *Siegfried*, a generation later, the god is altogether different. He has seemingly gained the wisdom to accept the power of time and fate as well as accepting the most poignant of human challenges: surrender and withdrawal, passing and death. In his final testament before Erda in S-3-i, Wotan's true mettle shines through as the god commits himself to his own passing.

Rather than letting Wotan simply fade away, however, Wagner adds a dramatic postscript that is among his most brilliant inventions: the confrontation with Siegfried. It is a scene filled with rueful charm, warmth, and danger. We are torn, as is Wotan, by the incompatibility of youth and age, by the very moment when the new replaces the old, not out of will or wisdom but by an inexorable force of life. How vulnerable and human Wotan is at the last! Despite all his emotional experience and intellectual resolution, he is goaded by the rough and uncaring boy into a final grasp at survival. Before we watch Siegfried ascend through the flames to his own great glory and beginning, the old man sadly picks up the shattered fragments of his spear and disappears.

MUSIC

There is no specific Wotan motive in *The Ring*. Rather, several motives refer directly to different aspects of his cosmic struggles. The first and perhaps most personal is 14–Valhalla, which as place and concept is wholly Wotan's. It is the first major musical transformation or mutation in *The Ring*, as 14A, the most prominent of its four segments, develops directly out of 12–The Ring in the transitional music between R-i and R-ii.

Wotan's worldly authority is generally associated with 24–Spear, an assertive descending scale. In V-2-i the formidable motive of 65–Frustration is introduced as Fricka thwarts Wotan's plan to redeem the ring and curse. This music, which does not stand alone in a traditional melodic sense, conveys emotions as insightfully as any in *The Ring*.

Wotan finally yields to his love for Brünnhilde as he departs from her in V-3-iii. Despite the godly significance of these events, the music of 78–Wotan's Love for Brünnhilde conveys the supremely human, personal aspect of the scene. Consistent with all we have learned about Brünnhilde and Wotan, the scene is also a paradigm of any father's tragic separation from a beloved daughter.

In S-1-ii Wotan appears as the Wanderer as we hear 88–The Wanderer, the slow, dignified passage that expresses his changed outlook on those events he is no longer determined to control.

As an individual, Wotan rises to his noblest height at the moment of self-renunciation. At the end of S-3-i he bequeaths his legacy and the future to Siegfried and Brünnhilde with the music of 101–World's Inheritance.

Wotan's last desperate act is to resist Siegfried and his own passing: 103–Resistance.

FRICKA
Consort of Wotan and Goddess of Family Values

SOURCES

Frigg appears in the Scandinavian *Prose Edda* and *Poetic Edda* as the wife of Odin and goddess of marriage. The *Edda* contains episodes in which Frigg complains of Odin's travels outside the circle of the gods. Fricka's jealousy is also founded in the *Edda*, in which Odin consorts with other women.[8] While Wagner's Fricka demands that Wotan destroy Siegmund, the Eddic Frigg opposes Odin's plan to destroy his favorite among two brothers. The mythologies make no mention of Fricka's chariot-pulling rams.

Grimm described Frigg as "the divine mother and guardian of marriages" even though, as E. Magee put it, "the demarcation-lines between [Fricka and Freia] were very fluid in the sources and Grimm spends several pages of his chapter on goddesses disentangling them."[9]

Wagner seems to have taken the Grimm summary literally. He reworked the character as little as any in *The Ring*, emphasizing her archetypal position as standard-bearer of the status quo in contrast to Wotan's revolutionary ideas. He did invent two details relating to Fricka—Wotan's risking, not losing, an eye to woo her, and her barrenness.

Biographers have sometimes speculated that Fricka reflects Wagner's view of his first wife, Minna. Wagner never addressed this issue directly.

RELATIONSHIPS

Wife of Wotan; sister of Freia, Froh, and Donner; stepmother of Brünnhilde, the other Valkyries, and Siegmund and Sieglinde.

APPEARANCES

R-ii

Chastises Wotan for pledging Freia to the giants, for his romantic roaming, and for trusting Loge.

Encourages Wotan to secure the gold from Alberich.

R-iv

Welcomes Wotan back from Nibelheim.

Counsels Wotan to give up the ring.

Rebukes Wotan for the humiliation of paying the gold to the giants.

Joins Wotan in entering Valhalla.

V-2-i

Attacks Wotan's support of the adulterous, incestuous Volsung twins.

Undermines Wotan's argument that Siegmund is a free agent, thereby causing Wotan to abandon his plan.

Secures Wotan's pledge that Hunding will defeat Siegmund.

COMMENTS

Like Erda, Fricka intervenes in the action of *The Ring* at one decisive moment. In V-2-i she not only forces Wotan to abandon his son, Siegmund, but she also has the broader impact of undermining his plan to escape from the problem of the ring. From this moment, Wotan accepts that he is caught in his own trap and begins to end his struggle against his own destiny.

With Hunding and Hagen, Fricka is among *The Ring*'s least sympathetic characters. In spite of ourselves, we have genuine feelings of compassion for Alberich, Fasolt, Mime, and even Fafner, to complement our disapproval or loathing. Fricka strikes us as a nag—possessive, loveless, inflexible—and relentless: she attacks Wotan, the Lord of Lights, constantly, bitterly, and across a wide range of subjects.

In fact, Fricka is resolute in upholding the values that she, as goddess, has the responsibility to represent: the sanctity of marriage and, by extension, the rule of law. She is a bulwark against wife stealing, adultery, and incest. She stands up for those, like Hunding, who are wronged and who pray to her for justice.

She also sounds distinctly contemporary when, at the outset, she scolds Wotan for the fraudulent contract with the giants: "you men firmly kept the women away so that, deaf and silent to us, you could deal alone with the giants." It is plausible that Fricka would never have made, or allowed Wotan to make, the disastrous pledge of Freia for Valhalla.

Fricka's power of persuasion in V-2 causes discomfort in Wotan and listeners alike. We want Wotan's plan, however amorphous, to succeed. We definitely want the young lovers, Siegmund and Sieglinde, to be allowed a chance for happiness. Like Wotan, we would like to brush Fricka aside but cannot. As Donington writes, "While her logic is in the main all too unassailable, it is ever so slightly but exasperatingly off the mark. There is no answering it, and yet we get caught up in it without being altogether convinced in our hearts, as opposed to our heads."[10]

Wotan acknowledges the power of his wife's argument all too well. Siegmund cannot be both Wotan's creation and an independent agent. Fricka wins: with a self-serving reminder about her own values and honor—and a smug parting comment to Brünnhilde, whom she envies as Wotan's favorite—she leaves the stage for good.

One supposes that she understands how hollow her victory is. She can not yet comprehend that Wotan's defeat means the end of all the gods, but she must know that by so humiliating her husband she has lost him forever. She can hardly savor her successful patronage of the vulgar Hunding. Her future may seem as barren to her as her childless marriage.

Fricka's victory sends Wotan into a deep tailspin. He will soon participate in the murder of his steadfast son and inflict a brutal and unfair punishment on his beloved daughter. But it is the dashing of his plan that causes his immediate anguish.

Donington casts this in Jungian terms, suggesting that Fricka's contribution (like Erda's and even Alberich's) is in the long run positive. Fricka is, after all, quite accurate in exposing the contradiction in Wotan's strategy. He gives up his tangled plan and begins to face the end that is inevitably coming to him and his era.[11]

This was never Fricka's intention, though. She struggled to maintain the status quo and the eternal supremacy of the gods. At the end, she sits by Wotan in Valhalla, awaiting the final conflagration in great fear, struck numb by Wotan's final will.

MUSIC

Fricka's music is not the most pervasive in *The Ring*. She commands only three major musical passages, yet each is unusually extended and vivid. Fricka is readily identified in R-ii by 15–Love's Enchantment, sometimes called Domestic Bliss, as she hopes that "a stately dwelling, splendidly appointed, might tempt [Wotan] to stay here and rest."

In V-2-i, 63–Fricka further emphasizes her insistent frustration of Wotan's plans and will. As she complains of Wotan's broken marriage vows, Fricka also introduces 64–Withered Love, a haunting corruption of 16B–Love, *The Ring*'s fundamental love motive.

FREIA

The Goddess of Love

SOURCES

In the Scandinavian sagas, Freyja is the goddess of love. In the Eddas, unlike *The Ring*, Freyja and Frey (Froh) come from a different race and are unrelated to Odin (Wotan) and Frigg (Fricka).[12]

Idunn, not Freyja, is, in E. Magee's words, "guardian of the apples of youth in the *Edda*,"[13] and it is Idunn who is bartered away to giants through the machinations of Loge. Wagner consolidated these aspects of Idunn into the figure of Freia.

Freia is also referred to in *The Ring* as Holda, a goddess from German mythology. Wagner makes a play on both names when Fasolt describes the goddess in R-ii: "Freia, the fair, Holda the free" [*Freia, die holde, Holda, die freie*].

RELATIONSHIPS

Sister of Fricka, Froh, and Donner; sister-in-law of Wotan.

APPEARANCES

R-ii

Seeks the protection of Wotan, Donner, and Froh from the giants, who claim her as wage for building Valhalla.

Is taken hostage by the giants until Wotan secures the gold.

R-iv

Is returned to the gods by the giants in exchange for the gold, which is measured
against her height.

COMMENTS

Of all the characters in *The Ring*, Freia has the clearest dramatic purpose and the
least delineated character. She is vital to the gods, keeping them eternally young
by tending the golden apples; without her they would fade and die. She is the center of Wotan's dilemma—his unworkable bargain with the giants. The entire second scene of *The Rhinegold* is directly focused on her. Her music spreads throughout *The Ring* with great significance.

Why is it, then, that she has almost nothing to say? Her emotions range only
from despair as hostage to relief at her release. The few lines she does sing have
no effect on the action. She *takes* no action at all.

Wagner surely intended all this; he was extremely careful about delineating his
characters, and he had almost thirty years to humanize Freia. He opted, instead,
to portray her as archetype and ideal.

A central issue of *The Ring* is whether a worthy aspiration for love can overcome a false quest for worldly power. Freia symbolizes the life-affirming, positive
aspects of love. She is depersonalized—her persona rendered virtually inert—
and this emphasizes her absolute and symbolic stature; if the gods exchange her
for corrupting power, they will fade and die, and will deserve to do so.

Wagner's treatment of Freia as archetype underscores the strong influence of
Greek drama on his own artistic standards and ideals. Nowhere are Wagner's pref-
erences for Greece so patent as in *The Rhinegold*.

MUSIC

The music of Freia, the goddess of love, is heard directly upon her entrance in
R-ii in agitated flight from the giants and in great distress. Two important elements associated with love are introduced by 16A– and 16B–Love.[14]

· The other music directly related to Freia is 21–Holda's Golden Apples, first
sung by Fafner in R-ii.

FASOLT
The Giant Who Loved Freia

SOURCES

Fasolt has his roots in the figure of Regin from the Scandinavian sagas. In the
Poetic Edda, the *Prose Edda*, and the *Volsunga Saga*, Regin, his father (Hreidmar),

and his brother (Fafnir)—they are not giants—capture Odin and Loki. Loki tricks the dwarf Andvari out of his gold and ring, paying these as ransom to Hreidmar. Regin and Fafnir kill their father for the gold, which Fafnir keeps for himself alone, turning himself into a serpent to hoard it. Regin is banished, not killed as Fasolt is, and he becomes foster father to Sigurd (Siegfried).

In making Regin a giant, Wagner drew on W. Müller's *Altdeutsche Religion*, in which Fasolt is mentioned as a storm-giant. Wilhelm Grimm's *Deutsche Helden-sage* describes Fasolt as a man for fair ladies.[15] Wagner may have chosen the name Fasolt both to draw on contemporary audiences' familiarity with the figure of Regin and to reinforce the effect of the *Stabreim* (see page 19) in his own poem, Fasolt as a counterpart to Fafner (as well as to Freia and Froh).

Thus Fafner emerges basically as described in the major sources, while Fasolt was fundamentally Wagner's invention, with aspects drawn from major and minor sources.

RELATIONSHIP

Brother of Fafner

APPEARANCES

R-ii

Claims Freia as wage for building Valhalla, warning Wotan about the sanctity of contracts and the value of women.

Takes Freia as hostage until Wotan returns with the gold.

R-iv

Returns Freia for the gold, Tarnhelm, and ring.

Demands his share from Fafner, seizes the ring, but is killed by Fafner.

COMMENTS

Fasolt is a striking example of how Wagner fused a detailed reading of the mythologies with his own best dramatic instincts. In the sources, giants are a natural enemy of heroes and gods—brutish, slow-witted, reliant on their physical strength. But in some stories they are more—an "old and dying order," in Jacob Grimm's words, possessed of an ancient innocence and wisdom.[16]

Rather than a simplistic villain, Wagner's Fasolt is an immensely individuated character who provides a deliberate contrast to his more brutish brother. He works honestly, according to contract; we are touched when he falls in love with the beautiful Freia, put up by Wotan as fair wage; he agrees only reluctantly to accept the gold in her place and takes no liberties while holding her hostage; finally, he appeals to the gods for fairness in securing his share of the fee. In fact, he equates the ring itself with the beauty of Freia's eyes.

Fasolt also reflects the simple wisdom of his race, a wisdom greater, in key aspects, than Wotan's. Fasolt reminds Wotan that his leadership of the "radiant, august" race of gods depends on his honoring his treaties and agreements. Further—and this point underlies so much of the tetralogy—Fasolt understands that the love of woman is worth more than gold, wealth, and power. This links Fasolt more with the primordial wisdom of Erda than with the base drives of his brother, Fafner.

MUSIC

Fasolt and Fafner enter R-ii to 17–Giants, which potently conveys their physical, plodding strength.

In R-ii Fasolt introduces two important aspects of the gods' preeminent position in the world: their political authority and their need to observe and uphold the rule of law. With 18–Power of the Gods, he reminds Wotan that "what you [gods] are, you are only by contracts: limited and well-defined is your power."

The motive 19–Treaty, related to 24–Spear, is introduced by Fasolt when he warns Wotan to honor the "solemn compact that your spear shows."

A charming transformation of a major motive occurs in R-ii when Fasolt recasts both segments of Freia's music (16A– and 16B–Love), first heard in association with Freia's agitated flight from the giants. Fasolt's restatement of this passage in 20–Love (Fasolt) is slowed and recolored in a way that expresses his heartfelt but hopeless aspiration "to win a woman, winsome and gentle, [who] will live with us poor creatures." This is a moment of unexpected, lyrical beauty, reinforcing Freia's symbolic association with the positive power of love.

FAFNER
The Ruthless Giant Who Gained the Ring

SOURCES

In the Scandinavian mythology, Fafnir is not a giant but a man, the brother of Regin and the son of Hreidmar. The three of them capture Odin and Loki and demand a ransom of gold. Loki, in turn, captures the dwarf Andvari and forces him to relinquish his hoard, which includes a magical ring (but no magic helmet). Fafnir and Regin kill their father for the gold, and Fafnir chases Regin away so that he can keep it all. He assumes the form of a serpent for this purpose.

Grimm speaks favorably of the innate innocence and wisdom of the race of giants. Wagner bestowed these qualities on Fafner's brother, Fasolt, but Fafner exhibits them only after he is mortally wounded in S-2-ii.

RELATIONSHIP

Brother of Fasolt

APPEARANCES

R-ii

Comes to collect Freia as wage for building Valhalla.

Knowing the value of Freia's apples to the gods, convinces Fasolt they should take the Nibelung gold instead.

Takes Freia hostage until Wotan delivers the gold.

R-iv

Delivers Freia in exchange for the gold, demanding also the Tarnhelm and ring.

Kills Fasolt when he seizes the ring; leaves with all the treasure.

S-2-i

In the form of a dragon, is warned by Alberich that an enemy approaches but does not give Alberich the ring. (Fafner is heard but not seen in this scene.)

S-2-ii

Wounded in the fight with Siegfried, warns the boy not to trust whoever has led him to Neidhöhle; dies.

Wotan   *Fricka*   *Fafner*

COMMENTS

By killing Fasolt, Fafner is the first to demonstrate the power of Alberich's curse. His brutal, unhesitating murder of his brother comes immediately after Erda's warning and stuns the gods and audience alike.

Fafner directly goes off to remote Neidhöhle and turns himself into a mighty dragon, his only purpose to hoard the Nibelung treasure. There he stays for a generation, the gold giving him neither pleasure nor power; in his curse Alberich has asserted that "each shall itch to possess it, but none in it shall find pleasure! Its owner shall guard it profitlessly, for through it he shall meet his executioner!" Thus Fafner perpetuates the curse.

Fafner is quite different from his love-struck brother. From the first he values Freia, who represents the positive force of love, less than the gold, and in this way joins Alberich in rejecting love. Fafner worries for the balance of power if Alberich wields the power of the ring, and he seems genuinely anxious to weaken the gods by withholding their life-sustaining apples. This overt hostility underscores the contentious political world of *The Rhinegold*, wherein giants, dwarfs, and gods are in constant struggle against each other.

Fafner exhibits no redeeming aspects. From the first he is ruthless, self-serving, mean-spirited, and single-minded. In the form of the dragon, he has no life: he is frozen in a single purpose—to keep the ring away from everyone else, just as Alberich had foretold.

But as he lies dying, we briefly glimpse a different Fafner. Seeming to feel relief rather than rancor, he asks who has killed him and who is behind this deed. He intuitively knows that Siegfried is the hero Alberich has prophesied in S-2-i but also that his death could not have been Siegfried's idea. He offers the boy valuable advice, soon to be confirmed by the Wood Bird's warning about Mime: whoever prompted him to kill Fafner now plots Siegfried's own death.

Sadly but without self-pity, Fafner informs Siegfried that he has killed the last of the giants, one who murdered his own brother for the "accursed gold." Only in death does Fafner regret his crime and gain relief from the curse.

MUSIC

Fafner shares with Fasolt the music of 17–Giants, heard on their initial appearance in R-ii (see chapter 3).

Wagner also gives effective musical shape to Fafner as dragon. The phrase is foreshadowed both in R-iii when Alberich takes the form of a huge serpent (Wagner's German word *Wurm* can mean both serpent and dragon) and in V-3-i when Siegrune and Schwertleite urge Sieglinde to take refuge in Neidhöhle. In the S-2 Prelude, 92–Fafner as Dragon is effectively played together with 17–Giants.

FROH
The Gentle God

SOURCES

Frey is, in Cooke's words, "the bright shining god"[17] of the *Poetic Edda*. He is brother to Freia but unrelated to Odin, Frigg, or Thor. In the *Prose Edda*, according to Cooke, "Frey is the most splendid of the gods. He rules over the rain and the sunshine, and over the fruits of the earth, and it is on him that one should call for fertility and peace. He also has power over the wealth of men."[18]

Froh is diminished at Wagner's hands as much as any *Ring* character. His glorious aspects in the mythologies are sharply curtailed in the interest of dramatic compression, but also so that he does not compete with the other leading male characters with whom Wagner is more concerned: Wotan, Siegmund, and Siegfried.

RELATIONSHIPS

Brother of Fricka, Freia, and Donner; brother-in-law of Wotan.

APPEARANCES

R-ii
Rushes in to save Freia from the giants but is held back by Wotan.
Encourages Wotan to secure the gold.

R-iv
Welcomes Wotan from Nibelheim and Freia from Riesenheim.
Helps pile up the gold for the giants.
Urges Wotan to give up the ring.
Conjures the Rainbow Bridge and crosses to Valhalla with the rest of the gods.

COMMENTS

It has become conventional to portray Froh in stage productions as superficial, ineffectual, even effeminate. In the 1993 Chicago *Ring*, he plays with a yo-yo, an unflattering personal symbol. This is a far cry from the "bright shining god" of the mythologies.

While Wagner deliberately diminished Froh's role and stature, the contemptuous treatment of our day is part of a wider problem. Contemporary *Ring* productions commonly overemphasize the negative aspects of the gods in *The Rhinegold*, including Wotan—but with the exception of the iconoclast demigod, Loge. This may have to do with a general cynicism toward established figures of authority and seems at the extreme to border on self-loathing.

However, portrayal of the gods in *The Rhinegold* as cardboard clowns leads to an interpretive dead end that makes its obvious point at the expense of a meaningful rendering of the work. To the extent that these characters are merely ridiculous, so is the audience discouraged from serious engagement with their problems. Wagner himself provides plenty of evidence for the foibles of the gods; stage directors needn't beat the point into the ground.

In the case of Froh, the derisive viewpoint suggests that he represents a hypocritical and ineffectual authority figure. As part of a privileged Establishment, he shows no interest in what might be called the legitimate rights of the Rhine Daughters, Nibelungs, and giants (although Froh urges Wotan to pay the ring over to them and helps Loge pile up the gold in R-iv). He threatens the giants loudly but fails to free Freia.

Froh's impotence results, at least in part, from Wotan's prohibition against the use of physical force. Wotan's spear is engraved with his pact with the giants, and as Law-Giver he is determined to preserve the legal authority of his contracts, even bad ones.

As Wagner differentiates between Fasolt and Fafner, so is Froh very different from his brother, Donner, the god of anger and thunder. It is no accident that, as the gods decline in Freia's absence at the end of R-ii, Froh complains of his waning heart while Donner remarks on the weakening of his hand. Bashing giants is almost Donner's *raison d'être*. Froh's feelings throughout his appearances in *The Rhinegold*, on the other hand, focus on the welfare of his sister, Freia. Of all the gods, he delights most in her liberation. On a familial level, this is admirable.

On a deeper level Froh, like Fasolt, has a central priority of *The Ring* quite right: while Wotan struggles ambivalently, Froh sees clearly that the value of Freia as woman and the personification of love is greater than the value of gold and worldly power. He does not hesitate to urge Wotan to give up the ring as Erda counsels.

Froh's one important action is to conjure the Rainbow Bridge and to invite the gods to cross to the protection of Valhalla. At this point, Wotan has already begun to see the illusion of it all. Froh longs for the beauty and peace that could exist for the race of gods. In this he is indeed naive.

MUSIC

Froh has three musically prominent moments that define his basic character and dramatic purpose. In R-ii he arrives with Donner in great excitement to save Freia. His urgent music, 23–Froh, is in fact a mutation of 21–Holda's Golden Apples.

In R-iv, Froh returns with Fricka and Donner to find that Wotan and Loge have succeeded in taking the gold from Alberich. As Freia approaches, Froh expresses his bliss upon her safe return, a further, arietta-like transformation of the motive 21–Holda's Golden Apples.

Froh is most memorably associated with the majestic music of the Rainbow Bridge, drawn directly from 2–Nature, as he bids the gods to "tread its terrorless path!" As Wagner weaves the extraordinary conclusion of *The Rhinegold*, we hear 12–The Ring, 14–Valhalla, 25–Loge, 40–Sword, and 41–Rhine Daughters' Lament. But the last thing we hear is Froh's 39–Rainbow Bridge as the gods cross over to the fortress they wrongly believe will isolate them from the troubles of the world.

DONNER
The God of Thunder and Anger

SOURCES

In the Scandinavian sagas Thor, the thunder god and scourge of giants, is a son of Odin by the earth goddess Jord. There is more space given to Thor in the Eddas than to Odin himself; in the nineteenth-century revival of the mythologies, he was perhaps the most popular of the gods.

Thor is an imposing figure, with a red beard that bristles when he becomes angry. His chariot is driven by two he-goats. He swings the great hammer, Mjoll-nir, made for him by dwarfs and used most often against giants; Donner's hammer was probably the best-known symbol to the first *Ring* audiences.

As in the treatment of Froh, Wagner greatly diminished Donner's role in *The Rhinegold*. He even took from Donner and gave to Wotan, as in the Eddic story of Donner's contest of wits with a dwarf, which provided the basis for the Wanderer's scene with Mime in S-1-ii.

RELATIONSHIPS

Brother of Freia, Froh, and Fricka; brother-in-law of Wotan.

APPEARANCES

R-ii

Charges in at Freia's call to save her from the giants, but is stopped by Wotan.

R-iv

Welcomes Wotan from Nibelheim.

Again threatens the giants when they measure the gold against Freia.

Urges Wotan to give up the ring.

Summons the mists into a storm cloud.

COMMENTS

Donner's case seems clear-cut: Wagner has sharply curtailed his great importance in the myths—his eminence as storm god, his adventures against the
giants, even his important lineage (he is the son of the Wotan and Erda figures).
Donner's dramatic function is to draw our attention, chiefly by means of contrast,
to the central figure of Wotan and his struggles as Warfather and Law-Giver.

Donner represents two related aspects of behavior that are reflected more
ambivalently in Wotan: anger and the use of force. Donner rages at any offense;
his instincts are to coerce and smash rather than to persuade. Significantly, when
the gods wane in Freia's absence near the end of R-ii and while Froh's heart is
stricken, it is Donner's hand that weakens and his hammer sinks.

Like Froh (and Erda and Fricka), Donner controls the action of *The Ring* at a
single moment. When Wotan, filled with dread by Erda's warning and Fasolt's
murder, speculates on the "unclean wages" that have won Valhalla, Donner literally clears the air by collecting the hanging sultry haze into a storm cloud. Wotan
is able to behold Valhalla once more, its shining radiance reflected in the evening
sun. With the other gods, Donner passes over the Rainbow Bridge to the safety of
the fortress.

MUSIC

Donner is associated with 43–Storm, foreshadowed at his entrance in R-ii. But he
makes his lasting mark in R-iv at 38–Donner's Call, which reappears in the stormy
V-1-Prelude. Donner summons the mists into a storm cloud for the one musical
moment in *The Ring* that is all his own, and it is among the most majestic in the
cycle. Like Donner, the music is straightforward and aggressive. It also has a
heroic bearing, qualities we do not see much of in this character. One wonders if
Wagner was being ironic, or if the music is so strong as to imbue Donner with
unintended value.

LOGE
Wit Without Wisdom, Craft Without Character

SOURCES

In the Scandinavian sagas, Loge is Loki, the mischief-maker, the teaser and taun-
ter of the gods. Many of the primary sources include the story of Loki's tricking
the dwarf Andvari out of his gold (see "Fasolt," pages 188–189).

Loge's association with fire probably comes from an entirely different figure,
the Eddic giant Logi, whom Grimm describes as "the natural force of fire."[19]

Wagner did not include Loge at all in his sketch of 1848. Subsequent reading of Weinhold's *Die Sagen von Loki* inspired him to interject the demigod as a major figure in *The Rhinegold*. Weinhold described Loge as more than a mere evildoer; he restored Loge, as E. Magee describes him, to "his original stature and dignity . . . [as] a god with a mission, albeit a negative one."[20]

RELATIONSHIPS

Loge is half god, half fire. This elemental aspect sets him apart from the rest of the gods.

APPEARANCES

R-ii

Summoned by Wotan, tells the gods that he has roamed the world looking for a substitute for Freia and love, but that only Alberich, in order to steal the gold and forge the ring of power, has renounced love.

His story causes the gods concern over Alberich and makes them covet the gold and ring for themselves. He suggests how to get them: "by theft!"

R-iii

Goes down to Nibelheim with Wotan, his trickery resulting in Alberich's capture.

R-iv

Observes Wotan's forcing the ring from Alberich, Freia's return, Erda's warning, and Fasolt's murder.

In an aside, expresses his contempt for the gods.

At Wotan's command, chastises the lamenting Rhine Daughters.

V-3-iii

Summoned by Wotan, forms a forbidding wall of flame around sleeping Brünnhilde.

T-3-iii

As fire, is carried by the ravens from Brünnhilde's rock and consumes Valhalla in flames.

(Loge also appears in the form of flames around Brünnhilde's rock in S-3-ii, T-Prologue, and T-1-iii, but he plays no active role in those scenes.)

COMMENTS

Loge is one the most original creations in *The Ring*. He has two distinct aspects: he appears in human form in *The Rhinegold* and thereafter as fire, an elemental and inanimate (but decidedly animated) force.

As half-god, he says he is "only half as glorious as you glorious ones!" This distinction underlies his ambivalent feelings toward the gods (and vice versa).

He is separated from the gods by more than blood and nature. Fricka, Froh, and Donner despise him; Wotan, his "only friend among all the gods, took [Loge] up when the rest mistrusted [him]." Freia was always ungenerous about sharing her life-sustaining apples with him, so he has learned to live without them, unlike the gods who have "staked all on the life-giving fruit."

Loge's apartness from the gods has no special basis in the mythologies, except that Loge openly satirizes them, but Wagner exploited his role to superb dramatic effect. For Loge is also detached from the struggle between gods, giants, and dwarfs in the universe of *The Rhinegold*. He seems to have no personal ambition for political power or godly responsibilities—such as protecting marriage or solemn contracts. Loge is a means, not an end.

As such, he represents pure intelligence. Nimble as a flickering flame, his wits allow him to run circles around all the others—even Wotan. Loge manipulates every individual character of *The Rhinegold* at one point or another; at times he, more than Wotan or Alberich, controls the course of the action.

Loge also has inherited from his earlier incarnations the ability to see things clearly, which allows him to exploit the other fellow's needs and goals. He keeps his own emotions—his resentment of the gods' feelings of superiority, for example—detached and under control. At the end of R-iv he is tempted to turn himself to flame and consume the whole corrupt lot (which he ultimately is made to do in T-3-iii); he says: "I'll think it over: who knows what I will do?"

But cynicism, not wisdom, is his path, despite several occasions when he appears to engage the ethical issues at hand. Four times in *The Rhinegold* he suggests that the gold be returned to the Rhine Daughters. We learn later (in T-1-iii, T-3-i, and T-3-iii) that this act might have helped to spare the gods.

But Loge's concern is more illusion than reality. A mischievous Loge dangles the solution in front of Wotan not because he desires it but because he knows, as the audience intuits, that Wotan will never accept it—at least not until it is too late. In this sense, Loge is what Karl Weinhold called the gods' "objectivized conscience" and "moral mirror";[21] their demise results from Wotan's conviction that the gods have no continuing moral right to exist.

Nor is repossession by the water maidens his only suggestion for the gold. Loge entices Wotan, Fricka, Mime, Fafner (R-ii), Fasolt (R-iv), and even Alberich, who is tricked into boastfully displaying it, with the ring's power. In Fasolt's case, Loge's intervention is immediately fatal.

At another point his limited moral sense is implied by his silence. When Erda is present in R-iv, Loge says nothing. Perhaps he knows to back off in the face of primordial wisdom, however inchoate.

Nor does Loge's advocacy of the Rhine Daughters survive Wotan's guilt-driven annoyance at their lament in R-iv. At Wotan's instructions, Loge cruelly makes sport of their (and the gods') predicament: "No more gleams the gold on you maidens: henceforth bask in bliss in the gods' new radiance!" Clever Loge thus elicits a cheap laugh from the gods; one is reminded of Rigoletto rubbing salt in the wounds of Monterone, for which he is cursed.

In the form of fire, Loge is not as dangerous as we might fear. In T-Prologue the Second Norn tells us that "to gain his freedom he gnawed and nibbled with his teeth at the notches in [Wotan's spear]," but Wotan then held him at Brünnhilde's rock. Loge's flames do not burn those who do not fear them. Anyone, even Gunther, could have walked through unhurt—needing only sufficient courage to do so.

Still, even passive and truncated, Loge gets his way. In T-3-iii Brünnhilde instructs Wotan's ravens to pass by her rock where the flames still flicker and to direct Loge to Valhalla. There we see him at last in all his destructive glory, as he consumes the hall and the assembled gods, heroes, and Valkyries. Loge, as remarkable as any character in *The Rhinegold* and a vivid presence in the following operas, blinds us with his destructive brilliance at the end. But it is a self-destructive brilliance as well, for without Wotan's will to sustain him, Loge must die out as surely as any fire when it has nothing left to feed on.

MUSIC

Loge is given three vivid musical aspects upon his first appearance in R-ii. These are played consecutively but are also separable—they will reappear throughout *The Ring*. The first, 25A–Loge (as Intelligence), expresses the flickering flame of Loge's quick, clearsighted, and mischievous wit.

The second, 25B–Loge (as Nature), is a churning figure suggesting Loge as a natural force and affirming his relationship to elemental nature and to other figures relating to nature, such as 8–Water Murmurs and 94–Forest Murmurs.

The third element, 25C–Loge (as Fire), centers on a falling step that comes at moments of high drama involving fire: Brünnhilde's Magic Fire (V-3-iii), Siegfried's ascent through the flames (S-3-iii), and the inferno at Valhalla (T-3-iii).

MIME
Wise Smith, the Other Nibelung

SOURCES

While a principal source for *The Valkyrie* and *Siegfried* stories, including Mime, is the *Volsunga Saga*, it is *Thidriks Saga* that gives Mime much of his special flavor. In it Mime is a man, not a dwarf, a smith who works at a "lonely forge in the forest."[22] Mime finds the orphan Siegfried and raises him. The boy is so unmanageable that Mime sends him to a dragon, hoping it will kill the boy. But Siegfried kills and eats the dragon, gaining the power to understand a bird who advises him to kill Mime. In the *Volsunga Saga*, it is Mime who gives Siegfried a sword and sends him to Brünnhilde.

Mime's account of the Nibelungs' plight, movingly told to Loge and Wotan in R-iii, is found in *Das Lied vom hürnen Seyfrid*. A story in the *Poetic Edda* provides the basis for Wotan's test of wits with Mime in S-1-ii.

Elizabeth Magee shows that Wagner's final account of the unfortunate smith relies heavily on secondary sources, especially Fouqué's dramatic poem *Sigurd*.[23]

Mime's kinship to Alberich is another of Wagner's inventions that tightens the *Ring* story.

RELATIONSHIPS

Brother of Alberich, foster father of Siegfried, uncle of Hagen.

APPEARANCES

R-iii

Enslaved by his brother Alberich, has forged the Tarnhelm, which Alberich
    seizes from him.
Tells Wotan and Loge of the Nibelungs' plight.

S-1-i

Has raised the orphan Siegfried but cannot reforge the sword, Notung.
Admits to Siegfried that he is not Siegfried's father (and mother, as he has
    claimed) and tells the boy that his real mother, Sieglinde, died giving birth to
    him.

S-1-ii

Loses a match of wits with the Wanderer, failing to ask what he needs to know:
    how to reforge Notung.
The Wanderer tells Mime he will lose is head to one "who has never learnt fear."

S-1-iii

His description of forest noises fails to teach Siegfried fear.
Plots Siegfried's death to gain the ring for himself.
Prepares a drugged drink while Siegfried reforges Notung.

S-2-ii

Brings Siegfried to Neidhöhle and leaves him to confront Fafner.

S-2-iii

After Siegfried has killed Fafner, quarrels with Alberich over the hoard.

Reveals his true, deadly intentions toward Siegfried, who can now read his heart. Siegfried kills Mime.

COMMENTS

As he should, Mime always provokes strong, mixed feelings. We take his word that the Nibelungs were happy smiths, forging ornamental trinkets for their women, before their enslavement by Alberich. (The *Ring* text also tells us, however, that the dwarf race was in habitual conflict with gods and giants.)

There is every reason to sympathize with his predicament in R-iii. He is psychologically and physically bullied by his own brother. He is oppressed absolutely, the only individual *Ring* character who is a direct victim of the ring's direct power (others are victimized by craving the ring or by the power of the curse on it).

Mime enlivens R-iii as a fourth dramatic element in the scene which would otherwise consist only of the confrontation between Wotan, Loge, and Alberich.[24] Alberich's renunciation of love for power becomes manifest in his brutal treatment of Mime. Getting to know Mime in R-iii also prepares us for the more central role he will play in S-1 and S-2.

In *Siegfried*, everyone seems to treat the little smith badly—Siegfried, the Wanderer (whom Mime eventually recognizes as Wotan), and Alberich. On occasion, Mime is capable of insight that transcends his self-pity. On the subject of learning fear, poor Mime, he observes ruefully, is an expert. He shows a flash of courage when he accepts the Wanderer's challenge: "Before [the Wanderer] my mother-wit melts away. But now I must show myself wise. Wanderer, ask on! Perhaps I'll be lucky enough to succeed in saving my dwarf's head."

He even proposes in S-2-iii that Alberich take the ring if Mime can keep only the Tarnhelm. Alberich immediately sees this as a dangerous ruse; invisibility would allow Mime to steal the ring and turn the tables on his brother, which in R-iii is what he said he wanted to do.

Audiences are commonly discomforted by Siegfried's relentless hostility toward the dwarf. Indeed Wagner has compressed much about Mime and Siegfried; the 1848 prose sketch portrays an initially harmonious relationship which is deleted in the final text.[25]

Some in today's audiences may consider Mime as a victim of society, but the case against him is overwhelming. As Siegfried's foster father, Mime is patently guilty of severely abusing the child solely in pursuit of his own greedy goals. The Wanderer and Alberich know that his plan is to use the boy to win the gold. The Wood Bird, who represents the inherent innocence of the natural world, warns Siegfried against "treacherous Mime." Even Fafner, whose innate wisdom is restored by his mortal wound, tells Siegfried that whoever encouraged him to kill Fafner is now plotting Siegfried's own death.

But Mime is most undone by his own words and heart. Tasting the dragon's blood has permitted Siegfried to understand Mime's real intentions. Here, in S-2-iii, Mime speaks from the heart:

> You and your kind have I always hated in my heart; from love I reared you not . . . the gold was what I toiled for. . . . You must pay me with your life . . . Now, my Volsung, you wolf's son! Drink and choke yourself to death.

MUSIC

Mime's personal music is built around a falling four-note phrase first heard in R-iii when he touchingly recounts the Nibelungs' happy past. In S-1-i, 82–Mime's Mission takes on a whining tone when Mime tries to manipulate Siegfried's sympathy.

Like other characters, Mime puts a personal stamp on additional motives that are not exclusively his. A good example occurs in R-iii when Loge and Wotan come upon him after Alberich has beaten him. His moaning suggests both 7–Woe and 30–Servitude, and the addition of a grace note imbues these motives with Mime's own wretchedness.

Mime is the only "enslaved" Nibelung to be individualized in *The Ring*. In a way he represents them all, and 28–Nibelungs, with its unmistakable image of forging, is strongly identified with the little smith (see "Nibelungs," page 204).

In R-iii Mime also introduces the motive of brooding and scheming; 79–Brooding reaches a definitive form in S-1-Prelude.

THE NIBELUNGS
First Slaves of the Ring

SOURCES

The emergence of the Nibelung story in the myths and sagas is uncertain and confusing. According to Cooke, a fifth-century Frankish lay depicted Siegfried winning a great treasure, the Nibelung hoard. In later retellings, the Burgundians of the lay became known as Nibelungs because of their association with the treasure. *Das Lied vom hürnen Seyfrid* first identifies King Nibelung and his sons as dwarfs, but the Nibelungs of *The Nibelungenlied* are human. Wagner himself linked the Nibelungs to the dwarf Alberich.

The etymology of the word *Nibelung* is also unclear. Both the Old Norse *nifl* and *nebel* mean "mist," which may imply that the ancient Nibelungs were denizens of the land of the mist—or land of the dead.

RELATIONSHIPS

The race of dwarfs. Chief among the Nibelungs are the brothers Alberich and Mime. Alberich is the father of Hagen by a mortal woman, so that Hagen is half Nibelung.

APPEARANCES

R-iii

They pile up the hoard at Alberich's command and depart screaming in terror.

R-iv

Again pile up the hoard at Alberich's command and depart in terror, as if struck.

COMMENTS

The Nibelungs are the exploited and enslaved. They appear in *The Ring* only twice, in R-iii and R-iv, both times bringing in the golden hoard. They have only one function: to mine the gold deep in the earth at Nibelheim. The hoard we see in R-iii is only a day's work, as Alberich boasts, "a paltry pile: it will increase boldly and mightily in the future." (Wagner's stage directions have the dwarfs enter in R-iii laden with both gold and silver handiwork; while they might logically mine silver as well as gold, other references to the hoard refer to gold only. Siegfried's horn, however, is silver.)

The Nibelungs, including Mime, are the only *Ring* characters who obey the direct commands of the ring's bearer. As a group— and unlike the Rhine Daughters, Valkyries, Norns, and even Gibichungs—they are wholly undifferentiated. They play no active dramatic role. They "speak" only once: a blood-curdling shriek of terror in R-iii (while the impressive shriek is often repeated in R-iv, Wagner's directions do not call for it).

We do know their past was happier. In R-iii Mime movingly sings of happier days before the ring: "Carefree smiths, once we created ornaments for our women, wondrous trinkets, dainty trifles for Nibelungs."

The future threatens a more ominous role: Alberich's plan to defeat the race of gods would turn the Nibelungs into warrior slaves. In R-iii he threatens Wotan: "Beware the nocturnal host when the Nibelung horde rises from the silent depths to the daylight!"

This danger has prompted Wotan to father the Valkyries so that by spurring mortal men to war and death, he can assemble a host of fallen heroes at Valhalla to act as warriors in his service. This part of Wotan's plan, at least, has been accomplished. He tells Brünnhilde in V-2-ii: "Listen carefully what the Wala [Erda] warned me of. Through Alberich's army our end is looming. . . . But now I do not fear his forces of darkness: my heroes would bring me victory."

If it makes sense to speculate on the world after *Twilight of the Gods*, ironically the Nibelungs seem to be among the survivors. They may be safe underground, unscathed by the inferno and flood of T-3-iii. Surely Wotan's seizure of the ring in R-iv has liberated them from Alberich's power, and the ring itself is washed clean of the curse in T-3-iii. Perhaps they are once again making beautiful trinkets for their women.

MUSIC

The Nibelungs will always be associated with the pulsating rhythm of hammering, fully developed as 28–Nibelungs during the transitional music between R-iii and R-iv as Wotan and Loge descend to Nibelheim.

The Nibelungs also introduce 33–Hoard as Alberich orders them to pile up that day's work.

The Nibelungs are the only characters to be commanded directly by the power of the ring and to obey it, mystically described as 31–Power of the Ring in both R-iii and R-iv.

ERDA
Earth Mother, Goddess of Earthly Wisdom

SOURCES

There is no clear reference to an earth goddess in the northern sagas, although, as Cooke reports, "both Eddas mention a certain Jord (Earth), on whom Odin begot Thor."[26] The myths do include earth spirits, *volva* or *wala*, who have mysterious powers of prophecy. The *Poetic Edda* includes two poems on which Wagner drew directly to frame Erda's two appearances in *The Ring*. In the first, the "Wise-Woman's Prophecy," the soothsayer foretells the gods' fate; in the second, "Baldr's Dream," Odin summons the *volva* to foretell the fate of his favorite son.

Erda did not appear in Wagner's sketch of 1848. His elevation of Erda to full-fledged Earth Mother may have been influenced more by the Greek myths than the Nordic, as well as by his specific dramatic needs. Wagner took the name Erda from Grimm; it is simply the Old High German word for Earth.[27]

RELATIONSHIPS

Mother of the three Norns, in her own words, "conceived before the start of time"; lover of Wotan; mother of Brünnhilde (with Wotan); possibly mother of the other Valkyries (with Wotan; the case can be made that Erda is, and is not, the mother of the eight Valkyries—see "Brünnhilde," pages 217–218).

APPEARANCES

R-iv

Advises Wotan to yield the ring to escape the "dark destruction" to which its
  possession dooms him; warns that a dark day dawns for the gods.

S-3-i

Is summoned from sleep by Wotan but becomes confused by his comments;
  can offer no further wisdom.

Is sent back down by Wotan to eternal sleep.

COMMENTS

In her cryptic appearance in R-iv, made apparently on her own initiative, Erda
decisively intervenes in the course of the drama. Although she is cloaked in mystery and the full meaning of her words is not fully grasped, her advice—to yield
the ring—is nevertheless clear. Wotan subsequently pursues and seduces her to
gain use of her wisdom, but his immediate response in R-iv is unequivocal: he
promptly gives up the ring to the giants.

In her much longer appearance in S-1-i, Erda is entirely passive. She comes
only when Wotan roughly summons her, she appears confused throughout the
scene, and she is dismissed without offering (or being in any condition to offer)
the wisdom he seeks.

Of all the major characters of *The Ring*, Erda is on stage the shortest period of
time. However, she has enormous impact and makes an unforgettable impression. Like Wotan, we are compelled to reflect on her purpose and mysteries.

Much about Erda seems clear. She is the Earth Mother, in the words of Deryck
Cooke, the "primordial wise-woman," the eternal feminine. "Far more even than
Loge, she is clearly independent of Wotan and the other gods, and she gives the
impression of being something greater than them . . . some fundamental wisdom
emerging from the unconscious—some basic intuition of what is ultimately right
and fitting."[28]

She is an archetype, with no earthly agenda or ambition. This is in sharp contrast to Wotan who, in *The Rhinegold*, is driven by human goals and vulnerabilities—political domination, wandering and wooing, the physical threat of enemies, the making of laws and treaties, compromise, and deceit.

Why does Erda intervene, and on Wotan's behalf? Despite their differences,
their shared godhood may still bind them. Most important, Erda is the first character in the *Ring* story to make manifest the power of fate. She is in the business
of foretelling the destiny of the world, and Wotan, the leader of the gods, is about
to make, or has already made, a colossal blunder.

A crucial distinction Erda makes on this point is often overlooked: the world of the gods is about to end in any case—by giving up the ring, Wotan will not escape this end but only the "dark destruction" that continued possession of the ring ensures. In Wagner's earlier sketch, Erda's advice is much more conventional: the gods will be destroyed *unless* Wotan gives up the ring. As we have seen (see page 29), Wagner explained this crucial change by saying that "The necessity of this downfall springs from our innermost feelings, as it does from the innermost feelings of Wotan."[29]

Against this fundamental power of destiny Wagner's characters posture a most human reaction—resistance. And while Wotan's fate is sealed by his dilemma, his offspring, first Siegmund and then Brünnhilde and Siegfried, defy fate and the old order with extraordinary results.

Erda's passivity and confusion in S-3-i is part of this process of change, the passing to a new order. Following Erda's appearance with Wotan, in S-3-ii Siegfried smashes Wotan's spear on his way to Brünnhilde and his own destiny: Siegfried is a principal agent of change, and the spear symbolizes the old authority.

In T-Prologue, we learn from the Norns, Erda's daughters, that the World Ash Tree has died and the "eternal" spring at its base has run dry. Their rope of fate breaks, representing the end of an era. As Wotan cruelly tells her in S-3-i, Erda's time has come to an end. No longer able to see the future or to intervene in it, she sinks back into eternal sleep.

MUSIC

Erda rises from the earth in R-ii in dramatic fashion, to the rising figure of 36–Erda, music that is unmistakably hers. It is taken directly from 2–Nature, turned to a somber minor key.

In R-iv, Erda also introduces the important 37–Downfall of the Gods, which is a falling inversion of 2–Nature and 36–Erda.

SIEGMUND
Heroic in Deed and Heart, Brünnhilde's Teacher

SOURCES

Siegmund is a major figure in the *Volsunga Saga*, the story of the Volsungs. Most major elements of his story in *The Valkyrie* appear in it. Wagner eliminated and compressed a great deal of material from the long and complicated saga; there, for example, Wotan is not Siegmund's father but causes him and Sieglinde to be born to an otherwise barren couple by providing the father with one of Holda's apples.

Siegmund also appears in the German *Nibelungenlied,* whose anonymous author describes him as king of the Netherlands and the father of Siegfried. However, the high birth of the Volsungs and the courtly manner of the *Nibelungenlied* in general did not provide Wagner with the milieu he wanted—the primitive, raw world he later found in the Scandinavian sagas.

Some further details, such as Siegmund's serpentine eyes, were drawn from the *Poetic Edda.* Others, such as Volse's sudden disappearance in the woods while hunting with the boy, were Wagner's invention.

As an intermediate or secondary source for his treatment of Siegmund, Wagner seems to have drawn most heavily on Wilhelm Grimm's scholarly *Die deutsche Heldensage.*[30]

RELATIONSHIPS

Son of Wotan (as Volse or Wolf) and a mortal Volsung woman, who is not named; twin brother and lover of Sieglinde; father of Siegfried (with Sieglinde); half-brother of Brünnhilde (through Wotan); half-brother of the Valkyries (through Wotan).

APPEARANCES

V-1-i

Pursued by enemies, takes refuge in Hunding's house.

Is refreshed by Sieglinde, in whom he takes a growing interest.

V-1-ii

Tells his story of family and flight.

Is recognized by Hunding as his enemy and is challenged to fight the next morning.

V-1-iii

Left alone, calls for the sword promised at his hour of need.

Is joined by Sieglinde, and they express their mutual love.

Discovering they are Volsung brother and sister, she gives him both name and sword.

V-2-iii

Comforts Sieglinde as she flees from Hunding.

V-2-iv

Refuses to follow Brünnhilde to Valhalla when told Sieglinde must stay behind.

Brünnhilde pledges to help him against Hunding.

V-2-v

Fights Hunding but is slain when Wotan intervenes by shattering his sword.

COMMENTS

Siegmund bursts upon *The Ring* at the beginning of V-1 like the storm that opens that opera and characterizes his plight. Within moments he sweeps us toward a desperate, blissful, and altogether human experience that contrasts sharply with the distant, cerebral sequence of events told in the mood and music of *The Rhinegold*. He crashes about into our hearts, defies the gods, and changes everything—and then he is gone as abruptly as he came.

How strange is this misfit, Siegmund! He is raised like an animal in the forest. Drawn to the human world, he is, by his own candid admission, at complete odds with it. Morally impetuous, whatever he thinks right others consider wrong, and what is wrong to him is approved by others. Whether seeking friends or courting women, "I was always unpopular."

Siegmund's account of his setbacks bears no hint of self-pity; if anything, he implies they are somehow justified. He asks only for what his father promised him—a sword. He does not wallow in his ill fortune, nor does he wish to expose Sieglinde to it.

And how he does care for Sieglinde. From the moment they lay eyes on each other, we know, as they do, that they are fated to be together. Wagner may have intended the considerable shock value of incest to underscore the concept of "unprecedented events" that both Wotan, and Wagner, advocated. To modern audiences, this hardly matters.

In V-1 the twins achieve an ecstatic passion probably not heard in opera before and rarely since. Wotan's punishment of Brünnhilde and their farewell makes V-3 one of Wagner's most moving acts. But the massive V-2 is the linchpin, the axis upon which the entire *Ring* cycle turns. Wotan's confrontation with Fricka, his introspective narration and abandonment of his plan, Brünnhilde's crucial encounter with Siegmund, and the climactic fight between Siegmund and Hunding (and their patrons)—these lead inexorably to the immolation scene of T-3.

In V-2 Siegmund passes every test of the heroic spirit. In just one night (one intermission, in fact) his world of ecstasy has turned to ashes. Sieglinde is mad with shame for her intimacy with Hunding and her fear of his pursuing hounds. Siegmund himself is doomed by Brünnhilde. He learns that his sword will shatter by the will of the very one who gave it to him, his own father. He is told his enemy, Sieglinde's bane, will kill him.

Against all this he is offered a place of everlasting glory—a place beside the immortals and the Warfather, abounding with attentive beauties and Brünnhilde herself—if he will just do what all heroes who look upon the Valkyrie are fated to do.

Siegmund's manly qualities shine here at their brightest: his defiance of his fated end is Promethean, his resolve is unshakable; he will kill both Sieglinde and their unborn child and spend eternity in Hell rather than abandon her for a single moment, even into the safety of Brünnhilde's care.

Above all, Siegmund's defiance is wrapped around a profound tenderness with which he protects and comforts Sieglinde before, after, and even during his confrontation with Brünnhilde. Is there another case in opera of such gentle loyalty in the face of such profound distress?

Thus Siegmund teaches by example and in the process alters the course of events. Siegmund does not simply persuade Brünnhilde to defy Wotan; he changes her. His uncompromising love for Sieglinde causes Brünnhilde to discard the values of godly obedience and war on which she has been raised in favor of new human ones—love, passion, compassion, and loyalty. In V-3-iii, she tells Wotan that "one man's love breathed this into my heart."

This change foreshadows Brünnhilde's loss of godhood in V-3, her opening to the full potential of human love at the end of *Siegfried*, and her ultimate act of sacrifice and redemption at the close of *Twilight*. This lesson in human wisdom is Siegmund's final gift; within moments he is betrayed and murdered.

MUSIC

In V-1 Siegmund (and Sieglinde) introduce a wealth of new musical material, especially around his flight, their Volsung origins, his mission, and their dawning love for each other.

Siegmund is closely associated with 43–Storm which opens V-1 and immediately warns us of the turbulent predicament in which he finds himself. Siegmund's own music, 44–Siegmund, includes a falling and rising motion, emphatically announced by a repeated figure.

Siegmund's and Sieglinde's feelings for each other grow, at least in part, from their shared background as Volsungs. The motive 47–Volsungs' Woe expresses the ill fate that has pursued them both. Siegmund is also associated with 51–Volsung Race, a phrase that first conveys a sense of distress and later of empowerment.

Weaponless and faced with Hunding's threat, Siegmund calls for the sword his father has promised him in time of greatest need (53–The Purpose of the Sword).

Above all, Siegmund is identified with 56–Spring Song, sung to Sieglinde in V-1-iii as part of their love music. This extended passage may be the closest thing to an aria in *The Ring*. As he prepares to extract Notung from the ash tree, Siegmund sings that "holiest love . . . burn[s] bright in my breast." The motive clearly restates 13–Renunciation of Love; this apparent contradiction—that Siegmund is affirming love here, not rejecting it—has been the subject of various explanations by Wagner critics.[31]

SIEGLINDE
Radiant Beauty in a Terrible World

SOURCES

In the *Nibelungenlied*, whose publication in 1755 largely initiated the revival in Germany of interest in the northern mythologies, Siegmund and Sieglinde are king and queen of the Netherlands and the parents of Siegfried. The enormous popularity of the work also stimulated Wagner's interest in the myths, but the chivalric bearing and courtly manners of its royal persons eventually were of no dramatic use to him.

In the Scandinavian *Volsunga Saga*, Signy (Sieglinde) is still the daughter of a king, Volsung, and becomes the reluctant wife of King Siggeir of Gothland (Hunding). With her twin brother Sigmund, she gives birth to Sinfiötli who avenges Siggeir's murder of King Volsung. Signy chooses to perish in Siggeir's flaming hall. In addition to providing a wealth of detail about the Volsungs, the more primitive, premedieval world of the *Volsunga Saga* appealed to Wagner. Sieglinde's flight into the forest in V-3-i is taken from *Thidriks Saga*.

Wagner's principal task was to compress this material, as E. Magee put it, into "the barest bones of the story: the twins, their union, Siegfried's conception, and Siegmund's death in consequence."[32]

RELATIONSHIPS

Daughter of Wotan (as Volse or Wolf) and a mortal Volsung woman, who is not named; legal wife of Hunding, the Neiding; twin sister and lover of Siegmund; mother of Siegfried (with Siegmund); half-sister of Brünnhilde and the Valkyries (through Wotan).

APPEARANCES

V-1-i

Discovers the fleeing Siegmund and offers him refreshment; love dawns between
them.

V-1-ii

With Hunding, listens to Siegmund's story with growing sympathy.
Tries but fails to show Siegmund the sword in the tree.
When Hunding threatens Siegmund, mixes a drugged drink for Hunding.

V-1-iii

After drugging Hunding, returns to Siegmund.
They pledge their love and discover they are brother and sister.
Gives Siegmund both name and sword.

V-2-iii

Fleeing Hunding and maddened by fear and shame, is comforted by Siegmund.

V-2-iv

Sleeps during Siegmund's confrontation with Brünnhilde.

V-2-v

Dreams of the attack on her childhood home.
Wakens to find Siegmund gone to fight Hunding.
Rushes to stop them, watches Siegmund fall, is carried off by Brünnhilde with
   the pieces of the shattered sword.

V-3-i

Taken by Brünnhilde to the other Valkyries, demands that Brünnhilde slay her.
Learns she is pregnant with a great hero, praises Brünnhilde for saving her, and
   escapes toward Neidhöhle, with the sword fragments, to bear Siegfried.

COMMENTS

Sieglinde is a towering heroine by conventional operatic standards. She is beautiful, victimized, brave, self-sacrificing, generous, and keen. Remarkable things happen to her—she suffers a loathsome, forced marriage; discovers and consummates true love; and flees in desperation. She sees her hero and lover murdered, begs for her own death, and ecstatically learns that she is with child and that her child will be a great hero for the future. The only mad scene in *The Ring* is hers.

By the higher standards of Wagnerian drama, she is a rich, complex character of great interest. She is resolute—if not ruthless—enough to drug her dreadful husband into sleep to permit Siegmund's escape. She displays a crisp deductive intelligence as the twins piece together their shared past. Defying convention, she gives herself without inhibition to her "friend" and brother. She is racked by inconsolable shame for the sexual pleasures Hunding has taken with her.

She is critical to the action and story. Her birth was part of Wotan's grand plan: she provides Siegmund with his name and weapon, and she gives birth to Siegfried.

She is given remarkable music. She sings one of only two love duets in *The Ring*, the one audiences generally prefer to the love music of Brünnhilde and Siegfried in S-3-iii. Her moments at "You are the spring" (V-1-iii) and "Oh, mightiest of miracles, most glorious of women" (V-3-i) are among the musical pinnacles of *The Ring*. She inspires both Siegmund's assertive passion in V-1 and his tender compassion in V-2.

She is perhaps the most purely sympathetic character in the cycle. Her one choice in crisis—abandoning her husband for Siegmund—has our full backing, however much Fricka may later complain of it. Her self-loathing in V-2 is not justified; she has been forced to lie with Hunding.

It might also be said that Sieglinde does not quite rise to the level of the foremost characters in *The Ring*. Our thoughts more often dwell on others, and the impression Sieglinde has made recedes as the drama moves on.

She plays a large role only in V-1. But Sieglinde is nearly elbowed aside by the dramatic power of the major players. Wotan, Brünnhilde, and Siegfried in particular are unlike any characters in opera before them. They are characters in process. They openly confront, reflect on, and are changed by enduring human problems—will, control, sexuality, relinquishment—conflicts into which audiences are drawn as much today as a century ago.

But Sieglinde is overshadowed only in relation to the unprecedented dramatic depth of those operatic giants around her. In all other ways she fulfills her promise to both drama and audience. She is a beacon of radiant beauty in the terrible world.

MUSIC

Sieglinde introduces musical material that sharply defines her own personality and growing relationship with Siegmund. Her personal motive, 45–Sieglinde, echoes 44–Siegmund, with which it is frequently joined.

In V-1-iii Sieglinde gives voice to the fullest flowering of 16B–Love, a principal love motive in *The Ring*. This motive has evolved throughout V-1 and reaches a definitive form in 57–Love (Sieglinde) at her words: "You are the spring for which I longed in the frosty winter time."

The last time we see her, Sieglinde emerges from the general agitation of V-3-i, piercing the air and our hearts with music that will conclude *The Ring* a generation later. Learning from Brünnhilde that she bears the child of Siegmund, who will become the greatest hero in the world, she praises Brünnhilde as "most glorious of women." Commonly known as a motive of redemption, 73–Redemption may in fact describe Brünnhilde herself, who will do the redeeming deed at the end of T-3-iii.

HUNDING
Fricka's Liege, Protected by Fricka

SOURCES

Hunding is drawn from the *Volsunga Saga*'s Siggeir, a famous and mighty king who seeks the hand of King Volsung's daughter, Signy (Sieglinde). Enmity arises between Siggeir and Volsung's son, Sigmund, when Sigmund draws a great sword from a tree and refuses to sell it to Siggeir. Sigmund is eventually killed by Siggeir's sons, one of whom is called Hunding.

Wagner took the sinister-sounding name Hunding from King Hunding, Siegmund's mortal enemy in the *Poetic Edda*. In *The Ring*, Hunding is a Neiding (there is a mean-spirited and treacherous King Nidung in both *Thidriks Saga* and the *Poetic Edda*).[33] According to E. Magee, Wagner had read Karl Simrock's dramatic poem, the *Amelungenlied*, in which "Nidung is a general term for an evil, cunning, envious person."[34] Neidings are also the villains of Wagner's stillborn prose sketch for an opera, *Wieland the Smith*.

RELATIONSHIPS

Husband of Sieglinde, member of the Neiding race, enemies of the Volsungs.

APPEARANCES

V-1-ii

Returns home to find Siegmund with his wife, Sieglinde.

Realizes that Siegmund is the enemy he has been hunting that day and challenges him to fight the next morning.

V-2-v

Pursuing Siegmund and Sieglinde, engages Siegmund in battle and kills him with Wotan's help.

Is dismissed by Wotan to death and Fricka.

COMMENTS

There have been many efforts to find redeeming qualities in Hunding. In Victorian times, he was sometimes excused as a protector of traditional virtues, a responsible, law-abiding citizen, an instrument of his patroness, Fricka. He is loyal to his own group, and he extends his patronage to his otherwise homeless wife. Most of all, he honorably respects the code of hospitality by providing a night's protection to his enemy, the violent, wife-stealing Siegmund.

None of this is very convincing. We do find complex human qualities in Hunding—Wagner never created hackneyed, one-dimensional characters, good or bad. Hunding exhibits a rough intelligence. For instance, he immediately recognizes the bond between Siegmund and Sieglinde in the shared snake markings of their eyes, which tells him (and us) something about their emerging relationship, incestuous and amorous, even before they recognize it themselves.

Hunding is a stark, theatrical presence, foreshadowing the figure of Hagen in *Twilight*. He provides dark contrast to the positive elements at work in V-1, which bring the happiest moments in *The Ring*: the love of Siegmund and Sieglinde and relief from the misfortune they have both known for so long. In this way, the memorable V-1 illuminates central issues of *The Ring*: love versus power; accepted social convention versus a newer, perhaps higher morality.

On these points Hunding is terribly exposed. He never exhibits any regard for Sieglinde, save possessing her. His spiritual alignment with Fricka is telling; they both accord a higher priority to the institution of marriage than to the qualities of love or lovelessness. As for the night's protection Hunding offers Siegmund, it is socially correct but hardly generous: his last words in V-1-ii warn Siegmund to be prepared to fight in the morning when he well knows that Siegmund is weaponless.

In the end the warrior Hunding, like Siegmund himself, is little more than a plaything of the gods. At the conclusion of V-2, all five characters present have reached important turning points: Wotan has slain his son and his hopes; Brünnhilde has willfully disobeyed Wotan; Siegmund is dead; and Sieglinde, bereft, wishes she were.

For Hunding alone, the fight with Siegmund is a moment of triumph. No audience savors his victory, however. Out of this general devastation, it is a consolation, albeit a small one, when Wotan contemptuously waves Hunding away to death and to Fricka.

MUSIC

The personal motive 48–Hunding is among the most patent in *The Ring*, emphatically announcing Hunding's appearance in the doorway of his hut.

The other significant passage introduced by Hunding is 49–Rights, in which he warns Siegmund to honor his holy hearth. This motive underlies 128–Vow of Atonement, which becomes the legal basis for Siegfried's murder by Hagen in T-3-ii.

BRÜNNHILDE
Radiant Eyes, Opened by Siegfried

SOURCES

The story of Brünnhilde's wooing by Siegfried was the subject of a premedieval lay; their story became associated with the Burgundian Gibichung lays through Siegfried's marriage into the Gibichung family (see "Gunther," pages 231–232). In these early tales, Brünnhilde is less important than Gutrune; she is a caricature of her later self, a virgin of superhuman strength whom Siegfried must wrestle to exhaustion so that Gunther may have her. Siegfried gives her ring to Gutrune, and she plots his murder in revenge.

In the *Nibelungenlied*, Brünnhilde is a Christian Queen of Iceland, beaten by Siegfried in an athletic competition of Olympian proportions. Forced to marry Gunther, she nevertheless avoids consummation of the marriage by binding him hand and foot each night and hanging him on a nail on the wall. She fades from the story as Kriemhild (Gutrune) and Siegfried take center stage.

As he did for Siegfried, Wagner stripped away the Christian, chivalric aspects of the medieval story and returned to the more primitive Scandinavian sources to create the Brünnhilde we know. *Thidriks Saga*, in addition to its pre-Christian treatment, also describes an earlier encounter between Siegfried and Brünnhilde. The *Poetic Edda* adds her punishment by Odin, her sleep in a ring of fire, and her awakening by a fearless hero, Sigurd.

RELATIONSHIPS

Daughter of Wotan and Erda; wife (and aunt, through Wotan) of Siegfried; sister or half-sister of the Valkyries (through Wotan and perhaps Erda); half-sister of Siegmund and Sieglinde (through Wotan); half-sister of the Norns (through Erda); stepdaughter of Fricka (through Wotan); relationships to Froh, Donner, and Freia (through Wotan).

APPEARANCES

V-2-i

Is instructed by Wotan to help Siegmund in the coming fight with Hunding.

V-2-ii

Listens to Wotan's narration of his dilemma.

Is told by Wotan that Siegmund must fall and is ordered to help Hunding against Siegmund.

V-2-iv

Tells Siegmund he must die and be carried by her to Valhalla.

Is persuaded by Siegmund's love for Sieglinde to defy Wotan and help the mortal twins.

V-2-v

Shields Siegmund from Hunding until Wotan intervenes.

Flees with Sieglinde and the sword's fragments.

V-3-i

Brings Sieglinde to the other Valkyries and asks for their help in escaping Wotan.

Tells Sieglinde she bears Siegmund's child; sends her into hiding.

V-3-ii

Confronts Wotan to give Sieglinde time to escape.

Is told by Wotan that she is banished from the gods and will be put to sleep for any man to claim her.

V-3-iii

Tries to persuade Wotan that she has obeyed his true will.

Begs for protection by fire from all but the greatest hero. Wotan relents; kissing away her godhood, he casts her into sleep, surrounded by fire, to be awakened only by a fearless hero.

S-3-iii

Is wakened by Siegfried's kiss. Greets the sun, day, and light, and tells Siegfried she loved him even before he was born.

Is frightened by her new human vulnerability and Siegfried's physical advances.

Laughing at death and bidding farewell to "Valhalla's glittering world," gives herself to Siegfried.

T-Prologue

Accepts the ring as pledge of Siegfried's love and gives him Grane in return.

Having given him her wisdom and protection, bids Siegfried off to valorous deeds.

T-1-iii

Rejects Waltraute's plea to save the gods by returning the ring to the Rhine Daughters.

Is subdued by Siegfried (in the form of Gunther); he seizes the ring and claims her as Gunther's wife.

T-2-iv

Arrives at the Gibichungs' hall with Gunther and is stunned to find that Siegfried is betrothed to Gutrune and does not recognize her.

Seeing the ring on Siegfried's finger, accuses him of treachery and claims she is his true wife.

Swears revenge against Siegfried.

T-2-v

Ruing her lost wisdom, plots Siegfried's death with Hagen and Gunther.

T-3-iii

Enters as Hagen fails to wrest the ring from dead Siegfried's hand and makes Gutrune understand that she, not Gutrune, was Siegfried's true wife.

Orders the vassals to build a funeral pyre for Siegfried; explains that Siegfried is the victim of the curse on the ring, which he gained as the unknowing pawn of Wotan.

Pledges to return the ring to the Rhine Daughters to cleanse it of the curse.

Sends the ravens back to Valhalla, with both news and Loge's fire, to end the
   reign of the gods. She ignites the funeral pyre.

Jumps on Grane and leaps into the flames to rejoin Siegfried.

COMMENTS

When we first see Brünnhilde at the beginning of V-2-i, the warrior maiden is
leaping from rock to rock, joyfully preparing for battle. It is an imposing projection of power, and we expect enormous things from the exuberant young woman.
We are not disappointed; Brünnhilde will emerge as a towering treasure of western music, but she will be quite different from our initial expectations of her.

This image of power belies an underlying reality: Brünnhilde in V-2-i is no
more than a part of Wotan. As her creator, he minces no words on this point:
"what else are you but my wish's blindly approving instrument?" He confides in
her in V-2-ii because he is convinced that in speaking to her he speaks only to
himself and his own will; she is terribly important to Wotan, but does not function independently.

By emphasizing her unquestioning obedience at this initial stage, Wagner
makes her subsequent defiance, which will do so much to change the course of
events in *The Ring*, all the more impressive. In V-2-iv, her next, crucial appearance, Brünnhilde defies Wotan's specific orders and agrees to help the (half-) mortal Siegmund against Hunding. In V-2-v she indeed helps Siegmund and then carries Sieglinde with the sword fragments away from Wotan.

In these and later actions, Brünnhilde behaves contrary to her nature as a
Valkyrie. She justifies her actions to Wotan in V-3-iii, first by saying that she has
done what Wotan wanted to do but could not, and so did not really defy him. Her
second explanation is more forthcoming: Siegmund's example of human love for
Sieglinde in V-2-iv has changed Brünnhilde. Not just in the ecstatic moment but
forever, she has come to understand that even mortal love is a higher calling than
the Valkyriehood for which she has been created.

The great irony is that Brünnhilde, with whom Wagner at first associates masculine and godly qualities of strength, knowledge, and self-confidence, gains this
level of wisdom from two mortal and in some ways pathetic primitives—Siegmund in V-2-iv and Siegfried in S-3-iii. She has learned that human instincts are
more trustworthy than the power machinations of the gods.

Brünnhilde's affirmation of human love—first between Siegmund and Sieglinde and then between herself and Siegfried—in this way illuminates a recurring theme of *The Ring*: the value of love over power. But we still wonder at her
conversion, no matter how carefully explained and how effectively dramatized,
because she and her uncaring sisters have been raised for one purpose: to pro-

voke men to battle and bring dead heroes to Valhalla where they will protect the gods.

The explanation may lie with her mother. After *The Rhinegold,* Wotan pursued Erda to gain knowledge that might help him avert the end of the gods which she has warned him about in R-iv. He later overcame her with love and "learned her secrets, but she exacted a fee from me: the world's wisest woman bore me you, Brünnhilde. With eight sisters I brought you up."

Wotan's words are ambiguous as to the maternity of the other Valkyries, and Erda might have given birth to them as well. Brünnhilde's actions of defiance, however, are incomprehensible to the other Valkyries when they learn of them in V-3-i. The Valkyries' purpose in no way draws on the insight and wisdom that Erda represents. Thus it may well be that among them only Brünnhilde is Erda's child.

At the end, then, Brünnhilde is no Valkyrie at all. Her journey in *The Ring* is a descent from Valhalla's lofty heights. Once she aligns herself with human values, Wotan strips her of her divine status and abandons her to the world of men. His taunts in V-3-ii are deliberately cruel: "she will sit by the fire and spin, the topic and butt of all jokers."

During her encounter with Siegfried in S-3-iii, it is Brünnhilde, not the naive boy, who fears the vulnerability of mortality and sex. In T-Prologue, she further relinquishes her godly (or masculine) attributes, voluntarily, by her love for Siegfried: "what the gods taught I have given [Siegfried] . . . Drained of knowledge but full of desire; rich in love but deprived of strength." In exchange for her wisdom, Siegfried gives her the ring.

When the crisis comes as she confronts Siegfried's apparent betrayal in T-2-iv and T-2-v, she feels her diminishment acutely: "where now is my wisdom to counter this confusion? Where are my spells to solve this riddle?" Bereft of her godly powers, she becomes the victim of human emotions with which she cannot now contend: hatred and vengefulness.

In T-3-iii Brünnhilde regains her senses. It is not just the enormity of Siegfried's foul murder that restores her clear and rightful judgment; she has had help. In T-3-i, the Rhine Daughters give up hope that Siegfried will return the ring to them, and they leave him: "a proud woman today will inherit your treasure: she will give us a better hearing. To her!" In T-3-iii, Gutrune says she has seen Brünnhilde that very night walking down by the river. During the immolation scene, Brünnhilde confirms she has met the Rhine Daughters: "wise sisters of the water's depths . . . I thank you for your good counsel."

At the end of *The Ring,* after four evenings and at least fifteen hours of music drama, Wagner leaves the stage to this extraordinary woman, Wotan's favorite, who has lost and gained so much. To her, at least, all is now clear. As ring bearer, she will follow Loge's advice and return the ring to the Rhine Daughters, advice she herself ignored in T-1-iii; for the moment, her act will save the world from the terrible threat of loveless tyranny.

The ring will be purified by fire, but the gods will not be redeemed. By her command fire will consume them, too, as they await the end that their fate, if not their folly, has made inevitable.

Finally, Brünnhilde returns to Siegfried, to be again at one with him. She describes this not as an act of redemption or self-destruction, or as having any purpose save "to be one with him." She is fulfilled in her own way and leaves it to us to ponder the rest.

MUSIC

It is not surprising that a great deal of remarkable music is focused on Brünnhilde and her difficult journey toward humanity. A true Valkyrie when we first see her, she briefly introduces 61–Valkyries at the beginning of V-2-i. She also foreshadows the exuberant Valkyrie cry of her sisters in V-3-i: 62–Hojotoho! seems to echo, or perhaps mock, 16B–Love.

During Brünnhilde's final confrontation with Wotan in V-3-iii, she reproaches her father for his unjust anger toward her. Later in the same scene, 74–Brünnhilde's Reproach becomes 75–Brünnhilde's Love for Wotan, the broadest expression of her compassionate love—for Wotan and for Wotan's love of Siegmund.

Brünnhilde's encounter with Siegfried in S-3-iii unleashes a wealth of new material about their emerging relationship, including 104–Awakening, 105–Love's Greeting, 106–Love's Ecstasy, 107–Immortal Beloved, 108–World's Treasure, and 109–Laughing at Death.

Their scene in T-Prologue introduces still more aspects of their now-consummated love: 114–Giving in Love and 116–Radiant Star, Victorious Light. The scene also includes music describing the human Brünnhilde, no longer godly but surely fulfilled: 113–The Woman Brünnhilde.

In T-2-v, with 142–Brünnhilde's Betrayal, she reveals Siegfried's point of vulnerability to Hagen, thereby permitting his murder.

The concluding music of *The Ring* is usually associated with redemption, but it is first heard in V-3-i when Sieglinde praises Brünnhilde for saving her and Siegmund's unborn son, who will become a hero: "Oh, mightiest of miracles, most glorious of women." Owen Lee believes that this magnificent passage in fact describes Brünnhilde herself.[35] It is with 73–Redemption that our own journey through *The Ring* ends.

THE VALKYRIES
Gerhilde, Helmwige, Waltraute, Schwertleite, Ortlinde, Siegrune, Grimgerde, Rossweisse
Warrior Maidens, Warfather's Arm

SOURCES

The mythical Valkyries may have historical, rather than mythological, roots in a primitive Teutonic war cult that participated in the sacrificial murder of prisoners to Odin. A few early lays refer to warrior maidens, human or godly. In one of these, the hero Hogni sees nine Valkyries ride past in the sky. This lay was incorporated into the Icelandic chronicles, including the *Prose Edda* of Snorri Sturluson, in which the Valkyries, according to Cooke, "fight alongside heroes and choose the slain for Valholl."[36]

Magee demonstrates that Wagner would have read about the Valkyries in any number of the Eddas.[37] He also relied heavily on secondary sources, including Frauer's study, *Die Walkyrien*, and Jacob Grimm's compilation, *Deutsche Mythologie*.

With the exceptions of Brünnhilde and Siegrune, Wagner's names for the warrior maidens are his own invention.

RELATIONSHIPS

Daughters of Wotan and an unnamed mother. Erda may or may not be the mother of the eight Valkyries—the evidence is inconclusive. Half-sisters or sisters to Brünnhilde (through Wotan and perhaps Erda); half-sisters to Siegmund and Sieglinde (through Wotan); relationships to the other gods through Wotan.

APPEARANCES

V-3-i

Assemble on a mountaintop to take fallen heroes to Valhalla.

Learn in consternation that Brünnhilde, who has arrived with Sieglinde, has disobeyed Wotan. They refuse to help but advise Sieglinde to flee to the forest to the east.

Form a protective ring around Brünnhilde to hide her from Wotan.

V-3-ii

Appeal to Wotan to moderate his punishment of Brünnhilde but are driven off by him.

T-1-iii

Waltraute appeals to Brünnhilde to redeem the gods by returning the ring to the Rhine Daughters, but she is rebuffed.

COMMENTS

"The Ride of the Valkyries" is a title Wagner used only for the concert piece without voices, which is quite different from the opening section of V-3-i. This most famous and maligned passage in *The Ring* serves important dramatic purposes. The boisterous, joking maidens and their spirited horses provide release and relief in between the somber and exhausting episodes of V-2 and the emotional intensity of V-3-iii. The exuberant interlude demonstrates Wagner's sound dramatic instincts for pacing an audience.

The Valkyries also illuminate, by contrast, the figure of Brünnhilde, who is given her own short "ride" at the beginning of V-2-i when she, too, is wholly god-oriented and obedient to the Warfather. Brünnhilde's disobedience, which the other Valkyries cannot comprehend, begins the most important transformation in *The Ring*: Brünnhilde's becoming human through her encounters with Siegmund, Wotan, and Siegfried.

Her half-sisters stand in stark contrast to her as their banter about the human carnage they are instructed to incite exposes them, in Deryck Cooke's words, as "cold, hard, inhuman instruments of Wotan guided only by military discipline, who regard human suffering and death as a joke."[38] At the same time, they remain cowed by Wotan's anger and cannot contemplate defiance of his will.

At the end, they stay in Valhalla at Wotan's side, impotent, consumed by the flames that sweep them away with the rest of the old order.

MUSIC

The Valkyries' music has become a cliche of advertising and film. This is partly explained, as Ernest Newman points out, by two common errors in the way the music is played: the dropping of the short note in each measure, and the emphasis being placed on the fourth rather than the first note in each measure.[39] Few would suggest that 61–Valkyries does not adequately characterize the eight exuberant sisters assembled at the beginning of V-3.

SIEGFRIED

The Longest Journey

SOURCES

There is no evidence that Siegfried was a historical figure. He appears to have originated in fifth-century Frankish lays, which include the fall of the Burgundians or Gibichungs (see "Gunther," pages 231–232). Siegfried, the dragon slayer, marries Gunther's sister and helps Gunther wed the powerful Brünnhilde, whom he subdues. Siegfried also takes a ring from her and gives it to Gutrune, whose prideful display of it angers Brünnhilde and induces her to plot Siegfried's death by one of Gunther's men.

Another lay that may have been current in the fifth century described Siegfried as the orphan son of Siegmund and Sieglinde. Siegfried was raised by a smith, killed a dragon, and secured a great treasure. In the twelfth century these lays were absorbed into both *Der Nibelunge Nôt* (The Nibelungs' Distress) and *Das Nibelungenlied*, which recount the story of Siegfried, Gunther, Gutrune, and Brünnhilde, but only hint at Siegfried's life beforehand. They also deal with the events following Siegfried's death, which were of no interest to Wagner.

It was the Siegfried as described in the *Nibelungenlied*, a "famous princeling. . . born of a noble line . . . a noble, gallant knight,"[40] who took center stage in the nineteenth-century revival of interest in northern mythology. Yet Wagner found this fine, courtly figure to be useless to him; he wrote in *A Communication to My Friends* (1851) that he had to go back past the poems of the Middle Ages

> to the foundations of the ancient German mythology [where I was able] to strip away one distorting veil after another which later poetry had thrown over it . . . [Siegfried] only fully enthralled me for the first time when I had succeeded in freeing him from all his later trappings, and saw him before me in his purest human form.[41]

Wagner reached the "foundations of the ancient German mythology" not in the German myths but in the Scandinavian sagas. The Eddas were of primary importance for Wagner's account of Siegfried's life.[42] *Thidriks Saga* was his source for much of Siegfried's early days, and he took additional material from the *Volsunga Saga*.

For Siegfried's oath, his physical invulnerability, the sun and light motif from S-3-iii, and other important details, Wagner relied on secondary sources— poems, essays, and the compilations of the Grimm brothers, Fouqué, and Simrock. Siegfried occupies *The Ring*'s center stage for a long time; Wagner focused his powers of selection, adaptation, and invention on the young hero as much as on any character in the operas.

RELATIONSHIPS

Son of Siegmund and Sieglinde; grandson of Wotan (as Volse or Wolf, with an unnamed, mortal Volsung woman); husband (and nephew, through Wotan) of Brünnhilde; distant relationships to gods and Valkyries (through Wotan).

APPEARANCES

S-1-i

Forces Mime to reveal the truth—that Mime is not Siegfried's father, that his
mother Sieglinde died giving birth to him, and that Mime has kept fragments
of his fallen father's sword.

S-1-iii

Demands that Mime take him to Fafner to learn fear.

Reforges Notung.

S-2-ii

Arrives at Neidhöhle.

Trying to imitate the Wood Bird, wakens Fafner. Fights and kills the dragon.

Told of the Nibelung treasure by the Wood Bird, enters Fafner's cave.

S-2-iii

Emerges from the cave with the ring and Tarnhelm.

Discerning Mime's true intention to poison him, kills the dwarf.

Appeals to the Wood Bird to provide a "good companion," and rushes after the
Wood Bird to find Brünnhilde.

S-3-ii

Encounters the Wanderer and asks him the way.

Discovers the old man is his "father's foe," shatters his spear, and climbs up
through the flames.

S-3-iii

Reaching Brünnhilde's rock, finds and awakens the maiden.

Inflamed with passion and overcoming Brünnhilde's doubts, embraces her as
wife.

T-Prelude

Emerging from the cave with Brünnhilde, is armed with Notung and Brünnhilde's shield and ready to perform deeds of valor.

Pledging his troth, gives Brünnhilde the ring and is given Grane in return.

T-1-ii

Comes ashore at the Gibichungs' hall, seeking Gunther.

Drinks the potion offered by Gutrune, forgets Brünnhilde, and falls in love with
Gutrune.

Determines to win Brünnhilde for Gunther so he can wed Gutrune.

Taking an oath of brotherhood with Gunther, departs with him for Brünnhilde's
rock.

T-1-iii

Appearing before Brünnhilde in Gunther's form, claims her as bride, seizes the ring, and drives her into the cave for the night.

Speaking in his natural voice, pledges to safeguard the bride's honor.

T-2-ii

Reappears at the Gibichungs' hall, tells Hagen and Gutrune that he has won Brünnhilde for Gunther, and that Brünnhilde and Gunther follow in a boat on the Rhine.

Assures Gutrune he has kept Brünnhilde's honor.

T-2-iv

Is accused by Brünnhilde of treachery, that he is her husband and has taken her.

Swears an oath on Hagen's spear point that Brünnhilde is lying.

T-2-v

Is carried through the hall on a shield in celebration of his wedding to Gutrune.

T-3-i

Losing his way during the hunt, encounters the three Rhine Daughters.

Is warned that he will be slain that very day if he keeps the ring, but ignores the threat.

T-3-ii

Resting with the Gibichungs, tries to cheer up Gunther by singing tales of his exploits. Drinks the second potion; remembering Brünnhilde, sings of their love.

Is speared in the back by Hagen and dies.

T-3-iii

Is carried back to the Gibichungs' hall where his arm rises menacingly when Hagen tries to grasp the ring.

Is immolated with Brünnhilde on the funeral pyre.

COMMENTS

If any *Ring* character has fallen short of audience expectations—sometimes even lowering estimations of the work itself—it is the hero, Siegfried. He has been faulted for many things. He treats Mime cruelly. He is impetuous, hot-headed, and prone to strike out when something is denied him. He cries for his mother when he is afraid, and he comes at Brünnhilde with sexual aggression.

Siegfried is expected to do great deeds, to change the world. Instead, after pledging his eternal fidelity to his wife, he betrays her for another. He has no interest in understanding either the power or danger of the ring. He pays no heed to sincere warnings but is vulnerable to the manipulations of Hagen.

It is sometimes suggested that Wagner's portrayal of Siegfried was mistaken, that Siegfried's shortcomings mirror the composer's personal failures inadvertently revealed in his hero, or that Wagner's conception of a true hero was warped by his own personal eccentricities. To the contrary, Wagner knew what he wanted to accomplish in his art: Siegfried came out the way Wagner wanted him to, faults and all.

No figure in *The Ring*, not even Wotan or Brünnhilde, undertakes a journey of self-discovery as profound or complex as that of the title figure of *Siegfried*. All opera characters face challenges, but Siegfried seeks and faces them directly as a result of his own will, courage, and intuition.

Rather than judging Siegfried as just a heroic archetype, we should fully consider the circumstances of his life. When the curtain rises at S-1-i, the only physical and emotional environment to which the boy has ever been exposed consists of the forest and Mime. He has never known, or known of, his true parents. Not a moment of genuine love has nurtured him. It is a wonder he is not even more vulgar.

S-1-i reveals two aspects of Siegfried far more important than his rough loathing of Mime: his innate intelligence and his sense of yearning, of longing. He knows intuitively that something is wrong in his life. He has observed the animals in the forest and discovered that they mate and have offspring that look like themselves. He longs for knowledge and companionship, and he rages, logically, against the instrument of his ignorance and deprivation who bears him no resemblance or genuine kindness, Mime. He has never known love but yearns for a companion. He has never felt fear but demands to know the dangers of the wider world.

As usual, Wagner wastes little time in advancing the story—Siegfried's liberation begins early in S-1-i. He forces Mime to admit that he is neither the boy's father nor mother (Mime had claimed to be both), that his mother died giving birth to him in the forest and left behind fragments of his fallen father's shattered sword. (Mime continues to conceal the identity of Siegfried's father.)

Siegfried is filled with hope and, as his father did, determines "to go forth from the forest into the world." Innocent but infantile nature stands in opposition to the human world beyond the forest; Siegfried's desire to go into the world reflects his intuitive drive for development and adulthood.

In S-1-iii Siegfried effects his own empowerment—he reforges Notung. To do so, he invents new forging techniques: the fragments must be shaved into filings, melted down, and cast anew, rather than merely soldered as recommended by the putative expert, Mime.

To save his head, Mime tries to teach fear to the boy, in the process lying once more: he says Sieglinde told him to do so. But Siegfried's curiosity and delight are aroused instead, and he determines to learn fear from Fafner "and then be off into the world!"

In S-2, Siegfried forces the confrontation with Fafner by demanding that the dragon teach him fear; Fafner is only too happy to oblige. This is a challenge of manhood, courage, and physical achievement—traditional tests for heroes—and Siegfried easily sails through. He neither enjoys nor gloats over Fafner's death, but regrets the loss of a worthy adversary. Even as Fafner dies, Siegfried asks for information about himself.

He must also dispose of the threat from Mime. Because of the taste of Fafner's blood, Siegfried can now read Mime's heart, and the dwarf, in the act of attempting to murder the boy, condemns himself.

But the most significant challenges come after these physical ones. To a radical transformation of the Horn Call music, Siegfried throws himself, exhausted, under a tree. He faces a new world alone—his mother is dead, his father fallen, and he has neither brother nor sister. A simple boy alone in the forest, Siegfried knows how little he knows. This is an acknowledgment of vulnerability and insecurity, and our hearts go out to him.

The Wood Bird answers his call for a companion, leading Siegfried in S-3 to two pivotal confrontations—liberation from parents and introduction to love. In Freudian terms, the symbolic murder of the father is necessary for emotional growth; Siegfried's shattering of the spear in S-3-ii has this effect (the Wanderer is more like Siegfried's father here than grandfather). This extraordinary encounter is filled with charm and reminiscence and belongs above all to the Wanderer/Wotan. We see him here at his most vulnerable and emotionally appealing, and for the last time. Nevertheless, Siegfried's instincts and courage serve him well again. Unknowing and insensitive as he still is, he must overcome the Wanderer if he is to reach his manhood.

Siegfried makes the ascent through the forbidding magic fire, another test of physical courage. As predicted, it does not deter one who does not know fear but leads rather to the final test: love. Siegfried has never seen a woman, and the sight of Brünnhilde floods him with confusing emotions, including, finally, fear.

The scene is sometimes remembered as an encounter between an awkward boy and a radiant, knowing woman. But midway through, it is Brünnhilde who is racked by doubt and regret and the uninhibited Siegfried who leads her to her new, human life. She is all theory and intellect and delay; he is driven by passion and the moment, and forces her to awaken. Siegmund once taught Brünnhilde a lesson in human fidelity in V-2-iv; now Siegfried teaches her to have faith in him and in herself alone.

At the beginning of *Twilight*, we see Siegfried completed as a man, ready to fulfill his mission and do great deeds. In fact, he accomplishes little. Worse, he bru-tally betrays and humiliates Brünnhilde, setting her on a course of vengeance that ultimately leads to his own destruction.

Siegfried's acts of betrayal are caused by Hagen's magic potion. To some, this dramatic device is archaic, unconvincing, and out of proportion, and the potion's power over him makes Siegfried seem less worthy. Yet *The Ring* is filled with magic powers, as are the mythological sources, and even under the evil potion Siegfried conducts himself as best he can, truthfully, and in accordance with heroic values.

More important, Brünnhilde reminds us at the last that Siegfried has always been manipulated by much greater influences—by Wotan, Alberich, and the problem of the ring. She places the blame squarely upon Wotan, who has created Siegfried and put him in harm's way in order to escape the ring's power. Wotan's betrayal of Siegfried leads Brünnhilde to do the deeds that will sweep away the gods and the old order. Thus Siegfried's life and death are at the heart of this momentous change.

The immolation of Siegfried and Brünnhilde can connote annihilation or evolution, death or transfiguration, or something else entirely. For Donington, "death in myth is transformation. . . . If we cannot understand this final theme of redemption, we cannot understand Wagner. It was his life-long preoccupation."[43] Siegfried's dead hand rises to rebuff Hagen and so fulfills Wotan's great idea of R-iv: "All Wotan's manhood, all Siegmund's, all Siegfried's are concentrated into the power of spirit which raises the dead man's arm . . . The ringing confidence of the sword's motive . . . rings with manhood."[44]

Brünnhilde's final action is momentous: her immolation both frees the world of the ring's curse and ends the reign of the gods. But her final words and last wish are for Siegfried alone: "to be one with him in the intensity of love! Siegfried! See! Your wife joyfully greets you!"

MUSIC

A great many musical ideas accompany Siegfried and his struggles, learning, adventures, and love. Two of these occur preponderantly as personal motives. The first, 72–The Heroic in Siegfried, is introduced by Brünnhilde in V-3-i when Sieglinde tells her she bears "the noblest hero in the world."

We first hear the second of Siegfried's personal motives, 80–Siegfried's Horn Call, when he exuberantly enters Mime's hut in S-1-i. Initially associated with his youthful energy, the figure grows in stature as Siegfried does, in the assertive horn call in S-2-ii, in the majestic fullness of life he has reached at T-Prologue, and in the blackness of death in the Funeral March.

Other musical fragments comment pertinently on Siegfried's drive for personal development, including 83–Yearning for Knowledge. This yearning, which will become his key to escape from Mime's forest prison, is paralleled in an equally insistent, instinctive longing for love, for emotional growth, in 84–Yearning for Love.

Siegfried's personal development through the course of the opera that bears his name leads to his increasing ability to articulate his mission; thus 86–Mission grows from 83–Yearning for Knowledge.

In the scenes between Siegfried and Brünnhilde in S-3-iii and T-Prologue, much new musical material centers on their mutual love, including 104–Awakening, 105–Love's Greeting, 106–Love's Ecstasy, and 107–Immortal Beloved. A further transformation of 86–Mission expresses their defiant, shared purpose: 109–Laughing at Death.

THE WOOD BIRD
Siegfried's Magical Friend

SOURCES
In *Thidriks Saga*, Siegfried is able to understand two birds after he kills and eats a dragon. One advises him to kill Mime. In the *Poetic Edda*, Sigurd is advised by a bird to take the treasure and awaken Brünnhilde.

RELATIONSHIPS
None.

APPEARANCES
S-2-ii
Tells Siegfried about the ring, Tarnhelm, and gold in Fafner's cave.

S-2-iii
Warns Siegfried about Mime's plan to murder him.
Tells Siegfried about Brünnhilde and leads him toward her.

S-3-ii
Directs Siegfried to a spot below Brünnhilde's rock, but sees Wotan and flies
  quickly away.

COMMENTS
The Wood Bird has the smallest singing role in *The Ring*. We do not know very much about the little bird that intervenes so significantly in Siegfried's life, but in the mythology, the ability to understand animals connotes both the benevolent aspect of magic and an affinity with nature.

Siegfried encounters the Wood Bird as he rests and it plays in the branches above him to the music of 94–Forest Murmurs. Here S-2 brings a potent sense of the underlying pulse of the natural world, as do R-Prelude and parts of R-i. The peace and repose of these moments contrast strongly with the strife, deceit, and carnage we have so far seen in S-2. Yet Siegfried also yearns to leave behind the infantile, passive life with which the forest is associated. The Wood Bird is an active agent of that change.

It gives Siegfried three pieces of advice that are accurate and extremely valuable to him: the information about the treasure in the cave, the warning about Mime, and the happy promise of Brünnhilde. The bird also appears in S-3-ii. Fluttering gaily ahead of Siegfried, it quickly disappears in alarm when it sees the Wanderer, who later warns Siegfried the bird flew away to save itself: "The lord of the ravens it learnt was here: woe to it if they catch it!"

Wagner might have provided Siegfried some other path to the treasure and Brünnhilde than the little bird. But in addition to its inherent charm, the Wood Bird reinforces Siegfried's alignment with the natural world and with the elements of fate, magic, and self-knowledge that will help shape his life and death.

MUSIC

The Wood Bird sings a series of lively motivic fragments in S-2-ii. These emerge out of the underlying context of 94–Forest Murmurs, the Wood Bird's link with nature. The first fragment, 95A–Wood Bird, is a restatement of 4–Rhine Daughters, who are also fundamentally innocent allies of the natural world.

In 95B–Wood Bird, the second fragment, the Wood Bird tells Siegfried that he can awaken and win Brünnhilde. This phrase was foreshadowed in 5–Warning in R-i, when Flosshilde cautions her sisters to guard the gold more carefully.

THE THREE NORNS
The End of an Era

SOURCES

The Icelandic *Prose Edda* of Snorri Sturluson, which provides the best medieval account of the world of the Scandinavian gods, includes the Nornir "who determine the fates of men at the well of wisdom by the world ash-tree."[45]

Wagner frequently relied on secondary sources to add details to the *Ring* story. For example, he drew on Fouqué's dramatic poem *Sigurd der Schlangentödter*, which includes an assemblage of Norns at Brünnhilde's rock.[46]

Wagner dispenses with their traditional names—Wurdur the oldest, Werdandi the middle in age, and Skuld the youngest—but he does preserve their relative ages and specific responsibilities for the past, present, and future, respectively. That Erda is their mother is another of Wagner's unifying inventions.

RELATIONSHIPS
Daughters of Erda (their father is not identified; in R-iv, Erda says they were "conceived before the start of time"). Half-sisters to Brünnhilde and possibly to the Valkyries, if Erda is considered their mother.

APPEARANCES
T-Prologue
Reviewing earlier events occurring both in and outside of the *Ring* story, they
    are unable to see the future clearly.
The rope of fate snaps as Alberich's "avenging curse" gnaws at its strands. With
    their knowledge at an end, they descend to Erda.

COMMENTS
The Norns serve a number of purposes in *The Ring* and serve them well. After the manic euphoria of the S-3-iii love scene and before the continuing rapture of Brünnhilde and Siegfried in the T-Prologue passage that follows, the Norns plunge us back into a dark and ominous world where the mystery of fate plays a central role. This reinforcement of the mythological foundation of *The Ring* reminds us that the lives of Siegfried and Brünnhilde will be played out as part of predestined, apocryphal events.

Theirs is also a world of reminiscence—much of what they say we already know, possibly because Wagner wrote the *Twilight* text first, not last, and some recounting of events seen in the preceding operas survived text revisions. But the Norn narration, like others in *The Ring*, is not a static repetition. We are provided new information about Wotan, the great World Ash Tree, the spring beside it, and the immolation of Valhalla.

One major event occurs in the scene: the rope of fate snaps, crystalizing a point toward which *The Ring* has been working since R-i and even before. This is the great historical dislocation that will engulf the race of gods and the Norns themselves. The Norn scene resonates with the ending of an era and uncertainty about the future.

The Norns in T-Prologue are as confused and impotent as Erda is in S-3-i. They know the world is changing, that something is undermining their powers of discernment and prophesy, but they do not understand what it is and are powerless to stop it. When the rope snaps, they huddle together in terror. They know their time is over. All they can do is sink down deep into the earth to join their mother in eternal sleep. We are left alone to watch the final events unfold.

MUSIC

The Norn scene sets the stage for the events that follow in *Twilight*. But what makes the scene so penetrating is the music, which in this scene, perhaps more than in any other, evokes reminiscence and presentiment, a sense both of what we have already experienced and of things to come.

Such evocation was among Wagner's primary objectives and is the true dramatic purpose of the recapitulative narration. By the end of the scene, we have heard versions of 104–Awakening, 2–Nature, 3–Rhine, 69–Fate, 12–The Ring, 89–World Ash Tree, 8–Water Murmurs, 31–Power of the Ring, 14A–Valhalla, 40–Sword, 70–Annunciation of Death, 18–Power of the Gods, 24–Spear, 37–Downfall, 25A–Loge, 76–Sleep, 9–Gold, 11–Rhinegold, 72–The Heroic in Siegfried, and 35–Curse. At no other point in *The Ring* are we so persuaded to take our minds off the words and eyes from the gloomy stage to give ourselves up to the sweeping, musical tapestry.

Of the minimal new thematic material introduced by the Norns, the most significant is 111–Rope of Fate.

GUNTHER
In the Shadow

SOURCES

Gunther is drawn from a historical person who may be the starting point for the Nibelung stories and sagas. According to Deryck Cooke, Gunther of the medieval sources is "a legendary transformation of a historical fifth-century Burgundian king, who is recorded in a Latin chronicle of the time (the *Lex Burgundiorum*) as Gunthaharius, a descendant of King Gibicha . . . the semi-mythical founder of the royal line of the Gibichungs."[47] In 437 A.D., Gunthaharius was defeated by the Huns of Attila. Attila died around 453 during his nuptials with a woman named Ildico (presumably a variation of the German root-syllable *Hild*), and there were rumors that he was murdered by the woman.

Cooke speculates that this account inspired one of the three first-millennium lays that could be the basis for the twelfth- and thirteenth-century chronicles of the northern gods and heroes. In the lay, Ildico becomes Gunther's sister and marries Attila, now called Etzel. To gain the Gibichung treasure, Etzel tricks and murders Gunther and his brothers and army. Gutrune murders Etzel in revenge.

The second basic lay tells the story of Gunther's marriage to Brünnhilde, assisted by Siegfried. The third deals mainly with Siegfried's earlier life and exploits.

The *Nibelungenlied* tells the story of Gunther's pursuit of and defeat by Etzel. In that poem Gunther and his brothers—the Burgundians—are called Nibelungs.[48] The reason the Burgundians are also called Nibelungs may come from their capture of the Nibelung treasure and their coming to be identified by it.

Wagner drew on Simrock's dramatic poem, the *Amelungenlied*, for details about the blood-brotherhood drink and oath depicted in T-1-ii. Once again, Wagner exercised great license and good dramatic judgment in shaping his own Gunther whose role has been radically reduced from its prominence in the sources.

RELATIONSHIPS

Son of King Gibich and Grimhilde; brother of Gutrune; half-brother of Hagen (through Grimhilde).

APPEARANCES

T-1-i

Is manipulated by Hagen to desire Brünnhilde as wife. Agrees to the plan to deceive Siegfried.

T-1-ii

Welcomes Siegfried, who drinks the potion offered by Gutrune, forgets Brünnhilde, and falls in love with Gutrune.

Brünnhilde   *Siegfried*   *Gunther*

Tells Siegfried that he longs for Brünnhilde; accepts Siegfried's offer to win her
for him, provided Siegfried can marry Gutrune.

Pledges blood-brotherhood with Siegfried and departs by boat with him for
Brünnhilde's rock.

T-2-iv

Arrives home with Brünnhilde and presents her to his vassals.

Announces his marriage and Gutrune's with Siegfried, shocking Brünnhilde.

Stunned and confused by Brünnhilde's accusations against Siegfried, urges
Siegfried to deny them.

T-2-v

Shamed by his own deception and convinced of Siegfried's, pushed by Hagen
and Brünnhilde, and desirous of the ring, agrees to Siegfried's murder.

T-3-ii

Gloomily joins Siegfried during the hunt. Listens in shock as Siegfried reveals
that he has, after all, lain with Brünnhilde.

Too late, fails to restrain Hagen.

T-3-iii

Accompanies Siegfried's corpse back to the Gibichungs' hall; tells Gutrune it
was Hagen who murdered the hero.

Resists Hagen's claim to the ring and is killed by Hagen.

COMMENTS

In T-Prologue, Siegfried departs from Brünnhilde to do great deeds in the world,
and the first place we see him go, in T-1-ii, is to Gunther, whose fame he has heard
sung "far along the Rhine." Siegfried tells the truth about Gunther's reputation,
but Hagen has lied to his half-brother in the preceding scene: "your standing is
still slight." Thus does Wagner place Gunther between the honest hero and complex villain of *Twilight*.

And there he stays. Wagner creates two views of Gunther. In his medieval context, Gunther (like Siegfried) is an admirable knight, acting in a straightforward
and honorable manner but victimized by the magic of Hagen's manipulation. Yet
a psychological weakness, a fatal vulnerability, plagues Gunther.

Hagen assures Gunther he is not up to the task of penetrating the flames to secure Brünnhilde; only Siegfried can accomplish this. Gunther admires Siegfried
for his surpassing fame and manliness. Gunther readily admits Hagen's superior
intelligence: "though I inherited the first-born's right, wisdom went to you alone."

Although the text is ambiguous, Gunther seems to have grown up in the
shadow of his father, King Gibich. His first words are to ask Hagen if he "maintains

Gibich's glory." And what must Gunther truly feel about his mother, Grimhilde, wife of a great king? Does he know that she sold herself for money to Alberich?

Like Gutrune, Gunther first joins the conspiracy without knowing that Siegfried has already wed Brünnhilde. Nor is the ring his objective. Thus we are obliged to distinguish between Gunther's (and Gutrune's) aspirations and Hagen's truly malevolent motives and actions. Gunther would likely have had nothing to do with Hagen's plot had he been fully aware of how it betrayed Siegfried. He is intuitively right to place his knightly trust in Siegfried in T-1-ii, and he seems reluctant to accept, in T-2-iv and T-2-v, that Siegfried has betrayed him and broken the oath of blood-brotherhood. He must be bullied by Brünnhilde and Hagen to agree to Siegfried's death, and in T-3-ii he tries, physically, to prevent Hagen from delivering the fatal blow, even though he has just been shocked to hear Siegfried proclaim "how ardently was I enfolded in fair Brünnhilde's arms."

Still, Gunther's moral weakness is patent; manipulated by Hagen, he contributes mightily to the destruction of Siegfried, Brünnhilde, his sister, and himself. It is with grave consequences that Siegfried identifies with Gunther and is taken in by his superficial attractiveness. To Donington, Gunther is part of Siegfried's "shadow," whom Siegfried mistakenly equates with his own "ego ideals," but whose values ultimately are counterfeit.

In any case, a shadow creates contrast as well as comparison. Wagner often uses one character to make a point about another. Gunther's play-acting at hero underscores the genuinely heroic nature of Siegfried, who could not knowingly have betrayed Brünnhilde, who has done genuinely heroic deeds, and who has no ambition for wealth and power.

MUSIC

Strong, manly, and warm, 119–Gunther carries within it all the deceptions of life. The motive of 124–Friendship characterizes the immediate and genuine regard Siegfried and Gunther feel for each other in T-1-ii. The oath of blood-brotherhood in T-1-ii will be used to help justify Siegfried's death. At first 127–Blood-Brotherhood projects noble purpose, but the motive suggests an overwhelming sense of regret as Gunther reluctantly joins the murder conspiracy in T-2-v.

HAGEN
The Ring's Last Victim

SOURCES

Hagen has no known historical relationship to the fifth-century Frankish leader, Gunthaharius, nor is it known if he appears in the early German lays that tell the story of Siegfried's murder. In the medieval Nibelung stories, however, Hagen emerges as liegeman and relative of Gunther and as champion of the Nibelungs (also known as Burgundians or Gibichungs) in their disastrous fight against the Huns.

In the *Nibelungenlied*, it is Hagen who murders Siegfried during a hunt to redeem Brünnhilde's honor. He also recounts Siegfried's earlier feats (killing the dragon and winning the treasure) when Siegfried arrives at Gunther's court. The second half of the *Nibelungenlied* tells how Gunther and Hagen lead their army in pursuit of Gunther's sister Kriemhild and her husband Etzel (Attila) to the Danube, where they are slaughtered by Etzel's army.

In the Scandinavian sources, Hogni (Hagen) is Gunnar's (Gunther's) full brother, and he advises against the killing of Sigurd. But in *Thidriks Saga*, of German origin but written in Bergen, Hagen is the son of Gunther's mother by an elf, has a terrifying appearance, and murders Siegfried.

Wagner's inventions add unity to the drama: Wagner makes Hagen Alberich's son and has the oath of blood-brotherhood taken on Hagen's spear.

RELATIONSHIPS
Son of Alberich (and Grimhilde, the wife of King Gibich and mother of Gunther and Gutrune); half-brother of Gunther and Gutrune (through Grimhilde); nephew of Mime (through Alberich).

APPEARANCES
T-1-i
Tempts Gunther to marry Brünnhilde and Gutrune to marry Siegfried. Convinces them to use a potion to make Siegfried desire Gutrune.

T-1-ii
Calls Siegfried to shore. Informs him of the Tarnhelm's powers.
Manipulates Siegfried to drink the potion offered by Gutrune and to take the oath of blood-brotherhood with Gunther.
Takes up the watch for Siegfried's return.

T-2-i
Alberich appears before the sleeping Hagen and urges him to secure the ring.

T-2-ii
Siegfried returns and tells Hagen and Gutrune that he has won Brünnhilde for Gunther.

T-2-iii
Calls the vassals together to greet Gunther and Brünnhilde.

T-2-iv

Manipulates Brünnhilde into accusing Siegfried. Takes Siegfried's and Brünnhilde's oaths on his spear point.

T-2-v

Learns from Brünnhilde that Siegfried's back is unprotected.

Goads Gunther to agree to Siegfried's death.

T-3-ii

Repeatedly asks Siegfried to sing of his exploits. Gives him the drink that
refreshes his memory so that Siegfried reveals he is Brünnhilde's husband.

Murders Siegfried.

T-3-iii

Tells Gutrune that Siegfried is dead.

Fights for the ring with Gunther and kills him.

Reaches for the ring but is stopped by Siegfried's dead hand.

Plunges into the flood after the ring, is carried down to the depths by the Rhine
Daughters.

COMMENTS

The Ring is filled with illusion—fire that does not burn, treasure that gives no
pleasure. Its characters are filled with ambition and longing; they struggle against
their destinies and strive for things they do not fathom.

Hagen is free of illusion. Gunther readily acknowledges his half-brother's
superior intelligence. He has useful knowledge—about Siegfried and Brünnhilde,
the Tarnhelm, and magic potions. Ever cynical, he knows how to exploit the
desires of those around him for his own purposes.

Until the end, he is the most successful character in *The Ring*. Unlike those of
most *Ring* characters, especially Wotan, Hagen's plans move promptly forward
exactly as he wishes. His victims, the radiant, glorious ones, rush toward their
destruction as they unwittingly do his bidding. He controls most of the action of
Twilight, appearing in the first two scenes of T-1, all five of T-2, and the last two
of T-3.

Hagen also has no illusions about the flaw that undermines any hopes for a
happy life. Like Siegmund and, indirectly, Siegfried, he has been given life only to
serve as instrument of another's will: Alberich fathered Hagen to gain back the
ring for himself, a single purpose born of vengeance and hatred. We hear about
Hagen as early as V-2-ii, when Wotan tells Brünnhilde that "the fruits of [Alber-
ich's] hatred a woman is carrying: his envy at full strength is sitting in her womb."

Hagen's ruthless manipulation is common in operatic villains, but like all
major *Ring* characters (one also thinks of Verdi's Iago), Hagen is richly multidi-

mensional. The T-2-i encounter between Hagen and Alberich, in the blackest hour before the dawn, is impressive enough because it provides our final glimpse of relentless Alberich who does most of the talking.

Yet we find ourselves looking at Hagen with unexpected interest. As Alberich's instrument, he is faithfully pursuing the ring. But he is also aware of the pain and the cost of doing his father's bidding, and he reveals a surprising resentment, even independence, from Alberich.

Far from joining in Alberich's long-winded enthusiasm for the dirty job of murdering Siegfried, Hagen, in remarkably few words, exposes the emptiness in which he has been trapped: "Prematurely old, pale and wan, I hate the happy and am never glad." He bears no gratitude toward his mother for giving him life; he knows that she was bought with gold by Alberich.

Near the end of their meeting Hagen says: "I will have the ring," and it is not entirely clear he means to hand it over to Alberich, whom he calls "hateful gnome." In T-3-iii, as he fights Gunther for the ring, he says: "Thus does his son demand the gnome's inheritance."

Ultimately, Hagen is another victim of the ring. Conceived in the hatred and envy of its curse, he becomes its servant while still unborn, before he has a conscious thought. The last, desperate words of *The Ring* are his, as he plunges after the Rhine Daughters and to his death: "Keep away from the ring!"

MUSIC

Hagen's personal motive is a plunging interval, which also becomes associated with the Gibichungs generally and the plot against Siegfried. 118–Hagen takes on its full and terrifying form in Hagen's Watch at the end of T-1-ii, but the phrase is first heard when Gunther addresses Hagen to open T-1-i.

A final iteration of the falling figure—initially heard in R-i with the first spoken word of *The Ring*, "Weia!"—is Hagen's ominous call to the Gibichung vassals: 137–Hoiho!

Foreshadowed by 134–Dawn in T-2-ii, 135–Grim Hagen conveys the relentless force of Hagen's plan, now in full force.

GUTRUNE
Sweet Sorrow of the Ring's Curse

SOURCES

Like Gunther, Gutrune can be traced to the Burgundians and, as Cooke tells it, the "semi-mythical" King Gibicha.[49] In the earliest stories, even in her relationship with Siegfried, Gutrune was more prominent than Brünnhilde.

In the *Nibelungenlied,* Gunther's sister is known as Kriemhild. At some point in the sources a distinction emerges between Kriemhild/Grimhild the mother and Gutrune the sister. In the *Volsunga Saga,* Grimhildur, the mother of the Gibichungs, masterminds the potion plot against Siegfried.[50] In *Das Lied vom hürnen Seyfrid,* Siegfried kills a dragon and a giant to rescue Gutrune.

Much as he expanded Brünnhilde's importance, Wagner diluted Gutrune's, diminishing both her dramatic role and her assertive character.

RELATIONSHIPS

Daughter of King Gibich and Grimhilde; sister of Gunther; half-sister of Hagen (through Grimhilde).

APPEARANCES

T-1-i

Joins the plot to win Siegfried through Hagen's potion.

T-1-ii

Offers the drugged drink to Siegfried, who forgets about Brünnhilde and falls in love with Gutrune.

T-2-ii

Welcomes Siegfried on his return from Brünnhilde's rock and secures Siegfried's assurances that he has respected Brünnhilde.

T-2-iv

With Siegfried, greets Gunther and Brünnhilde.

Asks Siegfried to deny Brünnhilde's accusation against him.

T-2-v

At the end of the scene, is carried aloft by vassals amid festive bridal preparations.

T-3-iii

Disturbed by bad dreams, looks for Brünnhilde and awaits Siegfried's return.

Sees Siegfried's corpse carried into the hall.

Watches as Hagen kills Gunther and tries to seize the ring.

Accuses Brünnhilde of jealously turning the men against Siegfried.

Understands at last that Brünnhilde was Siegfried's true wife and curses Hagen for the plot against them.

COMMENTS

Gutrune is destroyed by forces far stronger than she. She willingly takes part in the plot against Siegfried. She is not yet married and, against her better judgment, is convinced by Hagen that she can by magic win the greatest of heroes. By tradition, she is beautiful, but Wagner does not say this.

Like her brother Gunther, Gutrune projects aspects of both the medieval and modern worlds. As part of the former, she is merely demure. But as Wagner has shaped her, she is more complex and senses herself unworthy. Any woman might feel intimidated by the great Siegfried, but Gutrune seems to regard herself as less than other women; how could Siegfried ever love her, she says, when he could have his pick of the world's women! She is as vulnerable as Gunther to Hagen's insinuations about not being married and does not hesitate when Hagen convinces her that his magic can win Siegfried.

Gutrune has the ethical sense to know that her actions are deceptive. When the potion works on the hero, she cannot look Siegfried in the eyes; she leaves the hall, according to Wagner's stage directions, "with a gesture of feeling herself unworthy."

In T-2-ii she timidly but insistently seeks reassurance from Siegfried that he has not taken advantage of the magnificent Brünnhilde. She opens the final scene of *The Ring* as if she is frightened of Brünnhilde's shadow. Her honesty and perhaps insecurity allow her, once she is told the truth, to accept that Brünnhilde is Siegfried's true wife. Until that moment in T-3-iii, Gutrune does not know the extent of Hagen's deception, that is, that Siegfried and Brünnhilde were husband and wife before Siegfried arrived at the Gibichung hall; in T-1-i she is told only that the potion will bind Siegfried to her in love.

She therefore has every reason to think at first that the potion's magic will result not only in her own happiness, but in Siegfried's and Gunther's as well, since both will gain the wives they want. It is reasonable to expect that she, like Gunther, would have rejected Hagen's plan had she known she would be destroying Siegfried's and Brünnhilde's marriage in the process.

At the beginning of the immolation scene in T-3-iii, she is dissolved in grief, bent motionless over Gunther's body, "until the end." Her tragedy is complete, her life over. It would be fitting to assume that her heart breaks before fire and water sweep her, and so much else, into the past.

MUSIC

Gutrune is given music in 120–Gutrune that, properly sung, reveals her gentle modesty, her timid hopes for a glorious husband, and her treachery. Her opening words reflect her inner beauty and innate shyness. She sings not about herself but rather asks about Siegfried's heroic deeds.

Gutrune longs for Siegfried as husband and invites Hagen to tell her how she might win him, thus becoming directly involved in 122–Plotting.

As she approaches Siegfried bearing the magic potion, we hear 125–Gutrune's Treachery, a passage of warmth and delicacy sometimes considered Gutrune's personal music. Later, in quickened form, it will represent all the Gibichungs. Yet here, for all its sweetness, 125–Gutrune's Treachery defines Gutrune's role in the plot against Siegfried.

When Siegfried returns from Brünnhilde's rock, Gutrune greets him with soaring hopes in 136–Gutrune's Greeting; beyond her dreams, the plan seems to have worked.

THE GIBICHUNGS
Inheritors of the World

SOURCES
A fifth-century Latin chronicle, the *Lex Burgundiorum*, describes a Gunthaharius who ruled territory around the Rhine and was defeated by the Huns of Attila in 437 (see pages 231–232). Gunthaharius was a descendant of King Gibicha. The Gibichungs were also known as Burgundians.[51] In the medieval sources, the Gibichungs are subjects of Gunther.

RELATIONSHIPS
Vassals of Gunther, son of King Gibich.

APPEARANCES
T-2-iii

Upon Siegfried's return from Brünnhilde's rock, Hagen summons the vassals, who rush in to learn that Gunther approaches with a new wife.

Hagen urges them to prepare sacrifices to the gods and to drink in celebration until drunk. They marvel at Hagen's high spirits.

T-2-iv

The men greet Gunther and Brünnhilde. The women enter, in attendance to Siegfried and Gutrune.

In great confusion, the Gibichungs listen to Brünnhilde's accusation and Siegfried's oath of denial.

T-2-v

At the end of the scene, men and boys, women and girls enter as part of a festive bridal procession, bearing Siegfried and Gutrune aloft, while servants lead sacrificial beasts to the altar stones at the back.

T-3-ii

The men listen to Siegfried's narrative.

Shocked by Siegfried's murder, they carry the corpse back to the Gibichungs' hall.

T-3-iii

The Gibichungs watch in horror as Hagen kills Gunther and tries to seize the ring.

At Brünnhilde's order, the young men build a funeral pyre.

As Brünnhilde leaps into the pyre, the flames catch onto the hall, and the men and women crowd into the extreme front in terror.

From the ruins of the hall, the Gibichungs watch in great agitation as a glow in the sky grows in brightness until Valhalla and the gods seated there are consumed.

COMMENTS

We never see groups of Volsungs in *The Ring*, nor for that matter, members of Hunding's race, Neidings. The Nibelungs, the only crowd group in *The Ring* beside the Gibichungs, seem to be at the center of the drama when we witness their enslavement in R-iii, but we have only two brief glimpses of them.

By contrast, the Gibichungs, the only human group in *The Ring*, do not directly concern us much, but they actively and visibly take part in the action in T-2 and T-3. They react to events vocally, bang their weapons loudly, and jump into the Rhine to lay up Gunther's boat. They prepare to make wedding sacrifices to the same gods we first encountered in *The Rhinegold*. They ask questions and offer opinions.

Hagen makes some effort to manipulate them against Siegfried, without success. Oddly for one so incorrigible, he appeals to them in T-3-iii to confirm he is entitled to the ring on Siegfried's dead hand, much as Fasolt appealed to the gods as Fafner took over the hoard in R-iv.

The Gibichungs question, comment, worship, celebrate, and survive. All of this recalls nothing so much as a Greek chorus, which represented common humanity. For Wagner, Greek drama was the ideal in art, the starting point for his own critique of western culture and for the notion of fusing all the arts toward serious, socially uplifting purposes.

For all their struggles, the many contenders for love and power in the world have failed. Ancient primordial wisdom has settled into permanent sleep. A generation of gods is destroyed. The heroic children Wotan fostered are murdered or self-sacrificed. The Nibelung hordes will not rise up; their leader has lost all power. The last of the giants is dead.

At the last, the men and women watch in terror as the gods are consumed in flames. The Rhine has returned to its banks. It is common humanity, the Gibichungs, who will inherit the new world.

MUSIC

From the beginning of T-1-i, striking themes are introduced having to do with the Gibichungs. Most of these are also related to Gutrune, Gunther, or Hagen. The gentle 117–Treachery is transformed into an assertive phrase that represents the Gibichungs generally: 138–Gibichungs' Horn Call.

As Hagen tells the vassals about Gunther's new wife, they break into a song remarking on Hagen's rare good humor. This tune, 139–Vassals' Song, is a raucous restatement of 135–Dawn and 135–Grim Hagen, forming the only traditional chorus in *The Ring*.

With 140–Vassals' Greeting the vassals simply but enthusiastically greet Gunther and Brünnhilde as they step ashore in T-2-iv.

CHAPTER FIVE

CONCORDANCE

Boldly tread its terrorless path.
—Froh to the gods at the Rainbow Bridge, R-iv

THIS CHAPTER contains the first English-language concordance to *The Ring*. More than 160 principal words appear here in alphabetical order and in every context in which they occur in the opera librettos.

The concordance is a powerful tool for penetrating *The Ring* through its use of words. It offers a direct and simple way to look at how, when, where, and how often key words appear. Readers may also use this massive index to pursue particular thoughts—how does each character speak about the ring, for example?

For several reasons a concordance to the *Ring* texts is particularly apt. First, as we have seen in earlier chapters, the *Ring* librettos are unusually rich in meaning. They deal not just with actions and emotions, but with ideas, symbols, and complex psychological problems. Wagner himself wrote them and claimed, at least in his theoretical writings, that words are as important as the music itself.

Second, these librettos are also of great length and complexity. The Salter and Mann translations fill 264 pages. Stewart Spencer's translation of 1993 covers nearly three hundred pages, and Andrew Porter's is well over three hundred. Further, the texts are filled with names and events. As an index of key words, the concordance provides a new way to make sense of this wonderful but daunting story.

The concordance should be helpful to *Ring* newcomers and scholars alike. It can be used to clarify factual details: by looking up *Neiding*, for example, we can find the one place in the text that links Hunding to that race. We can also trace the prevalence of certain words through the tetralogy: *ring* is ubiquitous while *west, eagle,* and *Irming* may occur only once or twice.

Most important, beyond the quantitative data lie qualitative rewards. When we read through the full record of occurrences of *Fafner* and *sword,* we witness the evolution of the character and of the object and symbol. As Owen Lee wrote after reading a draft, "Alberich's character came together for me as never quite before when I read, in quick succession, what the others said about him."[1]

Of course, creating an English-language *Ring* concordance poses certain problems and requires some choices. First, the accuracy of a non-German concordance is as inherently imperfect as the translations of the texts themselves. This is a caution, not a prohibition. The translations used in this book are quite literal, so that even a concordance to the translations is highly accurate. And even if *The Ring* or any work is best understood in its original language, this tool should help to make the operas' pleasures more accessible to non-German speakers.

The words listed in the concordance include proper names, place names, specific objects, and some concepts of special significance, but not every noun in the text. An index to the key words appears at the start of the concordance, below. Under each key word, the entries appear in the order of their occurrence in the tetralogy. Each entry includes the quotation, the speaker, the opera, act, and scene, and the person being spoken to and/or the context.

The translations used for the concordance and throughout this book are by Lionel Salter *(The Rhinegold, Siegfried, Twilight of the Gods)* and William Mann *(The Valkyrie).* Some differences in spellings result from the use of two translators' renderings.

Readers will find this chapter easy to use. Because it is a concordance of English-language translations, the English word generally controls rather than the original German even if the term in English is not the exact counterpart of the German.

When the translation uses different words to describe the same German word, the English words appear as a cluster. For example, the German word *Hort* is translated as both "hoard" and "treasure." In this case, occurrences of both words appear under *hoard,* and the heading for *hoard* reads Hoard (Treasure). If you were to look up *treasure,* you would find only a cross reference: Treasure, see Hoard.

Different names for the same character or object are sometimes listed separately and cross-referenced. For example: Freia (see also Holda) and Holda (see also Freia). Words derived from the same root word in English are generally clustered under the same entry: Father (Battlefather, Warfather).

On a handful of occasions, the English translation omits the key German word altogether, and in such cases the German word appears in the concordance in brackets. Under the heading Erda (Wala), for example, [Wala] is added to the entry for clarification even though the English text at that point merely reads "woman."

Any omission from a quotation is indicated by ellipses or by a clarification in brackets. A clarification may also appear in brackets to complete a character's partial sentence or to supply other missing information.

Proper names are spelled uniformly throughout this book, even though Brünnhilde, Notung, Volse, and Nibelung are often rendered in the literature as Brunhilde or Brynhilde, Nothung, Volsa, and Niblung.

As this book is written by an American in the United States, American spelling and usage prevail over British.

KEY WORDS

Adultery (Cuckold)

Alberich

Alliance, see Treaty

Apples, see Golden Apples

Ash Tree (Primeval Ash, Tree [Esche],
    World Ash Tree)

Atonement

Bargain, see Treaty

Battlefather, see Father

Bear (Bearskin, Bruin)

Blood-Brotherhood

Boar

Bond, see Treaty

Bridge (Rainbow Bridge)

Brother-in-Law

Bruin, see Bear

Brünnhilde

Bruno

Castle, see Valhalla

Cheerful

Children of the Rhine, see Rhine
    Daughters

Compact, see Treaty

Contract, see Treaty

Covenant, see Treaty

Cuckold, see Adultery

Curse

Day (Daylight)

Divinity, see God

Donner

Dragon (Serpent, Snake)

Dream

Dusk, see Twilight

Earth Mother, see Mother

East (Eastward)

Eel

Erda (Wala)

Eye

Fafner (see also Giants)

Fasolt (see also Giants)

Fate

Father (Battlefather, Warfather; see also
    Volse, Wanderer, Wotan)

Fine-Wrought Gold, see Tarnhelm
Fir Tree
Flosshilde
Fort, Fortress, see Valhalla
Fox
Freia (see also Holda)
Fricka
Froh
Fruit, see Golden Apples

Gerhilde
Giants (see also Fafner, Fasolt)
Gibich (Gibichung; see also Gunther)
God (Divinity, Goddess, Godhead,
    Godlike)
Gold (Toy, Trinket; see also Hoard,
    Rhinegold)
Golden Apples (Apples, Fruit)
Grane
Grimgerde
Grimhilde
Gunther (see also Gibich)
Gutrune

Hagen
Hammer
Hawthorn
Hegeling
Hell, see Hella
Hella (Hell)
Helmet, see Tarnhelm
Helmwige
Hoard (Treasure; see also Gold)
Holda (see also Freia)
Horn
Hunding

Incest
Irming

King

Lime Tree
Loge

Magic (Spell)
Mime

Moon (Moonlight)
Mother (Earth Mother)
Music

Neidhöhle
Neiding
Nibelheim
Nibelung
Night
Norns
North
Notung (see also Sword)
Nymphs, see Rhine Daughters

Oath (Vow)
Ortlinde

Pact, see Treaty
Peace (Peaceful)
Primeval Ash, see Ash Tree

Rainbow Bridge, see Bridge
Rams
Ravens
Renunciation of Love
Revenge (Vengeance, Avenger)
Rhine
Rhine Daughters (Children of the Rhine,
    Nymphs, Rhinemaidens, Water
    Maidens, Watery Brood)
Rhinegold (see also Gold)
Rhinemaidens, see Rhine Daughters
Riesenheim
Ring
Rope
Rossweisse
Runes

Schwertleite
Serf, see Slave
Serpent, see Dragon
Shaft, see Spear
She-Wolf, see Wolf
Shield
Siegfried
Sieglinde

Siegmund

Siegrune

Sin

Sintolt

Slave (Serf)

Snake, see Dragon

Spear (Shaft, Spearpoint, Spearshaft)

Spell, see Magic

Spring (Springtime)

Spring (Well)

Star

Stronghold, see Valhalla

Sun (Sunlight)

Sword (see also Notung)

Tarnhelm (Fine-Wrought Gold, Helmet)

Throne

Toad

Toy, see Gold

Traitor, see Treachery

Treachery (Treason, Traitor)

Treason, see Treachery

Treasure, see Hoard

Treaty (Alliance, Bargain, Bond,
    Compact, Contract, Covenant, Pact)

Tree, see Ash Tree

Trinket, see Gold

Twilight (Dusk)

Twins

Valhalla (Castle, Fort, Fortress,
    Stronghold)

Valkyrie (Valkyriehood)

Volse (see also Father, Wanderer, Wotan)

Volsung

Vow, see Oath

Wala, see Erda

Waltraute

Wanderer (see also Father, Volse, Wotan)

Warfather, see Father

Water Maidens, see Rhine Daughters

Watery Brood, see Rhine Daughters

Wedding

Well, see Spring

Wellgunde

West

Wind

Winter

Wittig

Woeful

Woglinde

Wolf (She-Wolf, Wolf-Cub, Wolfskin)

Woman's Worth (Woman's Beauty,
    Woman's Grace)

World Ash Tree, see Ash Tree

Wotan (see also Father, Volse, Wanderer)

ADULTERY (Cuckold)

If you grant respectability to adultery, then go on boasting and sanctify the incestuous fruit of this liaison between twins.

> Fricka, V-2-i, to Wotan

Laughing you let go your rule over heaven—so as to gratify the mere pleasure and whim of those monstrous twins, your adultery's dissolute fruit.

> Fricka, V-2-i, to Wotan

Unceasingly you have cuckolded your faithful wife.

> Fricka, V-2-i, to Wotan

ALBERICH

Only one I saw who had forsworn love: for shining gold he had renounced woman's affection. . . . The Nibelung, night-Alberich, moped in vain for the maidens' favors.

> Loge, R-ii, to the gods

Alberich did not hesitate; boldly he gained the power of the spell: the ring became his.

　　Loge, R-ii, to Wotan

Alberich guards himself with guile; you must act shrewdly and subtly to bring the thief to justice and to return to the Rhinemaidens the gold, their shining toy; for that is what they beg of you.

　　Loge, R-ii, to Wotan

Nibelungs all, bow down to Alberich! . . . Listen for him, he is near, the Lord of the Nibelungs!

　　Alberich, R-iii, exulting in the power of the Tarnhelm

Alberich wrought for himself a golden ring from the Rhine's gold: . . . with it he has overcome us, the Nibelung's nocturnal race.

　　Mime, R-iii, to Wotan and Loge

[Alberich] bade me forge and weld for him a helmet: he gave exact orders how I was to make it . . . I wanted to keep the helmet for myself, and through its spell escape from Alberich's sway . . . snatch the ring from him, so that, as I now am a menial to this bully, I might be free and he my slave!

　　Mime, R-iii, to Loge

Beware! Alberich draws near.

　　Mime, R-iii, to Loge and Wotan

From Nibelheim's land of night we have heard new rumors: mighty marvels Alberich works here: greed drove us here as guests to gorge on them.

　　Wotan, R-iii, to Alberich

Faced with Alberich's work, who would not feel wonder?

　　Loge, R-iii, flattering the dwarf

Ha ha ha! Good Alberich! Good you villain! How quickly the dwarf turned to a monstrous dragon!

　　Wotan, R-iii, laughing at Alberich's serpent

Well now! Alberich has left you everything: now, bullies, loosen my bonds!

　　Alberich, R-iv, to Wotan and Loge

Born of night the fearful Nibelung Alberich broke night's bonds: he cursed love and through his curse won the glittering Rhinegold.

　　Wotan, V-2-ii, his narrative

Listen carefully what the Wala warned me of. Through Alberich's army our end is looming.

　　Wotan, V-2-ii, his narrative

I touched Alberich's ring: greedily I held his gold. The curse from which I fled still has not left me: I must forsake what I love.

　　Wotan, V-2-ii, his narrative

Only one thing I want now: the end, the end! And for that end Alberich is working.

　　Wotan, V-2-ii, his narrative

[Fafner] changed himself into the form of a dragon. In a cave he keeps watch over Alberich's ring.

    Schwertleite, V-3-i, to Brünnhilde and Sieglinde

In the earth's depths dwell the Nibelungs: Nibelheim is their land . . . . Black Alberich once ruled as their lord!

    Wotan, S-1-ii, answering Mime's first question

Even Alberich, who once thrust me in thrall, I now can compel to dwarf-drudgery; I shall go down there again as lord of the Nibelungs; the whole host shall be my slaves!

    Mime, S-1-iii, planning his revenge

Black Alberich, are you lurking here? Are you guarding Fafner's lair?

    The Wanderer, S-2-i, arriving at Neidhöhle

Well, Alberich, that went astray.

    The Wanderer, S-2-i, after the dwarf asks Fafner for the ring

How else could I seize the spoils, since Alberich is also after it? Now, my Volsung, you wolf's son! Drink and choke yourself to death!

    Mime, S-2-iii, revealing his heart to Siegfried

He whom I chose . . . has gained the Nibelung's ring . . . his nobility will quell Alberich's curse.

    The Wanderer, S-3-i, to Erda

Alberich once stole the Rhinegold. Do you know what happened to him?

    First Norn, T-Prologue

Gnome-father, fallen prince! Guardian of night, Lord of the Nibelungs! Alberich, hear me! Bid the Nibelung host once more obey you, Lord of the ring!

    Hagen, T-2-v, concluding T-2

ALLIANCE, see Treaty
APPLES, see Golden Apples

ASH TREE (Primeval Ash, Tree [Esche], World Ash Tree)
What is that bursting from the ash-tree's trunk? . . . Even the old ash-tree's trunk shone in a golden glow.

    Siegmund, V-1-iii, alone in Hunding's hut

A sword flashed in [the stranger's] hand. This he thrust into the tree [Esche] trunk.

    Sieglinde, V-1-iii, to Siegmund

Siegmund, where are you? . . . Your sword shatters in pieces. The tree [Esche] topples, the trunk breaks.

    Sieglinde, V-2-iii, hearing Hunding's dogs approaching

From the holiest branch of the primeval ash [Wotan] cut himself a shaft.

    The Wanderer, S-1-ii, to Mime

Notung is the name of the sword; Wotan thrust it into an ash-tree's trunk.

    Mime, S-1-ii, answering the Wanderer's second question

I burned the brown ash-tree to charcoal that now lies heaped on the hearth.

    Siegfried, S-1-iii, at the bellows

At the world ash-tree once I wove . . . In its cool shadow bubbled a spring . . . An intrepid god came to drink at the spring.

    First Norn, T-Prologue

From the world ash-tree Wotan then broke off a branch, a spearshaft the mighty one cut from the trunk. . . . The tree decayed and died, sadly the water dwindled in the well . . . So today I weave at the world ash-tree no more, and the fir must suffice me to fasten the rope.

    First Norn, T-Prologue

Then Wotan bade Valhalla's heroes hack to pieces the withered boughs of the world-ash . . . The ash-tree fell, the spring dried up forever! Today I fasten the rope to the jagged rock.

    Second Norn, T-Prologue

Still soars the stronghold the giants built, in its hall sits Wotan with his sacred clan of gods and heroes. A huge pile of logs is heaped up around the hall: this was once the world-ash!

    Third Norn, T-Prologue

The shattered spear's sharp splinters Wotan will one day plunge deep into the heart of the glow . . . And this the god will fling at the world-ash's piled-up logs.

    Third Norn, T-Prologue

He held the splinters of his spear: a hero had shattered the shaft. . . . He sent the nobles of Valhalla to the forest to fell the world-ash.

    Waltraute, T-1-iii, her narrative

ATONEMENT

Blood shall flow in torrents in full atonement to a friend!

    Gunther and Siegfried, T-1-i, swearing the consequences if the oath is broken

Brünnhilde, valiant woman, do you really recognize the ring? If it is that which you gave to Gunther, then it is his, and Siegfried obtained it by trickery, for which the traitor must atone.

    Hagen, T-2-iv

BARGAIN, see Treaty

BATTLEFATHER, see Father

BEAR (Bearskin, Bruin)

Why bring in a bear?

    Mime, S-1-i, to Siegfried

Bruin, ask for the sword!

    Siegfried, S-1-i, to Mime

On your way, Bruin: I don't need you now.

    Siegfried, S-1-i, to Mime

I suffer it gladly when you slay bears; but why bring a live beast home?

    Mime, S-1-i, to Siegfried

Out of the bushes came a bear, growling as he listened to me.

    Siegfried, S-1-i

Well, now listen to my horn. . . . Nothing better has yet come than wolf or bear. Now let me see what it will bring me; perhaps a dear companion!

    Siegfried, S-2-ii, to the Wood Bird

I slew a giant dragon for that ring: shall I give it to you now in exchange for a paltry bearskin?

    Siegfried, T-3-i, to the Rhine Daughters

BLOOD-BROTHERHOOD

Let the oath be of blood-brotherhood.

    Siegfried, T-1-ii, to Gunther

Glad and free may blood-brotherhood today blossom from our bond!

    Gunther and Siegfried, T-1-ii, having dripped their blood into the drinking horn

Blood-brotherhood I swore to Gunther: Notung, my trusty sword, guarded the oath of loyalty.

    Siegfried, T-2-iv, refuting Brünnhilde

We swore blood-brotherhood!

    Gunther, T-2-v, appalled at the thought of Siegfried's death

BOAR

Tomorrow let us blithely go out hunting: the hero will forge ahead of us: a boar will bring him down.

    Hagen, T-2-v, to Gunther

A wild boar's prey, Siegfried, your dead husband.

    Hagen, T-3-iii, when Gutrune asks what the procession is bringing

Do not reproach me! Complain to Hagen: he is the accursed boar who savaged this noble hero.

    Gunther, T-3-iii, to Gutrune

BOND, see Treaty

BRIDGE (Rainbow Bridge)

Brother, hither! Point out the path over the bridge!

    Donner, R-iv, to Froh

The bridge leads to the fortress, light but firm beneath your feet: boldly tread its terrorless path!

    Froh, R-iv, to the gods

BROTHER-IN-LAW

Where linger my brothers, who should bring help, since my brother-in-law abandons me in my weakness?

    Freia, R-ii

BRUIN, see Bear

BRÜNNHILDE

Brünnhilde must charge into battle, she must see [that] the Volsung wins.
> Wotan, V-2-i, to Brünnhilde

You still respected your wife to make the Valkyrie gang, and even Brünnhilde the bride of your desire, respect me as their sovereign.
> Fricka, V-2-i

Father, father, tell me, what is troubling you? . . . Confide in me, I am loyal to you. Look, Brünnhilde entreats you.
> Brünnhilde, V-2-ii, to Wotan

The world's wisest woman [Erda] bore me you, Brünnhilde. With eight sisters I brought you up; through you Valkyries I wanted to avert what the woman [Wala] told me to fear: a shameful end for the immortals.
> Wotan, V-2-ii, his narrative

As for Brünnhilde, she will regret her crime.
> Wotan, V-2-v, ending Act 2

With that swarthy Volsung Brünnhilde will still be waiting.
> Gerhilde, V-3-i, answering Helmwige's "We are only eight; one is still missing."
> (The German word *braunen* has been translated as "golden" or "tawny" as well as "swarthy.")

Brünnhilde's coming this way, riding furiously.
> Siegrune, V-3-i

Hoyotoho! Brünnhilde, hi!
> The Eight Valkyries, V-3-i

Heiaha, Brünnhilde, can't you hear us?
> Waltraute, V-3-i, as the Valkyrie approaches

From [Sieglinde's] brother Brünnhilde should today have withheld victory.
> Brünnhilde, V-3-i, to the Valkyries

Brünnhilde, terrible! Have you disobeyed Warfather's solemn orders, Brünnhilde?
> Six Valkyries, V-3-i

Brünnhilde, listen to the din of his approach.
> Six Valkyries, V-3-i, after Waltraute has alerted Brünnhilde that Wotan is coming

Stop, Brünnhilde!
> Wotan, V-3-i, as he comes near

Poor Brünnhilde! Vengeance is ablaze.
> All eight Valkyries, V-3-i, as Wotan nears

Where is Brünnhilde, where is the lawbreaker? Do you dare to hide the wicked girl from me?
> Wotan, V-3-ii, to the Valkyries

I know Brünnhilde is hiding from me among you. Shrink from her.
> Wotan, V-3-ii

Do you hear, Brünnhilde? . . . Do you hear my accusations, and do you hide in terror?
  Wotan, V-3-ii, to the hiding girl

Let cowards run away from Brünnhilde's rock!
  Wotan, V-3-iii, conjuring the magic fire

Siegfried now has slain the wicked dwarf! Now I know a wonderful wife for him . . .
Brünnhilde would be his!
  Wood Bird, S-2-iii, to Siegfried

The bride can never be won nor Brünnhilde awakened by a coward; only by one who
knows not fear!
  Wood Bird, S-2-iii, to Siegfried

This very day I vainly strove to learn fear from Fafner: now I burn with longing to learn
it from Brünnhilde.
  Siegfried, S-2-iii, responding to the Wood Bird

You mean the Valkyrie, the maid Brünnhilde? She flouted the father of the storms . . .
What the controller of combats longed to do but restrained himself against his will . . .
Brünnhilde in the brunt of battle—dared to accomplish for herself. The father of con-
flicts punished the maid.
  The Wanderer, S-3-i, to Erda

Brünnhilde, whom you bore me will waken to the hero [and] will do the deed that will
redeem the world.
  The Wanderer, S-3-i, to Erda

Go back yourself, braggart! I must go there, to the burning heart of the blaze, to Brünnhilde!
  Siegfried, S-3-ii, to the Wanderer

The flames that surrounded Brünnhilde's rock now burn within my breast! O woman,
now quench those flames!
  Siegfried, S-3-iii

No god ever came so close to me! . . . Sacrosanct I came from Valhalla! . . . O the shame
. . . He who woke me has wounded me. . . . I am Brünnhilde no more!
  Brünnhilde, S-3-iii

I have not yet broken Brünnhilde's sleep. Awaken, be my woman!
  Siegfried, S-3-iii

Awaken, Brünnhilde! . . . Laugh and live, sweetest delight! Be mine!
  Siegfried, S-3-iii

What you will be, be today! If my arms enfold you and hold you tight . . . then gone
would be the burning doubt whether Brünnhilde is now mine.
  Siegfried, S-3-iii

Brünnhilde lives, Brünnhilde laughs! Hail to the world in which Brünnhilde lives! She
is awake, alive, smiling at me. Effulgent shines Brünnhilde's star upon me!
  Siegfried, S-3-iii

With the spear's powerful point Wotan bade [Loge] burn round Brünnhilde's rock.
  Second Norn, T-Prologue

One thing I have grasped—that Brünnhilde lives for me; one lesson I have easily learned—to think of Brünnhilde!

    Siegfried, T-Prologue, to Brünnhilde

To win Brünnhilde!

    Siegfried, T-Prologue, explaining why he came through the flames

To waken Brünnhilde!

    Siegfried, T-Prologue, explaining why he tore off the maid's helmet

Think of the vows that unite us . . . then Brünnhilde will burn forever like a sacred flame in your breast!

    Brünnhilde, T-Prologue, to Siegfried

Now for the ring take my horse! . . . Grane fearlessly will follow you . . . often give Grane Brünnhilde's greeting!

    Brünnhilde, T-Prologue, to Siegfried

Sheltered by your shield, I can no longer count myself Siegfried, I am but Brünnhilde's arm.

    Siegfried, T-Prologue, to Brünnhilde

Could Brünnhilde but be your soul!

    Brünnhilde, T-Prologue, to Siegfried

Then you would be Siegfried and Brünnhilde.

    Brünnhilde, T-Prologue

Hail, Brünnhilde, radiant star!

    Siegfried, T-Prologue

Only he who breaks through the fire can be Brünnhilde's suitor.

    Hagen, T-1-i, to Gunther

Only [Siegfried] can win Brünnhilde?

    Gunther, T-1-i, to Hagen

If Siegfried brought home the bride to you, could Brünnhilde not be yours?

    Hagen, T-1-i, to Gunther

Brünnhilde!

    Hagen, T-1-ii, in an aside, after Siegfried tells him what was taken from the hoard: "A ring. . . . A wondrous woman keeps it."

Brünnhilde, to you I offer this first drink to faithful love!

    Siegfried, T-1-ii, as he drinks Gutrune's potion, unheard by the others

Only he who breaks through the fire . . . can be Brünnhilde's suitor.

    Gunther, T-1-ii, to Siegfried

I will bring you Brünnhilde.

    Siegfried, T-1-ii, to Gunther

Sailing off to woo Brünnhilde.

    Hagen, T-1-ii, telling Gutrune where Gunther and Siegfried are going

Brünnhilde! Sister! Are you asleep or awake?

    Waltraute, T-1-iii, calling ahead

Are you so brave as to offer Brünnhilde greeting without fear?
> Brünnhilde, T-1-iii, to Waltraute

For love of Brünnhilde you were bold enough to break the Father of Battle's ban?
> Brünnhilde, T-1-iii, to Waltraute

I pressed myself to [Wotan's] breast: then his fixed stare softened—he was thinking of you, Brünnhilde.
> Waltraute, T-1-iii, her narrative

Brünnhilde! A suitor has come whom your fire did not affright.
> Siegfried (as Gunther), T-1-iii

Now you are mine, Brünnhilde, Gunther's bride—now grant me your cave!
> Siegfried (as Gunther), T-1-iii, to Brünnhilde

From Brünnhilde's rock. There I drew the breath with which I called to you, so quick was my journey!
> Siegfried, T-2-ii, answering Hagen's "Hey, Siegfried, swift hero! Where have you stormed in from?"

Then you procured Brünnhilde?
> Hagen, T-2-ii, to Siegfried

I'll tell you both how I mastered Brünnhilde.
> Siegfried, T-2-ii, to Hagen and Gutrune

Is Brünnhilde following my brother?
> Gutrune, T-2-ii, to Siegfried

Did Brünnhilde take you for Gunther?
> Gutrune, T-2-ii, to Siegfried, who answers, "I resembled him to a hair: the Tarnhelm accomplished it, as Hagen rightly foretold."

Brünnhilde submitted to her husband throughout the bridal night. . . . Siegfried remained here with Gutrune.
> Siegfried, T-2-ii

Yet Brünnhilde was at his side?
> Gutrune, T-2-ii

Between east and west there lies the north: so near and so far was Brünnhilde.
> Siegfried, T-2-ii, pointing to his sword

Welcome Gunther's bride! Brünnhilde approaches with him.
> Hagen, T-2-iii, to the vassals

Home to the Rhine I bring you Brünnhilde, rarest of women. A nobler wife was never won. The race of Gibichungs was granted grace by the gods.
> Gunther, T-2-iv, presenting Brünnhilde

Two happy couples I see here on show: Brünnhilde and Gunther, Gutrune and Siegfried!
> Gunther, T-2-iv

What troubles Brünnhilde's brow?
> Siegfried, T-2-iv

Brünnhilde, valiant woman, do you really recognize the ring? If it is that which you gave to Gunther, then it is his, and Siegfried obtained it by trickery, for which the traitor must atone.
> Hagen, T-2-iv

Holy gods, rulers of heaven! . . . Cause Brünnhilde to break her heart, if only it will destroy her betrayer!
> Brünnhilde, T-2-iv

Brünnhilde, my bride! Restrain yourself!
> Gunther, T-2-iv

Brünnhilde's ring!
> Gunther, T-2-v, after Hagen tells him that he will have immense power if he
> obtains the ring

Is Brünnhilde causing him concern?
> Siegfried, T-3-ii, to Hagen, noting Gunther's gloominess

[The bird] still sat there and sang: ". . . Now I know a wonderful wife for him . . . he who can break through the blaze . . . Brünnhilde would be his." . . . How ardently was I enfolded in Brünnhilde's arms!
> Siegfried, T-3-ii, his narrative

Brünnhilde, holy bride! . . . Your wakener came and kissed you awake . . . Brünnhilde laughed in delight at him! . . . Sweet passing, blessed terror: Brünnhilde bids me welcome!
> Siegfried, T-3-ii, as he dies

Brünnhilde's laughter wakened me. Who was that woman I saw walking to the river bank? Brünnhilde frightens me! Is she at home? Brünnhilde! Brünnhilde! Her room is empty. Then it was she that I saw going to the Rhine!
> Gutrune, T-3-iii

Brünnhilde, black with jealousy! You brought this disaster on us!
> Gutrune, T-3-iii

Curses on you, Hagen . . . Suddenly I understand: Brünnhilde was his true love whom the draught drove from his mind!
> Gutrune, T-3-iii

Stack stout logs for me in piles there by the shore of the Rhine. . . . My own body longs to share the hero's holiest honor. Fulfill Brünnhilde's request.
> Brünnhilde, T-3-iii, immolation scene

Fly home, you ravens! Recount to your master what you have heard here by the Rhine! Pass by Brünnhilde's rock: direct Loge, who still blazes there, to Valhalla; for the end of the gods is nigh. Thus do I throw this torch at Valhalla's vaulting towers.
> Brünnhilde, T-3-iii, immolation scene

BRUNO
Quiet, Bruno [Brauner]! Don't disturb the peace.
> Helmwige, V-3-i, to her horse

CASTLE, see Valhalla

CHEERFUL
I can't call myself "Peaceful"; I wish I were called "Cheerful"; but "Woeful" has to be my name.
>   Siegmund, V-1-ii, to Sieglinde

CHILDREN OF THE RHINE, see Rhine Daughters
COMPACT, see Treaty
CONTRACT, see Treaty
COVENANT, see Treaty
CUCKOLD, see Adultery

CURSE
Hear me, ye waves: thus I curse love!
>   Alberich, R-i, to the Rhine Daughters

Hold firm to your bond! . . . I will curse all your wisdom if openly, honorably and freely you do not know to keep faith in your bond!
>   Fasolt, R-ii, to Wotan

[The ring] is easily won now without cursing love.
>   Froh, R-ii

Must . . . my curse serve but for your pleasure? Take heed, haughty god!
>   Alberich, R-iv, when Wotan demands the ring

Since by curse it came to me, accursed be this ring! . . . Keep it now, guard it well; my curse you cannot escape!
>   Alberich, R-iv, when he has lost the ring

Yield, Wotan, yield! Escape from the ring's curse.
>   Erda, R-iv

Terrible now I find the curse's power.
>   Wotan, R-iv, when Fafner has killed Fasolt

Born of night the fearful Nibelung Alberich broke night's bonds: he cursed love and through his curse won the glittering Rhinegold.
>   Wotan, V-2-ii, his narrative

He who cursed love . . . could cruelly use the spell of the ring for all noble people's unending disgrace.
>   Wotan, V-2-ii, his narrative, referring to Alberich

I touched Alberich's ring: greedily I held his gold. The curse from which I fled still has not left me: I must forsake what I love.
>   Wotan, V-2-ii, his narrative

Be off! Keep clear of the curse upon me. . . . I belonged to a man who obtained me without love. I am accursed.
>   Sieglinde, V-2-iii, to Siegmund

If, on account of our escape, I am not to curse you, maiden, then hear my solemn plea: plunge your sword into my heart.
>   Sieglinde, V-3-i, to Brünnhilde

Stop father! Stop your curse! Must the maiden wither and die for this man? Hear our entreaty! Terrible god, spare her this lamentable disgrace.

The Eight Valkyries, V-3-ii

Doomed to death through my curse is he who guards the treasure.

Alberich, S-2-i, to the Wanderer

[Siegfried's] nobility will quell Alberich's curse, for fear remains foreign to him.

The Wanderer, S-3-i, to Erda

I see the Nibelung's ring rise: an avenging curse gnaws at my strands.

Second Norn, T-Prologue

"If [Brünnhilde] would return the ring to the Rhine's daughters in its depths, from the weight of the curse would the gods and the world be free."

Waltraute, T-1-iii, her narrative, quoting Wotan

Valhalla and Nibelheim bow before him. Even my curse is blunted on that fearless hero: for he does not know the ring's value.

Alberich, T-2-i

Glad you will then feel if we free you from [the ring's] curse.

Rhine Daughters, T-3-i, to Siegfried

[He who fashioned the ring] laid on it a curse into all eternity to doom to death whoever wears it.

Rhine Daughters, T-3-i

Only [the Rhine's] waters can wash away the curse!

Rhine Daughters, T-3-i

Siegfried! . . . Beware! Avoid the curse! Nightly the weaving Norns twisted it into the rope of primeval law.

Rhine Daughters, T-3-i

My sword shattered a spear: even if they wove wild curses into it, Notung will sever for the Norns the eternal rope of primeval law.

Siegfried, T-3-i, to the Rhine Daughters

A dragon indeed once warned me of the curse, but did not teach me to fear it.

Siegfried, T-3-i, to the Rhine Daughters

Curses on you, Hagen, for suggesting to me the potion that snatched away [Brünnhilde's] husband.

Gutrune, T-3-iii

O you, heavenly custodian of oaths! . . . Hear my lament, mighty god! . . . You sacrificed [Siegfried] to the curse which had fallen on you.

Brünnhilde, T-3-iii, immolation scene

Accursed ring, terrible ring, I take your gold and now I give it away. . . . You swimming daughters of the Rhine, I thank you for your good counsel. . . . The fire that consumes me shall cleanse the ring from the curse! . . . Keep pure the gleaming gold that was disastrously stolen from you.

Brünnhilde, T-3-iii, immolation scene

DAY (Daylight)

There stands what we raised, brightly shining in the light of day: now pass in and pay us our fee!

> Fasolt, R-ii, to Wotan

Beware the nocturnal host when the Nibelung horde rises from the silent depths to the daylight!

> Alberich, R-iii, to Wotan

I hear [the Nibelungs] hauling the hoard from the depths to the daylight.

> Alberich, R-iv, to Wotan

A dark day dawns for the gods.

> Erda, R-iv, warning Wotan

Tomorrow arm yourself with stout weapons. I choose the day for fighting.

> Hunding, V-1-ii, to Siegmund

Night and darkness closed my eyes; then the blaze of her look fell on me: I knew warmth and daylight.

> Siegmund, V-1-iii, to himself

What I hid in my heart, what I am, bright as day it came to me . . . when in frosty lonely strangeness I saw my friend.

> Sieglinde, V-1-iii, to Siegmund

Volse promised me that in deepest distress I should one day find [the sword].

> Siegmund, V-1-iii

Are you trying to delude me, who day and night have been dogging your heels?

> Fricka, V-2-i, to Wotan

At last cheerful daylight smiles on me, now that the loathsome dwarf has left me.

> Siegfried, S-2-ii, to himself

Hail to thee, glorious day!

> Brünnhilde, S-3-iii, as she awakens

Emerge from the darkness and see: the day shines bright in the sun!

> Siegfried, S-3-iii, to Brünnhilde

Bright in the sun shines the day of my shame!

> Brünnhilde, S-3-iii, in reply to Siegfried

Hail to the day that gleams about us!

> Siegfried, S-3-iii

Is day dawning already?

> Second Norn, T-Prologue

Does day dawn?

> First Norn, T-Prologue

[So shall you be slain] and this very day.

> Rhine Daughters, T-3-i, to Siegfried

Three wild water-birds . . . sang to me there on the Rhine that this very day I should be slain.

> Siegfried, T-3-ii, to Hagen

DIVINITY, see God

DONNER

Donner, help! Come hither!
>Freia, R-ii, first mention of Donner

Donner and Froh, they are dreaming of food and shelter!
>Loge, R-ii, to the gods

From your hand, Donner, the hammer falls!
>Loge, R-ii, as Donner weakens in Freia's absence

Down, Donner! Roar where it helps, here your din avails you nothing.
>Fafner, R-iv, to the threatening Donner

Vapors to me! Donner, your master, summons you to his host. As I swing my hammer, hover here, misty moisture, hanging haze! Donner, your master, summons you.
>Donner, R-iv

You must kill a boar for Froh, and sacrifice a full-grown goat to Donner, but slaughter sheep for Fricka, that she may bless the marriage!
>Hagen, T-2-ii, to the vassals

Help, Donner! Roar forth in storm to silence this shameful infamy!
>Vassals, T-2-iv, in an uproar over Brünnhilde's accusation that Siegfried has broken his oath

DRAGON (Serpent, Snake)

Giant snake, curl and coil!
>Alberich, R-iii, commanding the Tarnhelm to change his shape

Terrible serpent, do not swallow me! Spare Loge's life!
>Loge, R-iii, feigning terror

Ha ha ha! Good Alberich! Good you villain! How quickly the dwarf turned to a monstrous dragon!
>Wotan, R-iii, laughs at Alberich's serpent

You swiftly made yourself into a giant snake; now that I have seen it I readily believe the marvel.
>Loge, R-iii, to Alberich

How like my wife she is! That snaky shiftiness gleams out of his eyes as well.
>Hunding, V-1-ii, to himself

[Fafner] changed himself into the form of a dragon. In a cave he keeps watch over Alberich's ring.
>Schwertleite, V-3-i

Only with the Wotan sword will a brave but stupid boy, Siegfried, slay the dragon.
>Mime, S-1-ii, answering the Wanderer

The dragon is after me. Fafner, Fafner!
>Mime, S-1-iii, to himself, in terror

I know an evil dragon who has killed and devoured many men.
>Mime, S-1-iii, to Siegfried

How will [Siegfried] slay the dragon if he does learn fear from it?
    Mime, S-1-iii

When [Siegfried] is weary from warring with the dragon, a drink will refresh him.
    Mime, S-1-iii, preparing the drugged drink

Is the dragon's destroyer at hand?
    Alberich, S-2-i

There lies the dragon. . . . Fafner, Fafner, dragon, waken!
    The Wanderer, S-2-i

Waken, Fafner! Waken, dragon!
    Alberich, S-2-i

Do you see that dark cavern's mouth there? In it dwells a dreadful savage dragon.
    Mime, S-2-ii, to Siegfried

So that his venomous saliva shan't harm me, I'll keep to the side of the dragon.
    Siegfried, S-2-ii

A serpent's tail he twists about him.
    Mime, S-2-ii

Tell me this: has the dragon a heart?
    Siegfried, S-2-ii, to Mime

Certainly, boy, the dragon's lies there, too.
    Mime, S-2-ii, explaining to Siegfried that Fafner's heart lies where it does in all
    men or beasts.

You must hear and see the dragon itself, then your senses will reel!
    Mime, S-2-ii, to Siegfried

When the sun is high, look out for the dragon.
    Mime, S-2-ii, to Siegfried

Mime, if you wait at the spring, I'll certainly let the dragon go there. I'll thrust Notung
into his guts only after he's gulped you down, too.
    Siegfried, S-2-ii

In your death, dragon, you seem wise.
    Siegfried, S-2-ii

The dreaded dragon—didn't you kill it?
    Mime, S-2-iii, to Siegfried

More than the dragon I hate the one who made me kill it!
    Siegfried, S-2-iii, to Mime

Lie there, too, grisly dragon.
    Siegfried, S-2-iii, pushing Fafner's body in front of the cave

That was the effect of a savage dragon's blood that I killed at Neidhöhle.
    Siegfried, S-3-ii, explaining to the Wanderer why he can understand the Wood
    Bird

I slew a savage dragon who grimly had long guarded [the ring].
    Siegfried, T-Prologue, to Brünnhilde

A gigantic dragon guarded the Nibelung's hoard at Neidhöhle: Siegfried closed its ravening jaws and slew it with his conquering sword.

Hagen, T-1-i, to Gunther and Gutrune

This must be he who slew the dragon. It is Siegfried, certainly no other!

Hagen, T-1-i, as Siegfried approaches

I almost forgot the treasure, so poorly do I prize its possession! I left it in a cavern where once a dragon guarded it.

Siegfried, T-1-ii

Wotan's spear was split by the Volsung who slew the dragon Fafner in combat and innocently gained the ring.

Alberich, T-2-i, to Hagen

Not strong enough, indeed, to oppose the dragon, which was destined for the Volsung alone, but to inexorable hate I bred Hagen, who now shall avenge me and obtain the ring in defiance of the Volsung and Wotan!

Alberich, T-2-i

The dragon-killer overcame the danger: the hero Siegfried kept him safe.

Hagen, T-2-iii, to the vassals

From no woman did the ring come to me . . . I know it well as the prize of the battle I once fought at Neidhöhle, when I slew the fierce dragon.

Siegfried, T-2-iv

I slew a giant dragon for that ring: shall I give it to you now in exchange for a paltry bearskin?

Siegfried, T-3-i, to the Rhine Daughters

As you slew the dragon . . .

Flosshilde, T-3-i, to Siegfried, explaining with Wellgunde that he too will be slain if he does not return the ring

A dragon indeed once warned me of the curse, but did not teach me to fear it.

Siegfried, T-3-i, to the Rhine Daughters

Mime was the name of a surly dwarf [who brought me up to] kill for him a dragon in the forest who sluggishly guarded a treasure there.

Siegfried, T-3-ii, his narrative

I killed the dragon Fafner. . . . From the dragon's blood . . . I could straightaway understand what the birds were singing.

Siegfried, T-3-ii, his narrative

DREAM

Up, leave dreams' delightful deceit!

Fricka, R-ii, to Wotan

As in my dreams I desired it, as my will directed, strong and fair it stands on show, sublime, superb structure!

Wotan, R-ii, beholding Valhalla

Donner and Froh, they are dreaming of food and shelter.

Loge, R-ii

Does a mist deceive me? Does a dream mock me?
> Loge, R-ii, as the gods fade in Freia's absence

A dream of love comes to my mind as well: burning with longing I have seen you before.
> Siegmund, V-1-iii, to Sieglinde

[Sieglinde] seems lifeless though she is alive: her sorrow is soothed by a smiling dream.
> Siegmund, V-2-v

My sleep is dreaming, my dreaming meditation.
> Erda, S-1-i, responding to Wotan

So now in sleep close your eyes: in dream behold my downfall!
> The Wanderer, S-3-i, to Erda

[Wotan] sighed deeply, closed his eyes, and as if in a dream whispered these words: "If [Brünnhilde] would return the ring to the Rhine's daughters in its depths, from the weight of the curse would the gods and the world be free."
> Waltraute, T-1-iii, to Brünnhilde

What tales of tortured dreams do you tell in such distress?
> Brünnhilde, T-1-iii, to Waltraute

Bad dreams disturbed my sleep.
> Gutrune, T-3-iii

DUSK, see Twilight

EAGLE
An eagle has swooped down to tear me to pieces!
> Brünnhilde, T-1-iii, seized with horror at the figure of Gunther

EARTH MOTHER, see Mother

EAST (Eastward)
Which of you sisters has flown eastwards?
> Brünnhilde, V-3-i, to the Valkyries

Away to the east stretches a forest.
> Siegrune, V-3-i

Hurry away, then, toward the east.
> Brünnhilde, V-3-i, to Sieglinde

Neidhöhle it is named, to the east, on the fringe of the forest.
> Mime, S-1-iii, to Siegfried

EEL
Well, if my skin revolts you, flirt with the eels!
> Alberich, R-i, to Wellgunde

ERDA (Wala)
The eternal world's first ancestress [Welt Ur-Wala], Erda, warns you.
> Erda, R-iv, answering Wotan's question, "Who is this woman who threatens?"

Dread and fear fetter my mind; how to end it Erda must teach me.
    Wotan, R-iv

Erda, the sacred and wisest of women [Wala], told me to give up the ring . . . As a god
I longed for knowledge. . . . With the magic of love I overpowered the woman [Wala],
brought down her pride in wisdom, and she talked to me.
    Wotan, V-2-ii, his narrative

The world's wisest woman [Erda] bore me you, Brünnhilde. With eight sisters I brought
you up; through you Valkyries I wanted to avert what the woman [Wala] told me to
fear: a shameful end for the immortals.
    Wotan, V-2-ii, his narrative

Listen carefully to what the Wala warned me of. Through Alberich's army our end is
looming.
    Wotan, V-2-ii, his narrative

Only one thing I want now: the end, the end! And for that end Alberich is working. Now
I understand the hidden meaning of the wise woman's [Wala's] words.
    Wotan, V-2-ii, his narrative

Waken, Wala! Wala, awake! . . . Erda! Erda! Eternal woman! From your hollow home rise
to the heights! . . . Erda! Erda! Eternal woman! Waken, awake! Wala! Awake!
    The Wanderer, S-3-i

To Wotan I bore a wish-maiden . . . why do you wake me, and not seek enlightenment
from Erda and Wotan's child?
    Erda, S-3-i, to the Wanderer

Why did you come and disturb the Wala's sleep?
    Erda, S-3-i, to the Wanderer

Whatever now befalls, to the ever-young the god gladly yields. Descend then, Erda,
mother of fear.
    The Wanderer, S-3-i

EYE (Eyelids)
Now [the waking sun] kisses [the gold's] eyes to open them.
    Flosshilde, R-i, as the sunlight spreads through the water

Does the gnome know nothing of the eyes of gold, which in turn wake and sleep?
    Wellgunde, R-i, to Alberich

So as to win you for my wife I sacrificed [put at risk] one of my eyes to woo you.
    Wotan, R-ii, to Fricka

Sleep softly sealed your eyes while we two, unsleeping, built the fort.
    Fasolt, R-ii, to Wotan

The light has faded from your eyes!
    Loge, R-ii, as the gods wither in Freia's absence

Hand and head, eye and ear are not more my own than this shining ring!
    Alberich, R-iv, to Wotan

The stars of her eyes still shine on me. . . . So long as I see those lovely eyes I cannot
tear myself away from the woman.
    Fasolt, R-iv, seeing Freia through the gold

The sun's eye sheds its evening beams; in its glorious gleam the castle shines in splendor.
    Wotan, R-iv, beholding Valhalla

He is still breathing; he's only closed his eyes.
    Sieglinde, V-1-i, discovering Siegmund

My eyes enjoy the blessed pleasure of what I see.
    Siegmund, V-1-i, seeing Sieglinde for the first time

Night fell on my eyelids, but now the sun shines on me anew.
    Siegmund, V-1-i, to Sieglinde

That snaky shiftiness gleams out of [Siegmund's] eyes as well.
    Hunding, V-1-ii, to himself

What is the light bursting from the ash-tree's trunk? My eyes are blinded by the flashing light. . . . Night and darkness closed my eyes; then the blaze of her look fell on me. . . . Then the blossom faded, the light went out. Night and darkness close my eyes: deep in the recesses of my heart an invisible fire burns on.
    Siegmund, V-1-iii, to himself

[The stranger's] hat was pulled down so as to cover one eye. But the glint of the other made them all afraid . . . To me alone his eye suggested sweet, longing sadness.
    Sieglinde, V-1-iii, her narrative

Through woods and meadows [spring's] breath blows, wide open its eyes are smiling.
    Siegmund, V-1-iii, the Spring Song

When my eyes saw you, you belonged to me.
    Sieglinde, V-1-iii, to Siegmund

O let me come close up to you and clearly see the noble light that shines in your eyes.
    Sieglinde, V-1-iii, to Siegmund

Rapturously my eyes gloat on you.
    Siegmund, V-1-iii, to Sieglinde

I've set eyes on you before. . . . The fire in your eyes has blazed at me before.
    Sieglinde, V-1-iii, to Siegmund

Into the depths and up to the heights, everywhere you looked with lecherous eyes to see how your changing fancy might be gratified.
    Fricka, V-2-i, to Wotan

Where are you, Siegmund? . . . Let the stars in your eyes shine on me once again.
    Sieglinde, V-2-iii, hysterically

Oh, speak, father. Look me in the eyes. Silence your rage, control your anger.
    Brünnhilde, V-3-iii, to Wotan

Because my eyes are yours I held to the one thing which the alternative forced you in a painful dilemma summarily to turn your back on.
    Brünnhilde, V-3-iii, to Wotan

I saw Siegmund's eyes . . . my eyes beheld what deep in my breast my heart sensed with noble throbbing.
    Brünnhilde, V-3-iii

If I must lose you whom I loved . . . laughing joy of my eyes: then a bridal fire shall burn for you, as it never burned for any bride! . . . That bright pair of eyes that often I fondled with smiles, . . . that radiant pair of eyes that often in tempests blazed at me . . . for the last time let them delight me today with farewell's last kiss! May their star shine for that happier man: for the luckless immortal they must close in parting. For thus the god departs from you, thus he kisses your godhead away!

> Wotan, V-3-iii, to Brünnhilde, whom he kisses long on the eyes

As soon as I set eyes on you, I see that all you do is evil.

> Siegfried, S-1-i, to Mime

My ears do not believe you. I'll credit only the evidence of my eyes: what proof supports your story?

> Siegfried, S-1-i, when Mime tells him of his birth

To protect myself from his swishing tail I'll keep my eyes on the brute [Fafner].

> Siegfried, S-2-ii, to Mime

With drooping ears and bleary eyes—away with the goblin! I never want to see him again.

> Siegfried, S-2-ii, on Mime

Like the roedeer's surely shone her soft lustrous eyes.

> Siegfried, S-2-ii, thinking of his mother

You bright-eyed boy, who do not know yourself, I will tell you whom you have murdered.

> Fafner, S-2-ii, to Siegfried

From the blue heaven [the sun's] eye gazes steeply down on to my head.

> Siegfried, S-2-iii, hot from killing Fafner and Mime

The father of conflicts punished the maid: in her eyes he pressed sleep.

> The Wanderer, S-3-i, to Erda

So now sleep on, close your eyes: in dream behold my downfall!

> The Wanderer, S-3-i, to Erda

But under [your hat] an eye is missing!

> Siegfried, S-3-ii, to the Wanderer

With the eye which is missing from its mate you yourself are looking at the one that remains to me for sight.

> The Wanderer, S-3-ii, to Siegfried

What is that shining in my face? What glittering suit of steel? Are my eyes still dazzled by the flames?

> Siegfried, S-3-iii

A fiery anxiety fills my eyes: my senses swim and swoon! . . . How shall I wake the maid so that she opens her eyes? But when she opens her eyes, will the light dazzle me?

> Siegfried, S-3-iii, discovering Brünnhilde

Hail to the earth that nourished me, that I can see those eyes whose light now delights me!

> Siegfried, S-3-iii, when Brünnhilde awakes

Your eyes alone might see me, you alone might waken me!
        Brünnhilde, S-3-iii, to Siegfried

The light of your eyes is bright to my sight . . . but what your song says to me I cannot understand.
        Siegfried, S-3-iii, to Brünnhilde

My eyes feast on your heavenly mouth, but my lips burn in passionate thirst to seek refreshment in the pasture of your eyes.
        Siegfried, S-3-iii, to Brünnhilde

Doleful darkness clouds my sight: my eyes dim, their light fades.
        Brünnhilde, S-3-iii, in fear at the loss of her wisdom

Night affrights your confined eyes. . . . Emerge from the darkness and see: the day shines bright in the sun!
        Siegfried, S-3-iii, to Brünnhilde

So do not touch me, do not upset me! Ever bright and happy will you then smile out of my eyes into yours.
        Brünnhilde, S-3-iii, to Siegfried

If our eyes kindle, and we breathe each other's breath, eye to eye, mouth to mouth, then you are to me what fearfully you were and will be.
        Siegfried, S-3-iii, to Brünnhilde

As my eyes devour you, are you not blinded?
        Brünnhilde, S-3-iii, to Siegfried

As our glowing eyes scorch one another, as our arms passionately clasp each other, my daring and courage return to me.
        Siegfried, S-3-iii, to Brünnhilde

An intrepid god came to sing at the spring [of wisdom]; one of his eyes he paid as forfeit forever.
        First Norn, T-Prologue

O sacred gods! Supreme beings! Feast your eyes on this dedicated pair!
        Brünnhilde, T-Prologue

You who have seared my sight with your glance, why do you lower your eyes before me? . . . Ah, fairest, maid! Close your eyes: their rays burn the heart in my breast.
        Siegfried, T-1-ii, to Gutrune, after drinking the potion

Are they good runes I read in [Gutrune's] eyes?
        Siegfried, T-1-ii

[Wotan] sighed deeply, closed his eyes, and as if in a dream whispered these words: "If she would return the ring to the Rhine's daughters in its depths, from the weight of the curse would the gods and the world be freed."
        Waltraute, T-1-iii, to Brünnhilde

Empty and idle seems your story to me; in your eyes, so exhausted, glow flickering flames.
        Brünnhilde, T-1-iii, to Waltraute

My eyes grow dim . . .
        Brünnhilde, T-2-iv, fainting

A single flicker of [Siegfried's] flashing eyes such as lighted on me from his lying face, would make your highest courage falter in fear!
>   Brünnhilde, T-2-v, to Hagen

If [Siegfried] let us have [the ring], we would no longer envy your [the sun's] bright eyes.
>   The Three Rhine Daughters, T-3-i

Brünnhilde, holy bride! Awake! Open your eyes! . . . Ah, her eyes, forever open!
>   Siegfried, T-2-ii, as he dies

Dear sister, open your eyes, speak to me!
>   Gunther, T-3-iii, comforting Gutrune

I am his rightful spouse, to whom Siegfried swore eternal vows before ever he set eyes on you.
>   Brünnhilde, T-3-iii, to Gutrune

FAFNER (see also Giants)

Fasolt and Fafner, have you yet felt my hammer's heavy blow?
>   Donner, R-ii, to the giants

I found Fasolt and Fafner reliable: not a stone but was firm in its place.
>   Loge, R-ii, to the gods

From afar Fasolt and Fafner are approaching; they are bringing Freia back.
>   Loge, R-iv, to Wotan

One of the giants, to whom I once gave the accursed gold as payment for work, he, Fafner, guards the treasure for which he slew his brother.
>   Wotan, V-2-ii, his narrative

Away to the east stretches a forest: Fafner carried off the Nibelung treasure into it.
>   Siegrune, V-3-i

Fafner, the fearsome dragon lurks in the dark forest . . . He guards the Nibelung's gold there.
>   Mime, S-1-i, to himself

Siegfried's youthful strength might well destroy Fafner's body: he would win for me the Nibelung's ring.
>   Mime, S-1-i, to himself

How shall I lead this hothead to Fafner's lair?
>   Mime, S-1-i, to himself

Fasolt and Fafner . . . envied the Nibelung's power; they won . . . the ring . . . Fasolt was slain, and as a savage dragon Fafner now guards the gold.
>   The Wanderer, S-1-ii, answering Mime's second question

A wise Nibelung watches over Siegfried, who must slay Fafner for him so that he may gain the ring and become master of the treasure. What sword must Siegfried now flourish, fit for Fafner's death?
>   The Wanderer, S-1-ii, his second question to Mime

Now, Fafner's courageous conqueror, listen, ruined dwarf: "Only one who has never felt fear shall forge Notung anew."
>   Wotan, S-1-ii, to Mime

The dragon is after me. Fafner, Fafner!

> Mime, S-1-iii, to himself, in terror

Fafner will teach you fear if you follow me to his lair.

> Mime, S-1-iii, to Siegfried

[My head] will fall to the boy if Fafner does not teach him fear! . . . How can he gain the ring for me?

> Mime, S-1-iii, watching Siegfried

He'll forge the sword and slay Fafner . . . The treasure and the ring will fall to him: how can I retrieve his gains?

> Mime, S-1-iii, to himself

He's shaping himself a sharp sword to slay Fafner, the dwarf's foe: I've brewed a deceptive draught to trap Siegfried when Fafner falls.

> Mime, S-1-iii, watching Siegfried

In the forest at night I keep watch over Neidhöhle. . . . Is the dragon's destroyer at hand? Is it he who is to slay Fafner?

> Alberich, at the beginning of S-2

Black Alberich, are you lurking here? Are you guarding Fafner's lair?

> The Wanderer, S-2-i, arriving at Neidhöhle

A hero is approaching to rescue the treasure; the Nibelungs crave for the gold; Fafner, who guards the ring, falls.

> The Wanderer, S-2-i, to Alberich

Quarrel with Mime, not me: your brother brings you danger; he is leading here a lad who must kill Fafner for him.

> The Wanderer, S-2-i, to Alberich

Waken, Fafner! Waken, dragon! A mighty hero is approaching to pit himself against your power.

> Alberich, S-2-i, to Fafner

Fafner and Siegfried, Siegfried and Fafner, oh if they'd only kill each other!

> Mime, S-2-ii, to himself

Of the towering race of giants, the brothers Fasolt and Fafner both now are dead. For the accursed gold gained from the gods I dealt death to Fasolt. He who defended the hoard as a dragon, Fafner, last of the giants, has fallen to a fresh-faced hero.

> Fafner, S-2-ii, mortally wounded by Siegfried

Let your beauty serve as witness to today: . . . that I vanquished Fafner in fight.

> Siegfried, S-2-iii, contemplating the ring

Siegfried! . . . The treasure in Fafner's keeping, the gold was what I toiled for.

> Mime, S-2-iii, revealing his heart to Siegfried

This very day I vainly strove to learn fear from Fafner: now I burn with longing to learn it from Brünnhilde.

> Siegfried, S-2-iii, responding to the Wood Bird

Wotan's spear was split by the Volsung who slew the dragon Fafner in combat and innocently gained the ring.

> Alberich, T-2-i, to Hagen

I killed the dragon Fafner. . . . From the dragon's blood . . . I could straightaway understand what the birds were singing.

> Siegfried, T-3-ii, his narrative

FASOLT (see also Giants)
Save me, sister! Protect me, brother! From yonder mountain menacing Fasolt would come to force me, Holda, away.

> Freia, R-ii, her first words

Fasolt and Fafner, have you yet felt my hammer's heavy blow?

> Donner, R-ii, to the giants, on saving Freia

I found Fasolt and Fafner reliable: not a stone but was firm in its place.

> Loge, R-ii, to the gods

From afar Fasolt and Fafner are approaching; they are bringing Freia back.

> Loge, R-iv, to Wotan

Fasolt and Fafner . . . envied the Nibelung's power; they won . . . the ring . . . Fasolt was slain, and as a savage dragon Fafner now guards the gold.

> The Wanderer, S-1-ii, answering Mime's second question

Of the towering race of giants, the brothers Fasolt and Fafner both now are dead. For the accursed gold gained from the gods I dealt death to Fasolt. He who defended the hoard as a dragon, Fafner, last of the giants, has fallen to a fresh-faced hero.

> Fafner, S-2-ii, mortally wounded by Siegfried

FATE
She who granted you a wretched fate, the Norn, did not love you.

> Hunding, V-1-ii, to Siegmund

You, Volsung—listen well to me—you have been chosen by fate.

> Brünnhilde, V-2-iv, when Siegmund refuses to follow her to Valhalla

I made you disposer of fates, but you disposed fate against me.

> Wotan, V-3-ii, to Brünnhilde

If anyone disobeys me and clings to [Brünnhilde] in her sadness—that fool shall share her fate.

> Wotan, V-3-ii, warning the eight Valkyries

Do you want to enjoy my ecstasy and share my fate?

> Brünnhilde, T-1-iii, to Waltraute

FATHER (Battlefather, Warfather; see also Volse, Wanderer, Wotan)
Father warned us of such a foe.

> Flosshilde, R-i, when Alberich appears

Father [told us of the power of the ring], and ordered us to guard the gleaming treasure skillfully.

> Flosshilde, R-i, to her sisters

"Wolf" was my father.

> Siegmund, V-1-ii

Do tell us more, stranger: where is your father now?

> Sieglinde, V-1-ii, to Siegmund

Many of the pursuers fell to the "Wolves". . . . But I was separated from my father. . . . Only a wolfskin I found in the forest. It lay empty before me. I did not find my father.
    Siegmund, V-1-ii

My father promised me a sword . . . Volse, Volse, where is your sword?
    Siegmund, V-1-iii

But did you name Wolf as your father?
    Sieglinde, V-1-iii

If "Volse" was your father and you are a "Volsung" it was for you [the old man] thrust his sword in the tree—so let me call you by the name I love: Siegmund so I name you.
    Sieglinde, V-1-iii

Let me warn you, Father, make ready yourself. You have to withstand a violent storm. Fricka, your wife, approaches in her chariot drawn by rams.
    Brünnhilde, V-2-i

Much as it grieved me I had to bear it when you went into battle with those uncouth girls that a wanton fancy caused you to father.
    Fricka, V-2-i, to Wotan

The father of hosts is waiting for you. Let him tell you what plans he has made.
    Fricka, V-2-i, to Brünnhilde

The outcome made Fricka laugh. Father, what must your child be told?
    Brünnhilde, V-2-ii, to Wotan

Father, father, tell me, what is troubling you? . . . Confide in me, I am loyal to you. Look, Brünnhilde entreats you.
    Brünnhilde, V-2-ii

I have never seen the father of victories like this . . . O my poor Volsung! In your deepest sorrow I, your friend, must disloyally forsake you.
    Brünnhilde, V-2-ii, after Wotan leaves

To the Lord of Battles [Walvater] who chose you I shall lead you. You will follow me to Valhalla.
    Brünnhilde, V-2-iv, to Siegmund

In the hall of Valhalla shall I find Battlefather alone?
    Siegmund, V-2-iv, to Brünnhilde

In Valhalla shall I find Volse, my own father?
    Siegmund, V-2-iv, to Brünnhilde

You will find your father there, Volsung.
    Brünnhilde, V-2-iv, answering Siegfried's question

If only Father would come home! He's still in the woods with the boy. Mother, Mother, I am afraid. The strangers do not look friendly . . . Siegmund, ha!
    Sieglinde, V-2-v, dreaming

Battlefather would give us an angry welcome if he saw us arrive without [Brünnhilde].
    Waltraute, V-3-i, after learning that Brünnhilde is with Siegfried

The father of battles is pursuing me.
    Brünnhilde, V-3-i

Battlefather is chasing you? You're running away from him?
    The Eight Valkyries, V-3-i, to Brünnhilde

Look to the north, see if Warfather is coming.
    Brünnhilde, V-3-i, to the Valkyries

Battlefather is riding his sacred horse.
    Six Valkyries, V-3-i, to Brünnhilde

Brünnhilde, terrible! Have you disobeyed Warfather's solemn orders, Brünnhilde?
    Six Valkyries, V-3-i

There's a wild neighing from Warfather's horse.
    Rossweisse, Grimgerde, and Schwertleite, V-3-i, as Wotan approaches

[My horse] has never run away from Warfather.
    Rossweisse, V-3-i, denying Brünnhilde the use of her horse

I must obey our father.
    Helmwige, V-3-i, to Brünnhilde

Keep for [your unborn son] the sword's fragments. From his father's battlefield I luckily brought them.
    Brünnhilde, V-3-i, to Sieglinde

Father, how have your daughters provoked you into this mad rage?
    The Eight Valkyries, V-3-ii

Here I am, father: pronounce your punishment.
    Brünnhilde, V-3-ii

Stop father! Stop your curse! Must the maiden wither and die for this man? Hear our
entreaty! Terrible god, spare her this lamentable disgrace.
    The Eight Valkyries, V-3-ii

Oh, speak, father. . . . Silence your rage, control your anger, and clearly explain to me
my hidden guilt.
    Brünnhilde, V-3-iii

You have renounced Warfather, he cannot choose for you.
    Wotan, V-3-iii

The father brought food to the nest.
    Siegfried, S-1-i, to Mime on the forest animals

I am both your father and your mother.
    Mime, S-1-i, to Siegfried

A fish never had a toad for a father!
    Siegfried, S-1-i, to Mime

From you I must first discover who are my mother and father?
    Siegfried, S-1-i, to Mime

What father? What mother? Idle question!
    Mime, S-1-i, to Siegfried

Who are my father and mother?
    Siegfried, S-1-i, repeats

I am neither your father nor of your family.
> Mime, S-1-i, admits to Siegfried

Now I ask, what was my father called?
> Siegfried, S-1-i, to Mime

I never saw [your father]. . . . To my care [Sieglinde] entrusted her fatherless child.
> Mime, S-1-i, answering Siegfried

Your mother gave me this . . . a shattered sword! She said your father carried it when he fell in his last fight.
> Mime, S-1-i, to Siegfried

You are not my father . . . I flee from here . . . nevermore, Mime to see you again!
> Siegfried, S-1-i, to Mime

My father's blade befits me well: I'll forge the sword myself.
> Siegfried, S-1-iii, to Mime

Notung, Notung, trusty sword! . . . The steel snapped for my dying father, his living son fashioned it anew.
> Siegfried, S-1-iii, completing the sword

[Mime's] not my father, how glad I am of that. . . . What did my father look like? Ha! Like me, of course!
> Siegfried, S-2-ii

I am so alone. I have no brothers or sisters: my mother is dead, my father was slain: their son never saw them!
> Siegfried, S-2-iii, to the Wood Bird

You mean the Valkyrie, the maid Brünnhilde? She flouted the father of the storms. . . . The father of conflicts punished the maid.
> The Wanderer, S-3-i, to Erda

My father's foe! . . . Flourish your spear: my sword will smash it to pieces!
> Siegfried, S-3-ii, to the Wanderer

Be glad, o hero, as you greet my father's hall.
> Gunther, T-1-ii, welcoming Siegfried

I can offer neither land nor people, nor father's house . . . All I have is a sword . . . May the sword be witness to my oath! I offer it with myself in alliance.
> Siegfried, T-1-ii, to Gunther

For love of Brünnhilde, you were bold enough to break the Father of Battle's ban?
> Brünnhilde, T-1-iii, to Waltraute

No more to war has Wotan sent us . . . The Father of Battles shunned Valhalla's brave heroes. . . . He roamed the world as the Wanderer.
> Waltraute, T-1-iii, her narrative

Gnome-father, fallen prince! Guardian of night, Lord of the Nibelungs! Alberich, hear me! Bid the Nibelung host once more obey you, Lord of the ring!
> Hagen, T-2-v, concluding T-2

Once [the depths] were bright, when safe and glorious our father's gold gleamed there. Rhinegold! Lustrous gold!
> Rhine Daughters, T-3-i, at the beginning of T-3

My father's blade I forged anew: I made Notung hard as nails.
>Siegfried, T-3-ii, his narrative

FINE-WROUGHT GOLD, see Tarnhelm

FIR TREE
So today I weave at the world ash-tree no more, and the fir must suffice me to fasten the rope.
>First Norn, T-Prologue

FLOSSHILDE
Flosshilde, swim! Woglinde's escaping: help me capture the truant!
>Wellgunde, R-i, playing in the waters

May the stiff curls of your wiry hair flow round Flosshilde forever!
>Flosshilde, R-i, mocking Alberich

FORT, FORTRESS, see Valhalla

FOX
A Wolf [my father] was to craven foxes! . . . His [real] name was "Volse."
>Siegmund, V-1-iii, to Sieglinde

Resting in the bushes, roedeer also paired off, and so even did wild foxes and wolves.
>Siegfried, S-1-i, to Mime

What's wrong with you, fool? . . . Are you a bird or a fox?
>Mime, S-1-i, to Siegfried

FREIA (see also Holda)
The fortress fills you with joy, but I fear for Freia.
>Fricka, R-ii, to Wotan

Thus shamelessly you brazenly bartered Freia, my lovely sister, and rejoiced at the base bargain.
>Fricka, R-ii, to Wotan

I will not yield our good Freia: in truth, I never had any such intention.
>Wotan, R-ii, to Fricka, on his bargain with the giants

When [Loge] counseled this contract, he promised to deliver Freia: on him I now rely.
>Wotan, R-ii, to Fricka

Where linger my brothers, who should bring help, since my brother-in-law abandons me in my weakness? Donner, help! Come hither! Rescue Freia, my Froh!
>Freia, R-ii

Freia the fair, Holda the free, it was agreed we should take home.
>Fasolt, R-ii, to Wotan, on the giants' fee

Think of some other fee: I cannot sell Freia.
>Wotan, R-11, to Fasolt

Custody of Freia serves little purpose; but to carry her off from the gods is worth much. [The gods] will waste away if they are forced to forego Freia. So let her be taken from their midst!
>Fafner, R-ii, to Fasolt

No other [fee]: only Freia!
> Fasolt, R-ii, to Wotan

To me, Freia! Let her be, rascal! Froh will protect the fair one.
> Froh, R-ii, to Freia and the giants

When those who built the castle stipulated Freia as payment, you know that I agreed only because you undertook to redeem the noble pledge.
> Wotan, R-ii, to Loge, who responds, "To consider with the utmost care how to release her—that I promised."

Concerned but for you, I looked about, feverishly ransacking the ends of the earth to find a substitute for Freia, such as would be fair to the giants.
> Loge, R-ii, to the gods

Believe me, that glittering gold is worth more than Freia: for eternal youth he gains who commands it by gold's magic.
> Fafner, R-ii, to Fasolt

Freia may stay with you in peace; an easier fee I've found in settlement: we rough giants would be satisfied with the Nibelung's shining gold.
> Fafner, R-ii, to Wotan

Then the time will be up and Freia forfeit: she will go with us forever!
> Fasolt, R-ii, to Wotan, continuing Fafner's threat: "Till evening—pay due heed—we will hold her as hostage."

Through the ford across the Rhine wade the giants. Freia hangs, far from happy, over the ruffians' shoulders!
> Loge, R-ii

I have it! Hear what it is you lack! Of Freia's fruit you have not yet eaten today.
> Loge, R-ii, to the gods, as they fade

To me Freia has always been ungenerous, niggardly with the precious fruit: for I am only half as godlike as you glorious ones.
> Loge, R-ii, to the gods

Freia the kind, Freia we must deliver.
> Wotan, R-ii, to Loge

From afar Fasolt and Fafner are approaching; they are bringing Freia back.
> Loge, R-iv, to Wotan

By craft and force we carried out the task: there lies what will free Freia.
> Loge, R-iv, pointing out the gold to Fricka, Donner, and Froh

Then Freia's form shall be the measure.
> Wotan, R-iv, answering Fasolt's plea, "If she is to be banished from my mind, the hoard of treasure must be heaped so high that it completely hides the lovely one from my sight."

I'll hasten to put an end to Freia's shame.
> Froh, R-iv, helping Loge pile up the gold for the giants

Let's have peace! I think Freia is covered now.
> Wotan, R-iv, separating Donner and Fafner

Freia the fair I see no more . . . Ah, her gaze still gleams on me here.

> Fasolt, R-iv, seeing Freia through the pile of gold

It's all over then; our first bargain stands: Freia follows us forever!

> Fasolt, R-iv, when Wotan refuses to give up the ring

Come to me, Freia! You are freed. Brought back, restore to us our youth!

> Wotan, R-iv, as he gives up the ring

You longed more for the maid than for the gold . . . If you had won Freia you would not have shared her: so, as I am dividing the treasure, I rightly retain the greater half for myself.

> Fafner, R-iv, to Fasolt

Mine is the ring: for it I gave up Freia's gaze!

> Fasolt, R-iv, to Fafner

Now blink at Freia's gaze: the ring you will not touch again!

> Fafner, R-iv, killing Fasolt

May Freia welcome you in the name of all women.

> Gutrune, T-2-ii, welcoming Siegfried as he returns from Brünnhilde's rock

FRICKA

Was Fricka truly free from like thirst when she herself begged me for the building?

> Wotan, R-ii, to Fricka, after she has chastised him for bartering Freia in his thirst for power

How is it with Fricka? Is she displeased with Wotan's grey gloom that suddenly turns him into a greybeard?

> Loge, R-ii, to Fricka, as the gods pale in Freia's absence

Let me warn you, Father, make ready yourself. You have to withstand a violent storm. Fricka, your wife, approaches in her chariot drawn by rams.

> Brünnhilde, V-2-i

What troubles Fricka let her freely say.

> Wotan, V-2-i

The outcome made Fricka laugh. Father, what must your child be told?

> Brünnhilde, V-2-ii, to Wotan

I provoked [Siegmund] to boldness against the council of the gods: against the vengeance of the gods his only protection now is the sword, which a god's favor bestowed on him . . . It was easy for Fricka to spot the trick . . . I must yield to her will.

> Wotan, V-2-ii, his narrative

Fight purely for Fricka, guard marriage for her and its vows. . . . I cannot will a free man to life: you must therefore fight for Fricka's subjects.

> Wotan, V-2-ii, to Brünnhilde

Come here, you blackguard wooer, let Fricka smite you down here.

> Hunding, V-2-v, pursuing Siegmund

Fight now yourself or Fricka will let you down. For look! From your house, from the homely tree-trunk I fearlessly pulled out the sword: now taste its cutting power!

> Siegmund, V-2-v, to Hunding

Be off, slave. Kneel before Fricka: tell her that Wotan's spear avenged what caused her shame. Go! Go!

Wotan, V-2-v, to Hunding

When Fricka made your own intentions foreign to you, when you took her point of view, you were your own enemy.

Brünnhilde, V-3-iii, to Wotan

You must kill a boar for Froh, and sacrifice a full-grown goat to Donner, but slaughter sheep for Fricka, that she may bless the marriage!

Hagen, T-2-iii, telling the vassals what they should do

FROH

Rescue Freia, my Froh!

Freia, R-ii

To me, Freia! Let her be rascal! Froh will protect the fair one.

Froh, R-ii, to Freia and Fafner

Donner and Froh, they are dreaming of food and shelter!

Loge, R-ii, to the gods

Courage, Froh, it is but early yet!

Loge, R-ii, as Froh weakens in Freia's absence

Help me, Froh!

Loge, R-iv, asks for help to pile up the gold

You must kill a boar for Froh, and sacrifice a full-grown goat to Donner, but slaughter sheep for Fricka, that she may bless the marriage!

Hagen, T-2-iii, telling the vassals what they should do

FRUIT, see Golden Apples

GERHILDE

Grimgerde, Gerhilde, lend me your horse. Schwertleite, Siegrune, look how afraid I am.

Brünnhilde, V-3-i

GIANTS (see also Fafner, Fasolt)

You men firmly kept the women away so that, deaf and silent to us, you could deal alone with the giants.

Fricka, R-ii, to Wotan

With quick strides the giants approach: where loiters your crafty helper [Loge]?

Fricka, R-ii, to Wotan

A simple giant thus counsels you: wise one, weigh his words.

Fasolt, R-ii, to Wotan

Many a time have I paid giants their due.

Donner, R-ii, to the giants

What bargain did I conclude? That which you contracted with the giants in council?

Loge, R-ii, responding to Wotan

Concerned but for you, I looked about, feverishly ransacking the ends of the earth to find a substitute for Freia, such as would be fair to the giants.

Loge, R-ii, to the gods

Freia may stay with you in peace; an easier fee I've found in settlement: we rough giants would be satisfied with the Nibelung's shining gold.

> Fafner, R-ii, to Wotan

Through the ford across the Rhine wade the giants. Freia hangs, far from happy, over the ruffians' shoulders!

> Loge, R-ii

You staked all on the life-giving fruit: this the giants knew well; your life they laid against it: now take care to defend it.

> Loge, R-ii, to the gods

From the giants' grasp our fair one approaches.

> Donner, R-iv

Listen, you giants! Come back and wait: you shall be given the gold.

> Donner, R-iv

You giants, take your ring!

> Wotan, R-iv, giving up the ring

The ring that [Alberich] made I took from him by a trick. But I did not return it to the Rhine; with it I paid the price for Valhalla, the castle that the giants built me, from which I ruled the world.

> Wotan, V-2-ii, his narrative

One of the giants, to whom I once gave the accursed gold as payment for work, he, Fafner, guards the treasure for which he slew his brother.

> Wotan, V-2-ii, his narrative

The best sword that ever I forged would hold firm in the fist of a giant.

> Mime, S-1-i, to himself

He babbles of giants and brave battles.

> Siegfried, S-1-i, on Mime

On the earth's face flourishes the race of giants; Riesenheim is their land.

> The Wanderer, S-1-ii, answering Mime's second question

Custody of the world lies in the hand that controls the spear, clasped in Wotan's fist. Before him bowed the Nibelung host; his commands quelled the crew of giants; they all forever obey the mighty lord of the spear.

> The Wanderer, S-1-ii, answering Mime's third question

My ring recompensed the giants for their toil.

> Alberich, S-2-i, to the Wanderer

You dare not snatch back from the giants what you paid them as quittance: you yourself would shatter your spear's shaft.

> Alberich, S-2-i, to the Wanderer

Unlike the stupid giants I will use the power of the ring: . . . I will storm Valhalla's heights with Hella's hosts.

> Alberich, S-2-i, threatening Wotan

Of the towering race of giants, the brothers Fasolt and Fafner both now are dead. For the accursed gold gained from the gods I dealt death to Fasolt. He who defended the hoard as a dragon, Fafner, last of the giants, has fallen to a fresh-faced hero.

Fafner, S-2-ii, mortally wounded by Siegfried

Where have you the ring now? The giants tore it from your timorous hands! [Note that Wotan, not the giants, took the ring from Alberich in R-iv.]

Mime, S-2-iii, to Alberich

If you slew this giant, who induced you to face the fearful dragon?

The Wanderer, S-3-ii, to Siegfried

Still soars the stronghold the giants built.

Third Norn, T-Prologue

GIBICH (Gibichung; see also Gunther)
Hagen, tell me, hero, can I hold my head high on the Rhine? Does Gunther maintain Gibich's glory?

Gunther, T-1-i, at the beginning of T-1

I know of good things which the Gibichung has not yet won.

Hagen, T-1-i, to Gunther

I see Gibich's children in the summer of their ripe strength—you, Gunther, unwived, you, Gutrune, without a husband.

Hagen, T-1-i

In his restless quest he may well roam even to the Gibich shores by the Rhine.

Hagen, T-1-i, as Siegfried approaches

To Gibich's stalwart son.

Siegfried, T-1-i, calling out his destination to those on shore

Which is Gibich's son?

Siegfried, T-1-ii, arriving at Gunther's hall

Welcome, o guest, to the house of Gibich! His daughter offers you this drink.

Gutrune, T-1-ii, to Siegfried

The wind wafts Gibich's son on his way to woo a wife.

Hagen, T-1-ii, Hagen's watch

I am a Gibichung, and Gunther is the name of the hero whom, woman, you must follow.

Siegfried (as Gunther), T-1-iii, to Brünnhilde

Bid me welcome, Gibich's child! I bring you good news.

Siegfried, T-2-ii, to Gutrune

You, Hagen, please call the vassals to the Gibich hall for the wedding!

Gutrune, T-2-ii, preparing for Gunther and Brünnhilde's return

Hoiho! You Gibich vassals, rouse yourselves!

Hagen, T-2-iii

Home to the Rhine I bring you Brünnhilde, rarest of women. A nobler wife was never won. The race of Gibichungs was granted grace by the gods.

Gunther, T-2-iv, presenting Brünnhilde

Hail to you, fortunate Gibichung!
> Vassals, T-2-iv, to Gunther

Up, Gunther, noble Gibichung! . . . Why do you sit there so sadly?
> Hagen, T-2-v

GOD (Divinity, Goddess, Godhead, Godlike)
You must grant me, as a god, that, even confined in the fortress, I must win the outside world over to myself.
> Wotan, R-ii, to Fricka

The lovely goddess, bright and light, of what use is her charm to you louts?
> Wotan, R-ii, to Fasolt

Custody of Freia serves little purpose; but to carry her off from the gods is worth much.
> Fafner, R-ii, to Fasolt

I, your only friend among all the gods, took you up when the rest mistrusted you.
> Wotan, R-ii, to Loge

How goes it with the glorious gods?
> Loge, R-ii

I am only half as godlike as you glorious ones!
> Loge, R-ii

Without the apples, old and grey, hoary and haggard, withered, the scorn of all the world, the race of gods will die.
> Loge, R-ii

All you gods I'll grip in my golden grasp.
> Alberich, R-iii, to Wotan

My curse serve but for your pleasure? Take heed, haughty god!
> Alberich, R-iv, when Wotan demands the ring

All that is shall come to an end. A dark day dawns for the gods.
> Erda, R-iv, to Wotan

Cruel god, give in to them!
> Fricka, R-iv, urging Wotan to give up the ring to the giants

They hasten to their end, though they think themselves strong and enduring . . . To burn them who once tamed me, rather than foolishly end with the blind, even though they be the most godlike gods, does not seem stupid to me.
> Loge, R-iv, as the gods prepare to cross over to Valhalla

Hear what Wotan wills for you. No more gleams the gold on you maidens: henceforth bask in bliss in the gods' new radiance!
> Loge, R-iv, to the Rhine Daughters

Is it the end, then, of the everlasting race of gods, since you brought those wild Volsungs to birth?
> Fricka, V-2-i, to Wotan

So alone [a hero] will be fit to do the deed which, much as the gods need it, a god is nevertheless prevented from doing.
> Wotan, V-2-i, to Fricka

What marvels could heroes perform that their gods were unable to do, by whose favor alone men can act?

Fricka, V-2-i

You alone inspire these whom you praise so to a goddess. . . . This Volsung you shall not keep for yourself. In him I find only you, since through you alone he can act boldly.

Fricka, V-2-i

Yes, the sword, the magical, strong flashing sword that you, the god, gave to your son.

Fricka, V-2-i, telling Wotan to take away the sword

Siegmund, as a slave, must be my victim. He, whose master you are, your slave and bondsman, must he exact the obedience of your immortal wife? . . . My husband . . . would not profane a goddess so!

Fricka, V-2-i, to Wotan

We gods will disappear, if today in a decent and respectable manner my rights aren't upheld by that bold girl. The Volsung shall die for my honor. Do I have Wotan's oath on it?

Fricka, V-2-i

O shameful affliction! Distress for the gods! Distress for the gods!

Wotan, V-2-ii

Erda, the sacred and wisest of women [Wala], told me to give up the ring . . . As a god I longed for knowledge. . . . With the magic of love I overpowered the woman [Wala], brought down her pride in wisdom, and she talked to me.

Wotan, V-2-ii, his narrative

I became ruler through treaties; by my treaties I am now enslaved. Only one person could do what I may not: a hero whom I have never stooped to help. A stranger to the god . . . This man opposed to the gods who will fight for me, this friendly foe, how can I find him? . . . What a predicament for a god, a grievous disgrace!

Wotan, V-2-ii, his narrative

I provoked [Siegmund] to boldness against the council of the gods: against the vengeance of the gods his only protection now is the sword, which a god's favor bestowed on him.

Wotan, V-2-ii, his narrative

What deeply revolts me I bequeath to [Alberich], the empty glory of divinity: greedily feed your hate on it!

Wotan, V-2-ii, concluding his narrative

From [Sieglinde's] brother Brünnhilde should today have withheld victory. But I protected Siegmund with my shield, disobeying the god who killed him himself with his spear. Siegmund fell, but I fled far away with his wife.

Brünnhilde, V-3-i, to the Valkyries

At the gods' solemn banquets you will never hand the drinking horn graciously to me again. . . . From the company of gods you are cut off.

Wotan, V-3-ii, to Brünnhilde

Stop father! Stop your curse! Must the maiden wither and die for this man? Hear our entreaty! Terrible god, spare her this lamentable disgrace.

The Eight Valkyries, V-3-ii

While life and breath last, the god must never see you again.
    Wotan, V-3-iii, to Brünnhilde

(Do not forget it, you god!)
    Brünnhilde, V-3-iii, reminding Wotan she is a part of him

Only one shall win the bride, one freer than I, the God!
    Wotan, V-3-iii

Thus the God departs from you, thus he kisses your godhood away!
    Wotan, V-3-iii

In the cloudy heights live the gods: Valhalla is their dwelling . . . Wotan, Lord of Light, rules over them.
    The Wanderer, S-1-ii, answering Mime's third question

To my hoard will flock gods and heroes: at my nod the world will kneel.
    Mime, S-1-iii, to himself

Well, laugh then, you frivolous, pleasure-seeking crew of gods! I shall yet see you all overthrown. So long as the gold gleams in the light, a knowing one keeps watch.
    Alberich, S-2-i, watching the Wanderer ride away

For the accursed gold gained from the gods I dealt death to Fasolt.
    Fafner, S-2-ii, mortally wounded by Siegfried

I will not let you go, mother . . . you once thrust the thorn of anxiety into Wotan's bold heart . . . Tell me now: how can the god conquer his cares?
    The Wanderer, S-3-i, to Erda

Fears of the gods' downfall grieves me not, since now I will it so! . . . Whatever now befalls, to the ever-young the god gladly yields. Descend then, Erda, mother of fear.
    The Wanderer, S-3-i

Hail to thee, gods! . . . I am awake and can see! It is Siegfried who has awakened me.
    Brünnhilde, S-3-iii

No god ever came so close to me! . . . Sacrosanct I came from Valhalla! . . . O the shame . . . He who woke me has wounded me. . . . I am Brünnhilde no more!
    Brünnhilde, S-3-iii, resisting Siegfried's advance

Farewell, Valhalla's glittering world! . . . Farewell, resplendent pomp of the gods!
    Brünnhilde, S-3-iii

At the world ash-tree once I wove . . . In its cool shadow bubbled a spring . . . An intrepid god came to drink at the spring.
    First Norn, T-Prologue

Still soars the stronghold the giants built: in its hall sits Wotan with his sacred clan of gods and heroes.
    Third Norn, T-Prologue

The end of the eternal gods will then fall forever. If you would know more, then wind the rope anew.
    Third Norn, T-Prologue

By the magic of his spear Wotan tamed [Loge]; he gave the god advice.
    Second Norn, T-Prologue

The shattered spear's sharp splinters Wotan will one day plunge deep into the heart of the glow . . . And this the god will fling at the world-ash's piled-up logs.

    Third Norn, T-Prologue

What the gods taught me I have given you—a rich hoard of holy runes.

    Brünnhilde, T-Prologue, to Siegfried

O sacred gods! . . . Feast your eyes on this dedicated pair!

    Brünnhilde, T-Prologue

When I protected Siegmund against the god—wrongly, I know—I was nevertheless fulfilling his wish.

    Brünnhilde, T-1-iii, to Waltraute

Then the severe god has still not softened?

    Brünnhilde, T-1-iii, to Waltraute

What ill has befallen the eternal gods?

    Brünnhilde, T-1-iii, to Waltraute

He sent the nobles of Valhalla to the forest to fell the world-ash. . . . He summoned the council of the gods . . . So he sits . . . the spear's splinters held in his hand; Holda's apples he will not touch.

    Waltraute, T-1-iii, her narrative

Amazement and awe struck the gods numb. He sent his two ravens on their travels: if ever they return with good tidings then once more, for the last time, the god will smile into eternity.

    Waltraute, T-1-iii, her narrative

If [Brünnhilde] would return the ring to the Rhine's daughters in its depths, from the weight of the curse would the gods and the world be freed.

    Waltraute, T-1-iii, her narrative, quoting Wotan

From the gods' holy heaven . . . I was banished . . . I do not grasp what I am told.

    Brünnhilde, T-1-iii, to Waltraute

More than the heaven of Valhalla, more than the glory of the gods, is this ring to me: one glance at its gleaming gold . . . weighs more with me than the eternal joy of all the gods! For from it shines Siegfried's love on me like a blessing—Siegfried's love!

    Brünnhilde, T-1-iii, to Waltraute

This is what the ring means to me! Go back to the gods' holy council. Tell them this about my ring: I will never renounce love . . . though Valhalla's sublime splendor collapse in ruins!

    Brünnhilde, T-1-iii, to Waltraute

Woe to you, sister! Woe to Valhalla's gods!

    Waltraute, T-1-iii, as she leaves Brünnhilde

Siegfried! Siegfried returning? . . . Into the arms of my god!

    Brünnhilde, T-1-iii, hearing Siegfried's horn call

He who once wrested the ring from me, Wotan the rabid robber, was overthrown by one of his own offspring: to the Volsung he lost his authority and power; with all the gods gathered round him in anguish he awaits his end.

    Alberich, T-2-i, to Hagen

Drink deep till drunkenness overcomes you! All in honor of the gods, that they may bless the marriage!

>Hagen, T-2-iii, to the vassals

Home to the Rhine I bring you Brünnhilde, rarest of women. A nobler wife was never won. The race of Gibichungs was granted grace by the gods.

>Gunther, T-2-iv, presenting Brünnhilde

Holy gods, rulers of heaven! . . . Cause Brünnhilde to break her heart, if only it will destroy her betrayer!

>Brünnhilde, T-2-iv

Omniscient god of vengeance, Wotan, witness of oaths and guardian of vows, look upon us!

>Brünnhilde and Gunther, T-2-v

O you, heavenly custodian of oaths! . . . Hear my lament, mighty god! . . . You sacrificed [Siegfried] to the curse which had fallen on you . . . All is now clear to me! I hear your ravens stirring too; with dreaded desired tidings I now send them both home. Rest, rest now, o god!

>Brünnhilde, T-3-iii, immolation scene

The end of the gods is nigh. Thus do I throw this torch at Valhalla's vaulting towers.

>Brünnhilde, T-3-iii, immolation scene

GOLD (Toy, Trinket; see also Hoard, Rhinegold)
Badly you guard the sleeping gold.

>Flosshilde, R-i, chastising Woglinde and Wellgunde

Guard the gold! Father warned us of such a foe.

>Flosshilde, R-i, when Alberich appears

Does the gnome know nothing of the eyes of gold which in turn wake and sleep?

>Flosshilde, R-i, to Alberich

Does the gold serve only for your water games?

>Alberich, R-i, to the Rhine Daughters

He would not scorn the gold's splendor if he were aware of all its wonders.

>Woglinde, R-i, referring to Alberich

Do you not know to whom alone it is given to shape the gold?

>Wellgunde, R-i, to Flosshilde

Only he who forswears love's power, only he who forfeits love's delight, only he can attain the magic to fashion the gold into a ring.

>Woglinde, R-i

I will put out your light, wrench the gold from the rock, forge the ring of revenge; for hear me, ye waves: thus I curse love!

>Alberich, R-i, to the Rhine Daughters

Rescue the gold!

>Wellgunde, R-i, as Alberich escapes

Only one I saw who had forsworn love: for shining gold he had renounced woman's affection.

>Loge, R-ii, to the gods

For the glittering toy, torn from the deep, the daughters made moan to me: to you, Wotan, they appeal to bring the thief to justice, and to give the gold back to the waters.
> Loge, R-ii, to Wotan

I grudge the gnome this gold; much harm the Nibelung has already done us.
> Fasolt, R-ii, to Fafner

New mischief will the Nibelung plot against us if the gold gives him power.
> Fafner, R-ii, to Fasolt

You there, Loge! Say without lies: of what great value is the gold then, that it satisfies the Nibelung?
> Fafner, R-ii, to Loge

It is a toy in the depths of the water, to give pleasure to laughing children.
> Loge, R-ii, to Fafner, on the gold

I have heard talk of the Rhine's gold: its glittering glow hides runes of riches; a ring would give unbounded power and wealth.
> Wotan, R-ii, to Loge

Would the golden trinket's glittering gems equally serve as fair adornment for women too?
> Fricka, R-ii, to Loge, who answers, "A wife could ensure her husband's fidelity if she decked herself with the bright ornament."

Could my husband win this gold for himself?
> Fricka, R-ii, to Loge

A magic spell turns the gold into a ring. No one knows it; but anyone can easily acquire it who renounces blissful love.
> Loge, R-ii, responding to Wotan

Alberich guards himself with guile; you must act shrewdly and subtly to bring the thief to justice and to return to the Rhinemaidens the gold, their shining toy; for that is what they beg of you.
> Loge, R-ii, to Wotan

Believe me, that glittering gold is worth more than Freia: for eternal youth he gains who commands it by gold's magic.
> Fafner, R-ii, to Fasolt

Freia may stay with you in peace; an easier fee I've found in settlement: we rough giants would be satisfied with the Nibelung's shining gold.
> Fafner, R-ii, to Wotan

Come, Loge, come down with me! We will descend to Nibelheim: I will procure the gold.
> Wotan, R-ii

You others wait here till evening: our loss of youth I'll banish with redeeming gold!
> Wotan, R-ii, to the other gods

Alberich wrought for himself a golden ring from the Rhine's gold: . . . with it he has overcome us, the Nibelung's nocturnal race.
> Mime, R-iii, to Wotan and Loge

Through the ring's gold, [Alberich's] greed divines where a new gleam is concealed in the clefts: there we have to track and trace it, dig it out, without pause or peace, to pile up our master's hoard.

    Mime, R-iii, to Wotan and Loge

Out of here, all of you! Hurry below! Find me gold from the new veins! My whip waits for those that don't dig deep!

    Alberich, R-iii, to the Nibelungs

Allured by gold, for gold alone shall you hunger.

    Alberich, R-iii, threatens Wotan

The treasure and your gleaming gold.

    Wotan, R-iv, naming the ransom to set Alberich free

You call the ring your own? Are you raving, shameless gnome? Tell me truly, from whom did you take the gold from which you made the ring? Was it your own, that you wickedly stole it from the water's depths? Ask the Rhine's daughters whether they gave you for your own their gold that you robbed for the ring.

    Wotan, R-iv, to Alberich

How gladly you yourself would have robbed the Rhine of its gold had you so easily found the way to forge it!

    Alberich, R-iv, to Wotan

Must this fatal fearful deed . . . lightly serve you as a royal toy, my curse serve but for your pleasure?

    Alberich, R-iv

Since its gold gave me measureless might, now may its magic bring death to whoever wears it.

    Alberich, R-iv, placing his curse on the ring

The ransom lies ready: now the amount of gold shall be fully measured.

    Wotan, R-iv, to the giants

Insatiable! Can't you see that all the gold [Hort] has gone?

    Loge, R-iv, to Fafner

On Wotan's finger still glints a ring of gold: give it here to fill the crack!

    Fafner, R-iv, responding to Loge

This gold belongs to the Rhinemaidens. Wotan will give it back to them. [Wotan refuses.]

    Loge, R-iv, to Fafner, who has demanded Wotan's ring

Do not hold the gold back!

    Froh, R-iv, urging Wotan

Listen, you giants! Come back and wait: you shall be given the gold.

    Donner, R-iv

You longed more for the maid than for the gold.

    Fafner, R-iv, to Fasolt

Your foes fell each other for the gold that you gave up.

    Loge, R-iv, to Wotan

Rhinegold! Rhinegold! Purest gold! . . . Give us the gold! O give us its glory again!
> Rhine Daughters, R-iv, appealing to the gods

The children of the Rhine lament their looted gold.
> Loge, R-iv

Hear what Wotan wills for you. No more gleams the gold on you maidens: henceforth bask in bliss in the gods' new radiance!
> Loge, R-iv, to the Rhine Daughters

Rhinegold! Rhinegold! Purest gold! If but your bright gleam still glittered in the deep!
> Rhine Daughters, nearing the end of R-iv

One of the giants, to whom I once gave the accursed gold as payment for work, he, Fafner, guards the treasure for which he slew his brother.
> Wotan, V-2-ii, his narrative

I touched Alberich's ring: greedily I held his gold. The curse from which I fled still has not left me: I must forsake what I love.
> Wotan, V-2-ii, his narrative

Fafner, the fearsome dragon lurks in the dark forest . . . He guards the Nibelung's gold there.
> Mime, S-1-i, to himself

Fasolt and Fafner . . . envied the Nibelung's power; they won . . . the ring . . . Fasolt was slain, and as a savage dragon Fafner now guards the gold.
> The Wanderer, S-1-ii, answering Mime's second question

The glittering ring that my brother wrought, on which he laid a mighty spell, the shining gold that makes one master—I have won it!
> Mime, S-1-iii, after Siegfried has reforged the sword

Besides you, only [Mime] covets the gold.
> The Wanderer, S-2-i, to Alberich

A hero is approaching to rescue the treasure; two Nibelungs crave for the gold; Fafner, who guards the ring, falls.
> The Wanderer, S-2-i, to Alberich

Well, laugh then, you frivolous, pleasure-seeking crew of gods! I shall yet see you all overthrown. So long as the gold gleams in the light, a knowing one keeps watch.
> Alberich, S-2-i, watching the Wanderer ride away

For the accursed gold gained from the gods I dealt death to Fasolt.
> Fafner, S-2-ii, mortally wounded by Siegfried

Villain, are you greedy for my gold?
> Alberich, S-2-iii, to Mime

Was it you who robbed the Rhine of gold for the ring? Was it you who cast the spell that clings to the ring?
> Alberich, S-2-iii, to Mime

What use you are to me I don't know, but I took you from the pile of heaped gold because I was guided by good advice. So let your beauty serve as witness to today . . . that I vanquished Fafner in fight.
> Siegfried, S-2-iii, contemplating the ring

The treasure in Fafner's keeping, the gold was what I toiled for.

> Mime, S-2-iii, revealing his heart to Siegfried

More than the heaven of Valhalla, more than the glory of the gods, is this ring to me: one glance at its gleaming gold . . . weighs more with me than the eternal joy of all the gods! For from it shines Siegfried's love on me like a blessing—Siegfried's love!

> Brünnhilde, T-1-ii, to Waltraute

The golden ring, that is what we must obtain! A wise woman lives for the Volsung's love: if ever she advised him to return the ring to the Rhinemaidens . . . then my gold would be lost and no ruse could ever retrieve it. So aim for the ring without delay!

> Alberich, T-2-i, to Hagen

Once [the depths] were bright, when safe and glorious our father's gold gleamed there. Rhinegold! Lustrous gold!

> Rhine Daughters, T-3-i, at the beginning of T-3

Dame Sun, send us the hero who will give us back the gold! . . . Rhinegold! Lustrous gold!

> Rhine Daughters, T-3-i

A gold ring gleams on your finger.

> Wellgunde, T-3-i, following Woglinde's question, "Siegfried, what will you give us if we grant you your quarry?"

From the Rhine's gold the ring was wrought. He who cunningly fashioned it . . . laid on it a curse into all eternity to doom to death whoever wears it.

> Rhine Daughters, T-3-1

Accursed ring, terrible ring, I take your gold and now I give it away. . . . You swimming daughters of the Rhine, I thank you for your good counsel. . . . The fire that consumes me shall cleanse the ring from the curse! . . . Keep pure the gleaming gold that was disastrously stolen from you.

> Brünnhilde, T-3-iii, immolation scene

GOLDEN APPLES (Apples, Fruit)

Golden apples grow in [Freia's] garden; only she knows how to tend them! By eating the fruit, her kindred are endowed with eternal, never-aging youth.

> Fafner, R-ii, to Fasolt

The golden apples in [Freia's] garden make you hearty and young when you eat them every day.

> Loge, R-ii, to the gods

You staked all on the life-giving fruit: this the giants knew well; your life they laid against it: now take care to defend it.

> Loge, R-ii, to the gods

Without the apples, old and grey, hoary and haggard, withered, the scorn of all the world, the race of gods will die.

> Loge, R-ii, to the gods

So [Wotan] sits . . . the spear's splinters held in his hand; Holda's apples he will not touch.

> Waltraute, T-1-iii, her narrative

GRANE

How Grane is panting after riding so fast!
> Grimgerde, V-3-i

Down to earth plunges strong Grane.
> Brünnhilde, S-3-iii

I see Grane there, my trusty steed . . . Siegfried woke him along with me.
> Waltraute, V-3-i

Now for the ring take my horse! . . . Grane fearlessly will follow you . . . often give Grane Brünnhilde's greeting!
> Brünnhilde, T-Prologue, to Siegfried

Tend Grane well for me! You never held the bridle of a horse of nobler breed.
> Siegfried, T-1-ii, to Hagen

Grane, my steed, greetings! . . . Radiant in the fire, there lies your lord, Siegfried, my blessed hero. . . . Heiajoho! Grane! Greet your master! Siegfried! See! Your wife joyfully greets you!
> Brünnhilde, T-3-iii, immolation scene

GRIMGERDE

Grimgerde and Rossweisse!
> Waltraute, V-3-i, greeting her sisters

Greetings, you riders, Rossweisse and Grimgerde!
> Helmwige, Ortlinde, and Siegrune, V-3-i

Grimgerde, Gerhilde, lend me your horse. Schwertleite, Siegrune, look how afraid I am.
> Brünnhilde, V-3-i

GRIMHILDE

She who bore us both as brothers, Dame Grimhilde, bade me observe [your legitimate title].
> Hagen, T-1-i, to Gunther

Praised be Grimhilde, who gave us such a brother!
> Gunther, T-1-i, on Hagen's plan

GUNTHER (see also Gibich)

Hagen, tell me, hero, can I hold my head high on the Rhine? Does Gunther maintain Gibich's glory?
> Gunther, at the beginning of T-1-i

I see Gibich's children in the summer of their ripe strength—you, Gunther, unwived, you, Gutrune, without a husband.
> Hagen, T-1-i

I, Gunther, am the one you seek.
> Gunther, T-1-ii, to Siegfried

Gunther, what is your sister's name?
> Siegfried, T-1-ii, suddenly inflamed with passion for Gutrune

Gunther, have you a wife?
>   Siegfried, T-1-ii

I am a Gibichung, and Gunther is the name of the hero whom, woman, you must follow.
>   Siegfried (as Gunther), T-1-iii, to Brünnhilde

By husband's right [the ring] must be given to Gunther; with it you shall be married to him!
>   Siegfried (as Gunther), T-1-iii, to Brünnhilde

Now you are mine, Brünnhilde, Gunther's bride—now grant me your cave!
>   Siegfried (as Gunther), T-1-iii, to Brünnhilde

Did Brünnhilde take you for Gunther?
>   Gutrune, T-2-ii, to Siegfried, who answers affirmatively

[Brünnhilde] surrendered—to Gunther's strength. . . . Brünnhilde submitted to her husband throughout the bridal night. . . . Siegfried remained here with Gutrune.
>   Siegfried, T-2-ii, to Gutrune

How now did Gunther take [Brünnhilde] over from you?
>   Gutrune, T-2-ii, to Siegfried

Gunther in a trice changed places with me: through the Tarnhelm's power I wished myself swiftly here. A strong wind now wafts the lovers up the Rhine.
>   Siegfried, T-2-ii, answering Gutrune

Why does the horn blast? . . . Hagen! Hagen! . . . Is Gunther in need? . . . Ho! Hagen!
>   Vassals, T-2-iii

You must greet Gunther, who has taken a wife.
>   Hagen, T-2-iii, to the vassals

Welcome Gunther's bride! Brünnhilde approaches with him.
>   Hagen, T-2-iii, to the vassals

Welcome Gunther! Hail!
>   Vassals, T-2-iii

Greetings, Gunther! Hail to you and your bride!
>   Vassals, T-2-iv

Two happy couples I see here on show: Brünnhilde and Gunther, Gutrune and Siegfried!
>   Gunther, T-2-iv

Gunther's gentle sister married to me, as you to Gunther.
>   Siegfried, T-2-iv, revealing to Brünnhilde that she is married to Gunther

I . . . to Gunther . . . ? You lie!
>   Brünnhilde, T-2-iv, to Siegfried, shocked to hear him say she is married to Gunther

Gunther, your wife is not well!
>   Siegfried, T-2-iv, when Brünnhilde asks, "Does Siegfried not know me?"

Brünnhilde, valiant woman, do you really recognize the ring? If it is that which you gave to Gunther, then it is his, and Siegfried obtained it by trickery, for which the traitor must atone.
>   Hagen, T-2-iv

Blood-brotherhood I swore to Gunther: Notung, my trusty sword, guarded the oath of loyalty.

Siegfried, T-2-iv, refuting Brünnhilde

Did he [Siegfried] tarnish Gunther's honor?

Vassals, T-2-iv

Gunther, control your wife who shamelessly slanders you!

Siegfried, T-2-iv

Up, Gunther, noble Gibichung! . . . Why do you sit there so sadly?

Hagen, T-2-v

Drink, Gunther, drink! Your brother offers it to you!

Siegfried, T-3-ii, offering the drinking horn

Hey, Gunther, morose man! If you would like me to, I will sing you stories of my boyhood days.

Siegfried, T-3-ii

GUTRUNE

I see Gibich's children in the summer of their ripe strength—you, Gunther, unwived, you, Gutrune, without a husband.

Hagen, T-1-i

Siegfried, the Volsung's offspring: . . . Siegmund and Sieglinde . . . engendered this noblest of sons. . . . Him I would wish for Gutrune's husband.

Hagen, T-1-i

Your request would soon persuade [Siegfried] if Gutrune had previously captured his heart.

Hagen, T-1-i, persuading Gunther that Siegfried can help him win Brünnhilde

Gutrune.

Gunther, T-1-ii, answering Siegfried's question, "Gunther, what is your sister's name?"

I fear no fire, and will win the woman for you . . . if I may have Gutrune for my wife.

Siegfried, T-1-ii, to Gunther

I gladly grant you Gutrune.

Gunther, T-1-ii, to Siegfried

Is Gutrune awake?

Siegfried, T-2-ii, to Hagen

Hoiho, Gutrune, come forth! Siegfried is here.

Hagen, T-2-ii

Brünnhilde submitted to her husband throughout the bridal night. . . . Siegfried remained here with Gutrune.

Siegfried, T-2-ii

Two happy couples I see here on show: Brünnhilde and Gunther, Gutrune and Siegfried!

Gunther, T-2-iv

Siegfried here . . . ! Gutrune . . . ?
>   Brünnhilde, T-2-iv, unable to comprehend that Siegfried has married Gutrune

Siegfried? Gutrune's husband?
>   Gibichung women, T-2-iv, when Brünnhilde claims she is married to Siegfried

Gutrune's husband?
>   Vassals, T-2-iv

But Gutrune . . . how can we justify ourselves to her?
>   Gunther, T-2-v, to Hagen

Gutrune is the sorcery that lured my husband away. May anguish overcome her!
>   Brünnhilde, T-2-v

Had I not given Gutrune my word, I would cheerfully have chosen for myself one of these pretty women!
>   Siegfried, T-3-i, as the Rhine Daughters swim away

Up, Gutrune! Greet Siegfried! The mighty hero is coming home.
>   Hagen, T-3-iii

Gutrune, dear sister, open your eyes, speak to me!
>   Gunther, T-3-iii

Would you lay hands on Gutrune's inheritance, shameless son of a gnome?
>   Gunther, T-3-iii

HAGEN

Hagen, tell me, hero, can I hold my head high on the Rhine? Does Gunther maintain Gibich's glory?
>   Gunther, T-1-i, at the beginning of T-1

You mocking, hateful Hagen! How could I capture Siegfried?
>   Gutrune, T-1-i

Now say: what think you of Hagen's scheme?
>   Hagen, T-1-i, to Gutrune

Hagen, you keep guard over the hall!
>   Gunther, T-1-ii, about to leave with Siegfried

Are you asleep, Hagen, my son?
>   Alberich, T-2-i, at the beginning of T-2

Hagen, my son, hate the happy . . . He who once wrested the ring from me, Wotan the rabid robber, was overthrown by one of his own offspring: to the Volsung he lost his authority and power; with all the gods gathered round him in anguish he awaits his end. . . Are you asleep, Hagen, my son?
>   Alberich, T-2-i

Valhalla and Nibelheim bow before [Siegfried]. Even my curse is blunted on that fearless hero: for he does not know the ring's value . . . Do you sleep, Hagen, my son?
>   Alberich, T-2-i

Not strong enough, indeed to oppose the dragon, which was destined for the Volsung alone, but to inexorable hate I bred Hagen, who now shall avenge me and obtain the

ring in defiance of the Volsung and Wotan! Do you swear it, Hagen, my son?
> Alberich, T-2-i

Do you swear it, Hagen, my hero?
> Alberich, T-2-i, to Hagen, who has assured him that he will regain the ring

Keep faith, Hagen, my son! Beloved hero!
> Alberich, T-2-i

Hoiho, Hagen, weary man! Can you see me coming?
> Siegfried, T-2-ii, appearing suddenly on the shore

I resembled [Gunther] to a hair: the Tarnhelm accomplished it, as Hagen rightly foretold.
> Siegfried, T-2-ii, answering Gutrune's question, "Did Brünnhilde take you for Gunther?"

You, Hagen, please call the vassals to the Gibich hall for the wedding!
> Gutrune, T-2-ii, preparing for Gunther and Brünnhilde's return

Why does the horn blast? . . . Hagen! Hagen! . . . Is Gunther in need? . . . Ho! Hagen!
> Vassals, T-2-iii

Hagen, what do you bid us do?
> Vassals, T-2-iii

Good fortune and prosperity now smile on the Rhine if grim Hagen can be so merry!
> Vassals, T-2-iii

Help, Hagen! Help my honor! Help your mother, who bore me too!
> Gunther, T-2-v

Hagen, what are you doing? What have you done?
> Vassals, T-3-ii, after Hagen has struck Siegfried

Hagen, what have you done?
> Gunther, T-3-ii, after Hagen has struck Siegfried

What has happened? Hagen! I did not hear his horn!
> Gutrune, T-3-iii, concerned to know Siegfried's fate

Hagen . . . is the accursed boar who savaged this noble hero.
> Gunther, T-3-iii, to Gutrune

I, Hagen, struck him dead. He was forfeit to my spear . . . I now demand this ring.
> Hagen, T-3-iii

Curses on you, Hagen . . . Suddenly I understand: Brünnhilde was his true love whom the draught drove from his mind!
> Gutrune, T-3-iii

HAMMER

Hold, hothead! Violence avails naught! My spearshaft protects bonds: spare your hammer's haft.
> Wotan, R-ii, to Donner

From your hand, Donner, the hammer falls!
> Loge, R-ii, as Donner weakens in Freia's absence

Vapors to me! Donner, your master, summons you to his host. As I swing my hammer, hover here, misty moisture, hanging haze! Donner, your master, summons you.

 Donner, R-iv

No dwarf hammer can subdue [the sword splinters'] hardness.

 Mime, S-1-i, to himself

HAWTHORN

The Hawthorn pricks no more; [Hagen] has been appointed bridal herald.

 Vassals, T-2-iii

HEGELING

Sintolt the Hegeling.

 Helmwige, V-3-i, answering Waltraute's question, "Who is hanging on your saddle?" Sintolt is a fallen hero of the Hegeling race.

HELL, see Hella

HELLA (Hell)

Hel, the land of the dead. . . .
Hel is not like the Christian Hell, but more like the ancient Greek Hades
—a realm of the 'shades' of the dead, guilty or innocent.
 —Deryck Cooke[2]

O shame upon him who made my sword . . . If I must die I shall not go to Valhalla. Let Hell [Hella] hold me fast.

 Siegmund, V-2-iii, to Brünnhilde

Unlike the stupid giants I will use the power of the ring: . . . I will storm Valhalla's heights with Hella's hosts.

 Alberich, S-2-i, threatening Wotan

Have you come from Hella's hordes of night?

 Brünnhilde, T-1-iii, to Siegfried (as Gunther)

HELMET, see Tarnhelm

HELMWIGE

Here, Helmwige, bring your horse here.

 Gerhilde, V-3-i, opening Act 3

Helmwige, listen.

 Brünnhilde, V-3-i

HOARD (Treasure; see also Gold)

Father [told us of the power of the ring], and ordered us to guard the gleaming treasure skillfully.

 Flosshilde, R-i, to her sisters

Through the ring's gold, [Alberich's] greed divines where a new gleam is concealed in the clefts: there we have to track and trace it, dig it out, without pause or peace, to pile up our master's hoard.

 Mime, R-iii, to Wotan and Loge

Idle herd, pile up the hoard there in heaps! . . . Despicable dogs, put down the treasure!
>   Alberich, R-iii, to the Nibelungs

Do you see the hoard that my henchmen have heaped up for me? . . . That is today's, a paltry pile: it will increase boldly and mightily in the future
>   Alberich, R-iii, to Loge

But what help is the hoard to you since Nibelheim is joyless and treasure can buy nothing?
>   Wotan, R-iii, responding to Alberich

Nibelheim's night serves me to create treasure and conceal treasure; but with the hoard . . . I will win the whole world for my own.
>   Alberich, R-iii, to Wotan

If your masterly cunning can win, with your treasure, all you demand, I must acclaim you the mightiest. . . . But I deem it significant above all that those who heaped the hoard, the Nibelung host, obey you ungrudgingly.
>   Loge, R-iii, to Alberich

The treasure and your gleaming gold.
>   Wotan, R-iv, naming the ransom Alberich must pay to free himself

But if I keep only the ring, I could easily spare the treasure.
>   Alberich, R-iv, to himself

Will you yield the treasure?
>   Wotan, R-iv, to Alberich

I've called the Nibelungs to me: obedient to their master, I hear them hauling the hoard from the depths to the daylight. Now loosen my burdensome bonds!
>   Alberich, R-iv, to Wotan

Bring it there as I command! Pile the hoard into a heap! Shall I help you cripples? Don't glance over here! . . . Off to your pits!
>   Alberich, R-iv, to the Nibelungs

A golden ring rests upon your finger: do you hear, gnome? That, in my view, belongs to the hoard.
>   Wotan, R-iv, demanding the ring from Alberich

If [Freia] is to be banished from my mind, the hoard of treasure must be heaped so high that it completely hides the lovely one from my sight.
>   Fasolt, R-iv

These poles we've planted to the measure of the pledge: now fill the space full with the hoard.
>   Fafner, R-iv, to the gods, measuring the gold against Freia

The hoard is used up.
>   Loge, R-iv, when the gold is piled up

You longed more for the maid than for the gold . . . If you had won Freia you would not have shared her: so, as I am dividing the treasure, I rightly retain the greater half for myself.
>   Fafner, R-iv, to Fasolt

I call on you as judges: in justice divide the treasure fairly between us.
    Fasolt, R-iv, to the gods

Let [Fafner] take the treasure: only keep control of the ring!
    Loge, R-iv, advises Fasolt

One of the giants, to whom I once gave the accursed gold as payment for work, he, Fafner, guards the treasure for which he slew his brother.
    Wotan, V-2-ii, his narrative

Away to the east stretches a forest: Fafner carried off the Nibelung treasure into it.
    Siegrune, V-3-i

In the earth's depths dwell the Nibelungs: Nibelheim is their land . . . Black Alberich once ruled as their lord! A magic ring's masterful might subjugated the slaving mass to him. The shimmering hoard of rich treasure they heaped up for him.
    Wotan, S-1-ii, answering Mime's first question

A wise Nibelung watches over Siegfried, who must slay Fafner for him so that he may gain the ring and become master of the treasure. What sword must Siegfried now flourish, fit for Fafner's death?
    Wotan, S-1-ii, asking Mime the second question

He'll forge the sword and slay Fafner . . . The treasure and the ring will fall to him: how can I retrieve his gains?
    Mime, S-1-iii, to himself

With the same sword that [Siegfried] won for himself I will easily remove him from my way and win the ring and treasure for myself. Well, wise Wanderer, do you still deem me dull?
    Mime, S-1-iii

To my hoard will flock gods and heroes: at my nod the world will kneel.
    Mime, S-1-iii, to himself

With my treasure you paid your debts.
    Alberich, S-2-i, to the Wanderer

Doomed to death through my curse is he who guards the treasure: who shall inherit it? Will the envied treasure again belong to the Nibelungs?
    Alberich, S-2-i, to the Wanderer

Will you keep your hands off the hoard?
    Alberich, S-2-i, to the Wanderer

A hero is approaching to rescue the treasure; two Nibelungs crave for the gold; Fafner, who guards the ring, falls.
    The Wanderer, S-2-i, to Alberich

Someone has come [who will] reward you with your life if for your life you will repay him with the treasure that you guard.
    The Wanderer, S-2-i, calling to Fafner

Give me the ring as reward, and I will prevent the fight; you can watch over your hoard and live long in peace.
    Alberich, S-2-i, to Fafner

He who defended the hoard as a dragon, Fafner, last of the giants, has fallen to a fresh-faced hero.

> Fafner, S-2-ii, mortally wounded by Siegfried

The Nibelung's treasure now belongs to Siegfried! Now he'll find the hoard in the cave! If he wants to take the Tarnhelm, it will help him perform wondrous deeds; but if he could get the ring it would make him ruler of the world!

> Wood Bird, S-2-ii, first words to Siegfried

Siegfried! . . . The treasure in Fafner's keeping, the gold was what I toiled for.

> Mime, S-2-iii, revealing his heart to Siegfried

As you were smelting your sword I was brewing this broth; drink it now, and I will win your trusty sword and with it the helmet and treasure.

> Mime, S-2-iii, revealing his heart to Siegfried

Lie here in the cavern on the treasure.

> Siegfried, S-2-iii, throwing Mime's body into the cave

Guard the glittering treasure, together with your booty-envying enemy: may you both find rest now!

> Siegfried, S-2-iii, having thrown Mime's body into the cave and Fafner's body in front of the entrance

What the gods taught me I have given you—a rich hoard of holy runes.

> Brünnhilde, T-Prologue, to Siegfried

A gigantic dragon guarded the Nibelung's hoard at Neidhöhle: Siegfried closed its ravening jaws and slew it with his conquering sword.

> Hagen, T-1-i, to Gunther and Gutrune

I have heard tell of the Nibelung hoard.

> Gunther, T-1-i

But rumor names you as lord of the Nibelung hoard.

> Hagen, T-1-ii, to Siegfried

I almost forgot the treasure, so poorly do I prize its possession! I left it in a cavern where once a dragon guarded it.

> Siegfried, T-1-ii, to Hagen

Did you take nothing else from the hoard?

> Hagen, T-1-ii, to Siegfried, who answers, "A ring. . . . A wondrous woman keeps it."

Mine is the treasure, to me it must belong.

> Hagen, T-2-v, near the end of T-2

Farewell, Siegfried! Stubborn man, a proud woman today will inherit your treasure.

> Rhine Daughters, T-3-i

Mime was the name of a surly dwarf [who brought me up to] kill for him a dragon in the forest who sluggishly guarded a treasure there.

> Siegfried, T-3-ii, his narrative

One [bird] sat on a bough and sang, "Hey! Siegfried now owns the Nibelung treasure! Now he'll find the hoard in the cave!"

> Siegfried, T-3-ii, his narrative

"[Siegfried] must not trust the treacherous Mime! Only for him is he to gain the treasure."

> Siegfried, T-3-ii, his narrative, quoting the Wood Bird

HOLDA (see also Freia)

Save me, sister! Protect me, brother! From yonder mountain menacing Fasolt would come to force me, Holda, away.

> Freia, R-ii, her first words

Freia the fair, Holda the free, it was agreed we should take home.

> Fasolt, R-ii, to Wotan, on the giants' fee

I still see the gleam of Holda's hair: throw that wrought object on the pile!

> Fafner, R-iv, when the gold is piled up

Dare I hope so? Do you think Holda truly worth this ransom?

> Freia, R-iv, hoping Wotan will give up the ring

Holda's apples [Wotan] will not touch.

> Waltraute, T-1-iii, to Brünnhilde, her narrative

HORN

Listen! The horns, do you hear them call? . . . Hunding has woken from deep sleep. Wildly [the dogs] cry to heaven for the broken marriage vows. Where are you, Siegmund? . . . That is Hunding's horn.

> Sieglinde, V-2-iii

In the depths of the forest I set my horn waking the echo.

> Siegfried, S-1-i, to Mime

I made you toys and a resounding horn.

> Mime, S-1-i, to Siegfried

Well, now listen to my horn. . . . Nothing better has yet come than wolf or bear. Now let me see what it will bring me; perhaps a dear companion!

> Siegfried, S-2-ii, to the Wood Bird

The horn sounds from the Rhine.

> Gunther, T-1-i, hearing Siegfried approach

It is [Siegfried] who gaily blows his horn.

> Hagen, T-1-i

Why does the horn blast? . . . Hagen! Hagen! . . . Is Gunther in need? . . . Ho! Hagen!

> Vassals, T-2-iii

I hear his horn.

> Woglinde, T-3-i, as Siegfried approaches

Was that his horn? . . . Was that his horn? No! No sign of life! If only I could see Siegfried soon.

> Gutrune, T-3-iii

What has happened? Hagen! I did not hear his horn!

> Gutrune, T-3-iii, answered by Hagen's "A pallid hero can blow it no more."

HUNDING

This house and this woman belong to Hunding.

> Sieglinde, V-1-i, to Siegmund

I will wait for Hunding.

> Siegmund, V-1-i, to Sieglinde

The roof that shelters you, the house that protects you, have Hunding for landlord. When you leave here and travel west, in wealthy estates there dwell the kinsmen who guard Hunding's honor.

> Hunding, V-1-i, to Siegmund

Hunding is sound asleep. I made him a drugged drink.

> Sieglinde, V-1-iii, to Siegmund

The men of his family sat in the room here, they were guests at Hunding's wedding. He was marrying a woman who, without being asked, robbers had made his wife.

> Sieglinde, V-1-iii

Brünnhilde must charge into battle, she must see the Volsung wins. Let Hunding decide where he belongs, I do not require him in Valhalla.

> Wotan, V-2-i, to Brünnhilde

I have observed Hunding's distress; he called on me to revenge him.

> Fricka, V-2-i, to Wotan

You must kill Siegmund and procure victory for Hunding.

> Wotan, V-2-ii, to Brünnhilde

Listen! The horns, do you hear them call? . . . Hunding has woken from deep sleep. Wildly [the dogs] cry to heaven for the broken marriage vows. Where are you, Siegmund? . . . That is Hunding's horn.

> Sieglinde, V-2-iii

Hunding will kill you in battle.

> Brünnhilde, V-2-iv, to Siegmund

You must threaten me with stronger blows than Hunding's.

> Siegmund, V-2-iv, to Brünnhilde

Hunding, Siegmund, if only I could see them!

> Sieglinde, V-2-v

INCEST

If you grant respectability to adultery, then go on boasting and sanctify the incestuous fruit of this liaison between twins.

> Fricka, V-2-i, to Wotan

IRMING

Ortlinde's mare carries Wittig the Irming.

> Schwertleite, V-3-i. Wittig is a fallen hero of the Irming race.

KING

Mime the bold, Mime is king, prince of the elves, ruler of all! Hi, Mime! How lucky you are!

> Mime, S-1-iii

Does the stingy, shabby slave coolly and brazenly claim to be made king?
>Alberich, S-2-iii, to Mime

LIME TREE
I'll seek cool shade under the lime tree.
>Siegfried, S-2-iii

LOGE
Did you not see Loge?
>Wotan, R-ii, to Fricka, who answers, "You always prefer to trust that trickster!"

To turn to use foe's jealousy, only craft and cunning will serve, such as Loge artfully employs. When he counseled this contract, he promised to deliver Freia: on him I now rely.
>Wotan, R-ii, to Fricka

Loge delays too long!
>Wotan, R-ii, to himself

Loge at last! Is this how you hasten to right the evil bargain that you concluded?
>Wotan, R-ii

Your name is Loge, but I call you Liar!
>Froh, R-ii

Leave my friend in peace! You know not Loge's wiles: his counsel is of richer weight when he delays in giving it.
>Wotan, R-ii, to Froh and Donner

Ingratitude is always Loge's lot!
>Loge, R-ii, beginning his narrative

I promised the maidens to tell you this: now Loge has kept his word.
>Loge, R-ii, ending his narrative

You there, Loge! Say without lies: of what great value is the gold then, that it satisfies the Nibelung?
>Fafner, R-ii

To control this ring seems wise to me. But how, Loge, can I learn the art of forging this gem?
>Wotan, R-ii

Come, Loge, come down with me! We will descend to Nibelheim: I will procure the gold.
>Wotan, R-ii

Who would have given you light and warming flames if Loge had not smiled on you? What would have been the use of your forging if I had not fired the forge? I am your kinsman and was your friend: your thanks do not seem very warm.
>Loge, R-iii, to Alberich, on their past friendship

Loge laughs now with the elves of light, the cunning rogue: if, false one, you're their friend as you once were friend to me, ha ha!
>Alberich, R-iii, responding to Loge

Loge thinks himself the most artful; others always seem stupid to him.
>> Alberich, R-iii, to Loge

Do you think I lie and boast like Loge?
>> Alberich, R-iii

Terrible serpent, do not swallow me! Spare Loge's life!
>> Loge, R-iii, feigning terror at Alberich's serpent

The wrought helmet that Loge is holding there, now kindly give it back to me.
>> Alberich, R-iv, to Wotan

By treaties I made alliance with powers concealing evil. Loge cunningly tempted me and now has fluttered away.
>> Wotan, V-2-ii, his narrative

Loge, listen! Harken here! . . . Arise, magic flame, girdle the rock with fire for me! Loge! Loge! Come here!
>> Wotan, V-3-iii, conjuring the magic fire

Loge's legions ring the rock with fire.
>> First Norn, T-Prologue

I cannot clearly recall the glorious past, when Loge once flared into fiery flame.
>> First Norn, T-Prologue

Fly home, you ravens! Recount to your master what you have heard here by the Rhine! Pass by Brünnhilde's rock: direct Loge, who still blazes there, to Valhalla; for the ends of the gods is nigh. Thus do I throw this torch at Valhalla's vaulting towers.
>> Brünnhilde, T-3-iii, immolation scene

MAGIC (Spell)
Only he who forfeits love's delight, only he can attain the magic to fashion the gold into a ring.
>> Woglinde, R-i

A magic spell turns the gold into a ring.
>> Loge, R-ii, to Wotan

That glittering gold is worth more than Freia: for eternal youth he gains who commands it by gold's magic.
>> Fafner, R-ii, to Fasolt

At the might of [the ring's] magic we tremble and marvel.
>> Mime, R-iii, to Wotan and Loge

Hypocrite, how well it worked for you that I the Nibelung, in shame and distress, maddened by fury, gained the terrible magic whose work now gaily gladdens you!
>> Alberich, R-iv, to Wotan

May [the ring's] magic bring death to whoever wears it!
>> Alberich, R-iv, pronouncing his curse

[Sieglinde] draws me to her in longing, she hurts me with sweet magic.
>> Siegmund, V-1-iii, to himself

Love's magic bewitched them. Who will atone to me for love's power?
    Wotan, V-2-i, defending the twins to Fricka

Take away [the sword's] magic, let it break in your serf's hands.
    Fricka, V-2-i, to Wotan

With the magic of love I overpowered [Erda], brought down her pride in wisdom and now she talked to me.
    Wotan, V-2-ii, his narrative

Deep as a spell [Zauberfest] sleep subdues my beloved's sorrow and pain.
    Siegmund, V-2-v

A magic ring's masterful might subjugated the slaving mass to [Alberich].
    The Wanderer, S-1-ii, to Mime

The glittering ring that my brother wrought, on which he laid a mighty magic spell . . . I have won it!
    Mime, S-1-iii

What have you ever known, bungler, about the black art? The magic ring put the dwarf and his skill at my service.
    Alberich, S-2-iii, to Mime

Strong is the summons of your song: mighty the lure of its magic.
    Erda, S-3-i, to whomever has summoned her

I will not let you go, mother, for magic lends me might.
    The Wanderer, S-3-i, to Erda

Without [Siegfried's] knowing, I enveloped him in my magic, which now protects him from wounds.
    Brünnhilde, T-2-v, to Hagen

MIME

Hi, Mime! Merry Dwarf! What tweaks and torments you so?
    Loge, R-iii, in Nibelheim

I would help you, Mime!
    Loge, R-iii

But what, Mime, gave [Alberich] the power to bind you?
    Loge, R-iii

Come here, Mime, you shabby scamp! Have you been chattering to this pair of tramps? . . . Mime shall stand bail that no one idles, or feel the lash of my whip.
    Alberich, R-iii

I had Mime, the most skillful smith, fashion [the Tarnhelm] for me.
    Alberich, R-iii, to Loge

Patience! He who made the old one can make another: mine is still the might that Mime obeys. Yet it's hard to leave my most cunning weapon to my crafty foes!
    Alberich, R-iv, to himself

Much you've taught me, Mime . . . [but not] how to tolerate you.
    Siegfried, S-1-i

I long to seize you by your nodding neck and make an end of your obscene blinking! That's how I've learnt, Mime, to endure you.
    Siegfried, S-1-i

Thus you too love your Mime—you must love him!
    Mime, S-1-i, to Siegfried

What the bird is to the fledgling . . . such to you, my lad, is sage, attentive Mime.
    Mime, S-1-i, to Siegfried

O Mime, if you're so wise explain something else to me. . . . Now where, Mime, have you your loving wife, that I may call her mother?
    Siegfried, S-1-i, to Mime

What trouble Mime took, what kindness and consideration he showed!
    Mime, S-1-i, to Siegfried

My rightful sword I'll brandish! Get up! Quickly, Mime!
    Siegfried, S-1-i

You are not my father . . . I flee from here . . . nevermore, Mime to see you again!
    Siegfried, S-1-i

So, Mime, sharpen your wits!
    The Wanderer, S-1-ii

Quick, how goes it with the sword? . . . Mime, you coward! Where are you!
    Siegfried, S-1-iii

But how can you bring it me, Mime? How, coward, could you teach me?
    Siegfried, S-1-iii, asking to be taught fear

Hey, Mime! Quick, what is this sword called that I've split into splinters?
    Siegfried, S-1-iii

Mime the craftsman is now learning cooking: he's lost his taste for forging. I have smashed all his swords. . . . A stranger must teach me [fear]: the best that Mime can do brings nothing home to me.
    Siegfried, S-1-iii, watching Mime

Then truly Mime's toil will be over: others will make eternal wealth for him. Mime the bold, Mime is king, prince of the elves, ruler of all! Hi, Mime! How lucky you are!
    Mime, S-1-iii, to himself

See, Mime, you smith, how sharp is Siegfried's sword!
    Siegfried, S-1-iii, completing the sword and concluding S-1

Quarrel with Mime, not me: your brother brings you danger; he is leading here a lad who must kill Fafner for him. . . . The Nibelung is using him for his own ends. . . . The boy knows nothing of the ring, but Mime will tell him.
    The Wanderer, S-2-i, to Alberich

Contend with your brother Mime.
    The Wanderer, S-2-i, to Alberich

Now, Mime, you must leave me to myself.
    Siegfried, S-2-ii, arriving at Neidhöhle

You'll thank me for bringing you and remember how Mime loves you.
> Mime, S-2-ii, to Siegfried

Mime, if you wait at the spring, I'll certainly let the dragon go there. I'll thrust Notung into his guts only after he's gulped you down, too.
> Siegfried, S-2-ii

If Mime had a son wouldn't he be the image of Mime?
> Siegfried, S-2-ii, resting under the lime tree

He must not trust the treacherous Mime! Let Siegfried listen alertly to the villain's lying words! He can now understand what Mime is thinking in his heart: this is how the taste of blood affected him.
> Wood Bird, S-2-iii, second advice to Siegfried

Hear what Mime means! Here, take and drink this draught!
> Mime, S-2-iii, offering Siegfried the poisoned draught

Mime, a deceitful dwarf, led me . . . but the dragon itself incited me to the sword-stroke which slew it.
> Siegfried, S-3-ii, to the Wanderer

Watch out, I say, that you don't fare like Mime!
> Siegfried, S-3-ii, taunting the Wanderer

Mime was the name of a surly dwarf: in the grip of envy he brought me up so that once the child had grown into a strong man he would kill for him a dragon in the forest who sluggishly guarded a treasure there.
> Siegfried, T-3-ii, his narrative

I gathered up the ring and Tarnhelm: I listened again to the delightful songster . . . "Hey! Siegfried now owns the helmet and the ring. He must not trust the treacherous Mime! Only for him is he to gain the treasure . . . He has designs on Siegfried's life. Oh, Siegfried must not trust Mime!"
> Siegfried, T-3-ii, his narrative

Did you repay Mime?
> Vassals, T-3-ii

What [Mime] could not forge he could still feel!
> Hagen, T-3-ii, after Siegfried tells him that his sword Notung killed Mime

MOON (Moonlight)
I must proclaim you the mightiest: for moon, stars and the radiant sun can do no other but serve you too.
> Loge, R-iii, flattering Alberich

In the spring moonlight you shine brightly . . . rapturously my eyes gloat on you.
> Siegmund, V-1-iii, to Sieglinde

MOTHER (Earth Mother)
Prematurely I was bereft of mother and sisters . . . Slaughtered lay my mother's brave body.
> Siegmund, V-1-ii

Mother, Mother, I am afraid. The strangers do not look friendly.
> Sieglinde, V-2-v, dreaming restlessly

Save me, girl; save a mother.
> Sieglinde, V-3-i, to Brünnhilde

The mother suckled the whelps. There I learned what love was: I never took cubs from their mother's care. Now where, Mime, have you your loving wife, that I may call her mother?
> Siegfried, S-1-i, to Mime

Did you really make me without a mother?
> Siegfried, S-1-i, to Mime

I am both your father and mother.
> Mime, S-1-i, to Siegfried

Who are my mother and father?
> Siegfried, S-1-i, to Mime

What father? What mother? Idle question!
> Mime, S-1-i, to Siegfried

Who are my father and mother?
> Siegfried, S-1-i, repeats

Then my mother died of me?
> Siegfried, S-1-i, to Mime

Your mother commanded me so to call you: as Siegfried you would be strong and handsome.
> Mime, S-1-i, answering Siegfried's question, "Now say: why am I called Siegfried?"

Now tell me, what was my mother's name?
> Siegfried, S-1-i, to Mime

But my mother mentioned [my father's] name?
> Siegfried, S-1-i, to Mime

Your mother gave me this . . . a shattered sword! She said your father carried it when he fell in his last fight.
> Mime, S-1-i, to Siegfried

Long ago I emerged from my mother's womb.
> Mime, S-1-ii, to the Wanderer

I am repeating your mother's advice . . . not to let you go into the world's wiles until you had learnt fear.
> Mime, S-1-iii, to Siegfried

Notung is the name of the trusty sword: your mother told me so.
> Mime, S-1-iii, to Siegfried

But what did my mother look like? I can't imagine that at all. . . . Do all men's mothers die of their sons? That would be sad indeed! Ah, if I her son could see my mother, my mother, a mortal woman! . . . If I understood [the bird's] sweet song, it would surely be saying something to me, perhaps about my dear mother?
> Siegfried, S-2-ii, resting under the lime tree

I am so alone. I have no brothers or sisters: my mother is dead, my father was slain: their son never saw them!
    Siegfried, S-2-iii, to the Wood Bird

The Valkyrie, Wotan's child, suffered the fetters of sleep while her omniscient mother slept? Does he who taught defiance punish defiance?
    Erda, S-3-i, to the Wanderer

I will not let you go, mother . . . you once thrust the thorn of anxiety into Wotan's bold heart . . . Tell me now: how can the god conquer his cares?
    The Wanderer, S-3-i, to Erda

The earth-mother's wisdom is drawing to an end: your wisdom will wither before my will. Do you know what is Wotan's will?
    The Wanderer, S-3-i, to Erda

Whatever now befalls, to the ever-young the god gladly yields. Descend then, Erda, mother of fear.
    The Wanderer, S-3-i

My senses swim and swoon! Whom can I call on to help me? Mother, mother! Think of me! . . . O mother, mother, this is your valiant child!
    Siegfried, S-3-iii, at first seeing Brünnhilde

Hail to my mother that bore me . . . that I can see those eyes whose light now delights me!
    Siegfried, S-3-iii, as Brünnhilde wakens

O hail to the mother that bore you! . . . Your eyes alone might see me.
    Brünnhilde, S-3-iii

Then my mother did not die? Was she only asleep?
    Siegfried, S-3-iii, to Brünnhilde

You dearest child! Your mother will not come back to you.
    Brünnhilde, S-3-iii, to Siegfried

To mother!
    Second Norn, T-Prologue, after the rope has snapped

Remember the might that you command, if you share the mettle of the mother who bore you.
    Alberich, T-2-i, to Hagen

Though my mother gave me valor I have no mind to thank her for falling victim to your guile.
    Hagen, T-2-i

Help, Hagen! Help my honor! Help your mother, who bore me too!
    Gunther, T-2-v

Now it is mixed, it overflows: let it be a refreshment for Mother Earth!
    Siegfried, T-3-ii, mixing his drink with Gunther's

I have heard children cry to their mother when sweet milk had been spilled; but no lament reached my ear fitting for this supreme hero.
    Brünnhilde, T-3-iii, to the Gibichungs

MUSIC

In the depths of the forest I set my horn waking the echo: with my music I asked, Would I be gladdened with a good friend's company?

> Siegfried, S-1-i, to Mime

NEIDHÖHLE

Neidhöhle it is named, to the east, on the fringe of the forest.

> Mime, S-1-iii, to Siegfried

[The world] is quite near to Neidhöhle.

> Mime, S-1-iii, to Siegfried

In the forest at night I keep watch over Neidhöhle. . . . Is the dragon's destroyer at hand? Is it he who is to slay Fafner?

> Alberich, S-2-i, at the beginning of S-2

To Neidhöhle I have come by night: whom do I descry there in the darkness?

> The Wanderer, S-2-i, joining Alberich

That was the effect of a savage dragon's blood that I killed at Neidhöhle.

> Siegfried, S-3-ii, explaining to the Wanderer why he can understand the Wood Bird

A gigantic dragon guarded the Nibelung's hoard at Neidhöhle: Siegfried closed its ravening jaws and slew it with his conquering sword.

> Hagen, T-1-i, to Gunther and Gutrune

From no woman did the ring come to me . . . I know it well as the prize of the battle I once fought at Neidhöhle, when I slew the fierce dragon.

> Siegfried, T-2-iv

NEIDING

Those ruffians [Neidinge] started a fierce attack on us.

> Siegmund, V-1-ii, to Sieglinde and Hunding

NIBELHEIM

From Nibelheim's night I'd gladly draw near if you'd but come down to me.

> Alberich, R-i, to the Rhine Daughters

Come, Loge, come down with me! We will descend to Nibelheim: I will procure the gold.

> Wotan, R-ii

Here's Nibelheim: through the pale mist what fiery sparks are flashing?

> Loge, R-iii, to Wotan

From Nibelheim's land of night we have heard new rumors: mighty marvels Alberich works here: greed drove us here as guests to gorge on them.

> Wotan, R-iii, to Alberich

Envy led you to Nibelheim: that I well know, bold guests.

> Alberich, R-iii, in response to Wotan

But what help is the hoard to you since Nibelheim is joyless and treasure can buy nothing?

> Wotan, R-iii

Nibelheim's night serves me to create treasure and conceal treasure; but with the hoard . . . I will win the whole world for my own.

> Alberich, R-iii, to Wotan

In the earth's depths dwell the Nibelungs: Nibelheim is their land.

> Wotan, S-1-ii, answering Mime's first question

Valhalla and Nibelheim bow before [Siegfried].

> Alberich, T-2-i, to Hagen

NIBELUNG

If you'd dive down, the Nibelung would freely frisk and frolic with you.

> Alberich, R-i, to the Rhine Daughters

Mock on then! The Nibelung nears your toy!

> Alberich, R-i, to the Rhine Daughters

The Nibelung, night-Alberich, moped in vain for the maidens' favors.

> Loge, R-ii

I grudge the gnome this gold; much harm the Nibelung has already done us.

> Fasolt, R-ii, to Fafner

New mischief will the Nibelung plot against us if the gold gives him power.

> Fafner, R-ii, to Fasolt

You there, Loge! Say without lies: of what great value is the gold then, that it satisfies the Nibelung?

> Fafner, R-ii, to Loge

Freia may stay with you in peace; an easier fee I've found in settlement: we rough giants would be satisfied with the Nibelung's shining gold.

> Fafner, R-ii, to Wotan

It will be easy for you, with cunning craft, which we in quarrels could never command, to fetter the Nibelung firmly.

> Fafner, R-ii, to Wotan

Nibelungs all, bow down to Alberich! . . . Listen for him, he is near, the Lord of the Nibelungs!

> Alberich, R-iii, exulting in the power of the Tarnhelm

Alberich wrought for himself a golden ring from the Rhine's gold . . . with it he has overcome us, the Nibelung's nocturnal race.

> Mime, R-iii, to Wotan and Loge

Carefree smiths, once we created ornaments for our women, wondrous trinkets, dainty trifles for Nibelungs, and lightly laughed at our work.

> Mime, R-iii, to Wotan and Loge

Friends to you; we will free the Nibelung people from their misery.

> Loge, R-iii, to Mime, who has asked who Loge and Wotan are

Beware the nocturnal host when the Nibelung horde rises from the silent depths to the daylight!

> Alberich, R-iii, threatens Wotan

But I deem it significant above all that those who heaped the hoard, the Nibelung host, obey you ungrudgingly.

> Loge, R-iii, to Alberich

I've called the Nibelungs to me: obedient to their master, I hear them hauling the hoard from the depths to the daylight.

> Alberich, R-iv, to Wotan

Hypocrite, how well it worked for you that I the Nibelung, in shame and distress, maddened by fury, gained the terrible magic whose work now gaily gladdens you!

> Alberich, R-iv, to Wotan

Thus, in direst distress, the Nibelung blesses his ring! Keep it now, guard it well; my curse you cannot escape!

> Alberich, R-iv, to Wotan, cursing the ring

Born of night the fearful Nibelung Alberich broke night's bonds: he cursed love and through his curse won the glittering Rhinegold.

> Wotan, V-2-ii, his narrative

With baleful rage the Nibelung nurses his grudge.

> Wotan, V-2-ii, his narrative

Of the Nibelung I recently heard a rumor that a woman was overpowered by the dwarf and seduced for money. . . . Then take my blessing, Nibelung's son. What deeply revolts me I bequeath to you.

> Wotan, V-2-ii, his narrative

Away to the east stretches a forest: Fafner carried off the Nibelung treasure into it.

> Siegrune, V-3-i

Fafner, the fearsome dragon lurks in the dark forest . . . He guards the Nibelung's gold there.

> Mime, S-1-i, to himself

Siegfried's youthful strength might well destroy Fafner's body: he would win for me the Nibelung's ring.

> Mime, S-1-i, to himself

Nibelung hatred, trouble and toil will not knit Notung together for me, nor wield the sword into a whole!

> Mime, S-1-i, to himself

In the earth's depths dwell the Nibelungs: Nibelheim is their land.

> The Wanderer, S-1-ii, answering Mime's first question

Fasolt and Fafner . . . envied the Nibelung's power; they won . . . the ring . . . Fasolt was slain, and as a savage dragon Fafner now guards the gold.

> The Wanderer, S-1-ii, answering Mime's second question

Custody of the world lies in the hand that controls the spear, clasped in Wotan's fist. Before him bowed the Nibelung host; his commands quelled the crew of giants; they all forever obey the mighty lord of the spear.

> The Wanderer, S-1-ii, answering Mime's third question

A wise Nibelung watches over Siegfried, who must slay Fafner for him so that he may gain the ring and become master of the treasure. What sword must Siegfried now flourish, fit for Fafner's death?

> The Wanderer, S-1-ii, asking Mime the second question

Even Alberich, who once thrust me in thrall, I now can compel to dwarf-drudgery; I shall go down there again as lord of the Nibelungs; the whole host shall be my slaves!

> Mime, S-1-iii, planning his revenge

Will the envied treasure again belong to the Nibelungs?

> Alberich, S-2-i, to the Wanderer

Quarrel with Mime, not me: your brother brings you danger; he is leading here a lad who must kill Fafner for him. . . . The Nibelung is using him for his own ends.

> The Wanderer, S-2-i, to Alberich

A hero is approaching to rescue the treasure; two Nibelungs crave for the gold; Fafner, who guards the ring, falls.

> The Wanderer, S-2-i, to Alberich

The Nibelung's treasure now belongs to Siegfried!

> Wood Bird, S-2-ii, first words to Siegfried

Though in fury and loathing I flung the world to the Nibelung's envy, now to the valiant Volsung I leave my heritage.

> The Wanderer, S-3-i, to Erda

He whom I chose . . . has gained the Nibelung's ring.

> The Wanderer, S-3-i, to Erda

I see the Nibelung's ring rise: an avenging curse gnaws at my braided strands.

> Second Norn, T-Prologue

A gigantic dragon guarded the Nibelung's hoard at Neidhöhle: Siegfried closed its ravening jaws and slew it with his conquering sword.

> Hagen, T-1-i, to Gunther and Gutrune

I have heard tell of the Nibelung hoard.

> Gunther, T-1-i

The Nibelungs are [Siegfried's] slaves.

> Hagen, T-1-i, to Gunther

Rumor names you as lord of the Nibelung hoard.

> Hagen, T-1-ii, to Siegfried

I know the Tarnhelm, the Nibelung's most skillful handiwork.

> Hagen, T-1-ii, when Siegfried mentions the helmet

His own bride [Siegfried] brings back to the Rhine: but to me he brings—the ring! You sons of freedom . . . you will yet serve the Nibelung's son.

> Hagen, T-1-ii, Hagen's watch

The Nibelung's ring.

> Hagen, T-2-v, contradicting Gunther, who asks if they will obtain "Brünnhilde's ring."

Guardian of night, Lord of the Nibelungs! Alberich, hear me! Bid the Nibelung host once more obey you, Lord of the ring!
> Hagen, concluding T-2

One [bird] sat on a bough and sang, "Hey! Siegfried now owns the Nibelung treasure!"
> Siegfried, T-3-ii, his narrative

NIGHT

From Nibelheim's night I'd gladly draw near.
> Alberich, R-i, to the Rhine Daughters

Night and mist, like to no one!
> Alberich, R-iii, invoking invisibility as he first tests the Tarnhelm

From Nibelheim's land of night we have heard new rumors.
> Wotan, R-iii, to Alberich

Nibelheim's night serves me to create treasure and conceal treasure.
> Alberich, R-iii, to Wotan

Night draws on; from its envy [Valhalla] now offers shelter.
> Wotan, R-iv

Night fell on my eyelids, but now the sun shines on me anew.
> Siegmund, V-1-i, regarding Sieglinde

This night I put you up. But tomorrow arm yourself.
> Hunding, V-1-ii, to Siegmund

Prepare my night drink and wait till I come to bed.
> Hunding, V-1-ii, to Sieglinde

Night and darkness closed my eyes; then the blaze of her look fell on me. . . . Night and darkness close my eyes: Deep in the recesses of my heart an invisible fire burns on.
> Siegmund, V-1-iii, to himself

I made [Hunding] a drugged drink: use the night to save yourself.
> Sieglinde, V-1-iii, to Siegmund

Are you trying to delude me, who day and night have been dogging your heels?
> Fricka, V-2-i, to Wotan

Born of night the fearful Nibelung Alberich broke night's bonds.
> Wotan, V-2-ii, his narrative

In the forest at night I keep watch over Neidhöhle.
> Alberich, at the beginning of S-2

To Neidhöhle I have come by night.
> The Wanderer, S-2-i, to Alberich

A whole night through we two have wandered in the woods.
> Siegfried, S-2-ii, to Mime

My eyes dim, their light fades: night falls on me.
> Brünnhilde, S-3-iii

Night affrights your confined eyes. Emerge from the darkness, and see.
> Siegfried, S-3-iii, to Brünnhilde

Dusk of the gods, let your darkness descend! Night of annihilation, let your mist fall!
> Brünnhilde, S-3-iii

It is still night. Why are we not spinning and singing?
> Third Norn, T-Prologue

Night is fading; I can discern no more.
> First Norn, T-Prologue

One night you must wait by the bank in the boat.
> Siegfried, T-1-ii, to Gunther

Have you come from Hella's hordes of night?
> Brünnhilde, T-1-iii, to Siegfried (as Gunther)

Night is falling: in your abode must you be wedded to me.
> Siegfried (as Gunther), T-1-iii, to Brünnhilde

Guardian of the night, Lord of the Nibelungs! Alberich, hear me. Bid the Nibelung host once more obey you, Lord of the ring!
> Hagen, concluding T-2

Dame Sun sends down her rays of light; night lies in the depths: once they were bright.
> Rhine Daughters, at the beginning of T-3

Avoid the curse! Nightly the weaving Norns twisted it into the rope of primeval law.
> Rhine Daughters, T-3-i, to Siegfried

NORNS

My womb bore three daughters, conceived before the start of time: what I see, the Norns nightly tell you.
> Erda, R-iv, to Wotan

She who granted you a wretched fate, the Norn, did not love you.
> Hunding, V-1-ii, to Siegmund

While I sleep the Norns are awake . . . Why not ask the Norns?
> Erda, S-3-i, to the Wanderer

Subservient to the world spin the Norns: nothing can they alter or deflect.
> The Wanderer, S-3-i, to Erda

You, Norns, snap your rope of symbols! Dusk of the gods, let your darkness descend! . . . Siegfried's star now shines upon me.
> Brünnhilde, S-3-iii

Siegfried! . . . Avoid the curse! Nightly the weaving Norns twisted it into the rope of primeval law.
> Rhine Daughters, T-3-i

My sword shattered a spear: even if they wove wild curses into it, Notung will sever for the Norns the eternal rope of primeval law.
> Siegfried, T-3-i, responding to the Rhine Daughters

NORTH

There's a thunderstorm coming from the north.
> Ortlinde, V-3-i

The furious huntsman [Wotan] who's hunting me in his anger, he's coming, he's coming from the north.
> Brünnhilde, V-3-i

Darkness is moving this way from the north.
> Waltraute, V-3-i, as Wotan approaches

From the north I throw [the rope] back to you. Spin, sister, and sing!
> The Third Norn, T-Prologue

The rope is too slack, it does not reach me. If I am to direct its end to the north, it must be stretched tighter!
> The Third Norn, T-Prologue, just before the rope snaps

NOTUNG (see also Sword)
"Notung," "Notung," I name you sword. "Notung," "Notung," precious blade . . . come from your scabbard to me.
> Siegmund, V-1-iii

Now follow me far from here, out into springtime's smiling house. For protection you'll have "Notung" the sword, even if Siegmund expires with love.
> Siegmund, V-1-iii

Our enemy . . . will die here at my hand when Notung devours his heart. Then you will be revenged.
> Siegmund, V-2-iii, to Sieglinde

Two lives smile on you here: take them, Notung, precious sword.
> Siegmund, V-2-iv, threatening to kill Sieglinde and the unborn child

Notung will pay [Hunding] his due.
> Siegmund, V-2-v. He rushes off to face Hunding

With Notung's fragments [Siegfried] could not taunt me.
> Mime, S-1-i, to himself

One sword only will suffice for the deed; only Notung can serve my envy if swaggering Siegfried wields it. But I can't wield it, that sword Notung.
> Mime, S-1-i, to himself

Nibelung hatred, trouble and toil will not knit Notung together for me, nor wield the sword into a whole!
> Mime, S-1-i, to himself

Notung is the name of the sword; Wotan thrust it into an ash-tree's trunk.
> Mime, S-1-ii, answering the Wanderer's second question

Who will weld the sturdy splinters of the sword Notung?
> The Wanderer, S-1-ii, posing the third question to Mime, who cannot answer

Now, Fafner's courageous conqueror, listen, ruined dwarf: "Only one who has never felt fear shall forge Notung anew."
> The Wanderer, S-1-ii, to Mime

The sword? The sword? How can I weld it? "Only one who has never felt fear shall forge Notung anew."
> Mime, S-1-iii

Notung is the name of the trusty sword: your mother told me so.
    Mime, S-1-iii

Notung, Notung, trusty sword!
    Siegfried, S-1-iii, pulling on the bellows

Notung, Notung, trusty sword! Now the splinters of your steel are molten! . . . Soon I will swing you as my sword!
    Siegfried, S-1-iii, at the bellows

Now sweat once more so that I can weld you, Notung, my sword!
    Siegfried, S-1-iii, thrusting the steel into the fire again

Notung, Notung, trusty sword! . . . The steel snapped for my dying father, his living son fashioned it anew . . . Notung, Notung, trusty sword!
    Siegfried, S-1-iii, completing the sword and concluding S-1

I'll thrust Notung into [Fafner's] haughty heart! Is that what's called fear?
    Siegfried, S-2-ii, to Mime

Mime, if you wait at the spring, I'll certainly let the dragon go there. I'll thrust Notung into his guts only after he's gulped you down, too.
    Siegfried, S-2-ii

Lie there, murderous beast: you have Notung through your heart.
    Siegfried, S-2-ii, having struck Fafner

Notung has settled envy's wages.
    Siegfried, S-2-iii, having killed Mime

Now, Notung, be witness that my wooing was chaste. Keeping faith with my brother, separate me from his bride!
    Siegfried, T-1-iii, in his natural voice, concluding T-1

Blood-brotherhood I swore to Gunther: Notung, my trusty sword, guarded the oath of loyalty.
    Siegfried, T-2-iv, refuting Brünnhilde

You lie, deceitful hero, and call your sword in false witness! . . . Serenely on the wall reposed Notung, faithful friend, when its lord wed his beloved.
    Brünnhilde, T-2-iv, accusing Siegfried

My sword shattered a spear: even if they wove wild curses into it, Notung will sever for the Norns the eternal rope of primeval law.
    Siegfried, T-3-i, to the Rhine Daughters

My father's blade I forged anew: I made Notung hard as nails.
    Siegfried, T-3-ii, his narrative

Notung felled the villain!
    Siegfried, T-3-ii, answering the vassals' question, "Did you repay Mime?"

NYMPHS, see Rhine Daughters

OATH (Vow)
Both sword and woman will be mine. Fiercely in my heart burns the oath that makes you my noble wife.
    Siegmund, V-1-iii, to Sieglinde

It is about marriage, a holy vow, vilely flouted, I am complaining.

    Fricka, V-2-i, to Wotan

Unholy I consider the vow that unites without love.

    Wotan, V-2-i, to Fricka

Oh! Why do I protest about marriage and its vows since you were the first to break them?

    Fricka, V-2-i, to Wotan

We gods will disappear, if today in a decent and respectable manner my rights aren't upheld by that bold girl. The Volsung shall die for my honor. Do I have Wotan's oath on it?

    Fricka, V-2-i

Take my oath!

    Wotan, V-2-i, to Fricka

Fight purely for Fricka, guard marriage for her and its vows. . . . I cannot will a free man to life: you must therefore fight for Fricka's subjects.

    Wotan, V-2-ii, to Brünnhilde

Listen! The horns, do you hear them call? . . . Hunding has woken from deep sleep. Wildly [the dogs] cry to heaven for the broken marriage vows.

    Sieglinde, V-2-iii

Does he who defends the right and preserves vows banish right and rule by perjury?

    Erda, S-3-i, to the Wanderer

Think of the vows that unite us; think of our mutual trust.

    Brünnhilde, T-Prologue, to Siegfried

May my body bear witness to my oath!

    Gunther, T-1-ii, to Siegfried

I can offer neither land nor people, nor father's house . . . All I have is a sword . . . May the sword be witness to my oath! I offer it with myself in alliance.

    Siegfried, T-1-ii, to Gunther

Then let us swear an oath.

    Gunther, T-1-ii, after Siegfried has promised to bring back Brünnhilde

Let the oath be of blood-brotherhood.

    Siegfried, T-1-ii, to Gunther

Thus I take the oath.

    Gunther, T-1-ii, swearing blood-brotherhood to Siegfried

Why did you not join in the oath?

    Siegfried, T-1-ii, to Hagen

Blood-brotherhood I swore to Gunther: Notung, my trusty sword, guarded the oath of loyalty.

    Siegfried, T-2-iv, refuting Brünnhilde

Swear an oath!

    Vassals, T-2-iv

I will silence [Brünnhilde's] accusation and swear an oath: which of you will venture his weapon on it?

> Siegfried, T-2-iv, to the Gibichungs

I will lay my spear-point on it: it will vouch for the honor of the oath.

> Hagen, T-2-iv

Shining spear . . . aid my eternal oath! On the spear-point I take this vow: spear-point, mark my words!

> Siegfried, T-2-iv

Shining spear . . . aid my eternal oath! On the spear-point I take this vow: spear-point, mark my words! . . . This man has broken his entire oath and now has perjured himself!

> Brünnhilde, T-2-iv

Oaths and perjury are idle words! Search for something stronger to sharpen your spear if you wish to assail the strongest!

> Brünnhilde, T-2-v, when Hagen asks whether Siegfried's perjury will protect him from Hagen's spear

Siegfried shall die! . . . He has betrayed his solemn oath . . . Omniscient god of vengeance, Wotan, witness of oaths and guardian of vows, look upon us! Bid your awesome heavenly hosts hearken here to this vow of vengeance.

> Brünnhilde and Gunther, T-2-v

He swore oaths—and does not keep them!

> Rhine Daughters, T-3-i, leaving Siegfried

You never were his true wife . . . I am his rightful spouse, to whom Siegfried swore eternal vows before ever he set eyes on you.

> Brünnhilde, T-3-iii, to Gutrune

No man more honest ever took an oath; none more true made a treaty; . . . yet none so betrayed all oaths, all treaties, his truest love! Do you know why this was?

> Brünnhilde, T-3-iii, immolation scene

O you, heavenly custodian of oaths! . . . Hear my lament, mighty god!

> Brünnhilde, T-3-iii, immolation scene

ORTLINDE
Put your stallion next to Ortlinde's mare.

> Ortlinde, V-3-i

Ortlinde's mare carries Wittig the Irming.

> Schwertleite, V-3-i

PACT, see Treaty

PEACE (Peaceful)
You bound us, who were free, to keep peace: I will curse all your wisdom and flee from your peace if . . . you do not know to keep faith in your bond!

> Fasolt, R-ii, to Wotan

Freia may stay with you in peace; an easier fee I've found in settlement: we rough giants would be satisfied with the Nibelung's shining gold.

Fafner, R-ii, to Wotan

Leave me in peace.

Mime, R-iii, to Loge

We have to track and trace [the gold], dig it out, without pause or peace, to pile up our master's hoard.

Mime, R-iii, to Wotan and Loge

Let's have peace! I think Freia is covered now.

Wotan, R-iv, restraining Donner

Leave me in peace! The ring I'll not surrender.

Wotan, R-iv, to the other gods

I can't call myself "Peaceful."

Siegmund, V-1-ii, to Sieglinde and Hunding

Woman, you asked; now you know why I am not called "Peaceful."

Siegmund, V-1-ii, to Sieglinde

And "Peaceful" may you not, being happy, be named?

Sieglinde, V-1-iii, to Siegmund

Sleep on now until the battle has been fought and peace brings you joy.

Siegmund, V-2-v, holding Sieglinde

Have I found myself a way to peace?

Mime, S-1-iii, to himself, hatching the plot against Siegfried

So, shameless one, leave us now in peace.

Alberich, S-2-i, to the Wanderer

Give me the ring as reward, and I will prevent the fight; you can watch over your hoard and live long in peace.

Alberich, S-2-i, to Fafner

I'll just hack off the boy's head: then I shall have peace and the ring too!

Mime, S-2-iii, again revealing his heart to Siegfried

Laughing hero! Leave me, oh leave me in peace.

Brünnhilde, S-3-iii, to Siegfried

Divine peace now floods my being.

Brünnhilde, S-3-iii

PRIMEVAL ASH, see Ash Tree
RAINBOW BRIDGE, see Bridge

RAMS

Let me warn you, Father, make ready yourself. You have to withstand a violent storm. Fricka, your wife, approaches in her chariot drawn by rams.

Brünnhilde, V-2-i

RAVENS

[The little bird] flew from you to save itself! The lord of the ravens it learnt was here: woe to it if they catch it! You shall not take the way it showed!

>   The Wanderer, S-3-ii, warning Siegfried

Amazement and awe struck the gods numb. He sent his two ravens on their travels: if ever they return with good tidings . . . the god will smile into eternity.

>   Waltraute, T-1-iii, her narrative

Can you also understand those ravens' cry? To me they cry revenge!

>   Hagen, T-3-ii, as Siegfried turns his back to Hagen

I hear your ravens stirring too; with dreaded desired tidings I now send them both home. Rest, rest now, o god!

>   Brünnhilde, T-3-iii, immolation scene

Fly home, you ravens!

>   Brünnhilde, T-3-iii

RENUNCIATION OF LOVE

Only he who forswears love's power, only he who forfeits love's delight, only he can attain the magic to fashion the gold into a ring.

>   Woglinde, R-i

Then we are secure and free from care, for everything that lives wants love: no one will reject love.

>   Wellgunde, R-i

I will put out your light, wrench the gold from the rock, forge the ring of revenge; for hear me ye waves: thus I curse love!

>   Alberich, R-i, to the Rhine Daughters

Concerned but for you, I looked about, feverishly ransacking the ends of the earth to find a substitute for Freia, such as would be fair to the giants. . . . Only one I saw who had forsworn love: for shining gold he had renounced woman's affection. . . . Night-Alberich . . . stole from [the Rhine Daughters] the Rhinegold; he now esteems it earth's most precious prize, greater than a woman's grace.

>   Loge, R-ii, to the gods, suggesting a substitute wage for the giants

A magic spell turns the gold into a ring. No one knows it; but anyone can easily acquire it who renounces blissful love. That you will not do.

>   Loge, R-ii, responding to Wotan

[The ring] is easily won now without cursing love.

>   Froh, R-ii

As I renounced love, all living things shall renounce it!

>   Alberich, R-iii, warns Wotan

Go back to the gods' holy council. Tell them this about my ring: I will never renounce love . . . though Valhalla's sublime splendor collapse in ruins!

>   Brünnhilde, T-1-iii, to Waltraute

He does not realize that he renounced it.

>   Rhine Daughters, T-3-i, who have said about Siegfried: "A glorious gift was granted him."

RHINE

The Rhine's innocent children bewailed their plight to me.

> Loge, R-ii, to the gods

I have heard talk of the Rhine's gold: its glittering glow hides runes of riches; a ring would give unbounded power and wealth.

> Wotan, R-ii, to Loge

Through the ford across the Rhine wade the giants.

> Loge, R-ii

I will gladly lead you steeply down: shall we journey through the Rhine?

> Loge, R-ii, to Wotan, as they depart for Nibelheim

Not through the Rhine!

> Wotan, R-ii, answering Loge

Alberich wrought for himself a golden ring from the Rhine's gold: . . . with it he has overcome us, the Nibelung's nocturnal race.

> Mime, R-iii, to Wotan and Loge

How gladly you yourself would have robbed the Rhine of its gold had you so easily found the way to forge it!

> Alberich, R-iv, to Wotan

The ring that [Alberich] made I took from him by a trick. But I did not return it to the Rhine; with it I paid the price for Valhalla, the castle that the giants built me, from which I ruled the world.

> Wotan, V-2-ii, his narrative

Was it you who robbed the Rhine of gold for the ring? Was it you who cast the spell that clings to the ring?

> Alberich, S-2-iii, to Mime

Hagen, tell me, hero, can I hold my head high on the Rhine? Does Gunther maintain Gibich's glory?

> Gunther, T-1-i, at the beginning of T-1

In his restless quest he may well roam even to the Gibich shores by the Rhine.

> Hagen, T-1-i, as Siegfried approaches

The horn sounds from the Rhine.

> Gunther, T-1-i, hearing Siegfried approach

Far along the Rhine have I heard of your fame.

> Siegfried, T-1-ii, to Gunther

The wind wafts Gibich's son on his way to woo a wife. . . . His own bride [Siegfried] brings back to the Rhine: but to me he brings—the ring!

> Hagen, T-1-ii, on watch

Gunther in a trice changed places with me: through the Tarnhelm's power I wished myself swiftly here. A strong wind now wafts the lovers up the Rhine.

> Siegfried, T-2-ii, to Gutrune

Good fortune and prosperity now smile on the Rhine if grim Hagen can be so merry!

> Vassals, T-2-iii

Home to the Rhine I bring you, Brünnhilde, rarest of women.
> Gunther, T-2-iv, presenting Brünnhilde

From the Rhine's gold the ring was wrought. He who cunningly fashioned it laid on it a curse into all eternity to doom to death whoever wears it.
> Rhine Daughters, T-3-i, to Siegfried

[Restore the ring to us] to hide it deep in the Rhine.
> Wellgunde and Flosshilde, T-3-i, warning Siegfried that he will be slain if he doesn't obey the Rhine Daughters' demand to return the ring to them

I would have caught three wild water-birds who sang to me there on the Rhine that this very day I should be slain.
> Siegfried, T-3-ii, to the Gibichungs

Brünnhilde! Brünnhilde! Her room is empty. Then it was she that I saw going to the Rhine!
> Gutrune, T-3-iii

Stack stout logs for me in piles there by the shore of the Rhine.
> Brünnhilde, T-3-iii, immolation scene

Fly home, you ravens! Recount to your master what you have heard here by the Rhine!
> Brünnhilde, T-3-iii, immolation scene

RHINE DAUGHTERS (Children of the Rhine, Nymphs, Rhinemaidens, Water Maidens, Watery Brood)

Hey, hey, you nymphs! How inviting you look.
> Alberich, R-i

Do you feed only on fraud, you faithless brood of nymphs?
> Alberich, R-i

Coquet in the dark, brood of the waters! I will put out your light.
> Alberich, R-i

For the glittering toy torn from the deep, the daughters made moan to me: to you, Wotan, they appeal to bring the thief to justice, and to give the gold back to the waters.
> Loge, R-ii, to the gods

Alberich guards himself with guile; you must act shrewdly and subtly to bring the thief to justice and to return to the Rhinemaidens the gold, their shining toy; for that is what they beg of you.
> Loge, R-ii, to Wotan

The Rhinemaidens? What is this counsel to me?
> Wotan, R-ii, to Loge

I wish to know nothing of that watery brood: many a man—to my sorrow—have they lured with their seductive sport.
> Fricka, R-ii, to Wotan

The Rhinemaidens appealed to you: can they hope for a hearing?
> Loge, R-ii, to Wotan

You call the ring your own? . . . Ask the Rhine's daughters whether they gave you for your own their gold that you robbed for the ring.
> Wotan, R-iv, to Alberich

This gold belongs to the Rhinemaidens. Wotan will give it back to them.
> Loge, R-iv, to Fafner, who has demanded Wotan's ring

The children of the Rhine lament their looted gold.
> Loge, R-iv, to Wotan

Accursed nymphs! Stop them annoying us!
> Wotan, R-iv, to Loge

You there in the water, why wail to us? Hear what Wotan wills for you. No more gleams the gold on you maidens: henceforth bask in bliss in the gods' new radiance!
> Loge, R-iv

If [Brünnhilde] would return the ring to the Rhine's daughters in its depths, from the weight of the curse would the gods and the world be free.
> Waltraute, T-1-iii, her narrative, quoting Wotan

Return it to the Rhinemaidens!
> Waltraute, T-1-iii, to Brünnhilde, urging her to give up the ring

To the Rhinemaidens? I? The ring? Siegfried's pledge of love? Are you out of your mind?
> Brünnhilde, T-1-iii, answering Waltraute

A wise woman lives for the Volsung's love: if ever she advised him to return the ring to the Rhinemaidens . . . then my gold would be lost and no ruse could ever retrieve it. So aim for the ring without delay!
> Alberich, T-2-i, to Hagen

I will never give [the ring] to you nymphs!
> Siegfried, T-3-i

Hey! You merry water-maidens! Come quickly! I'll give up the ring!
> Siegfried, T-3-i

You swimming daughters of the Rhine, I thank you for your good counsel.
> Brünnhilde, T-3-iii, immolation scene

RHINEGOLD (see also Gold)
Rhinegold! Rhinegold! Dazzling delight, how brightly and bravely you laugh! . . . Rhinegold! Rhinegold! Heiajaheia!
> Rhine Daughters, R-i, as the gold is first illuminated by the rays of the rising sun

Have you never heard of the Rhinegold?
> Rhine Daughters, R-i, responding to Alberich

He who from the Rhinegold fashioned the ring that would confer on him immeasurable might could win the world's wealth for his own.
> Wellgunde, R-i, explaining to Alberich

In revenge the robber [Alberich] stole from [the Rhine Daughters] the Rhinegold; he now esteems it earth's most precious prize, greater than woman's grace.
> Loge, R-ii, to the gods and giants

Till evening—pay due heed—we will hold [Freia] as hostage: we shall return; but when we come, if as ransom the bright gleaming Rhinegold is not lying ready—
    Fafner, R-ii, to Wotan

Rhinegold! Rhinegold! Purest gold! . . . Give us the gold! O give us its glory again!
    Rhine Daughters, R-iv, appealing to the gods

Rhinegold! Rhinegold! Purest gold! If but your bright gleam still glittered in the deep!
    Rhine Daughters, R-iv

Born of night the fearful Nibelung Alberich broke night's bonds: he cursed love and through his curse won the glittering Rhinegold.
    Wotan, V-2-ii, his narrative

Alberich once stole the Rhinegold. Do you know what happened to him?
    First Norn, T-Prologue

Once [the depths] were bright, when safe and glorious our father's gold gleamed there. Rhinegold! Lustrous gold!
    Rhine Daughters, T-3-i, at the beginning of T-3

Dame Sun, send us the hero who will give us back the gold! . . . Rhinegold! Lustrous gold!
    Rhine Daughters, T-3-i

RHINEMAIDENS, see Rhine Daughters

RIESENHEIM
Only at the boundary of Riesenheim do they make a pause.
    Loge, R-ii, watching the giants depart with Freia

At Riesenheim's towering boundary we stopped to rest: honorably we tended the pledge for the pact.
    Fasolt, R-iv, to the gods

On the earth's face flourishes the race of giants; Riesenheim is their land.
    The Wanderer, S-1-ii, answering Mime's second question

RING
He who from the Rhinegold fashioned the ring that would confer on him immeasurable might could win the world's wealth for his own.
    Wellgunde, R-i, explaining to Alberich

Only he who forswears love's power, only he who forfeits love's delight, only he can attain the magic to fashion the gold into a ring.
    Alberich, R-i, to the Rhine Daughters

I will put out your light, wrench the gold from the rock, forge the ring of revenge; for hear me, ye waves: thus I curse love!
    Woglinde, R-i

If [the gold] were fashioned into a round ring, it would bestow supreme power and win its master the world.
    Loge, R-ii, to Fafner

I have heard talk of the Rhine's gold: its glittering glow hides runes of riches; a ring would give unbounded power and wealth.

Wotan, R-ii, to Loge

A wife could ensure her husband's fidelity if she decked herself with the bright ornament that dwarfs forge to shine, toiling in the power of the ring.

Loge, R-ii, responding to Fricka

To control this ring seems wise to me. But how, Loge, can I learn the art of forging this gem?

Wotan, R-ii, to Loge

A magic spell turns the gold into a ring. No one knows it; but anyone can easily acquire it who renounces blissful love. That you will not do.

Loge, R-ii, to Wotan

You are too late also. Alberich did not hesitate; boldly he gained the power of the spell: the ring became his.

Loge, R-ii, to Wotan

The dwarf would have dominion over us all if the ring were not wrested from him.

Donner, R-ii, to the gods, learning of Alberich's control of the ring

I must have the ring!

Wotan, R-ii

Alberich wrought for himself a golden ring from the Rhine's gold: . . . with it he has overcome us, the Nibelung's nocturnal race.

Mime, R-iii, to Wotan and Loge

Through the ring's gold, [Alberich's] greed divines where a new gleam is concealed in the clefts: there we have to track and trace it, dig it out, without pause or peace, to pile up our master's hoard.

Mime, R-iii, to Wotan and Loge

I wanted to keep the helmet for myself, and through its spell escape from Alberich's sway . . . snatch the ring from him, so that, as I now am a menial to this bully, I might be free and he my slave!

Mime, R-iii, to Loge

Tremble with terror, abject throng: at once obey the master of the ring!

Alberich, R-iii, to the Nibelungs

Boldly you fingered a ring before which your people trembled in fear. But if in sleep a thief stole upon you and by stealth snatched the ring, how, wise one, would you guard yourself?

Loge, R-iii, to Alberich

But if I keep only the ring I could easily spare the treasure: for to win new wealth and joyfully increase it would soon be done at the ring's command.

Alberich, R-iv, to himself, when Wotan demands the gold

A golden ring rests upon your finger: do you hear, gnome? That, in my view, belongs to the hoard.

Wotan, R-iv, demanding the ring from Alberich

The ring?

> Alberich, R-iv, to Wotan, who has demanded the ring

My life, but not the ring!

> Alberich, R-iv, answering Wotan's "To be freed you must forfeit it."

I require the ring: with your life do what you will!

> Wotan, R-iv, to Alberich

I lose limb and life if I must lose the ring too; hand and head, eye and ear are not more my own than this shining ring!

> Alberich, R-iv, to Wotan

You call the ring your own? Are you raving, shameless gnome? Tell me truly, from whom did you take the gold from which you made the ring? Was it your own, that you wickedly stole it from the water's depths? Ask the Rhine's daughters whether they gave you for your own their gold that you robbed for the ring.

> Wotan, R-iv, to Alberich

Take heed, haughty god! If I sinned, I sinned only against myself: but you, immortal one, sin against all that was, is and shall be if recklessly you seize my ring!

> Alberich, R-iv, to Wotan

Surrender the ring! No right to it can your prattle prove.

> Wotan, R-iv, seizing the ring from Alberich

Since by curse it came to me, accursed be this ring! . . . The ring's master to the ring a slave, until again I hold in my hand what was stolen! Thus, in direst distress, the Nibelung blesses his ring!

> Alberich, R-iv, after Wotan seizes the ring

On Wotan's finger still glints a ring of gold: give it here to fill the crack!

> Fafner, R-iv, to Loge

What? This ring?

> Wotan, R-iv, answering Fafner

Your promise does not bind me: the ring remains with me as booty.

> Wotan, R-iv, rejecting Loge's suggestion to return the ring to the Rhine
> Daughters

I will not surrender the ring!

> Wotan, R-iv, answering Fafner's demand, "But you must yield it here towards the
> ransom."

Give up the ring!

> Donner, R-iv, to Wotan

Leave me in peace! The ring I'll not surrender.

> Wotan, R-iv, answering Donner

Yield, Wotan, yield! Escape from the ring's curse. To dark destruction irredeemably its possession dooms you.

> Erda, R-iv, her first words

I charge you, shun the ring!

> Erda, R-iv

You giants, take your ring!

> Wotan, R-iv, tossing the ring on the pile

Let [Fafner] take the treasure: only keep control of the ring!

> Loge, R-iv, advising Fasolt

Mine is the ring: for it I gave up Freia's gaze!

> Fasolt, R-iv, to Fafner

The ring is mine!

> Fafner, R-iv, as Fasolt tears the ring from Fafner's hand and cries "I hold it: it belongs to me."

Hold it fast in case it falls! [He kills Fasolt.] Now blink at Freia's gaze: the ring you will not touch again!

> Fafner, R-iv, to Fasolt

Great your gain when you won the ring; still more it profits you now that it is taken; you see, your foes fell each other.

> Loge, R-iv, to Wotan

The ring that [Alberich] made I took from him by a trick. But I did not return it to the Rhine; with it I paid the price for Valhalla, the castle that the giants built me, from which I ruled the world.

> Wotan, V-2-ii, his narrative

Erda, the sacred and wisest of women [Wala], told me to give up the ring.

> Wotan, V-2-ii, his narrative

If ever the ring were won back to [Alberich], then Valhalla would be lost. He who cursed love . . . could cruelly use the spell of the ring for all noble people's unending disgrace.

> Wotan, V-2-ii, his narrative

I anxiously deliberated with myself how the ring could be snatched from my enemy. One of the giants, to whom I once gave the accursed gold as payment for work, he, Fafner, guards the treasure for which he slew his brother. From him I would have to seize the ring.

> Wotan, V-2-ii, his narrative

I touched Alberich's ring: greedily I held his gold. The curse from which I fled still has not left me: I must forsake what I love.

> Wotan, V-2-ii, his narrative

[Fafner] changed himself into the form of a dragon. In a cave he keeps watch over Alberich's ring.

> Schwertleite, V-3-i, to Brünnhilde

Siegfried's youthful strength might well destroy Fafner's body: he would win for me the Nibelung's ring.

> Mime, S-1-i, to himself

Black Alberich once ruled as [the Nibelungs'] lord! A magic ring's masterful might subjugated the slaving mass to him. The shimmering hoard of rich treasure they heaped up for him.

> The Wanderer, S-1-ii, answering Mime's first question

Fasolt and Fafner . . . envied the Nibelung's power; they won . . . the ring . . . Fasolt was slain, and as a savage dragon Fafner now guards the gold.
    The Wanderer, S-1-ii, answering Mime's second question

A wise Nibelung watches over Siegfried, who must slay Fafner for him so that he may gain the ring and become master of the treasure. What sword must Siegfried now flourish, fit for Fafner's death?
    The Wanderer, S-1-ii, asking Mime the second question

How can he gain the ring for me?
    Mime, S-1-iii, watching Siegfried

He'll forge the sword and slay Fafner . . . The treasure and the ring will fall to him: how can I retrieve his gains?
    Mime, S-1-iii, to himself

With the same sword that [Siegfried] won for himself I will easily remove him from my way and win the ring and treasure for myself. Well, wise Wanderer, do you still deem me dull?
    Mime, S-1-iii, to himself

The glittering ring that my brother wrought, on which he laid a mighty spell, the shining gold that makes one master—I have won it!
    Mime, S-1-iii, when Siegfried has reforged the sword

Were I . . . as stupid as when you caught me . . . how easy it would prove to rob me of the ring again!
    Alberich, S-2-i, to the Wanderer

With my treasure you paid your debts; my ring recompensed the giants for their toil in building you your castle.
    Alberich, S-2-i

Unlike the stupid giants I will use the power of the ring: . . . I will storm Valhalla's heights with Hella's hosts.
    Alberich, S-2-i, threatening the Wanderer

Let him who wins the ring be its master.
    The Wanderer, S-2-i, to Alberich

The boy knows nothing of the ring, but Mime will tell him.
    The Wanderer, S-2-i, to Alberich

Am I contending with [Mime] alone for the ring?
    Alberich, S-2-i, to the Wanderer

A hero is approaching to rescue the treasure; two Nibelungs crave for the gold; Fafner, who guards the ring, falls.
    The Wanderer, S-2-i, to Alberich

[The boy] hankers for the golden ring alone: give me the ring as reward, and I will prevent the fight; you can watch over your hoard and live long in peace.
    Alberich, S-2-i, to Fafner

The Nibelung's treasure now belongs to Siegfried! Now he'll find the hoard in the cave. If wants to take the Tarnhelm, it will help him perform wondrous deeds; but if he could get the ring it would make him ruler of the world!

    Wood Bird, S-2-ii, first words to Siegfried

Was it you who robbed the Rhine of gold for the ring? Was it you who cast the spell that clings to the ring?

    Alberich, S-2-iii, to Mime

The magic ring put the dwarf and his skill at my service.

    Alberich, S-2-iii, to Mime

Where have you the ring now? The giants tore it from your timorous hands! [Note that Wotan, not the giants, took the ring from Alberich in R-iv.]

    Mime, S-2-iii, responding to Alberich

The ring should more rightly go to the mangiest dog than to you: never shall you gain the mighty ring, you lout!

    Alberich, S-2-iii, to Mime

Keep it then and guard it well, the gleaming ring! . . . I'll trade it to you for the gay toy of my Tarnhelm: we'd both be satisfied if we thus shared the spoils.

    Mime, S-2-iii, to Alberich, who refuses

Then neither ring nor Tarnhelm shall you have. I will not share with you!

    Mime, S-2-iii, to Alberich

And the ring, too!

    Mime, S-2-iii, noting Siegfried coming out of Fafner's cave with the ring

Damnation! The ring!

    Alberich, S-2-iii, also seeing Siegfried

Get him to give you the ring then! I'll soon win it for myself.

    Mime, S-2-iii, to Alberich

Hey! The helmet and the ring now belong to Siegfried!

    Wood Bird, S-2-iii, to Siegfried

So you would rob me of my sword and what it earned me, the ring and the booty?

    Siegfried, S-2-iii, to Mime

I'd nowhere be safe from you even if I had the ring. So with the sword . . . I'll just hack off the boy's head: then I shall have peace and the ring too!

    Mime, S-2-iii, again revealing his heart to Siegfried

He whom I chose . . . has gained the Nibelung's ring.

    The Wanderer, S-3-i, to Erda

I see the Nibelung's ring rise: an avenging curse gnaws at my braided strands.

    Second Norn, T-Prologue

In return for your tuition I give you this ring.

    Siegfried, T-Prologue, to Brünnhilde

Now for the ring take my horse! . . . Grane fearlessly will follow you . . . often give Grane Brünnhilde's greeting!

    Brünnhilde, T-Prologue, to Siegfried

A ring. . . . A wondrous woman keeps it.
> Siegfried, T-1-ii, referring to Brünnhilde, in answer to Hagen's question, "Did
> you take nothing else from the hoard?"

His own bride [Siegfried] brings back to the Rhine: but to me he brings—the ring! You
sons of freedom . . . you will yet serve the Nibelung's son.
> Hagen, T-1-ii, on watch

If [Brünnhilde] would return the ring to the Rhine's daughters in its depths, from the
weight of the curse would the gods and the world be free.
> Waltraute, T-1-iii, her narrative, quoting Wotan

The ring on your hand . . . for Wotan's sake, throw it away!
> Waltraute, T-1-iii, to Brünnhilde

The ring! Away?
> Brünnhilde, T-1-iii, to Waltraute

To the Rhinemaidens? I? The ring? Siegfried's pledge of love? Are you out of your mind?
> Brünnhilde, T-1-iii, answering Waltraute's entreaty to return the ring to the
> Rhine Daughters

More than the heaven of Valhalla, more than the glory of the gods, is this ring to me:
one glance at its gleaming gold . . . weighs more with me than the eternal joy of all the
gods! For from it shines Siegfried's love on me like a blessing—Siegfried's love!
> Brünnhilde, T-1-iii, to Waltraute

This is what the ring means to me! Go back to the gods' holy council. Tell them this
about my ring: I will never renounce love . . . though Valhalla's sublime splendor collapse in ruins!
> Brünnhilde, T-1-iii, to Waltraute

To horse, away! You shall not take the ring from me!
> Brünnhilde, T-1-iii, to Waltraute

Stand back! Fear this token! You cannot compel me into shame as long as this ring
shields me.
> Brünnhilde, T-1-iii, to Siegfried (as Gunther), who answers, "By husband's right
> it must be given to Gunther; with it you shall be married to him!"

Stand back, you robber . . . The ring makes me stronger than steel: never shall you steal
it from me.
> Brünnhilde, T-1-iii, to Siegfried (as Gunther)

He who once wrested the ring from me, Wotan the rabid robber, was overthrown by
one of his own offspring: to the Volsung he lost his authority and power; with all the
gods gathered round him in anguish he awaits his end.
> Alberich, T-2-i, to Hagen

Wotan's spear was split by the Volsung who slew the dragon Fafner in combat and innocently gained the ring.
> Alberich, T-2-i, to Hagen

Valhalla and Nibelheim bow before him. Even my curse is blunted on that fearless
hero: for he does not know the ring's value.
> Alberich, T-2-i, to Hagen

The golden ring, that is what we must obtain! A wise woman lives for the Volsung's love: if ever she advised him to return the ring to the Rhinemaidens . . . then my gold would be lost and no ruse could ever retrieve it. So aim for the ring without delay!

    Alberich, T-2-i, to Hagen

Not strong enough, indeed to oppose the dragon, which was destined for the Volsung alone, but to inexorable hate I bred Hagen, who now shall avenge me and obtain the ring in defiance of the Volsung and Wotan!

    Alberich, T-2-i, to Hagen

I will have the ring: possess yourself in patience.

    Hagen, T-2-i, to Alberich

Ah! The ring . . . on his hand! He . . . ? Siegfried . . . ?

    Brünnhilde, T-2-iv

I saw a ring on your hand. . . . How came you to get the ring from me?

    Brünnhilde, T-2-iv, to Siegfried

I did not get this ring from him [Gunther].

    Siegfried, T-2-iv, to Brünnhilde

As you took from me this ring . . . demand back the pledge!

    Brünnhilde, T-2-iv, to Gunther

The ring? I did not give him one.

    Gunther, T-2-iv, deeply bewildered, to Brünnhilde

Where have you hidden the ring you wrenched from me?

    Brünnhilde, T-2-iv, to Gunther

Ah! It was he who tore the ring from me: Siegfried, the thieving deceiver!

    Brünnhilde, T-2-iv, bursting out in rage

From no woman did the ring come to me . . . I know it well as the prize of the battle I once fought at Neidhöhle, when I slew the fierce dragon.

    Siegfried, T-2-iv

Brünnhilde, valiant woman, do you really recognize the ring? If it is that which you gave to Gunther, then it is his, and Siegfried obtained it by trickery, for which the traitor must atone.

    Hagen, T-2-iv

Immense power will be yours if you obtain from him the ring.

    Hagen, T-2-v, to Gunther, referring to Siegfried

Brünnhilde's ring!

    Gunther, T-2-v, to Hagen

The Nibelung's ring.

    Hagen, T-2-v, to Gunther

Mine is the treasure, to me it must belong. So let the ring be wrested from him. Gnome-father, fallen prince! Guardian of night, Lord of the Nibelungs! Alberich, hear me! Bid the Nibelung host once more obey you, Lord of the ring!

    Hagen, T-2-v, concluding T-2

A gold ring gleams on your finger.
> Wellgunde, T-3-i, to Siegfried, whom Woglinde has asked, "Siegfried, what will you give us if we grant you your quarry?"

I slew a giant dragon for that ring: shall I give it to you now in exchange for a paltry bearskin?
> Siegfried, T-3-i, to the Rhine Daughters

Laugh if you like! . . . Though you long for the ring, I will never give it to you nymphs!
> Siegfried, T-3-i, to the Rhine Daughters

If they came back to the water's edge, they could have the ring. Hey! You merry water-maidens! Come quickly! I'll give you the ring!
> Siegfried, T-3-i

. . . that is enclosed in the ring.
> Woglinde and Wellgunde, T-3-i, completing Flosshilde's warning to Siegfried, "Keep it, hero, until you learn the calamity."

You retain the ring at your peril.
> Wellgunde, T-3-i, to Siegfried

From the Rhine's gold the ring was wrought. He who cunningly fashioned it laid on it a curse into all eternity to doom to death whoever wears it.
> Rhine Daughters, T-3-i, to Siegfried

. . . and this very day: this we tell you, if you do not restore the ring to us . . .
> Three Rhine Daughters, T-3-i, to Siegfried, warning him that he should return the ring to the Rhine

A ring would win me the world's wealth: for the gift of love I'd gladly relinquish it . . . But by threatening life and limb . . . you will not wrest the ring from me!
> Siegfried, T-3-i, responding to the Rhine Daughters' warning

Only the ring. . .
> Flosshilde, T-3-i, telling of Siegfried's desire to retain the ring, which, Wellgunde adds, "dooms him to death"

. . . the ring alone he seeks to retain!
> Rhine Daughters, T-3-i

One [bird] sat on a bough and sang, "Hey! Siegfried now owns the Nibelung treasure! Now he'll find the hoard in the cave! If he would take the Tarnhelm it would serve him for mighty deeds; but if he could get the ring it would make him ruler of the world!"
> Siegfried, T-3-ii, his narrative

The ring and Tarnhelm, did you take them away?
> Hagen, T-3-ii, to Siegfried

I gathered up the ring and Tarnhelm.
> Siegfried, T-3-ii, to Hagen

I, Hagen, struck [Siegfried] dead. He was forfeit to my spear . . . I now demand this ring.
> Hagen, T-3-iii

Give the ring here!
> Hagen, T-3-iii, after killing Gunther

Accursed ring, terrible ring, I take your gold and now I give it away. . . . You swimming daughters of the Rhine, I thank you for your good counsel. . . . The fire that consumes me shall cleanse the ring from the curse! You in the water, wash it away and keep pure the gleaming gold that was disastrously stolen from you.

    Brünnhilde, T-3-iii, immolation scene

Keep away from the ring!

    Hagen, T-3-iii, the last words of *The Ring*

ROPE

With a rough rope I bridled [the bear] and brought him to ask you, rogue, for the sword.

    Siegfried, S-1-i, to Mime

The Norns are awake: they weave the rope, and zealously spin what I know.

    Erda, S-3-i, to Wotan

You, Norns, snap your rope of symbols! Dusk of the gods, let your darkness descend! . . . Siegfried's star now shines upon me.

    Brünnhilde, S-3-iii

While we spin and sing, what will you wind the rope on?

    Second Norn, T-Prologue, to the first

Come fair, come foul, I'll twine the rope and sing.

    First Norn, T-Prologue

So today I weave at the world ash-tree no more, and the fir must suffice me to fasten the rope.

    First Norn, T-Prologue

The ash-tree fell, the spring dried up forever! Today I fasten the rope to the jagged rock.

    Second Norn, T-Prologue

The end of the eternal gods will then fall forever. If you would know more, then wind the rope anew.

    Third Norn, T-Prologue

Do you want to know when that will be? Pass me the rope, sisters!

    Third Norn, T-Prologue, referring to Wotan's setting fire to the piled up logs

I can no longer find the strands of the rope.

    First Norn, T-Prologue

The jagged edge is cutting into the rope.

    Second Norn, T-Prologue

The rope is too slack, it does not reach me. . . . It has snapped.

    Third Norn, T-Prologue

Siegfried! . . . Avoid the curse! Nightly the weaving Norns twisted it into the rope of primeval law.

    Rhine Daughters, T-3-i

My sword shattered a spear: even if they wove wild curses into it, Notung will sever for the Norns the eternal rope of primeval law.

    Siegfried, T-3-i, to the Rhine Daughters

ROSSWEISSE

Grimgerde and Rossweisse!
>Waltraute, V-3-i, greeting her sisters

Greetings, you riders. Rossweisse and Grimgerde!
>Helmwige, Ortlinde, and Siegrune, V-3-i

Rossweisse, my sister, lend me your racehorse.
>Brünnhilde, V-3-i

RUNES

Runes of honestly concluded covenants Wotan carved in the spearshaft . . . An audacious hero shattered the spear in conflict.
>Second Norn, T-Prologue

What the gods taught me I have given you—a rich hoard of holy runes.
>Brünnhilde, T-Prologue, to Siegfried

Are they good runes I read in her eyes?
>Siegfried, T-1-ii, ardently looking at Gutrune

SCHWERTLEITE

Grimgerde, Gerhilde, lend me your horse. Schwertleite, Siegrune, look how afraid I am.
>Brünnhilde, V-3-i

SERF, see Slave
SERPENT, see Dragon
SHAFT, see Spear
SHE-WOLF, see Wolf

SHIELD

If half so stoutly as my arms my spear and shield had stuck to me, I'd never have run from my foes. But my spear and shield were smashed.
>Siegmund, V-1-i, to Sieglinde

With spear and shield I protected [the girl] for a long time until my spear and shield were cut from me in the fight.
>Siegmund, V-1-ii

Your eternal wife's sacred honor [Brünnhilde's] shield will protect today.
>Fricka, V-2-i, to Wotan

But I protected Siegmund with my shield, disobeying the god who killed him himself with his spear.
>Brünnhilde, V-3-i, to the Valkyries

I made you bearer of my shield, but you raised that shield against me.
>Wotan, V-3-ii, to Brünnhilde

Siegfried, Siegfried! . . . Even before you were born my shield protected you: so long have I loved you, Siegfried!
>Brünnhilde, S-3-iii

I see the shield there that sheltered heroes . . . No longer [does it] shield or protect me.
>Brünnhilde, S-3-iii

A wondrous maid has pierced my heart, a woman has wounded my head: I came here without a shield or helmet.
    Siegfried, S-3-iii

Think of the woman beneath the shield whom you found fast asleep.
    Brünnhilde, T-Prologue, to Siegfried

Sheltered by your shield, I can no longer count myself Siegfried, I am but Brünnhilde's arm.
    Siegfried, T-Prologue, to Brünnhilde

SIEGFRIED

Let me give [your unborn son] his name. "Siegfried," joyous in victory.
    Brünnhilde, V-3-i, to Sieglinde

Siegfried's youthful strength might well destroy Fafner's body: he would win for me the Nibelung's ring.
    Mime, S-1-i, to himself

One sword only will suffice for the deed; only Notung can serve my envy if swaggering Siegfried wields it.
    Mime, S-1-i, to himself

[Sieglinde] died, but Siegfried, he survived.
    Mime, S-1-i, to Siegfried

Now say: why am I called Siegfried?
    Siegfried, S-1-i, to Mime

Your mother commanded me so to call you: as Siegfried you would be strong and handsome.
    Mime, S-1-i, to Siegfried

Stop! Stop! Where are you going? Hey, Siegfried! Siegfried!, hey!
    Mime, S-1-i, as the boy runs off into the forest

The Volsungs are the love-children that Wotan fathered and fondly cherished . . . from them sprung Siegfried, the strongest scion of the Volsungs.
    Mime, S-1-ii, answering the Wanderer's first question

A wise Nibelung watches over Siegfried, who must slay Fafner for him so that he may gain the ring and become master of the treasure. What sword must Siegfried now flourish, fit for Fafner's death?
    The Wanderer, S-1-ii, asking Mime the second question

Only with the Wotan sword will a brave but stupid boy, Siegfried, slay the dragon.
    Mime, S-1-ii, answering the Wanderer's second question

I've brewed a deceptive draught to trap Siegfried when Fafner falls.
    Mime, S-1-iii, watching Siegfried

Smite the false, fell all knaves! See, Mime, you smith, how sharp is Siegfried's sword.
    Siegfried, S-1-iii, completing the sword and concluding S-1

Fafner and Siegfried, Siegfried and Fafner, oh if they'd only kill each other!
    Mime, S-2-ii, to himself

Tell me where I came from: in your death, dragon, you seem wise. You will know from my name: I am called Siegfried.
>   Siegfried, S-2-ii, to the dying Fafner

Siegfried . . . !
>   Fafner, S-2-ii, replies to Siegfried, then dies

The Nibelung's treasure now belongs to Siegfried!
>   Wood Bird, S-2-ii, first words to Siegfried

Against you I will call in Siegfried and his doughty sword.
>   Mime, S-2-iii, threatening Alberich

Hey! The helmet and the ring now belong to Siegfried!
>   Wood Bird, S-2-iii, to Siegfried

He must not trust the treacherous Mime! Let Siegfried listen alertly to the villain's lying words! He can now understand what Mime is thinking in his heart: this is how the taste of blood affected him.
>   Wood Bird, S-2-iii, second advice to Siegfried

Welcome, Siegfried! Tell me, valiant one, have you learnt fear?
>   Mime, S-2-iii, to Siegfried

Siegfried! . . . The treasure in Fafner's keeping, the gold was what I toiled for . . . Siegfried, my son, you can see for yourself, you must pay me with your life!
>   Mime, S-2-iii, revealing his heart to Siegfried

Siegfried now has slain the wicked dwarf! Now I know a wonderful wife for him . . . Brünnhilde would be his!
>   Wood Bird, S-2-iii, to Siegfried

There I see Siegfried coming.
>   The Wanderer, S-3-ii

I am Siegfried, and I awoke you.
>   Siegfried, S-3-iii, at Brünnhilde's awakening

Hail to thee, gods! . . . I am awake and can see! It is Siegfried who has awakened me.
>   Brünnhilde, S-3-iii

Siegfried, Siegfried! . . . Even before you were born my shield protected you: so long have I loved you, Siegfried!
>   Brünnhilde, S-3-iii

O Siegfried, Siegfried! . . . I have always loved you; for I alone divined Wotan's thought . . . my love for you!
>   Brünnhilde, S-3-iii

I see Grane there, my trusty steed . . . Siegfried woke him along with me.
>   Brünnhilde, S-3-iii

O Siegfried, Siegfried! See my anguish! . . . O Siegfried! . . . Wealth of the world! . . . Leave me in peace. . . . Do not destroy your beloved! . . . O Siegfried! Radiant youth! Love yourself and let me be.
>   Brünnhilde, S-3-iii

O Siegfried! I have always been yours!
>   Brünnhilde, S-3-iii

Whether I am now yours? Siegfried, Siegfried, do you not see me? . . . Siegfried, do you not fear, do you not fear this wild passionate woman?
    Brünnhilde, S-3-iii

Siegfried's star now shines upon me.
    Brünnhilde, S-3-iii

Sheltered by your shield, I can no longer count myself Siegfried, I am but Brünnhilde's arm.
    Siegfried, T-P, to Brünnhilde

Then you would be Siegfried and Brünnhilde.
    Brünnhilde, T-Prologue

Hail, Siegfried, victorious light!
    Brünnhilde, T-Prologue

Siegfried, the Volsung's offspring: . . . Siegmund and Sieglinde . . . engendered this noblest of sons. . . . Him I would wish for Gutrune's husband.
    Hagen, T-1-i, to Gunther and Gutrune

A gigantic dragon guarded the Nibelung's hoard at Neidhöhle: Siegfried closed its ravening jaws and slew it with his conquering sword.
    Hagen, T-1-i, to Gunther and Gutrune

And Siegfried won [the Nibelung hoard] in combat?
    Gunther, T-1-i, to Hagen

If Siegfried brought home the bride to you, could Brünnhilde not be yours?
    Hagen, T-1-i, to Gunther

You mocking, hateful Hagen! How could I capture Siegfried?
    Gutrune, T-1-i

Were Siegfried to . . . drink of that spiced draught, he would completely forget that . . . a woman had ever come near him. Now say: what think you of Hagen's scheme?
    Hagen, T-1-i, to Gutrune

I wish I could see Siegfried.
    Gutrune, T-1-i

This must be he who slew the dragon. It is Siegfried, certainly no other!
    Hagen, T-1-i, as the boat approaches

Hail, Siegfried, dear hero!
    Hagen, T-1-ii, upon Siegfried's arrival

You called me Siegfried: have you seen me before?
    Siegfried, T-1-ii, to Hagen

You need give me nothing, Siegfried: I'd be giving a mere trifle in exchange if for your helmet you took all I had.
    Gunther, T-1-ii

Siegfried?
    Gutrune, T-1-ii, asking Hagen where Siegfried has gone

Siegfried—mine!
    Gutrune, T-1-ii, when Hagen tells her Siegfried seeks her as wife

[Give up] Siegfried's pledge of love? Are you out of your mind? . . . For from it shines Siegfried's love on me like a blessing—Siegfried's love!

Brünnhilde, T-1-iii, to Waltraute

Siegfried! Siegfried returning? . . . Into the arms of my god!

Brünnhilde, T-1-iii, hearing Siegfried's horn call

Hey, Siegfried, swift hero! Where have you stormed in from?

Hagen, T-2-ii, as the hero suddenly appears

Hoiho, Gutrune, come forth! Siegfried is here.

Hagen, T-2-ii

Brünnhilde submitted to her husband throughout the bridal night. . . . Siegfried remained here with Gutrune.

Siegfried, T-2-ii, assuring Gutrune

Siegfried! Mightiest of men! I am in awe of you!

Gutrune, T-2-ii

The hero Siegfried kept [Gunther] safe.

Hagen, T-2-iii, to the vassals

Two happy couples I see here on show: Brünnhilde and Gunther, Gutrune and Siegfried!

Gunther, T-2-iv

Siegfried here . . . ! Gutrune . . . ?

Brünnhilde, T-2-iv, when Siegfried asks, "What troubles Brünnhilde's brow?"

Does Siegfried not know me?

Brünnhilde, T-2-iv, followed by Siegfried's, "Gunther, your wife is not well!"

Ah! The ring . . . on his hand! He . . . ? Siegfried . . . ?

Brünnhilde, T-2-iv, seeing the ring on Siegfried's finger

Ah! It was he who tore the ring from me: Siegfried, the thieving deceiver!

Brünnhilde, T-2-iv, bursting out in rage

Brünnhilde, valiant woman, do you really recognize the ring? If it is that which you gave to Gunther, then it is his, and Siegfried obtained it by trickery, for which the traitor must atone.

Hagen, T-2-iv

Siegfried? Gutrune's husband?

Gibichung women, T-2-iv, when Brünnhilde claims she is married to Siegfried

Disloyal, Siegfried? Did you indeed deceive?

Gutrune, T-2-iv

On Siegfried, who betrayed you.

Hagen, T-2-v, to Brünnhilde, offering to take revenge

On Siegfried? You?

Brünnhilde, T-2-v, to Hagen

How well I know Siegfried's conquering might. . . Whisper wise advice how the hero may fall to my spear.

Hagen, T-2-v, to Brünnhilde

Naught can help save Siegfried's death!
  Hagen, T-2-v, to Gunther

Siegfried's death!
  Gunther, T-2-v, horror struck

Siegfried shall die to redeem himself and you!
  Brünnhilde, T-2-v, to Gunther and Hagen

Then Siegfried is doomed!
  Gunther, T-2-v, to Hagen and Bruunnhilde, sighing deeply

Siegfried shall die! . . . He has betrayed his solemn oath.
  Brünnhilde and Gunther, T-2-v

Siegfried!
  Rhine Daughters, T-3-i, greeting the hero

Tell us, Siegfried, tell us!
  Rhine Daughters, T-3-i

Siegfried, what will you give us if we grant you your quarry?
  Woglinde, T-3-i

Siegfried! Siegfried! Siegfried!
  Rhine Daughters, T-3-i, and Wellgunde warns, "You retain the ring at your peril."

Siegfried! Siegfried! . . . Beware! Avoid the curse! Nightly the weaving Norns twisted it into the rope of primeval law.
  Rhine Daughters, T-3-i

Farewell, Siegfried! Stubborn man, a proud woman today will inherit your treasure.
  Rhine Daughters, T-3-i

Now we must hear the marvels of Siegfried and his hunting.
  Hagen, T-3-ii, as the Gibichungs join him

I heard say, Siegfried, that you could understand birdsong: is this so?
  Hagen, T-3-ii

One [bird] sat on a bough and sang, "Hey! Siegfried now owns the Nibelung treasure!"
  Siegfried, T-3-ii, his narrative

I listened again to the delightful songster . . . "Hey! Siegfried now owns the helmet and the ring. He must not trust the treacherous Mime! Only for him is he to gain the treasure; . . . He has designs on Siegfried's life. Oh, Siegfried must not trust Mime!"
  Siegfried, T-3-ii, his narrative

[The bird] still sat there and sang: "Hey! Siegfried now has slain the wicked dwarf!"
  Siegfried, T-3-ii, his narrative

Was that his horn? . . . Was that his horn? No! No sign of life! If only I could see Siegfried soon!
  Gutrune, T-3-iii

Up, Gutrune! Greet Siegfried! The mighty hero is coming home.
  Hagen, T-3-iii

A wild boar's prey, Siegfried, your dead husband.
  Hagen, T-3-iii, to Gutrune

Siegfried—Siegfried slain! Away, faithless brother . . . They have killed Siegfried!
>Gutrune, T-3-iii

You never were his true wife . . . I am his rightful spouse, to whom Siegfried swore eternal vows before ever he set eyes on you.
>Brünnhilde, T-3-iii, to Gutrune

Grane, my steed, greetings! . . . Radiant in the fire, there lies your lord, Siegfried, my blessed hero. . . . Heiajoho! Grane! Greet your master! Siegfried! See! Your wife joyfully greets you!'
>Brünnhilde, T-3-iii, immolation scene, her last words

SIEGLINDE

Are you Siegmund whom I see here? I am Sieglinde who longed for you: your own sister you have won and the sword as well.
>Sieglinde, V-1-iii

Smile on love and bless Siegmund and Sieglinde's union.
>Wotan, V-2-i, to Fricka

May Siegmund embrace Sieglinde there [in Valhalla]?
>Siegmund, V-2-iv, to Brünnhilde

She must still breathe the air of earth. You will not see Sieglinde there, Siegmund.
>Brünnhilde, V-2-iv

Wherever Sieglinde lives, in pleasure or sorrow, Siegmund will also stay.
>Siegmund, V-2-iv, to Brünnhilde

Stop, Volsung, hear what I say. Sieglinde shall live and Siegmund live with her. . . . For you, Siegmund, I'll procure favor and victory.
>Brünnhilde, V-2-iv

This is Sieglinde, Siegmund's sister and wife. Wotan is fuming with rage against the Volsungs.
>Brünnhilde, V-3-i, to the Valkyries

Farewell, luckless Sieglinde blesses you.
>Sieglinde, V-3-i, to Brünnhilde, her last words

By tearing myself from you I have saved [the Volsungs]. Sieglinde is carrying the holiest of issue.
>Brünnhilde, V-3-iii, to Wotan

She who in grief gave you to me may have been called Sieglinde.
>Mime, S-1-i, to Siegfried

The Volsungs are the love-children that Wotan fathered and fondly cherished . . . Siegmund and Sieglinde were sired by Volse . . . from them sprung Siegfried, the strongest scion of the Volsungs.
>Mime, S-1-ii, answering the Wanderer's first question

Siegfried, the Volsung's offspring: . . . Siegmund and Sieglinde . . . engendered this noblest of sons.
>Hagen, T-1-i, to Gunther and Gutrune

SIEGMUND

If "Volse" was your father and you are a "Volsung," it was for you [the old man] thrust his sword in the tree—so let me call you by the name I love: Siegmund so I name you.
Sieglinde, V-1-iii

Siegmund I am called and Siegmund I am, let this sword, which I fearlessly hold, bear witness. Volse promised me that in deepest distress I should one day find it.
Siegmund, V-1-iii

You see Siegmund, the Volsung, woman! As wedding gift he brings this sword.
Siegmund, V-1-iii

Now follow me far from here, out into springtime's smiling house. For protection you'll have "Notung" the sword, even if Siegmund expires with love.
Siegmund, V-1-iii

Are you Siegmund whom I see here? I am Sieglinde who longed for you: your own sister you have won and the sword as well.
Sieglinde, V-1-iii

Smile on love and bless Siegmund and Sieglinde's union.
Wotan, V-2-i, to Fricka

Siegmund won [the sword] himself in adversity.
Wotan, V-2-i, to Fricka, who has told Wotan to take away "the magical, strong flashing sword that you, the god, gave to your son."

Siegmund, as a slave, must be my victim. He, whose master you are, your slave and bondsman, must he exact the obedience of your immortal wife?
Fricka, V-2-i

Forbid her to let Siegmund win.
Fricka, V-2-i, arguing that Wotan must not let Brünnhilde help Siegmund

I called her to horse for Siegmund.
Wotan, V-2-i, to Fricka as Brünnhilde approaches

But the "Volsung" Siegmund, does he not act on his own?
Brünnhilde, V-2-ii, to Wotan

Then will you deprive Siegmund of victory?
Brünnhilde, V-2-ii, to Wotan

You love Siegmund; out of love for you, I know, I must protect the Volsung.
Brünnhilde, V-2-ii, to Wotan

You must kill Siegmund and procure victory for Hunding. . . . Siegmund wields a conquering sword: he will hardly die a coward.
Wotan, V-2-ii, to Brünnhilde

Do not provoke me. Remember what I commanded. Siegmund shall die. This is the Valkyrie's task.
Wotan, V-2-ii, to Brünnhilde

Look, your brother is holding his bride. Siegmund is your companion.
Siegmund, V-2-iii, comforting Sieglinde

Wildly [the dogs] cry to heaven for the broken marriage vows. Where are you, Sieg-mund? . . . That is Hunding's horn.

> Sieglinde, V-2-iii

No sword will serve when [Hunding's gang's] dogs attack. Throw it away, Siegmund. Siegmund, where are you? . . . Your sword shatters in pieces. The tree [Esche] topples, the trunk breaks. Brother, my brother, Siegmund—Ah!

> Sieglinde, V-2-iii

Siegmund, look at me. I am she whom you will follow soon.

> Brünnhilde, V-2-iv, beginning the annunciation scene

May Siegmund embrace Sieglinde there [in Valhalla]?

> Siegmund, V-2-iv, , to Brünnhilde

She must still breathe the air of earth. You will not see Sieglinde there, Siegmund.

> Brünnhilde, V-2-iv

Wherever Sieglinde lives, in pleasure or sorrow, Siegmund will also stay.

> Siegmund, V-2-iv

Siegmund, confide your wife to me; my protection shall enfold her firmly.

> Brünnhilde, V-2-iv

Stop, Volsung, hear what I say. Sieglinde shall live and Siegmund live with her. . . . For you, Siegmund, I'll procure favor and victory.

> Brünnhilde, V-2-iv

Rely on your sword and wield it boldly. The weapon will be true to you, just as the Valkyrie will truly protect you. Farewell, Siegmund, beloved hero.

> Brünnhilde, V-2-iv

If only Father would come home! He's still in the woods with the boy. Mother, Mother, I am afraid. The strangers do not look friendly . . . Siegmund, Siegmund! Siegmund, ha!

> Sieglinde, V-2-v, dreaming

Hunding, Siegmund, if only I could see them!

> Sieglinde, V-2-v

Strike [Hunding], Siegmund! Rely on your sword.

> Brünnhilde, V-2-v

This is Sieglinde, Siegmund's sister and wife. Wotan is fuming with rage against the Volsungs.

> Brünnhilde, V-3-i, to the Valkyries

From [Sieglinde's] brother Brünnhilde should today have withheld victory. But I pro-tected Siegmund with my shield, disobeying the god who killed him himself with his spear. Siegmund fell, but I fled far away with his wife.

> Brünnhilde, V-3-i, to the Valkyries

I would have been struck down by the same weapon that killed Siegmund. . . . Far from Siegmund, Siegmund, from you! O let death cover me.

> Sieglinde, V-3-i, to Brünnhilde

I knew one thing, that you loved the Volsung. . . . The alternative alone you had to see . . . that you must deny Siegmund your support.

> Brünnhilde, V-3-iii, to Wotan

I only saw what you could not see. I could not help seeing Siegmund. . . . Victory or death to share with Siegmund: I only knew that this was the lot I must choose. One man's love breathed this into my heart; one will it was that allied me with the Volsung.

    Brünnhilde, V-3-iii, to Wotan

[Sieglinde] is looking after the sword which you made for Siegmund.

    Brünnhilde, V-3-iii

The Volsungs are the love-children that Wotan fathered and fondly cherished . . . Siegmund and Sieglinde were sired by Volse . . . from them sprung Siegfried, the strongest scion of the Volsungs.

    Mime, S-1-ii, answering the Wanderer's first question

Notung is the name of the sword; Wotan thrust it into an ash-tree's trunk . . . Only Siegmund the valiant was victorious.

    Mime, S-1-ii, answering the Wanderer's second question

Siegfried, the Volsung's offspring: . . . Siegmund and Sieglinde . . . engendered this noblest of sons.

    Hagen, T-1-i, to Gunther and Gutrune

When I protected Siegmund against the god—wrongly, I know—I was nevertheless fulfilling his wish.

    Brünnhilde, T-1-iii, to Waltraute

SIEGRUNE

Here, Siegrune. Where were you dawdling so long?

    Waltraute, V-3-i

Grimgerde, Gerhilde, lend me your horse. Schwertleite, Siegrune, look how afraid I am.

    Brünnhilde, V-3-i

SIN

Take heed, haughty god! If I sinned, I sinned only against myself: but you, immortal one, sin against all that was, is and shall be if recklessly you seize my ring!

    Alberich, R-iv, to Wotan

SINTOLT

Sintolt the Hegeling.

    Helmwige, V-3-i, answering Waltraute's question, "Who is hanging on your
    saddle?" Sintolt is a fallen hero of the Hegeling race.

I always saw them at enmity, Sintolt and Wittig.

    Gerhilde, V-3-i, to Schwertleite

SLAVE (Serf)

I wanted to keep the helmet for myself, and through its spell escape from Alberich's sway . . . snatch the ring from him, so that, as I now am a menial to this bully, I might be free and he my slave!

    Mime, R-iii, to Loge

Crushed! Shattered! Of wretches the wretchedest slave!

    Alberich, R-iv

The ring's master to the ring a slave, until again I hold in my hand what was stolen! Thus, in direst distress, the Nibelung blesses his ring!

> Alberich, R-iv, curses the ring

With slaves no nobleman will fight . . . Siegmund, as a slave, must be my victim. He, whose master you are, your slave and bondsman, must he exact the obedience of your immortal wife?

> Fricka, V-2-i

Then take away [the sword's] magic. Let it break in your serf's hand.

> Fricka, V-2-i, answering Wotan's "I cannot strike [Siegmund] down. He found my sword."

Be off, slave. Kneel before Fricka: tell her that Wotan's spear avenged what caused her shame. Go! Go!

> Wotan, V-2-v, to Hunding

I shall go down there again as Lord of the Nibelungs; the whole host shall be my slaves!

> Mime, S-1-iii

Does the stingy, shabby slave coolly and brazenly claim to be made king?

> Alberich, S-2-iii, to Mime

The Nibelungs are [Siegfried's] slaves.

> Hagen, T-1-i, to Gunther

SNAKE, see Dragon

SPEAR (Shaft, Spearpoint, Spearshaft)

The marks of solemn compact that your spear shows, are they but sport to you?

> Fasolt, R-ii, to Wotan

Hold, hothead! Violence avails naught! My spearshaft protects bonds: spare your hammer's haft.

> Wotan, R-ii, to Donner, who threatens the giants

If half so stoutly as my arms my spear and shield had stuck to me, I'd never have run from my foes. But my spear and shield were smashed.

> Siegmund, V-1-i, to Sieglinde

With spear and shield I protected [the girl] for a long time until my spear and shield were cut from me in the fight.

> Siegmund, V-1-ii, to Sieglinde and Hunding

Get back from my spear; to pieces with the sword.

> Wotan, V-2-v, intervening in the fight between Siegmund and Hunding

Be off, slave. Kneel before Fricka: tell her that Wotan's spear avenged what caused her shame. Go! Go!

> Wotan, V-2-v, to Hunding

From [Sieglinde's] brother Brünnhilde should today have withheld victory. But I protected Siegmund with my shield, disobeying the god who killed him himself with his spear. Siegmund fell, but I fled far away with his wife.

> Brünnhilde, V-3-i, to the Valkyries

Let all trace of [my] body be destroyed by your spear; but do not be so cruel as to condemn [me] to vilest disgrace.

Brünnhilde, V-3-iii, to Wotan

Whosoever fears the tip of my spear shall never pass through the fire!

Wotan, V-3-iii, concluding *The Valkyrie*

Never shall the spear decay; with its point Wotan governs the world . . . Solemn treaties with symbols of trust he carved in its shaft. Custody of the world lies in the hand that controls the spear, clasped in Wotan's fist. Before him bowed the Nibelung host; his commands quelled the crew of giants; they all forever obey the mighty lord of the spear.

The Wanderer, S-1-ii, to Mime's third question

[Notung] was snapped on Wotan's spear.

Mime, S-1-ii, answering the Wanderer's second question

What once you promised the obstinate pair still remains today inscribed on the mighty shaft of your spear. You dare not snatch back from the giants what you paid them as quittance: you yourself would shatter your spear's shaft.

Alberich, S-2-i, to the Wanderer

No written treaty of trust bound you, villain, to me: my spear subjugated you by its power.

The Wanderer, S-2-i, to Alberich

If you do not fear the fire, then my spear must bar your way! . . . This shaft once shattered the sword you bear: once again then let it break on the eternal spear!

The Wanderer, S-3-ii, threatening Siegfried

My father's foe! . . . Flourish your spear: my sword will smash it to pieces!

Siegfried, S-3-ii, to the Wanderer

With his spear in splinters, has the coward escaped me?

Siegfried, S-3-ii, after the Wanderer disappears

Wotan then broke off a branch, a spearshaft the mighty one cut from the trunk. . . . The tree decayed and died: sadly the water dwindled in the well.

First Norn, T-Prologue

Runes of honestly concluded covenants Wotan carved in the spearshaft . . . An audacious hero shattered the spear in conflict.

Second Norn, T-Prologue

By the magic of his spear Wotan tamed [Loge]; he gave the god advice. To gain his freedom he gnawed and nibbled with his teeth at the notches in the shaft: then with the spear's powerful point Wotan bade him burn round Brünnhilde's rock.

Second Norn, T-Prologue

The shattered spear's sharp splinters Wotan will one day plunge deep into the heart of the glow.

Third Norn, T-Prologue

[Wotan] held the splinters of his spear: a hero had shattered the shaft. . . . He sent the nobles of Valhalla to the forest to fell the world-ash. . . . He summoned the council of the gods . . . So he sits . . . the spear's splinters held in his hand; Holda's apples he will not touch.

> Waltraute, T-1-iii, her narrative

Wotan's spear was split by the Volsung who slew the dragon Fafner in combat and innocently gained the ring.

> Alberich, T-2-i, to Hagen

I will silence [Brünnhilde's] accusation and swear an oath: which of you will venture his weapon on it?

> Siegfried, T-2-iv

I will lay my spear-point on it: it will vouch for the honor of the oath.

> Hagen, T-2-iv, answering Siegfried

Shining spear . . . aid my eternal oath! On the spear-point I take this vow: spear-point, mark my words!

> Siegfried, T-2-iv

Shining spear . . . aid my eternal oath! On the spear-point I take this vow: spear-point, mark my words!

> Brünnhilde, T-2-iv

Shall [Siegfried's] perjury protect him from my spear?

> Hagen, T-2-v, to Brünnhilde

Oaths and perjury are idle words! Search for something stronger to sharpen your spear if you wish to assail the strongest!

> Brünnhilde, T-2-v, to Hagen

Well I know Siegfried's conquering might . . . Whisper wise advice how the hero may fall to my spear.

> Hagen, T-2-v, to Brünnhilde

And there my spear shall strike!

> Hagen, T-2-v, when Brünnhilde reveals that Siegfried's back is vulnerable

My sword shattered a spear: even if they wove wild curses into it, Notung will sever for the Norns the eternal rope of primeval law.

> Siegfried, T-3-i

I, Hagen, struck him dead. He was forfeit to my spear . . . I now demand this ring.

> Hagen, T-3-iii

SPELL, see Magic

SPRING (Springtime)
Look, the spring smiles into the room. . . . In a gentle light springtime shines out. . . . The stout doors yielded too, for stubborn and hard they kept us from the spring. To its sister here it flew. Love decoyed the spring. . . . Love and Spring are united.

> Siegmund, V-1-iii, to Sieglinde

You are the spring for which I longed in the frosty winter time.

> Sieglinde, V-1-iii, in response

In the spring moonlight you shine brightly, nobly haloed with waving hair.
> Siegmund, V-1-iii, to Sieglinde

Now follow me far from here, out into springtime's smiling house. For protection you'll have "Notung" the sword, even if Siegmund expires with love.
> Siegmund, V-1-iii

What wrong did those two do when spring united them in love?
> Wotan, V-2-i, to Fricka

SPRING (Well)
I'll lie down by the spring there.
> Mime, S-2-ii, to Siegfried

Mime, if you wait at the spring, I'll certainly let the dragon go there. I'll thrust Notung into his guts only after he's gulped you down, too. So take my advice and don't rest by the spring.
> Siegfried, S-2-ii

At the world ash-tree once I wove . . . In its cool shadow bubbled a spring . . . An intrepid god came to drink at the spring.
> First Norn, T-Prologue

Wotan then broke off a branch, a spearshaft the mighty one cut from the trunk. . . . The tree decayed and died: sadly the water dwindled in the well . . . So today I weave at the world ash-tree no more, and the fir must suffice me to fasten the rope.
> First Norn, T-Prologue

The ash-tree fell, the spring dried up forever!
> Second Norn, T-Prologue

STAR
[Does not the gnome know] of the wondrous star in the waters' depths that shines, all-glorious, through the waves?
> Woglinde, R-i, as the sun illuminates the Rhinegold

I must acclaim you the mightiest: for moon, stars and the radiant sun can do no other but serve you too.
> Loge, R-iii, flattering Alberich

The stars of her eyes still shine on me: through a crack I cannot but see them!
> Fasolt, R-iv, seeing Freia through the piles of gold

Let the stars in your eyes shine on me again.
> Sieglinde, V-2-iii, hysterical when she cannot see Siegmund

For the last time let [your radiant eyes] delight me today with farewell's last kiss! May their star shine for that happier man!
> Wotan, V-3-iii, to Brünnhilde

Dusk of the gods, let your darkness descend! . . . Siegfried's star now shines upon me.
> Brünnhilde, S-3-iii

Effulgent shines Brünnhilde's star upon me!
> Siegfried, S-3-iii

Hail, Brünnhilde, radiant star!
> Siegfried, T-Prologue

Lustrous gold! How brightly you once shone, majestic star of the deep! . . . How happily you shone then, free star of the deep!
> Rhine Daughters, T-3-i

STRONGHOLD, see Valhalla

SUN (Sunlight)
The waking sun laughs in the depths.
> Woglinde, R-i

I must acclaim you the mightiest: for moon, stars and the radiant sun can do no other but serve you too.
> Loge, R-iii, flattering Alberich

The sun's eye sheds its evening beams; in its glorious gleam the castle shines in splendor.
> Wotan, R-iv

Now the sun shines on me anew.
> Siegmund, V-1-i, regarding Sieglinde

Like a blessing on me shone the sunlight.
> Siegmund, V-1-iii

Sun and clouds, just as they are, appeared reflected in the sparkling stream.
> Siegfried, S-1-i, to Mime

[What] glistens and gleams in the sunlight's glow?
> Mime, S-1-iii, hallucinating

When the sun is high, look out for the dragon: it will crawl from its cave . . . to drink at the stream.
> Mime, S-2-ii, to Siegfried

The sun stands high: from the blue heaven its eye gazes steeply down on to my head.
> Siegfried, S-2-iii

The laughing face of the radiant sun gleams through the billowing clouds.
> Siegfried, S-3-iii, reaching Brünnhilde's rock

Hail to thee, sun!
> Brünnhilde, S-3-iii, first words upon awakening

Emerge from the darkness, and see: the day shines bright in the sun!
> Siegfried, S-3-iii, to Brünnhilde

Bright in the sun shines the day of my shame!
> Brünnhilde, S-3-iii, answering Siegfried

Hail to the sun that shines upon us!
> Siegfried, S-3-iii

Dame Sun sends down her rays of light; night lies in the depths.
> Rhine Daughters, T-3-i

Dame Sun, send us the hero who will give us back the gold.
> Rhine Daughters, T-3-i

Like sunlight his clear radiance shines on me: he was the purest, he who betrayed me!

    Brünnhilde, T-3-iii, contemplating Siegfried's face after he has died

SWORD (see also Notung)

My father promised me a sword . . . Volse, Volse, where is your sword? The stout sword that I shall wield in adversity.

    Siegmund, V-1-iii

Let me show you a sword: o if only you could get it!

    Sieglinde, V-1-iii, to Siegmund

A sword flashed in [the stranger's] hand. This he thrust in the tree trunk . . . The sword remains silently there. . . . I know too for whom alone he fixed the sword in the tree.

    Sieglinde, V-1-iii, to Siegmund

Both sword and woman will be [mine]. Fiercely in my heart burns the oath that makes you my noble wife.

    Siegmund, V-1-iii, to Sieglinde

If "Volse" was your father and you are a "Volsung," it was for you [the old man] thrust his sword in the tree—so let me call you by the name I love: Siegmund so I name you.

    Sieglinde, V-1-iii

Siegmund I am called and Siegmund I am, let this sword, which I fearlessly hold, bear witness. Volse promised me that in deepest distress I should one day find it.

    Siegmund, V-1-iii

"Notung," "Notung," I name you sword. "Notung," "Notung," precious blade . . . come from your scabbard to me!

    Siegmund, V-1-iii

You see Siegmund, the Volsung, woman! As wedding gift he brings this sword.

    Siegmund, V-1-iii

Now follow me far from here, out into springtime's smiling house. For protection you'll have "Notung" the sword, even if Siegmund expires with love.

    Siegmund, V-1-iii

I am Sieglinde who longed for you: your own sister you have won and the sword as well.

    Sieglinde, V-1-iii, to Siegmund

Take away the sword which you gave him.

    Fricka, V-2-i, to Wotan

The sword?

    Wotan, V-2-1, to Fricka

Yes, the sword, the magical, strong flashing sword that you, the god, gave to your son.

    Fricka, V-2-i, to Wotan

You created the adversity for him, just like the flashing sword. . . . It was for him you thrust the sword into the tree trunk.

    Fricka, V-2-i, to Wotan

I cannot strike [Siegmund] down. He found my sword.

    Wotan, V-2-i, to Fricka

I provoked [Siegmund] to boldness against the council of the gods: against the vengeance of the gods his only protection now is the sword, which a god's favor bestowed on him.

> Wotan, V-2-ii, his narrative

Siegmund wields a conquering sword: he will hardly die a coward.

> Wotan, V-2-ii, telling Brünnhilde she must kill Siegmund

No sword will serve when [Hunding's gang's] dogs attack. Throw it away, Siegmund. Siegmund, where are you? . . . Your sword shatters in pieces. The tree [Esche] topples, the trunk breaks. Brother, my brother, Siegmund—Ah!

> Sieglinde, V-2-iii

Do you know this sword? He who made it for me promised me victory.

> Siegmund, V-2-iv, to Brünnhilde

He who made it for you has decreed your death. He will take the power from the sword.

> Brünnhilde, V-2-iv, to Siegmund

O shame upon him who made my sword . . . If I must die I shall not go to Valhalla. Let Hell [Hella] hold me fast.

> Siegmund, V-2-iv, to Brünnhilde

This sword which in trust a traitor gave me: this sword, which cowardly must betray me to my foe; if it may not avail against my foe, then let it avail against my friend. Two lives smile on you here: take them, Notung, precious sword.

> Siegmund, V-2-iv, threatening to kill the pregnant Sieglinde

Rely on your sword and wield it boldly. The weapon will be true to you, just as the Valkyrie will truly protect you. Farewell, Siegmund, beloved hero.

> Brünnhilde, V-2-iv

Fight now yourself or Fricka will let you down. For look! From your house, from the homely tree-trunk I fearlessly pulled out the sword: now taste its cutting power!

> Siegmund, V-2-v, to Hunding

Strike [Hunding], Siegmund! Rely on your sword.

> Brünnhilde, V-2-v, intervening in the fight

Get back from my spear; to pieces with the sword.

> Wotan, V-2-v, intervening in the fight

I would have been struck down by the same weapon that killed Siegmund. . . . Far from Siegmund, Siegmund from you! . . . If, on account of our escape, I am not to curse you, maiden, then hear my solemn plea: plunge your sword into my heart.

> Sieglinde, V-3-i, to Brünnhilde

Keep for [your unborn son] the sword's fragments. From his father's battlefield I luckily brought them. He will forge them anew and one day wield the sword.

> Brünnhilde, V-3-i, to Sieglinde

[Sieglinde] is looking after the sword which you made for Siegmund.

> Brünnhilde, V-3-iii, to Wotan

The best sword that ever I forged would hold firm in the fist of a giant . . . There is one sword [Siegfried] could not shatter.

> Mime, S-1-i, to himself

One sword only will suffice for the deed; only Notung can serve my envy if swaggering Siegfried wields it. But I can't wield it, that sword Notung.
    Mime, S-1-i, to himself

The best sword that ever I forged will never do for the one deed I desire.
    Mime, S-1-i, to himself

Bruin, ask for the sword!
    Siegfried, S-1-i

Hey, send [the bear] off! There lies the sword, prepared and polished today.
    Mime, S-1-i

With a rough rope I bridled [the bear] and brought him to ask you, rogue, for the sword.
    Siegfried, S-1-i, to Mime

Do you call this puny pin a sword?
    Siegfried, S-1-i, to Mime

He babbles of giants and brave battles . . . wants to make weapons and forge swords . . . I'd melt him down along with his sword.
    Siegfried, S-1-i, about Mime

Your mother gave me this . . . a shattered sword! She said your father carried it when he fell in his last fight.
    Mime, S-1-i, to Siegfried

My rightful sword I'll brandish! Get up! Quickly, Mime!
    Siegfried, S-1-i, to Mime

For this very day, I swear, I must have that sword.
    Siegfried, S-1-i, to Mime

What do you want with the sword today?
    Mime, S-1-i, to Siegfried

Nibelung hatred, trouble and toil will not knit Notung together for me, nor wield the sword into a whole!
    Mime, S-1-i, to himself

What sword must Siegfried now flourish, fit for Fafner's death?
    The Wanderer, S-1-ii, asking Mime the second question

Notung is the name of the sword; Wotan thrust it into an ash-tree's trunk . . . only Siegmund the valiant was victorious . . . it was snapped on Wotan's spear . . . only with the Wotan sword will a brave but stupid boy, Siegfried, slay the dragon.
    Mime, S-1-ii, answering the Wanderer's second question

Who will weld the sturdy splinters of the sword Notung?
    The Wanderer, S-1-ii, posing the third question to Mime

The sword! Alas, my head swims! . . . Who will shape the sword if my skill is insufficient?
    Mime, S-1-ii, responding to the Wanderer

Quick, how goes it with the sword? . . . Mime, you coward! Where are you?
    Siegfried, S-1-iii, to Mime

Say, what are you doing there? Sharpening the sword for me?
    Siegfried, S-1-iii, to Mime

The sword? The sword? How can I weld it? "Only one who has felt fear shall forge Notung anew."
    Mime, S-1-iii, half aside

What use is the stoutest of swords if fear remains foreign to you?
    Mime, S-1-iii, to Siegfried

Make the sword. I mean to wield it in the world.
    Siegfried, S-1-iii, to Mime

The sword? Alas!
    Mime, S-1-iii, to Siegfried

My father's blade befits me well: I'll forge the sword myself.
    Siegfried, S-1-iii, to Mime

Take that mush away! . . . I can't fire a sword with pulp.
    Siegfried, S-1-iii, rejecting Mime's solder

He's succeeding with the sword.
    Mime, S-1-iii, watching Siegfried

Hey, Mime! Quick, what is this sword called that I've split into splinters?
    Siegfried, S-1-iii

Notung is the name of the trusty sword: your mother told me so.
    Mime, S-1-iii, to Siegfried

Notung, Notung, trusty sword!
    Siegfried, S-1-iii, pulling on the bellows

He'll forge the sword and slay Fafner . . . The treasure and the ring will fall to him: how
can I retrieve his gains?
    Mime, S-1-iii, to himself

With the same sword that [Siegfried] won for himself I will easily remove him from my
way and win the ring and treasure for myself. Well, wise Wanderer, do you still deem
me dull?
    Mime, S-1-iii, to himself

Notung, Notung, trusty sword! Now the splinters of your steel are molten! . . . Soon I
will swing you as my sword!
    Siegfried, S-1-iii, at the bellows

Now sweat once more so that I can weld you, Notung, trusty sword!
    Siegfried, S-1-iii, thrusting the steel into the fire again

I have smashed all [Mime's] swords.
    Siegfried, S-1-iii

Hammer, shape me a sturdy sword. . . . Hammer, shape me a sturdy sword.
    Siegfried, S-1-iii, as he hammers the blade

He's shaping himself a sharp sword to slay Fafner, the dwarf's foe: I've brewed a deceptive draught to trap Siegfried when Fafner falls.
    Mime, S-1-iii, watching Siegfried

Notung, Notung, trusty sword! . . . The steel snapped for my dying father, his living son fashioned it anew . . . Notung, Notung, trusty sword! . . . Smite the false, fell all knaves! See, Mime, you smith, how sharp is Siegfried's sword.

> Siegfried, S-1-iii, completing the sword and concluding S-1

Bold is the boy's strength, and sharply cuts his sword.

> The Wanderer, S-2-i, to Fafner

The dead can tell no tales. Then lead me, my living sword.

> Siegfried, S-2-ii, pulling Notung from Fafner's breast

Against you I will call in Siegfried and his doughty sword.

> Mime, S-2-iii, threatening Alberich

As you were smelting your sword I was brewing this broth; drink it now, and I will win your trusty sword and with it the helmet and treasure.

> Mime, S-2-iii, revealing his heart to Siegfried

So you would rob me of my sword and what it earned me, the ring and the booty?

> Siegfried, S-2-iii, to Mime

I'd nowhere be safe from you even if I had the ring. So with the sword . . . I'll just hack off the boy's head: then I shall have peace and the ring too!

> Mime, S-2-iii, again revealing his heart to Siegfried

Taste my sword, loathsome babbler!

> Siegfried, S-2-iii, as he kills Mime

Mime, a deceitful dwarf, led me . . . but the dragon itself incited me to the sword-stroke which slew it.

> Siegfried, S-3-ii, to the Wanderer

Who made the sword so sharp and solid that it felled so strong a foe?

> The Wanderer, S-3-ii, asks Siegfried

I forged it myself since the smith couldn't: else I'd still be swordless.

> Siegfried, S-3-ii, to the Wanderer

But who made the splinters from which you forged yourself the sword?

> The Wanderer, S-3-ii, persisting to question Siegfried

How do I know? I only know that the fragments would have been useless had I not forged the sword afresh.

> Siegfried, S-3-ii, to the Wanderer

If you do not fear the fire, then my spear must bar your way! . . . This shaft once shattered the sword you bear: once again then let it break on the eternal spear!

> The Wanderer, S-3-ii, threatening Siegfried

My father's foe! . . . Flourish your spear: my sword will smash it to pieces!

> Siegfried, S-3-ii, answering the Wanderer

Come, my sword, sever the iron!

> Siegfried, S-3-iii, bending over the sleeping Brünnhilde, lifting the breastplate and discovering she is not a man

I see the breastplate's shining steel; a sharp sword cut it in two . . . I am exposed and unprotected, defenseless, a weak woman!

> Brünnhilde, S-3-iii

A gigantic dragon guarded the Nibelung's hoard at Neidhöhle: Siegfried closed its ravening jaws and slew it with his conquering sword.
  Hagen, T-1-i, to Gunther and Gutrune

I can offer neither land nor people, nor father's house . . . All I have is a sword . . . May the sword be witness to my oath! I offer it with myself in alliance.
  Siegfried, T-1-ii, to Gunther

Blood-brotherhood I swore to Gunther: Notung, my trusty sword, guarded the oath of loyalty.
  Siegfried, T-2-iv, refuting Brünnhilde

Lo, you lie, deceitful hero, and call your sword in false witness! . . . Serenely on the wall reposed Notung, faithful friend, when its lord wed his beloved.
  Brünnhilde, T-2-iv

Who will offer me a sword with which to sever my bonds?
  Brünnhilde, T-2-v

My sword shattered a spear: even if they wove wild curses into it, Notung will sever for the Norns the eternal rope of primeval law.
  Siegfried, T-3-i

[The] pupil's enterprise had to . . . weld into a sword again the pieces of a shattered weapon. My father's blade I forged anew: I made Notung hard as nails.
  Siegfried, T-3-ii, his narrative

Deceiving his wife, loyal to his friend, with his sword he separated himself from his own true love, alone dear to him.
  Brünnhilde, T-3-iii, immolation scene

TARNHELM (Fine-Wrought Gold, Helmet, Wrought Object)
Come here, crafty dwarf! You shall be pitilessly pinched by me if you haven't, on time, finished making what I ordered, the fine-wrought gold.
  Alberich, opening R-iii

The helmet fits my head; will the spell work, too?
  Alberich, R-iii, to Mime, as Alberich inspects the Tarnhelm

[Alberich] bade me forge and weld for him a helmet: he gave exact orders how I was to make it . . . I wanted to keep the helmet for myself, and through its spell escape from Alberich's sway.
  Mime, R-iii, to Loge

He who planned the work and snatched it from me now has taught me—alas, too late—what cunning lay in the helmet.
  Mime, R-iii, to Loge

I had Mime, the most skillful smith, fashion it for me: the helmet allows me to transform myself swiftly at will, and change my shape. No one can see me, though he search for me; yet I am everywhere hidden from sight. Thus I can live carefree, safe even from you, kind, considerate friend!
  Alberich, R-iii, to Loge

The wrought helmet that Loge is holding there, now kindly give it back to me.
  Alberich, R-iv, to Wotan

I still see the gleam of Holda's hair: throw that wrought object on the pile!

Fafner, R-iv, when the gold is piled up, referring to the Tarnhelm

What, the helmet too?

Loge, R-iv, answering Fafner

The Nibelung's treasure now belongs to Siegfried! Now he'll find the hoard in the cave! If he wants to take the Tarnhelm, it will help him perform wondrous deeds; but if he could get the ring it would make him ruler of the world!

Wood Bird, S-2-ii, first words to Siegfried

Who made the Tarnhelm, which changes men's shapes?

Mime, S-2-iii, to Alberich

Keep it then and guard it well, the gleaming ring! . . . I'll trade it to you for the gay toy of my Tarnhelm: we'd both be satisfied if we thus shared the spoils.

Mime, S-2-iii, to Alberich

Share with you? And the Tarnhelm too? . . . Not a jot!

Alberich, S-2-iii, to Mime

Then neither ring nor Tarnhelm shall you have. I will not share with you!

Mime, S-2-iii, to Alberich

He is holding the Tarnhelm!

Alberich, S-2-iii, as Siegfried emerges from Fafner's cave

Hey! The helmet and the ring now belong to Siegfried!

Wood Bird, S-2-iii, to Siegfried

As you were smelting your sword I was brewing this broth; drink it now, and I will win your trusty sword and with it the helmet and treasure.

Mime, S-2-iii, revealing his heart to Siegfried

I know the Tarnhelm, the Nibelung's most skillful handiwork.

Hagen, T-1-ii, when Siegfried says he has the Tarnhelm

You need give me nothing, Siegfried: I'd be giving a mere trifle in exchange if for your helmet you took all I had.

Gunther, T-1-ii

By the Tarnhelm's trickery I will change my shape to yours.

Siegfried, T-1-ii, explaining to Gunther how Siegfried will delude Brünnhilde

I resembled him to a hair: the Tarnhelm accomplished it, as Hagen rightly foretold.

Siegfried, T-2-ii, answering Gutrune's question, "Did Brünnhilde take you for Gunther?"

Gunther in a trice changed places with me: through the Tarnhelm's power I wished myself swiftly here. A strong wind now wafts the lovers up the Rhine.

Siegfried, T-2-ii, answering Gutrune

Believe me, I deplore it more than you that I did not better deceive [Brünnhilde]: I think perhaps the Tarnhelm only half hid me.

Siegfried, T-2-iv, to Gunther

One [bird] sat on a bough and sang, "Hey! Siegfried now owns the Nibelung treasure! Now he'll find the hoard in the cave! If he would take the Tarnhelm it would serve him for mighty deeds; but if he could get the ring it would make him ruler of the world!"
 Siegfried, T-3-ii, his narrative

The ring and Tarnhelm, did you take them away?
 Hagen, T-3-ii, to Siegfried

I gathered up the ring and Tarnhelm: I listened again to the delightful songster . . . "Hey! Siegfried now owns the helmet and the ring."
 Siegfried, T-3-ii, his narrative

THRONE
[Wotan] summoned the council of the gods; he took the throne in state . . . So he sits, speaking not a word, silent and solemn on his sacred throne.
 Waltraute, T-1-iii

TOAD
O might I, mute and amazed, see and hear only your toad-like form, your croaking voice!
 Flosshilde, R-i, teasing Alberich

So that the narrowest crevice might hold you, where a toad timidly hides.
 Loge, R-iii, challenging Alberich to make himself small

Crawl, crooked and grey toad!
 Alberich, R-iii, commands the Tarnhelm

There's the toad: seize it quickly!
 Loge, R-iii, to Wotan

A fish never had a toad for a father!
 Siegfried, S-1-i, to Mime

TOY, see Gold
TRAITOR, see Treachery

TREACHERY (Treason, Traitor)
Are you planning treachery? Betray our bond?
 Fasolt, R-ii, to Wotan

What a treacherous knave you have trusted!
 Fricka, R-ii, to Wotan, on Loge

Did I not have to avenge treason?
 Wotan, V-3-iii, to Brünnhilde

[Siegfried] must not trust the treacherous Mime!
 Wood Bird, S-2-iii

If . . . Siegfried obtained [the ring] by trickery . . . the traitor must atone!
 Hagen, T-2-iv

Treachery, to be revenged as never before!
 Brünnhilde, T-2-iv

Treachery? To whom?
 Gutrune, T-2-iv, confused by Brünnhilde's accusation

Treachery? Treachery?
  Vassals, T-2-iv

Treachery? To whom?
  Women, T-2-iv

Away, traitor, self betrayed!
  Brünnhilde, T-2-iv, to Gunther

"[Siegfried] must not trust the treacherous Mime!"
  Siegfried, T-3-ii, quoting the Wood Bird

TREASON, see Treachery
TREASURE, see Hoard

TREATY (Alliance, Bargain, Bond, Compact, Contract, Covenant, Pact)
By a contract I tamed [the giants'] insolent race into building me this sublime abode.
  Wotan, R-ii, to Fricka

Had I known of your contract I would have prevented the fraud.
  Fricka, R-ii, to Wotan

When [Loge] counseled this contract, he promised to deliver Freia: on him I now rely.
  Wotan, R-ii, to Fricka and Freia

They who betrayed you in this base pact have now all gone to ground.
  Fricka, R-ii, to Freia

Has this contract sent you off your heads? Think of some other fee: I cannot sell Freia.
  Wotan, R-ii, to the giants

Betray our bond? The marks of solemn compact that your spear shows, are they but sport to you?
  Fasolt, R-ii, to Wotan

Hold firm to your bond! What you are, you are only by contracts . . . I will curse all your wisdom if openly, honorably and freely you do not know to keep faith in your bond! . . . Do you now upset our bargain?
  Fasolt, R-ii, to Wotan

My spearshaft protects bonds: spare your hammer's haft.
  Wotan, R-ii, preventing Donner's attack on the giants

Is this how you hasten to right the evil bargain that you concluded?
  Wotan, R-ii, seeing Loge arrive

What? What bargain did I conclude?
  Loge, R-ii, to Wotan

Honorably we tended the pledge for the pact.
  Fasolt, R-iv, telling the gods that the giants have protected Freia's honor

It's all over then; our first bargain stands: Freia follows us forever!
  Fasolt, R-iv, when Wotan refuses to give up the ring

By treaties I made alliance with powers concealing evil. Loge cunningly tempted me and now has fluttered away.
  Wotan, V-2-ii, his narrative

I told you [Brünnhilde] to fetch . . . men, whose spirits we curbed, and through shady treaties deceitfully binding, held them to us in blind obedience. You were to spur them to storm and strife . . . so that hosts of bold warriors would gather in Valhalla's hall.
>   Wotan, V-2-ii, his narrative

These are the bonds that bind me. I became ruler through treaties; by my treaties I am now enslaved.
>   Wotan, V-2-ii, his narrative

Solemn treaties with symbols of trust [Wotan] carved in its shaft.
>   The Wanderer, S-1-ii, to Mime

No written treaty of trust bound you, villain, to me: my spear subjugated you by its power.
>   The Wanderer, S-2-i, to Alberich

Runes of honestly concluded covenants Wotan carved in the spearshaft . . . An audacious hero shattered the spear in conflict.
>   Second Norn, T-Prologue

In fragments fell the sacred register of contracts.
>   Second Norn, T-Prologue

Would you treat me with like disdain if I offered myself to you in bond?
>   Siegfried, T-1-ii, to Gutrune

Glad and free may blood-brotherhood today blossom from our bond!
>   Gunther and Siegfried, T-1-ii

If a brother breaks his bond . . .
>   Gunther, T-1-ii, taking the oath of blood-brotherhood

I abstain from hot-blooded bonds.
>   Hagen, T-1-ii, to Siegfried

For a broken bond blood alone can make amends!
>   Hagen, T-2-v, to Gunther

Did [Siegfried] break the bond?
>   Gunther, T-2-v, to Hagen

No man more honest ever took an oath; none more true made a treaty . . . yet none so betrayed all oaths, all treaties, his truest love! Do you know why this was?
>   Brünnhilde, T-3-iii, immolation scene

TREE, see Ash Tree
TRINKET, see Gold

TWILIGHT (Dusk)
Have you never felt, in the gloomy forest, when twilight falls in some dark spot . . . a grim horror?
>   Mime, S-1-iii, to Siegfried

Dusk of the gods, let your darkness descend!
>   Brünnhilde, S-3-iii

Evening twilight veils the sky: brighter blazes the guardian fire.
>   Brünnhilde, T-1-iii, as the flames around her rock become gradually brighter

TWINS

I came into the world one of two, I and a twin sister.
Siegmund, V-1-ii

If you grant respectability to adultery, then go on boasting and sanctify the incestuous fruit of this liaison between twins.
Fricka, V-2-i, to Wotan

Laughing you let go your rule over heaven—so as to gratify the mere pleasure and whim of those monstrous twins, your adultery's dissolute fruit.
Fricka, V-2-i, to Wotan

A vulgar human being has born you twins.
Fricka, V-2-i, to Wotan

VALHALLA (Castle, Fort, Fortress, Stronghold)

'Tis completed, the everlasting work: on the mountain peak stands the gods' stronghold, superbly soars the resplendent building!
Wotan, R-ii, contemplating the completed fortress

The fortress fills you with joy, but I fear for Freia. . . . The fort is finished, and forfeit is the pledge.
Fricka, R-ii, to Wotan

I well know what were the terms of those that built me yonder fortress.
Wotan, R-ii, to Fricka

But you, in building an abode, thought only of defenses and battlements: they would increase your dominion and power; only to arouse storms of unrest did this towering castle arise.
Fricka, R-ii, to Wotan

Though you wished, wife, to keep me in the castle, you must grant me, as a god, that, even confined in the fortress, I must win the outside world over to myself.
Wotan, R-ii, to Fricka

We two, unsleeping, built the fort . . . A lofty tower, door and gate guard and enclose the hall of the fine fortress.
Fasolt, R-ii, to Wotan

How foolishly you strive for towers of stone, and place in pledge woman's beauty for fortress and hall.
Fasolt, R-ii, to Wotan

The glorious fortress now firmly stands.
Loge, R-ii, to Wotan

When those who built the castle stipulated Freia as payment, you know that I agreed only because you undertook to redeem the noble pledge.
Wotan, R-ii, to Loge

The castle there was hard to build.
Fafner, R-ii, to Wotan

Does the noble fort not beckon to you, as it waits to welcome its owner to its shelter?
Fricka, R-iv, answered by Wotan's "With unclean wages I paid for that building!"

The bridge leads to the fortress.

> Froh, R-iv, to the gods

The castle shines in splendor . . . Thus I salute the fortress, safe from terror and dread. Wife, follow me and dwell with me in Valhalla!

> Wotan, R-iv

Let Hunding decide where he belongs, I do not require him in Valhalla.

> Wotan, V-2-i, telling Brünnhilde she must "charge into battle, she must see the Volsung wins"

The ring that [Alberich] made I took from him by a trick. But I did not return it to the Rhine; with it I paid the price for Valhalla, the castle that the giants built me, from which I ruled the world.

> Wotan, V-2-ii, his narrative

You [Valkyries] were to spur them to storm and strife . . . so that hosts of bold warriors would gather in Valhalla's hall.

> Wotan, V-2-ii, his narrative

If ever the ring were won back to [Alberich], then Valhalla would be lost. He who cursed love . . . could cruelly use the spell of the ring for all noble people's unending disgrace.

> Wotan, V-2-ii, his narrative

To the Lord of Battles [Walvater] who chose you I shall lead you. You will follow me to Valhalla.

> Brünnhilde, V-2-iv, to Siegmund

In the hall of Valhalla shall I find Battlefather alone?

> Siegmund, V-2-iv, to Brünnhilde

In Valhalla shall I find Volse, my own father?

> Siegmund, V-2-iv, to Brünnhilde

In Valhalla shall I be welcomed warmly by a woman?

> Siegmund, V-2-iv, to Brünnhilde

Then greet Valhalla for me, greet Wotan too, greet Volse for me and all the heroes, greet the lovely wishmaidens too. I will not follow you to them.

> Siegmund, V-2-iv, to Brünnhilde

O shame upon him who made my sword . . . If I must die I shall not go to Valhalla. Let Hell [Hella] hold me fast.

> Siegmund, V-2-iv

Of Valhalla's frigid joys please do not speak to me.

> Siegmund, V-2-iv

If we're all assembled then don't wait any longer. We'll make our way to Valhalla to bring Wotan his warriors.

> Rossweisse, V-3-i

I will never again send you from Valhalla, never again instruct you to fetch heroes from the wars.

> Wotan, V-3-ii, to Brünnhilde

If I must leave Valhalla . . . then let no cowardly boaster have me as his prize.
    Brünnhilde, V-3-iii

In the cloudy heights live the gods: Valhalla is their dwelling . . . Wotan, Lord of Light, rules over them.
    The Wanderer, S-1-ii, answering Mime's third question

My ring recompensed the giants for their toil in building you your castle.
    Alberich, S-2-i, to the Wanderer

Unlike the stupid giants I will use the power of the ring: . . . I will storm Valhalla's heights with Hella's hosts.
    Alberich, S-2-i, threatening the Wanderer

No god ever came so close to me! . . . Sacrosanct I came from Valhalla! . . . O the shame . . . He who woke me has wounded me. . . . I am Brünnhilde no more!
    Brünnhilde, S-3-iii

Farewell, Valhalla's glittering world! Let your proud fortress fall to dust!
    Brünnhilde, S-3-iii

Then Wotan bade Valhalla's heroes hack to pieces the withered boughs of the world-ash.
    Second Norn, T-Prologue

Still soars the stronghold the giants built.
    Third Norn, T-Prologue

My anxiety urges me back to Valhalla, as it drove me here to you.
    Waltraute, T-1-iii, to Brünnhilde

No more to war has Wotan sent us . . . The Father of Battles shunned Valhalla's brave heroes. . . . He roamed the world as the Wanderer.
    Waltraute, T-1-iii, her narrative

He held the splinters of his spear: a hero had shattered the shaft. . . . He sent the nobles of Valhalla to the forest to fell the world-ash.
    Waltraute, T-1-iii, her narrative

To end Valhalla's despair, throw the accursed thing in the water!
    Waltraute, T-1-iii, to Brünnhilde

More than the heaven of Valhalla, more than the glory of the gods, is this ring to me.
    Brünnhilde, T-1-iii, to Waltraute

This is what the ring means to me. Go back to the gods' holy council. Tell them this about my ring: I will never renounce love . . . though Valhalla's sublime splendor collapse in ruins!
    Brünnhilde, T-1-iii, to Waltraute

Woe to Valhalla's gods!
    Waltraute, T-1-iii, as she leaves Brünnhilde

Valhalla and Nibelheim bow before [Siegfried].
    Alberich, T-2-i, to Hagen

Fly home, you ravens! Recount to your master what you have heard here by the Rhine! Pass by Brünnhilde's rock: direct Loge, who still blazes there, to Valhalla; for the ends of the gods is nigh. Thus do I throw this torch at Valhalla's vaulting towers.

> Brünnhilde, T-3-iii, immolation scene

VALKYRIE (Valkyriehood)
You still respected your wife to make the Valkyrie gang, and even Brünnhilde the bride of your desire, respect me as their sovereign.

> Fricka, V-2-i, to Wotan

Keep the Valkyrie away from [Siegmund] too.

> Fricka, V-2-i, to Wotan

The Valkyrie shall do as she pleases.

> Wotan, V-2-i, to Fricka

The world's wisest woman bore me you, Brünnhilde. With eight sisters I brought you up; through you Valkyries I wanted to avert what the woman [Wala] told me to fear: a shameful end for the immortals.

> Wotan, V-2-ii, his narrative

Do not provoke me. Remember what I commanded. Siegmund shall die. This is the Valkyrie's task.

> Wotan, V-2-ii, to Brünnhilde

You have seen the Valkyrie's searing glance. Now you must go with her.

> Brünnhilde, V-2-iv, to Siegmund

Rely on your sword and wield it boldly. The weapon will be true to you, just as the Valkyrie will truly protect you. Farewell, Siegmund, beloved hero.

> Brünnhilde, V-2-iv

When the Valkyrie came to me, did she bring [Sieglinde] this marvelous comfort?

> Siegmund, V-2-v

I never saw such furious galloping by any Valkyrie.

> Rossweisse, V-3-i

Get the woman [Sieglinde] away if danger threatens her. None of the Valkyries dares protect her.

> Six Valkyries, V-3-i, to Brünnhilde

Wotan has told you what you once were. . . . Your Valkyriehood is over: from now on be what is still left for you to be.

> Wotan, V-3-ii, to Brünnhilde

You mean the Valkyrie, the maid Brünnhilde? She flouted the father of the storms.

> The Wanderer, S-3-i, to Erda

The Valkyrie, Wotan's child, suffered the fetters of sleep while her omniscient mother slept? Does he who taught defiance punish defiance?

> Erda, S-3-i, to the Wanderer

We Valkyries lie clasping [Wotan's] knees . . . He was thinking of you, Brünnhilde.

> Waltraute, T-1-iii, her narrative

VOLSE (see also Father, Wanderer, Wotan)
My father promised me a sword . . . Volse, Volse, where is your sword?
> Siegmund, V-1-ii

A Wolf (my father) was to craven foxes! . . . His name was Volse.
> Siegmund, V-1-iii, to Sieglinde

If "Volse" was your father and you are a "Volsung," it was for you [the old man] thrust his sword in the tree—so let me call you by the name I love: Siegmund so I name you.
> Sieglinde, V-1-iii

Siegmund I am called and Siegmund I am, let this sword, which I fearlessly hold, bear witness. Volse promised me that in deepest distress I should one day find it.
> Siegmund, V-1-iii

As Volse and like a wolf you prowled round the woods . . . You would sacrifice your wife to the she-Wolf's litter.
> Fricka, V-2-i, to Wotan

In Valhalla shall I find Volse, my own father?
> Siegmund, V-2-iv, answered by Brünnhilde's "You will find your father there, Volsung."

Then greet Valhalla for me, greet Wotan too, greet Volse for me and all the heroes, greet the lovely wishmaidens too. I will not follow you to them.
> Siegmund, V-2-iv

Siegmund and Sieglinde were sired by Volse . . . from them sprung Siegfried, the strongest scion of the Volsungs.
> Mime, S-1-ii, answering the Wanderer's first question

VOLSUNG
If "Volse" was your father and you are a "Volsung," it was for you [the old man] thrust his sword in the tree—so let me call you by the name I love: Siegmund so I name you.
> Sieglinde, V-1-iii

You see Siegmund, the Volsung, woman! As wedding gift he brings this sword.
> Siegmund, V-1-iii

Wife and sister you'll be to your brother. So let the Volsung blood increase.
> Siegmund, V-1-iii, concluding V-1

Brünnhilde must charge into battle, she must see the Volsung wins. Let Hunding decide where he belongs. I do not require him in Valhalla.
> Wotan, V-2-i, to Brünnhilde

Is it the end then, of the everlasting race of gods, since you brought those wild Volsungs to birth?
> Fricka, V-2-i, to Wotan

This Volsung you shall not keep for yourself. In him I find only you, since through you alone he can act boldly.
> Fricka, V-2-i, to Wotan

Hands off the Volsung!
> Fricka, V-2-i, answering Wotan's question, "What are you asking for?"

The Volsung shall die for my honor. Do I have Wotan's oath on it?
    Fricka, V-2-i

But the "Volsung" Siegmund, does he not act on his own?
    Brünnhilde, V-2-ii, to Wotan

You love Siegmund; out of love for you, I know, I must protect the Volsung.
    Brünnhilde, V-2-ii, to Wotan

I have never seen the father of victories like this . . . O my poor Volsung! In your deepest sorrow I, your friend, must disloyally forsake you.
    Brünnhilde, V-2-ii, after Wotan leaves

You will find your father there, Volsung.
    Brünnhilde, V-2-iv, answering Siegmund's question, "In Valhalla shall I find
    Volse, my own father?"

Volsung—listen well to me—you have been chosen by fate.
    Brünnhilde, V-2-iv, to Siegmund

Volsung, madman! Hear what I advise. Confide your wife to me for the sake of the child that she has got by your love.
    Brünnhilde, V-2-iv

Stop, Volsung, hear what I say. Sieglinde shall live and Siegmund live with her. . . . For you, Siegmund, I'll procure favor and victory.
    Brünnhilde, V-2-iv

With that swarthy Volsung Brünnhilde will still be waiting.
    Gerhilde, V-3-i, to Helmwige, who has noticed Brünnhilde's absence

This is Sieglinde, Siegmund's sister and wife. Wotan is fuming with rage against the Volsungs.
    Brünnhilde, V-3-i, to the Valkyries

Woe to this poor woman if Wotan finds her; he threatens destruction on all the Volsungs.
    Brünnhilde, V-3-i

Save the child that you received from him: a Volsung is growing in your womb.
    Brünnhilde, V-3-i, to Sieglinde

Did I order you to fight for the Volsung?
    Wotan, V-3-iii, to Brünnhilde

I knew one thing, that you loved the Volsung. . . . The alternative alone you had to see . . . that you must deny Siegmund your support.
    Brünnhilde, V-3-iii, to Wotan

Victory or death to share with Siegmund: I only knew that this was the lot I must choose. One man's love breathed this into my heart; one will it was that allied me with the Volsung.
    Brünnhilde, V-3-iii, to Wotan

The greatest hero—I know—will be born to the Volsung race.
    Brünnhilde, V-3-iii, to Wotan

Hold your tongue about the Volsung race! When I gave you up, I gave them up, too. Hatred demanded their annihilation!

Wotan, V-3-iii, to Brünnhilde

The Volsungs are the love-children that Wotan fathered and fondly cherished . . . Sieg-mund and Sieglinde were sired by Volse . . . From them sprung Siegfried, the strongest scion of the Volsungs.

Mime, S-1-ii, answering the Wanderer's first question

Now, my Volsung, you wolf's son! Drink and choke yourself to death!

Mime, S-2-iii, revealing his heart to Siegfried

Though in fury and loathing I flung the world to the Nibelung's envy, now to the valiant Volsung I leave my heritage.

The Wanderer, S-3-i, to Erda

Siegfried, the Volsung's offspring: . . . Siegmund and Sieglinde . . . engendered this no-blest of sons. . . . Him I would wish for Gutrune's husband.

Hagen, T-1-i

To the Volsung [Wotan] lost his authority and power; with all the gods gathered round him in anguish he awaits his end.

Alberich, T-2-i

Wotan's spear was split by the Volsung who slew the dragon Fafner in combat and in-nocently gained the ring.

Alberich, T-2-i, to Hagen

The golden ring, that is what we must obtain! A wise woman lives for the Volsung's love: if ever she advised him to return the ring to the Rhinemaidens . . . then my gold would be lost and no ruse could ever retrieve it.

Alberich, T-2-i, to Hagen

Not strong enough, indeed to oppose the dragon, which was destined for the Volsung alone, but to inexorable hate I bred Hagen, who now shall avenge me and obtain the ring in defiance of the Volsung and Wotan! Do you swear it, Hagen, my son?

Alberich, T-2-i

VOW, see Oath

WALA, see Erda

WALTRAUTE

Waltraute's voice, so welcome to me!

Brünnhilde, T-1-iii, hearing her sister's call

WANDERER (see also Father, Volse, Wotan)

The world calls me Wanderer; widely have I wandered already.

Wotan, S-1-ii, to Mime

Do not dally here, if the world calls you Wanderer.

Mime, S-1-ii

Much, Wanderer, have you told me of the earth's dark kernel.

Mime, S-1-ii

Much, Wanderer, have you told me of the rough surface of the earth.
> Mime, S-1-ii

You have solved the questions and redeemed your head: now, Wanderer, go on your way!
> Mime, S-1-ii

Wanderer, ask on! Perhaps I'll be lucky enough to succeed in saving my dwarf's head.
> Mime, S-1-ii

Well, Wanderer, do I keep my head this first time?
> Mime, S-1-ii

He's succeeding with the sword . . . The Wanderer knew it well. . . . [My head] will fall to the boy if Fafner does not teach him fear!
> Mime, S-1-iii, watching Siegfried

With the same sword that [Siegfried] won for himself I will easily remove him from my way and win the ring and treasure for myself. Well, wise Wanderer, do you still deem me dull?
> Mime, S-1-iii, to himself

I came to watch, not to act: who would bar the Wanderer's path?
> Wanderer, S-2-i, to Alberich

He is reflecting, reckoning up the value of his prize. Perhaps a wise Wanderer tarried here.
> Mime, S-2-iii, watching Siegfried

That is the Wanderer's way when he walks against the wind.
> The Wanderer, S-3-ii, when Siegfried asks why a large hat hangs down over the Wanderer's face

No more to war has Wotan sent us . . . The Father of Battles shunned Valhalla's brave heroes. . . . He roamed the world as the Wanderer.
> Waltraute, T-1-iii, her narrative

WARFATHER, see Father
WATER MAIDENS, see Rhine Daughters
WATERY BROOD, see Rhine Daughters

WEDDING
The men of his family sat in the room here, they were guests at Hunding's wedding.
> Sieglinde, V-1-iii

You, Hagen, please call the vassals to the Gibich hall for the wedding!
> Gutrune, T-2-ii

Women, lend a willing hand to the wedding!
> Siegfried, T-2-v

WELL, see Spring

WELLGUNDE
With Wellgunde there'd be two of us.
> Woglinde, R-i, inviting her sister to join her play

WEST

When you leave here and travel west, in wealthy estates there dwell the kinsmen who guard Hunding's honor.

> Hunding, V-1-ii, to Siegmund

WIND

That is the Wanderer's way when he walks against the wind.

> The Wanderer, S-3-ii, when Siegfried asks why a large hat hangs down over the Wanderer's face

Hence with you, raging storm-cloud, driven on the wind: never come my way again!

> Brünnhilde, T-1-iii, after Waltraute departs in a thundercloud

A strong wind now wafts the lovers up the Rhine.

> Siegfried, T-2-ii, to Gutrune

WINTER

Winter storms have vanished before Maytime. . . . Winter and storms vanish before their stout defense.

> Siegmund, V-1-iii, the Spring Song

You are the spring for which I longed in the frosty winter time.

> Sieglinde, V-1-iii, to Siegmund

WITTIG

Ortlinde's mare carries Wittig the Irming.

> Schwertleite, V-3-i. Wittig is a fallen hero of the Irming race.

I always saw them at enmity, Sintolt and Wittig.

> Gerhilde, V-3-i

WOEFUL

I named myself "Woeful" [Wehwalt].

> Siegmund, V-1-i, to Sieglinde

I can't call myself "Peaceful"; I wish I were called "Cheerful"; but "Woeful" has to be my name.

> Siegmund, V-1-ii, to Sieglinde and Hunding

Strange and brutal tales you tell us, bold guest, "Woeful" the "Wolf-cub"!

> Hunding, V-1-ii

I had to be called "Woeful": Woe is all I possess.

> Siegmund, V-1-ii

Are you really called "Woeful"?

> Sieglinde, V-1-iii, to Siegmund

Woeful! Woeful! Stand up and fight me, or my dogs will get you.

> Hunding, V-2-v

WOGLINDE

Woglinde, are you watching alone?

> Wellgunde, R-i, joining her playful sister

Flosshilde, swim! Woglinde's escaping.
>Wellgunde, R-i

Turn to me and do not heed Woglinde.
>Wellgunde, R-i, teasing Alberich

WOLF (She-Wolf, Wolf-Cub, Wolfskin)
"Wolf" was my father . . . Warlike and strong was Wolf . . . From scrapping and harrying we came home one day: there stood the Wolf's lair empty . . . Many years I passed with Wolf in the wild wood . . . But we two Wolves defended ourselves bravely. A "Wolf-cub" tells you this, and as "Wolf-cub" I'm known to many folk.
>Siegmund, V-1-i, to Sieglinde and Hunding

Strange and brutal tales you tell us, bold guest, "Woeful" the "Wolf-cub"! I fancy of that war-like couple I have heard dark tales, though I never knew "Wolf" or "Wolf-cub."
>Hunding, V-1-ii

Many of the pursuers fell to the "Wolves". . . . But I was separated from my father. . . . Only a wolfskin I found in the forest. It lay empty before me. I did not find my father.
>Siegmund, V-1-ii

My house will shelter you, "Wolf-cub," for today. For this night I put you up. But tomorrow arm yourself.
>Hunding, V-1-ii, to Siegmund

A man needs his armor. "Wolf-cub," I will meet you tomorrow. . . Be on your guard!
>Hunding, V-1-ii

But did you name Wolf as your father?
>Sieglinde, V-1-iii, to Siegmund

A Wolf he was to craven foxes! . . . His name was Volse.
>Siegmund, V-1-iii, answering Sieglinde

As Volse and like a wolf you prowled round the woods . . . you would sacrifice your wife to the she-Wolf's litter.
>Fricka, V-2-i

Resting in the bushes, roedeer also paired off, and so did even wild foxes and wolves.
>Siegfried, S-1-i, to Mime

Well, now listen to my horn. . . . Nothing better has yet come than wolf or bear. Now let me see what it will bring me; perhaps a dear companion!
>Siegfried, S-2-ii, to the Wood Bird

Now, my Volsung, you wolf's son! Drink and choke yourself to death!
>Mime, S-2-iii, revealing his heart to Siegfried

WOMAN'S WORTH (Woman's Beauty, Woman's Grace; see also "A Core Motive: Woman's Worth" in the Appendix)

For the idle toys of might and dominion would you, in blasphemous scorn, stake love and a woman's worth.
>Fricka, R-ii, to Wotan

How foolishly you strive for towers of stone, and place in pledge woman's beauty [Weibes Wonne].
>Fasolt, R-ii

In the whole wide world nothing is so rich that a man will accept it in lieu of woman's beauty and delight [Weibes Wonne und Wert]. Wherever there is life and being . . . I asked . . . what would a man think mightier than woman's beauty and delight.

> Loge, R-ii

[Alberich] now esteems [the Rhinegold] earth's most precious prize, greater than woman's grace [Weibes Huld].

> Loge, R-ii

WORLD ASH TREE, see Ash Tree

WOTAN (see also Father, Volse, Wanderer)
Wotan, husband, awake!

> Fricka, opening R-ii

Alas! Woe's me! Wotan forsakes me!

> Freia, R-ii, believing herself abandoned to the giants

A stately home, a stronghold, this was Wotan's wish.

> Loge, R-ii, to the gods

To you, Wotan, [the Rhine Daughters] appeal to bring the thief to justice, and to give the gold back to the waters.

> Loge, R-ii, to Wotan

Hear, Wotan, what we have at last to say!

> Fafner, R-ii

On what does Wotan brood so darkly? . . . How is it with Fricka? Is she displeased with Wotan's grey gloom that suddenly turns him into a greybeard?

> Loge, R-ii, as the gods weaken in Freia's absence

Wotan, unhappy man! See how your giddy thoughtlessness has brought disgrace and humiliation on us all!

> Fricka, R-ii

Fare thee well, Wotan.

> Donner, R-ii, as Wotan goes down to Nibelheim

On Wotan's finger still glints a ring of gold: give it here to fill the crack!

> Fafner, R-iv

This gold belongs to the Rhinemaidens. Wotan will give it back to them.

> Loge, R-iv, to the giants

Yield, Wotan, yield! Escape from the ring's curse. To dark destruction irredeemably its possession dooms you.

> Erda, R-iv, her first words

Desist Wotan, touch not the noble one, heed her words!

> Froh, R-iv, as Wotan tries to follow Erda

What can equal your luck, Wotan? . . . Your foes fell each other for the gold that you gave up.

> Loge, R-iv, after Fafner kills Fasolt

Why do you tarry, Wotan?

> Fricka, R-iv, as Wotan ponders Erda's warning

Hear what Wotan wills for you. No more gleams the gold on you maidens: henceforth bask in bliss in the gods' new radiance!

> Loge, R-iv, to the Rhine Daughters

The Volsung shall die for my honor. Do I have Wotan's oath on it?

> Fricka, V-2-i

Desirable maidens abound there in splendor. Wotan's daughter will gladly give you your drink.

> Brünnhilde, V-2-iv, answering Siegfried's question, "In Valhalla shall I be welcomed warmly by a woman?"

You are wonderful and I recognize the holy daughter of Wotan.

> Siegmund, V-2-iv, to Brünnhilde

Then greet Valhalla for me, greet Wotan too, greet Volse for me and all the heroes, greet the lovely wishmaidens too. I will not follow you to them.

> Siegmund, V-2-iv

Be off, slave. Kneel before Fricka: tell her that Wotan's spear avenged what caused her shame. Go! Go!

> Wotan, V-2-v, to Hunding

If we're all assembled then don't wait any longer. We'll make our way to Valhalla to bring Wotan his warriors.

> Rossweisse, V-3-i

This is Sieglinde, Siegmund's sister and wife. Wotan is fuming with rage against the Volsungs.

> Brünnhilde, V-3-i, to the Valkyries

Woe to this poor woman if Wotan finds her; he threatens destruction on all the Volsungs.

> Brünnhilde, V-3-i

Then quickly escape, and escape by yourself. I will stay here and face Wotan's vengeance.

> Brünnhilde, V-3-i, to Sieglinde

The wood would surely shelter her from Wotan's anger. The Master dislikes it and keeps away from the place.

> Brünnhilde, V-3-i

Furiously Wotan is riding to the rock.

> Waltraute, V-3-i

Wotan's getting off his horse, and he's angry. This way he hurries bent on revenge.

> The Eight Valkyries, V-3-i, hiding Brünnhilde

Wotan has told you what you once were. . . . Your Valkyriehood is over: from now on be what is still left for you to be.

> Wotan, V-3-ii, to Brünnhilde

When Wotan is at war I guard his back, and this time I only saw what you could not see.

> Brünnhilde, V-3-iii, to Wotan

In the cloudy heights live the gods: Valhalla is their dwelling . . . Wotan, Lord of Light, rules over them.

> Wanderer, S-1-ii, answering Mime's third question

He cut himself a shaft: though the trunk wither, never shall the spear decay; with its point Wotan governs the world . . . Custody of the world lies in the hand that controls the spear, clasped in Wotan's fist.

> Wanderer, S-1-ii, to Mime's third question

Wotan's eyes fell on me, peered into my cave.

> Mime, S-1-ii, to the Wanderer

Which is the race that Wotan oppressed and yet whose life is dearest to him?

> Wanderer, S-1-ii, posing the first question to Mime

The Volsungs are the love-children that Wotan fathered and fondly cherished.

> Mime, S-1-ii, answering the Wanderer's first question

Notung is the name of the sword; Wotan thrust it into an ash-tree's trunk . . . only Siegmund the valiant was victorious . . . it was snapped on Wotan's spear . . . only with the Wotan sword will a brave but stupid boy, Siegfried, slay the dragon.

> Mime, S-1-ii, answering the Wanderer's second question

To Wotan I bore a wish-maiden . . . why do you wake me, and not seek enlightenment from Erda and Wotan's child?

> Erda, S-3-i, to the Wanderer

The Valkyrie, Wotan's child [der Wala Kind], suffered the fetters of sleep while her omniscient mother slept? Does he who taught defiance punish defiance?

> Erda, S-3-i, to the Wanderer

I will not let you go, mother . . . you once thrust the thorn of anxiety into Wotan's bold heart . . . Tell me now: how can the god conquer his cares?

> Wanderer, S-3-i, to Erda

The earth-mother's wisdom is drawing to an end: your wisdom will wither before my will. Do you know what is Wotan's will?

> Wanderer, S-3-i, to Erda

O Siegfried, Siegfried! . . . I have always loved you; for I alone divined Wotan's thought . . . my love for you!

> Brünnhilde, S-3-iii

Wotan then broke off a branch, a spearshaft the mighty one cut from the trunk.

> First Norn, T-Prologue

Runes of honestly concluded covenants Wotan carved in the spearshaft . . . An audacious hero shattered the spear in conflict.

> Second Norn, T-Prologue

Then Wotan bade Valhalla's heroes hack to pieces the withered boughs of the world-ash.

> Second Norn, T-Prologue

Still soars the stronghold the giants built: in its hall sits Wotan with his sacred clan of gods and heroes.

> Third Norn, T-Prologue

By the magic of his spear Wotan tamed [Loge]; he gave the god advice. . . . With the spear's powerful point Wotan bade him burn round Brünnhilde's rock.

> Second Norn, T-Prologue

The shattered spear's sharp splinters Wotan will one day plunge deep into the heart of the glow . . . And this the god will fling at the world-ash's piled-up logs.

Third Norn, T-Prologue

Was it—to tell me—that Wotan has relaxed his rage against me?

Brünnhilde, T-1-iii, to Waltraute

Something different drove me in dread to defy Wotan's orders.

Waltraute, T-1-iii, to Brünnhilde

No more to war has Wotan sent us . . . The Father of Battles shunned Valhalla's brave heroes. . . . He roamed the world as the Wanderer.

Waltraute, T-1-iii, her narrative

The ring on your hand . . . for Wotan's sake, throw it away!

Waltraute, T-1-iii

Wotan! Wrathful, ruthless god! Alas! now I see the meaning of my sentence! You doom me to derision and distress!

Brünnhilde, T-1-iii, in an outburst of despair

Hagen, my son, hate the happy . . . He who once wrested the ring from me, Wotan the rabid robber, was overthrown by one of his own offspring: to the Volsung he lost his authority and power; with all the gods gathered round him in anguish he awaits his end.

Alberich, T-2-i

Wotan's spear was split by the Volsung who slew the dragon Fafner in combat and innocently gained the ring.

Alberich, T-2-i, to Hagen

Not strong enough, indeed to oppose the dragon, which was destined for the Volsung alone, but to inexorable hate I bred Hagen, who now shall avenge me and obtain the ring in defiance of the Volsung and Wotan! Do you swear it, Hagen, my son?

Alberich, T-2-i

You must slaughter sturdy steers; let Wotan's altar flow with their blood.

Hagen, T-2-iii, to the vassals

Siegfried shall die! . . . He has betrayed his solemn oath . . . Omniscient god of vengeance, Wotan, witness of oaths and guardian of vows, look upon us!

Brünnhilde and Gunther, T-2-v

APPENDIX

Staging *The Ring*
With a portfolio of photographs
373

A Core Motive: Woman's Worth
393

Possession of the Ring
397

Endings
399

✿
Staging The Ring

U PON WAGNER's death in 1883, absolute control of the Bayreuth Festival and thus determination of the "correct" approach to staging *The Ring* passed to his widow, Cosima. Directly in charge until 1907 and still influential until her own death in 1930, Cosima left a legacy of stifling conservatism. Hers was an iron-handed determination to reproduce the operas with scenery, costumes, vocalisms, and even gestures as approved in 1876 by Wagner himself.[1]

Siegfried, Cosima and Richard Wagner's son, took over the direction of Bayreuth in 1908 until his death, just four months after his mother's. Despite some significant changes, continuity and tradition remained stronger priorities for Siegfried than did innovation, much less iconoclasm. To be sure, nontraditional *Ring* productions were conceived and staged elsewhere before World War II, but in general Bayreuth succeeded in setting an accepted standard.

After 1950 and especially after 1976, a new era began, as much because of Bayreuth and the Wagner family as in spite of them. The two most influential *Ring* productions since 1876 were staged there. In 1951, the festival was permitted by the Allied Powers to reopen under the direction of Wagner's grandsons, Wieland and Wolfgang, the sons of Siegfried and his wife Winifred.

The 1951 staging of *The Ring* created a sensation and established what has become known as the New Bayreuth style, so successful that it obtained in the first four postwar cycles through the mid-1970s (see photographs 1 to 8 beginning on page 377). Characters wore simplified cloaks reminiscent of Greek dramas. The stage was stripped bare of props, furniture, rocks, castles, and caves; pervasive lighting largely replaced scenery. Singers appeared on a bare disc, and histrionic gestures—in fact, gestures of any kind—were suppressed.

The results were revelatory. Audiences were impelled toward the inner meaning of the work, for the psychological level of *The Ring* was never so patent. There was so little to look at that the music and words became the principal focus as if by default. Timelessness and universality of place strengthened the archetypal symbolism of the underlying mythologies. Although radically different in staging from what Richard Wagner had specified in his directives, the grandsons' productions were nevertheless true, indeed liberating, with respect to the intrinsic purposes and qualities of *The Ring.*

New Bayreuth dominated *Ring* productions around the world for twenty years, to the point of artistic exhaustion. A post–New Bayreuth reaction was inevitable, and in the early 1970s deliberately different productions of *The Ring* were staged, for example, in London (see photographs 20 and 21), Kassel, and even Milan. But the new freedom received its official blessing from Bayreuth itself.

Wieland Wagner died in 1966, and his brother Wolfgang became director of the festival. As he planned the cycle to be performed from 1976 to 1980, Wolfgang engaged the French modernist composer and conductor, Pierre Boulez—one of the few non-Germans invited to conduct at Bayreuth. By tradition, the conductor was permitted to select the producer, and when the Swedish film director, Ingmar Bergman, proved unavailable, Boulez turned to the French stage director, Patrice Chéreau.

Chéreau's staging of the tetralogy included explicit views of nineteenth-century Europe in the throes of the Industrial Revolution, suffering under the destructive grip of capitalism (see photographs 9 to 11). Moreover, Chéreau choreographed intensely realistic acting.

Revisionist *Ring* productions, those largely given over to the personal visions of the director and ignoring Wagner's set, costume, and stage directions, were fairly common by the 1970s. Yet Chéreau's staging on the sacrosanct stage of Bayreuth caused a second postwar sensation during the centennial of the first festival. Festspielhaus audiences at first reacted with unprecedented hostility to Chéreau's deliberate break with tradition. In time, however, the production accumulated a wide and telling critical approval, and by its 1980 close "the Chéreau" had established a new standard and new rules for *Ring* performance. The ovation at the final curtain is said to have lasted ninety minutes.

Overshadowed but not lost in all this was the impact of the conductor, Boulez. The cerebral Frenchman had so suppressed and clarified the orchestral sound that it was commonly likened to that of chamber music. There are famous stories about rebellious Bayreuth musicians demanding to be allowed to play louder.

Ironically, Boulez's deliberate musical reticence reinforced an impression that artistic primacy had passed from conductor to producer/director. In any case, the way was now fully open to any imaginable approach to *Ring* interpretation. The essential difference between the Wagner brothers' New Bayreuth style and Chéreau's *Ring* is that the former was a disciplined attempt to illuminate the composer's core intentions, while Chéreau's production was a personal reinterpretation superimposed on them. This distinction is more than semantic. Indeed, it is as common today to hear of Chéreau's *Ring*, or Götz Friedrich's or Harry Kupfer's, as Richard Wagner's *Ring*.

Since Chéreau, the assumption of unrestricted interpretive license has become the norm as the visual aspects of *The Ring* have been given over to the personal visions of producers, directors, and designers. This is not because the seneschals of this movement are less thoughtful or insightful or knowledgeable about *The Ring* than their predecessors—they are often more so. Images of hydroelectric dams and time tunnels can be striking and can resonate, at the moment, with the *Ring* story and music.

Nevertheless the era of personal-vision *Ring*s seems destined to pass, as much a victim of its overwhelming success as of its inherent contradictions. The outsized and outdated influence of the East German stage director Walter Felsenstein on such opera producers as Friedrich and Kupfer has helped exhaust post–New Bayreuth. Friedrich introduced the new style at Bayreuth in 1973 with a *Tannhäuser* that featured a Nazi-like governing class repressing revolutionary workers.[2] This approach surely has said all that it has to say, in *The Ring*, about a bleak, cynical world vision—without the benefit of, for example, Bertold Brecht's coherent dogmatism or cunning humor. It is significant and a hopeful sign that "East German" *Ring*s seem to be going the way of East Germany itself.

In the late 1980s, the Metropolitan Opera threw down a gauntlet of sorts by staging a new *Ring* that was called an expression of the New Romanticism by its set designer, Günther Schneider-Siemssen. No slavish imitation of 1876 Bayreuth, the production was nevertheless vividly literal, traditional, and realistic in comparison with other contemporary *Ring*s. The Metropolitan also undertook a deliberate effort to apply its vast technological capacities to realizing Wagner's almost unstageable special effects, often with stunning results. (Photos of Met stage settings illustrate the *Ring* story in chapter 2.)

Many critics were skeptical. In place of the grim, monochromatic counter-Wagnerian devices of post–New Bayreuth came a sense of natural beauty that had been fundamental to the composer's conception, this underscored by a pervasive awareness of love, beauty, innocence, and generosity—elements essential to making dramatic sense of their negative counterparts.

The Metropolitan *Ring* was a huge success with the public. Audiences flocked to New York, perhaps relieved that somebody still saw value in staging the work more or less in the manner Wagner directed. A few commentators bravely suggested that the general public might have a point.

The result is that *Ring* staging has reached another crossroads. The Met *Ring* did not carry the day for Wagner's stage directions, yet it helped expose the risks faced by those who succumb to the powerful temptation to reinterpret this vast, elusive music drama. Furthermore, virtually any approach to *The Ring* can still be

defended by reference to Wagner's life and writings, not to mention by the logically relativistic argument that producers and directors *always* interpret, that
every production of every opera is by definition personal.

Still, Wagner's overriding artistic objective was that all elements of the drama,
what is seen as well as heard, must be coordinated and complementary. Götz
Friedrich, who has produced *The Ring* in Berlin, London, and Hamburg, has said
that the first thing a *Ring* director must do is ask where the action takes place.[3]
But why? Wagner has already given us explicit set and stage directions, as well as
words and music. The problem with personal interpretations is more fundamental than whether the composer's specific staging instructions should be honored.
It is this: the priorities inherent in the operas are ignored at great peril. What is
heard in *The Ring* is far more important than what is *seen* (hence the real success
underlying the starkly nontraditional New Bayreuth style), and the music is more
central than the words.

As for visual contradictions to the words, Wagner himself created genuine
problems of realization. Few of us, for example, expect that a real horse will appear on stage to leap with Brünnhilde into the funeral pyre, though that is what
her words say.[4]

But it is more than simply a literal error if Siegmund and Sieglinde remark on
the sudden vision of a moonlit forest in V-1-iii while they (and we) remain
trapped, for example, in the same forestless, post-nuclear ruin we have been
looking at since the beginning of V-1-i. Especially depreciated in this case is the
fundamental dramatic device of contrast, the hope and beauty and affirmation
that resounds so honestly from the orchestra and young Volsungs out of their pre-
vious desolation. Wagner aligns these aspirations, as articulated by Siegmund,
with two powerful metaphors from the natural world: the passing of winter into
spring and the emergence from darkness into light (where the twins logically and
for the first time recognize their physiognomical similarities). Time and again we
find Wagner's solutions, in their details, both dramatically sensible and symboli-
cally persuasive.

Visual contradictions with the music (as opposed to text) can be more grievous still. Siegfried has all too often been portrayed as thuggish and insubstantial.
We know he is much more than this from his words alone. But the full reach and
color of Siegfried's personality come alive in his music, which also speaks to us,
unmistakably, of yearning, passion, generosity, modesty, and good humor. This is
the greater truth that we hear about the boy, as we hear it in the music of all the
Ring characters.

Wagner's music is always there to guide opera directors if, before they visual-
ize, they will *listen*.

Wieland Wagner's staging of the first postwar *Ring* at Bayreuth, 1951–1958, caused a sensation. The austere sets, costumes, and gestures exposed audiences as never before to the mythic and inner worlds of Wagner's music and drama.

1 Bayreuth, 1951. *The Rhinegold,* Scene iv.

2 Bayreuth, 1954. *Siegfried,* Act 3, Scene iii.

Wieland's brother Wolfgang Wagner designed the 1960–1964 cycle, which definitively projected major elements of the New Bayreuth style: expressive lighting virtually replaced sets and props, and the action took place on a huge disc representing the cosmos.

3 Bayreuth, 1962. *The Valkyrie,* Act 3, Scene iii.

4 Bayreuth, 1961. *Twilight of the Gods,* Act 2, Scene v.

Wieland Wagner's second *Ring* cycle was staged from 1965 to 1969. Mythic symbols were added to form a backdrop for the action. Having cleared the stage in 1951–1958, Wagner was "attempting to find his way back from abstraction to a real world, while resisting the real world of his grandfather," as Charles Osborne put it (*The World Theatre of Wagner*, 159).

5 Bayreuth, 1965. *The Rhinegold*, Scene ii.

6 Bayreuth, 1965. *Twilight of the Gods*, Act 2, Scene iv.

Wolfgang Wagner's second cycle was the last of the New Bayreuth productions to be seen at the Festspielhaus, although imitations continued to be staged elsewhere. The overwhelming and long-lasting success of New Bayreuth provided an impetus to find new solutions to *Ring* staging.

7 Bayreuth, 1974. *The Valkyrie,* Act 3, Scene ii.

8 Bayreuth, 1974. *Twilight of the Gods,* Act 2, Scene i.

The Chéreau *Ring*, designed by Richard Peduzzi, created a second postwar sensation at Bayreuth. It presented a highly personal interpretation, some said four unrelated interpretations, of Wagner's work. The explicitly referential sets and costumes usually evoked Europe during the Industrial Revolution, which was also Wagner's own day. While revisionist *Ring*s were common by the 1970s, Chéreau's vision, as realized by Peduzzi, was especially handsome, and its appearance in the Festspielhaus gave impetus to the notion that what Wagner asked us to see no longer mattered.

9 Bayreuth, 1979. *The Rhinegold*, Scene ii.

10 Bayreuth, 1979. *Siegfried*, Act 1, Scene iii.

11 Bayreuth, 1979. *Twilight of the Gods,* Act 1, Scene ii.

Peter Hall's Bayreuth *Ring,* 1983–1986, was plagued by serious musical problems. And in the wake of Chéreau's triumphant nontraditionalism, designer William Dudley's New Romanticism generally failed to satisfy critics.

12 Bayreuth, 1986. *The Valkyrie,* Act 1, Scene ii.

13 Bayreuth, 1985. *The Valkyrie,* Act 3, Scene iii.

14 Bayreuth, 1985. *Siegfried,* Act 1, Scene ii.

Bayreuth's *Ring* of 1988–1992, haunted by a vision of ruined landscapes and hopeless lives, paid homage to the postwar theater of East Germany. Harry Kupfer's conception and Hans Schavernoch's sets described an environmental nightmare: there was hardly a glimpse of natural beauty. Fortunately East Germany itself had ceased to exist by the end of the cycle.

15 Bayreuth, 1992. *The Valkyrie*, Act 3, Scene i.

16 Bayreuth, 1992. *Siegfried*, Act 1, Scene iii.

17 Bayreuth, 1992. *Twilight of the Gods,* Act 3, Scene iii.

The last word, or merely one of the latest, in personal, inscrutable *Ring*s? Here the work of the costume designer (Rosalie) may have upstaged both the music and the contribution by the producer (Alfred Kirchner). Wotan's blue rubber skirt and other concoctions may be remembered, with regret, for years.

18 Bayreuth, 1994. *The Rhinegold,* Scene ii.

19 Bayreuth, 1994. *Twilight of the Gods,* Act 1, Scene ii.

Sadler's Wells (now the English National Opera) staged a *Ring* cycle in English in the early 1970s, and its enormous success came as something of a surprise. Ralph Koltai's sets, all chrome, copper, and plastic, visualized Wagner's story as unfolding in a future world. Yet the real revelations were the inspired singing—especially that of Norman Bailey and Rita Hunter—and above all the superb playing of the orchestra under Sir Reginald Goodall.

20 London, early 1970s. *The Rhinegold,* Scene i.

21 London, early 1970s. *Siegfried,* Act 3, Scene iii.

Seattle Opera gained an international reputation by staging a naturalistic *Ring* in 1975 and for ten summers thereafter. In 1985 a new, nontraditional cycle was directed by François Rochaix. A coherent and imaginative interpretation, the production rendered Wotan as Wagner, cast as a theater director–author–magician. The signature vision of the cycle was the flying merry-go-round horses, a spectacular display that underlined the deliberate theatricality of the interpretation.

22 Seattle, 1987. *The Rhinegold,* Scene ii.

23 Seattle, 1987. *The Valkyrie*, Act 3, Scene i.

The Deutsche Oper brought its *Ring* from Berlin to Washington in the summer of 1989. The production was staged by Götz Friedrich, the preeminent East German *Ring* interpreter. Audiences were struck by the resemblance of the ubiquitous tunnel set with their own subway system. It was a dark and circular vision from which the performances never seemed to emerge.

24 Berlin-Washington, 1989. *The Rhinegold*, Scene iv.

The Staatsoper's *Ring* cycle was directed by Adolf Dresen, sets by Herbert Kapplmüller. The action took place on a human level in a setting that seemed almost smaller than life.

25 Vienna, 1992. *The Rhinegold,* Scene iv.

26 Vienna, 1993. *Twilight of the Gods,* Act 2, Scene iv.

August Everding directed the Chicago *Ring*, and John Conklin designed it. The complete cycle was first performed in 1996. The production projected a clean, traditional, and stylized reality, and included the New Bayreuth cosmic disc, slide projections, lasers, gymnast Valkyries, and bungee-jumping Rhine Daughters.

27 Chicago, 1992. *The Rhinegold,* Scene ii.

28 Chicago, 1992. *The Rhinegold,* Scene iv.

29 Chicago, 1993. *The Valkyrie*, Act 1, Scene ii.

A rare Paris *Ring*, designed and directed by Pierre Strosser. Its visual starkness, with a largely bare stage and nineteenth-century costumes, recalled the New Bayreuth style of 1951–1974.

30 Paris, 1994. *The Rhinegold*, Scene ii.

31 Paris, 1994. *The Valkyrie,* Act 3, Scene i.

A Core Motive: Woman's Worth

I N CHAPTER 3 we looked at some ways in which Wagner's music tells the story of *The Ring*. We explored in particular his use of musical phrases and fragments, or motives, to convey a sense of physical objects, inner feelings, dramatic situations, personality traits, and other elements of the drama. Here we will explore the remarkable narrative flexibility of Wagner's motivic system by tracing the important occurrences of a single motive, one of the most pervasive and appealing in *The Ring*: 27–Woman's Worth.

27–Woman's Worth

As we have frequently noted, numbering or labeling motives can be misleading because the musical fragments are never simply repeated; they are always evolving, conveying different shades of meaning in each dramatic situation.

A case in point is 27–Woman's Worth. At the first appearance of this motive, Loge comments directly on the value of "woman's beauty and delight," a theme related to Alberich's renunciation of love and to Wotan's pledge to the giants of Freia, the symbol of womanly love. The musical phrase recurs frequently throughout *The Ring*; forty-three occurrences are listed here. It is heard most often at times of high emotion and dramatic significance. We readily recognize it for its consistent, immediate impact. The phrase accompanies so many characters in such an unusually wide range of emotions and situations that it can be considered a core motive taking us to the very heart of the drama.

The citations below indicate where 27–Woman's Worth occurs. Words or orchestral parts heard at the same time as the musical fragment are in italics.

1. Loge to the gods (R-ii): In vain I searched, and see now full well that in the whole wide world nothing is so rich that a man will accept it in lieu of *woman's beauty and delight.*

2. Loge to the gods (R-ii): I asked and sought of all, where forces stir and seeds sprout: what would a man think mightier than *woman's beauty and delight?*

3. Loge to the gods, (R-ii): [Alberich] now esteems it earth's most precious prize, *greater than woman's grace.*

4. Loge to the gods (R-ii): Alberich did not hesitate; boldly he gained the power of the spell: *the ring became his.*

5. Froh to the gods (R-ii): It is easily won now *without cursing love.*

6. *Orchestra:* Transitional music between R-ii and R-iii

7. Loge to Wotan (R-iii): Now quickly up we go: *there [Alberich] will be ours.*

8. Alberich to himself, after Wotan has taken the ring (R-iv): *Of wretches the wretchedest slave!*

9. Fasolt to Wotan (R-iv): Know that to do without the woman saddens us sorely: if she is to be banished from my mind, the hoard of treasure must be heaped so high that it completely hides *the lovely one from my sight!*

10. Fasolt to the gods (R-iv): *I cannot tear myself away from the woman.*

11. Wotan to Freia (R-iv): Come to me, Freia! You are freed. Brought back, *restore to us our youth.*

12. Wotan to Brünnhilde (V-2-ii): My anger will never end. My misery is everlasting. *I am the saddest of all men.*

13. Wotan to Brünnhilde (V-2-ii): The fruits of [Alberich's] hatred a woman is carrying: his envy at full strength is sitting in her womb. *This miracle befell the loveless creature.*

14. Wotan to Brünnhilde (V-2-ii): Remember what I commanded. Siegmund shall die. This is the Valkyrie's task. *Orchestra.*

15. Wotan to Brünnhilde (V-3-iii): So easily did you imagine love's bliss was attained when burning pain had stabbed me to the heart, when desperate necessity had roused my anger, when love of the world allowed *the source of love to be curbed in my aching heart?*

16. Wotan to Brünnhilde (V-3-iii): Angry longing with its burning desires had formed my dread decision: in the ruins of my own world *I would end my endless sadness.*

17. The Wanderer to Erda (S-3-i): Subservient to the world spin the Norns: *nothing can they alter or deflect.*

18. Erda to the Wanderer (S-3-i): My mind grows misty with the deeds of men: even I, with all *my wisdom, once was overcome by a conqueror.* To Wotan I bore a wish-maiden.

19. The Wanderer to Erda (S-3-i): The consecrated one will waken only *when a man woos her for his wife.*

20. Erda to the Wanderer (S-3-i): You are not what you call yourself! Why did you come, wild and stubborn, and *disturb the Wala's sleep?*

21. The Wanderer to Erda (S-3-i): To you, wise one, I address these words so that you then may sleep *carefree forever.*

22. The Wanderer to Erda (S-3-i) : He whom I chose, *though he does not know me* . . . has gained the Nibelung's ring.

23. Siegfried, as he determines to waken Brünnhilde (S-3-iii): Then I will suck life from those sweetest lips, *though I die in doing so.*

24. Siegfried to Brünnhilde (S-3-iii): You have bound me in powerful bonds, but *no longer deprive me of my courage!*

25. First Norn to the other Norns (T-Prologue): I can no longer find the strands of the rope: the weft is tangled. *A confused sight provokes and perplexes my senses.*

26. *Orchestra:* Transitional music between T-Prologue and T-1-i (Siegfried's Rhine Journey)

27. Hagen to Gunther (T-1-i): He who truly knew how to use [the Nibelung hoard] *would indeed be master of the world.*

28. Hagen to Gutrune (T-1-i): Remember the potion in the chest; (more secretly) trust me, who obtained it: *it will bind to you in love* the hero whom you long for.

29. Hagen to himself (T-1-ii): His own bride [Siegfried] brings back to the Rhine; but to me he brings—the ring! *Orchestra.*

30. *Orchestra:* Transitional music between T-1-ii and T-1-iii.

31. Alberich to Hagen (T-2-i): Remember the might that you command, if you share the mettle *of the mother who bore you!*

32. Hagen to Alberich (T-2-i): *I hate the happy and am never glad!*

33. Alberich to Hagen (T-2-i): *Our one end now is to destroy [Siegfried]!*

34. Brünnhilde, accusing Siegfried before the Gibichungs (T-2-iv): *He wrung from me gratification and love.*

35. Siegfried to the Gibichungs (T-2-iv): *May those whom love gladdens be made as happy as is my elated heart.*

36. *Orchestra:* Transitional music between T-2-iv and T-2-v

37. Gunther to Brünnhilde and Hagen (T-2-v): O disgrace! O dishonor! Woe is me, *most wretched of men!*

38. Gunther to Hagen (T-2-v): Help, Hagen! Help my honor! *Help your mother, who bore me too!*

39. Hagen to Gunther, secretly (T-2-v): He [Siegfried] shall die—and you shall profit! Immense power will be yours if you obtain from him the ring *from which in death alone can he be parted.*

40. Rhine Daughters, demanding the ring from Siegfried (T-3-i): *Give it to us!*

41. Rhine Daughters to Siegfried (T-3-i): Glad will you then feel *if we free you from its curse.*

42. Siegfried to the Rhine Daughters (T-3-i): A dragon once warned me of the curse, *but did not teach me to fear it!*

43. Hagen to Gutrune (T-3-iii): The pallid hero can blow [his horn] no more; no more will he go off hunting or into battle, *nor woo lovely women.*

Possession of the Ring

O NCE Alberich has forged the golden ring, which he does between R-i and R-iii, it changes hands nine times through the rest of the drama. Here we trace that chain of possession. Stage directions are quoted from the G. Schirmer Vocal Scores or from the Salter or Mann translations; text translations are from Salter and Mann (see "The *Ring* Texts and Their Translations" in the Introduction).

1. Alberich (R-iii). Having renounced love at the end of R-i in order to gain the magic to forge the ring from the stolen gold, Alberich appears with the ring on his finger at the beginning of R-iii, dragging hapless Mime from a side cleft.

Later in the same scene, to demonstrate his new power to Wotan and Loge, Alberich "draws the ring from his finger, kisses it and stretches it out threateningly" to dismiss the Nibelungs: "Tremble with terror, abject throng: at once obey the master of the ring!" With a shriek, they do.

2. Wotan (R-iv). After securing the hoard and Tarnhelm from the bound Alberich and ignoring the Nibelung's dire warning, Wotan "seizes Alberich, and with violence draws the ring from his finger." Wotan contemplates the ring: "Now I possess what will make me the mightiest of mighty lords!"

3. Fafner (R-iv). Heeding Erda's admonition to yield the ring, Wotan throws it on the hoard: "You giants, take your ring!" Fafner begins to pack up the treasure in a sack.

4. Fasolt (R-iv). Fasolt appeals to the gods as judges to ensure a fair distribution with his brother, but Loge tells him: "Let him take the treasure: only keep control of the ring!" Fasolt throws himself on his brother and "wrests the ring from Fafner." Fasolt says: "I hold it: it belongs to me."

5. Fafner (R-iv). Fafner immediately strikes Fasolt with his club and "from the dying man he then hastily wrests the ring." As Fasolt dies, Fafner says: "Now blink at

Freia's gaze: the ring you will not touch again!" Fafner "puts the ring into the sack and quietly goes on packing the hoard."

6. Siegfried (S-2-iii). At the end of S-2-ii, after Siegfried has killed Fafner, the Wood Bird tells him that in Fafner's cave he will find the hoard, Tarnhelm, and ring which "would make him ruler of the world." He emerges in S-2-iii with both Tarnhelm and ring, and contemplating them says: "What use you are to me I don't know, but I took you from the pile of heaped gold because I was guided by good advice. So let your beauty serve as witness to today: the trinkets will be a reminder that I vanquished Fafner in fight, though I still haven't learnt fear!"

7. Brünnhilde (T-Prologue). As he is about to leave Brünnhilde for the world, Siegfried takes the ring off his finger and holds it out to her: "I must leave you here, my dearest, in the sacred custody of the fire; in return for your tuition I give you this ring." As Brünnhilde slips the ring on her finger, she says: "I prize this as my sole possession! Now for the ring take my horse!"

8. Siegfried (T-1-iii). Siegfried, who uses the Tarnhelm to assume Gunther's form, will take Brünnhilde as wife for Gunther. "Stretching out threateningly the finger on which she carries Siegfried's ring," she says: "Stand back! Fear this token! You cannot compel me into shame so long as this ring shields me." Siegfried says: "You impel me now to take it from you." After a struggle, he "seizes her by the hand and draws the ring from her finger."

9. Brünnhilde (T-3-iii). Brünnhilde "makes a sign to the Vassals to lift Siegfried's body onto the pyre; at the same time she draws the ring from Siegfried's finger and looks at it meditatively." She says: "Now I take up my inheritance. Accursed ring, terrible ring. I take your gold and now I give it away." She puts the ring on her finger.

10. Rhine Daughters (T-3-iii). After Brünnhilde's (and Siegfried's) immolation, the Rhine overflows its banks, and the Rhine Daughters appear on the waves. Hagen dives after them but is pulled into the depths. "Flosshilde, swimming in front of the others at the back, holds up the regained ring joyously." Illuminated by a growing red glow on the horizon, they "are seen, swimming in circles, merrily playing with the ring on the calmer waters of the Rhine, which has gradually returned to its natural bed."

Endings

A S IN *Hamlet*, most principal *Ring* characters fail to survive the end of *The Ring*. The drama is filled with notions of fate, endings, and death. In R-iv, Alberich warns that through his possession of the ring, its owner will "meet his executioner!" Wagner does not always explicitly reveal each character's final position. Some are surprising.

Here we recount each character's fate in *The Ring*. From the Rhine Daughters to the Gibichungs, twenty-five characters or groups are listed in order of initial appearance, as in chapter 4. Text quotations are taken from Salter's and Mann's translations. Stage directions are taken from the G. Schirmer Vocal Scores.

The Rhine Daughters. The first characters to appear in *The Ring* are the last major characters seen alive and prominently on stage. They ride the waves after the Rhine has overflowed its banks and after it has extinguished the fire that immolated Brünnhilde and Siegfried and burned down the Gibichungs' hall. Woglinde and Wellgunde embrace Hagen and drag him into the depths as they swim away. "Flosshilde, swimming in front of the others towards the back, holds up the regained ring joyously." As a red glow breaks forth from the clouds above, all three nymphs are "swimming in circles, merrily playing with the ring on the calmer waters of the Rhine which has gradually returned to its natural bed."

Alberich. Alberich is last seen at the end of T-2-i, having urged his son Hagen to persevere in the plot against Siegfried. Alberich has said that if Brünnhilde ever returned the ring to the Rhine Daughters, then "no ruse could ever retrieve it." Alberich presumably no longer poses a danger, but he is the only major character to survive and whose whereabouts at the end is unknown. One doubts that his ambition and hatred are quenched.

Wotan. Both the Norns and Waltraute have told us, in T-Prologue and T-1-iii, respectively, that Wotan sits in Valhalla, where he has assembled the other gods and his heroes. The remnants of the World Ash Tree have been piled up around the hall. Wotan awaits the end, but still hopes Brünnhilde will return the ring to the Rhine Daughters, thereby lifting the curse and freeing the gods.

Near the end of the immolation scene in T-3-iii, Brünnhilde directs Wotan's ravens to her rock, where Loge still burns. She tells them to carry fire to Valhalla, where they are to tell Wotan what has happened and to set Valhalla on fire. As she hurls the torch onto Siegfried's pyre, Brünnhilde says: "Thus do I throw this torch at Valhalla's vaulting towers." At the end, as the Rhine subsides into its bed, the Gibichung men and women see an increasingly bright glow in the sky. At its brightest, it illuminates the interior of Valhalla, where the gods sit assembled. Wagner's final stage directions are: "Bright flames appear to seize on the hall of the gods. As the gods become entirely hidden by the flames, the curtain falls."

Fricka. She perishes with Wotan at Valhalla.

Freia. She perishes with Wotan at Valhalla.

Fasolt. He is murdered by Fafner in a struggle for the ring in R-iv, the first victim of Alberich's curse.

Fafner. Having taken the form of a fearsome dragon to guard the hoard, Fafner is killed by Siegfried in S-2-ii.

Donner. He perishes with Wotan at Valhalla.

Froh. He also perishes with Wotan at Valhalla.

Loge. At the close of R-iv, Loge considers turning himself into a flickering flame to burn the gods rather than joining them in the end to which they unwittingly hasten. Ironically, at the end of T-3-iii the ravens carry the fire from Brünnhilde's rock to Valhalla to immolate the gods and heroes. As the curtain falls, "the gods become entirely hidden by the flames," so in a sense we see Loge at the end. However, Loge, like fire, lives only by feeding on others. Once he has consumed the gods, will he die out with them?

Mime. Mime's plot to kill Siegfried is undone in S-2-iii when Siegfried, having tasted the blood of the dragon Fafner, can hear the true intentions of Mime's heart. As Mime reveals his hatred and deadly intentions, Siegfried "as if seized by violent loathing . . . gives Mime a sharp stroke with his sword. Mime falls at once dead to the ground." Alberich's mocking laughter is heard from his hiding place.

The Nibelungs. The Nibelungs are last seen in R-iv, when they are summoned by Alberich to deliver up the hoard to Wotan. They are sent back down to the caverns of Nibelheim, and in all likelihood survive the cataclysms of T-3-iii. When the ring, cleansed of the curse, is returned to the Rhine Daughters, Alberich's mastery over them is undone. We might think of them as they once described themselves: "carefree smiths, once we created ornaments for our women, wondrous trinkets, dainty trifles for Nibelungs, and lightly laughed at our work."

Erda. At the end of S-3-i, Wotan has accepted a future given over to Siegfried and Brünnhilde. He commands Erda: "So now sleep on, close your eyes: in dream behold my downfall! . . . Descend then, Erda, mother of fear, of timeless sorrow! Away, away to endless sleep!" With closed eyes, she sinks down, beyond consciousness.

Siegmund. Near the end of V-2-iv, Siegmund determines he will fight Hunding to protect Sieglinde rather than enjoy the pleasures of Valhalla without her. Wotan, Siegmund's father, who first provided Siegmund with the mighty sword Notung, causes it to shatter in the fight. Hunding kills Siegmund with his spear.

Sieglinde. Sieglinde is the only *Ring* principal who dies offstage. We last see her in V-3-i, when she is told she bears Siegmund's son, who will be a mighty hero. She rushes off alone to give birth to the boy in the forest at Neidhöhle, near Fafner's cave, a place avoided by Wotan. Brünnhilde stays behind to face Wotan, giving Sieglinde time to escape.

In S-1-i, Mime tells Siegfried that he found the woman lying whimpering in the woods. He took her into his cave; "wretchedly she here gave it birth; back and forth she writhed . . . Great was her distress. She died, but Siegfried, he survived."

Hunding. The Neiding's death comes as small consolation to the terrible events at the end of V-2-v. Hunding has killed Siegfried with Wotan's help. Wotan gazes sadly at Siegmund's body and turns to Hunding: "Be off, slave. Kneel before Fricka; tell her that Wotan's spear has avenged what caused her shame. Go! Go!" With a contemptuous wave of Wotan's hand, Hunding falls dead.

Brünnhilde. The Valkyrie's spectacular death at the conclusion of *The Ring* closes Brünnhilde's great peroration, or summing up. She explains herself to Gutrune, accuses and forgives Wotan, and sends his ravens to burn Valhalla. By her death she will cleanse the ring of its curse and return it to the Rhine Daughters. This is an historic dislocation, the ending of an era. Yet her final thought and the ultimate purpose of her self-immolation is to rejoin her husband. "Siegfried! See! Your wife joyfully greets you!" She swings up onto Grane and spurs him to leap upon the pyre.

The Eight Valkyries. They perish with Wotan at Valhalla.

Siegfried. By the end of T-2, Siegfried is unknowingly poised to fall victim to Hagen's plan. He has been made to forget Brünnhilde and to fall in love with Gutrune. He has sworn an oath of blood-brotherhood with Gunther, won Brünnhilde for Gunther, wrenched the ring from her, and sworn an oath on Hunding's spear that he is not Brünnhilde's husband. In T-3-ii, he drinks another of Hagen's potions, which restores his memories of and love for Brünnhilde.

When two ravens rise up and fly off toward the Rhine, Hagen asks Siegfried if he can understand them as he once understood the Wood Bird. Siegfried rises to watch the ravens, turning his back to Hagen. "To me they cry revenge!" Hagen says, plunging into Siegfried's back the spear upon which Siegfried falsely swore. Siegfried turns and raises his shield as if to strike Hagen but instead falls back on it. Supported by two vassals, Siegfried is raised into a sitting position, opens his eyes, and sings radiantly of Brünnhilde. He falls back and dies.

The Wood Bird. The Wood Bird's final appearance is often missed by audiences or eliminated by stage directors. At the beginning of S-3-ii, it flies ahead of Siegfried, leading him to Brünnhilde. But as it comes on stage, it sees Wotan, the Wanderer, who later in the scene calls himself the Lord of the Ravens. The Wood Bird "flutters about in alarm and then disappears quickly towards the back." The Wanderer later tells Siegfried: "Woe to it if [the ravens] catch it!" We hope that it returns safely to the forest at Neidhöhle.

The Three Norns. At the end of the Norns' scene opening T-Prologue, the rope of fate snaps. The Norns know their eternal knowledge is at an end. They sink— "Down! To mother! Down!"—to join Erda in endless sleep.

Gunther. As Gunther grieves over Siegfried's body in T-3-iii, Hagen steps forward to demand the ring. Gunther claims it for himself, declaring that it is Gutrune's inheritance and that Hagen will never have it. They struggle, and Hagen kills him with a stroke of his sword.

Hagen. Following his foiled attempt to seize the ring from dead Siegfried's hand, Hagen listens with increasing anxiety as Brünnhilde declares she will return it to the Rhine Daughters. The appearance of the nymphs on the waves unhinges him. Throwing spear, shield, and helmet aside, he "rushes, as if mad, into the flood. Woglinde and Wellgunde embrace his neck with their arms and draw him with them into the depths as they swim away."

Gutrune. Toward the end of T-3-iii, Gutrune at last understands that Siegfried was Brünnhilde's true husband. "She turns away from Siegfried and, dissolved in grief, bends over Gunther's body: she remains motionless like this, until the end."

The Gibichungs. The Gibichung men and women are left on stage at the end of *The Ring*. As the flames from Siegfried's pyre catch onto the hall, they press to the front in terror. The Rhine overflows to extinguish the fire, and then subsides into its bed under the red sky. "From the ruins of the fallen hall, the men and women, in the greatest agitation, look on the growing firelight in the heavens." Valhalla is consumed. The Gibichungs are left, perhaps to inherit the earth.

DISCOGRAPHY

FOR MANY YEARS *Ring* listeners had to be content with a handful of recordings of the complete cycle; the release of each new one was an event of major proportions. Growing interest in *The Ring* and improvements in technology, however, have provided listeners (and viewers) with an ever-widening range of opportunities to enjoy the tetralogy outside the theater. James Levine, Bernard Haitink, and Daniel Barenboim have recorded complete versions in the last few years. Compact disc technology in particular has justified the rerelease of older versions, such as those conducted by Wilhelm Furtwängler, Clemens Krauss, and Hans Knappertsbusch. Laser discs and VCRs have even made visual performances of *The Ring* accessible, such as the Pierre Boulez and James Levine cycles.

Do we now have too many *Ring*s? We have had Herbert von Karajan's monumental studio recording since 1970. Do we need another Karajan, recorded live at Salzburg soon after his studio work and with many of the same singers? Do we need both Furtwängler versions, 1950 and 1953, and both Knappertsbusch recordings from the 1957 and 1958 Bayreuth festivals? How much does the new Barenboim/Bayreuth recording add?

These questions are rhetorical, of course. From an archival point of view, we only gain from a broadened historical record. Nor have any genuinely bad *Ring* recordings been issued. Each has included many of the best Wagner musicians of its time.

For the newcomer, however, the range of choices has become increasingly daunting. This discography is intended to help listeners find the most meaningful and pleasurable listening experiences.

I bring several personal perspectives, if not outright biases, to this analysis. My own serious exposure to *The Ring* on records came in the mid-1960s through the Georg Solti set. First impressions can be indelible: for me the Solti *is The Ring*.

Second, I also confess to a pronounced preference for modern recording technology. I would recommend a good cast brilliantly projected over giants of the past poorly heard. Even more, the orchestra—the primary vehicle of the *Ring* music—can only be satisfactorily heard in modern recordings.

Modern here usually refers to after 1958, the year of Solti's *The Rhinegold*. We are indeed fortunate to have the older versions with the magnificent singers they included. Generally, however, the historical recordings will be most appreciated by experienced *Ring* listeners.

Third, I prefer studio recordings to live. At the very least, studio productions can eliminate both extraneous noise and musical errors. At their best, recordings can be a unique musical event in themselves. The prospect of a permanent record should inspire producers to assemble the strongest possible casts and orchestras, performing (with retakes and splicing) at their highest levels. Knowing the home listener can hear but not see, studio engineers have the opportunity to concoct sounds more explicit, more thrilling, than anything we can hear in a theater. To me, a truly memorable recording from a single live performance is largely a matter of good fortune.

This review begins with the Solti recording. This monumental achievement established a standard and a context around which other recordings, both earlier and later, may be interpreted. It was the first technically modern cycle to be distinguished by an outstanding orchestra and cast; it has endured as the favored *Ring* to this day. Following the Solti in this selective discography are other recordings of the complete *Ring*, presented in chronological order. At the end are brief comments on special recordings of a single *Ring* opera and of a single *Ring* act.

The recordings described here feature distinguished musicians who have emerged at the top of their difficult professions. Each recording has special strengths and will resonate with different listeners. Readers are urged to consider other *Ring* discographies; among the best are *The Penguin Guide to Compact Discs and Cassettes* (1992), "Worthy Versions of 'The Ring': A Critical Selection" (a critics' survey that appeared in the *New York Times* on 16 April 1993), and Owen Lee's *Wagner's "Ring": Turning the Sky Round*.

Following the recording reviews (all are for compact discs) are cast lists and timings of selected important *Ring* recordings.

Recordings of the Complete Ring Cycle

Georg Solti. Vienna Philharmonic. Decca. Studio. 1958–1965.

R 414 101-2   V 414 105-2   S 414 110-2   T 414 115-2   Complete 414 100-2

The Solti *Ring* is still widely regarded as the greatest achievement in recorded music. Each opera won the Grand Prix du Disque Mondial as the best recording for the year it was released, and the *Twilight of the Gods* has been called "the best recording ever made of anything."[1] It was among the first recordings to exploit the new technologies of long-play and stereophonic sound, and thereby made a complete and vital performance of *The Ring* widely accessible for the first time. In doing that, the Solti, even more than the Bayreuth stage productions of the early 1950s, initiated the post–World War II *Ring* renaissance which continues to the present day. In sum, the Solti helped reestablish *The Ring* itself as an integral part of our musical present and future.

All commentators—those who favor the Solti and those who do not—agree on certain points: it glows with drive and focus, a sustained sense of purpose, and a passionate excitement. The first E-flat of *The Rhinegold*, played more assertively than

Wagner intended, leaves no doubt that an intense and purposeful dramatic journey has begun. Solti's conception is unapologetic and unpatronizing; he knows the high quality of this music.

Detractors find Solti's intensity to be manic, and some listeners are put off by it. But the nineteenth-century idiom of *The Ring* is deliberately awash in passionate engagement. The composer/dramatist's stage directions make this unmistakably clear: Wagner consistently calls for emotional extremes—ecstatic joy, deepest gloom, fervent longing. And Solti's emotional power, like Wagner's, is always reinforced by a pervasive musical intelligence. His phrasing and tempos convey a convincing dramatic posture. The strength of purpose does not overwhelm the subtleties of the score. Even at the orchestra's loudest, the individual elements are clearly articulated. The quiet passages are subtle and tender. The Vienna Philharmonic, in its component parts and in ensemble, rises to extraordinary levels of playing.

The producer of the Solti, John Culshaw, has written that "our basic concern was the sound which, whatever its texture at any given moment, was required always to be beautiful, balanced and yet well endowed with an indefinable something which I will call, for want of a better word, impact."[2] The recording abounds with special effects. The hissing steam as Notung is cooled, the tunnelled voices of Siegfried (as Gunther) and Fafner (as dragon), surely the best of all recorded thunder, Grane crashing into the flaming pyre, even Wotan stepping on toad/Alberich—these are things Wagner intended us to hear, and hearing them the way we do, we see them vividly in our mind's eye.

An enormous amount has been written about the singing in the Solti set. It is difficult to find the kind of weaknesses that detract from almost every other recorded *Ring*. The cast presents a hall of fame of postwar Wagner singers: Nilsson, Hotter, Flagstad, London, Frick, Windgassen, Ludwig, Watson, King, Neidlinger—the list is still astonishing thirty years after the fact. The lesser roles, from Wächter's Donner to Sutherland's Wood Bird, are sung at the same high level. Fischer-Dieskau's portrayal of Gunther, which animates that lesser character's tragic weaknesses, has become the stuff of legend.

Yet the Solti reflects not so much a golden age of Wagner singing as it does the end of one. Nilsson, widely regarded as the definitive Brünnhilde since the mid-1950s, was in the prime of her career, but Flagstad, London, Hotter, and especially Windgassen (a late substitute for Thomas) were very much in the home stretch of theirs. Their voices may have been in better form in other recordings, but each here clearly draws on vast experience and artistic intelligence to achieve convincing results.

Solti recorded *The Rhinegold* first (1958) and *The Valkyrie* last (1965), and the latter may be the weakest of the set. Even so, Hotter and Nilsson fashion the finest Wotan's Farewell (V-3-iii) that has been recorded. In *Siegfried* and *Twilight* the whole Solti team can do no wrong.

Although blessed by good fortune—available singers, time, and the opportunities to exploit new technologies—the Solti achievement was still no accident. For the first time the role of the recording producer (Culshaw) was featured, much as live performances rely on the stage director. Great attention to detail was harnessed to the uncompromising objective of rendering Wagner's *Ring*, not someone else's personal or political vision. The result is as close to the real *Ring* as we are likely ever to have.

Fortunately this most honored of all recordings may also be the best documented. Culshaw's book, *Ring Resounding*, is a brilliant memoir of the recording process (see Bibliography). A 1965 documentary of that process, *The Golden Ring*, was issued on videotape by the Decca Record Company in 1992 under license from BBC Enterprises Limited. Among its most powerful images is that of Solti repeatedly driving the orchestra to capture the wrenching irony of the blood-brotherhood music in T-2-v.

Wilhelm Furtwängler. Orchestra Sinfonica della Radio Italiana. Live concert. 1953.
Complete CZS7 67123-2

Furtwängler—with Bruno Walter, Clemens Krauss, Arturo Toscanini, and Hans Knappertsbusch—was part of a golden age of Wagner conducting, lasting roughly from the late 1920s through the 1950s. Furtwängler died in 1954, a year after this performance was recorded. Critical consideration of the man and his career has become caught up in his complex relationship with German politics during this period, in particular his mercurial dealings with Winifred Wagner and the Bayreuth Festival, as well as his rivalry there with Toscanini. (The Italian was a fixture at Bayreuth until the Nazi ascendancy; regrettably, his only extant *Ring* recordings consist of scattered excerpts.)

Whatever its limitations, this recording occupies a historic position both in *Ring* archives and in the development of recorded sound. The set was originally taped in 1953 by Radiotelevisione Italiana (RAI), one act at a time, before a live concert audience. The first LP set was not issued until 1972. The original analog tapes were digitally remastered for a second LP set in 1986. Finally, the source tapes were remastered again, with the latest denoising and declicking technologies, for a CD set. The resulting sound is a remarkable improvement over the first LPs (as well as over the other Furtwängler *Ring*, recorded live at La Scala in 1950 with Kirsten Flagstad as Brünnhilde).

In this *Ring*, the singers are vastly better than the orchestra. Many of the old masters, schooled in the Bayreuth tradition, are represented here. Furtwängler's mastery of the material is obvious, and he deftly paints the big picture. What a second-rate orchestra and archaic taping cannot provide is the small picture, the wealth of instrumental detail in which so many of *The Ring*'s secrets and pleasures reside.

The technical enhancements have made the Furtwängler a viable and listenable *Ring*, not just an artifact. As the critic Bernard Holland has put it, this is not the best choice for *Ring* newcomers; it is like "a postgraduate course . . . from which the expert researcher using proper tools can extract treasures."[3]

Clemens Krauss. Bayreuth Festival Orchestra. Foyer Laudis. Live. 1953.
R CF 2007   V CF 2008   S CF 2009   T CF 2010   Complete CF2011

Krauss's 1953 Bayreuth recording was not issued until 1988, and it has quickly become a preferred *Ring* for many. Krauss, a distinguished Wagnerian and a collaborator of

Strauss —he wrote the libretto for *Capriccio*—maintains a consistent and intelligent conception without sacrificing the spirit of the individual moment. *New York Times* critic John Rockwell has written that "his conducting combines the sweep and intensity of the Toscanini-Böhm modernist Wagner style with the Germanic brooding of Furtwängler in an utterly convincing blend of those seeming opposites."[4]

Krauss takes advantage of an experienced and talented team of singers assembled at the 1953 Bayreuth Festival. Unlike Solti, he had Hotter and Windgassen in their primes. There are few weaknesses. Resnik's Sieglinde, for example, is young and moving, and Vinay's Siegmund is manly, if anything too mature for the embattled Volsung. Some of the smaller roles, like Uhde's Donner and Steich's Wood Bird, are exceptionally strong.

The Krauss also boasts the best sound quality of the old (pre-Solti) recordings. Digital remastering has reduced extraneous noises. (Although Bayreuth audiences have always been unlikely to cough, they surprise by applauding prematurely before the conclusion of S-3-iii.) Most important, the archaic sound does not suffocate the passion of Krauss's reading.

Nevertheless, this *Ring* still suffers from technical limitations common in older live recordings. There is an incessant creaking at quieter moments—Krauss on his conductor's stool? Worse, an overall blending of sound overwhelms many individual details, especially in the orchestra, in which so much of *The Ring*'s meaning is articulated.

The most dangerous pitfall of live recordings is unfortunately demonstrated in S-1-iii. Windgassen enters into the forging scene a full measure behind the orchestra, and the entire scene remains an uncoordinated hash to the end. It is a spectacular failure, reflecting less on the musicianship of Windgassen and Krauss, two magnificent artists, than on the excruciating difficulty of opera performance generally and the risks of having only one chance at the recording tape.

Hans Knappertsbusch. Orchester der Bayreuther Festspiele. Melodram. Live. 1958.

R CDMP 441   V CDMP 442   S CDMP 443   T CDMP 444

This recording embodies a transition in *Ring* performance. The 1958 Bayreuth Festival saw the final performances of Wieland Wagner's revolutionary postwar *Ring*, first staged in 1951. It also marks the last time the legendary Knappertsbusch conducted *The Ring* at Bayreuth (he conducted *The Ring, Parsifal*, or *The Mastersingers* there every year from 1951 to 1964 except 1953).

Between 1951 and 1957, Bayreuth witnessed a remarkable continuity of personnel and purpose. Such singers as Hotter, Varnay, Neidlinger, Suthaus, and Kuen, German-trained in the Bayreuth tradition, had consistently appeared at the festival. The year 1958 saw large-scale changes, especially in *The Rhinegold*, in which only four roles were repeated from 1957, and in *The Valkyrie*, in which Vickers sang for the first and last time at Bayreuth.

Despite some unevenness in these first two operas, the changes seem hardly to have mattered to Knappertsbusch. By this time he, like many others, had become bored by the director's austere and ever-darkening approach to the stage. In his notes to this 1958 recording he joked that "now Wieland has finally succeeded in casting the spell of total gloom . . . . Most of the time I don't even know who is standing on stage."

Knappertsbusch seemed not really to mind. Unable to see the singers or to be seen clearly by them (Bayreuth singers always have difficulty finding the conductor in the sunken gloom of the mystic abyss), Knappertsbusch immerses himself in the score rather than the stage action, and the result is an especially musical cycle.

No other conductor gives off a greater sense of musical understanding of *The Ring*. This interpretation does not bear the lighter, more detached approach of the Boulez; Knappertsbusch is not afraid to rise to the dramatic moment, as when the thunderous bass underpins the introduction of the sword motive in R-iv, but he never indulges in overkill. He moves on to the next moment comfortably and easily.

The mixture of old and new in the cast adds special interest. Hotter is at his most handsomely commanding. Gorr seems to echo Flagstad's perfect phrasing as Fricka in her own majestic voice. Vickers, who was apparently never fully appreciated by the Wagner brothers and knew it, sounds more tentative than in the Karajan (and Leinsdorf) versions.

From Windgassen and Stolze, who also sang for Solti, Knappertsbusch extracts a pointed reading of the final encounter between Siegfried and Mime in S-2-iii, perhaps the least popular passage in *The Ring*. But Windgassen, who was carrying an incredible singing load at the 1958 festival, sounds less vibrant than usual. Even though he sang for the Solti recording even later in his career, the opportunity to sing shorter segments, to rest, and to repeat imperfect takes in the studio produced a stronger result. Varnay, who sang Brünnhilde in all eight of the original Wieland Wagner seasons, here sounds her most accomplished.

The recorded sound is improved over the Krauss (1953) version but falls short of the first good live recording, the Böhm. Even a hand as gifted as Knappertsbusch's fails to achieve full orchestral definition. Even so, he frequently uncovers harmonic events in ways unheard in other versions.

Karl Böhm. Orchester der Bayreuther Festspiele. Philips. Live. 1967.

R 412 475-2   V 412 478-2   S 412 483-2   T 412 488-2   Complete 420 325-2

This is a *Ring* of many strengths. It is the first modern (post-1958) set taken from live performance. Though the sound falls short of that of later live recordings—the Boulez and the Barenboim—it does reflect great advances in recorded sound technologies. In fact, the booklet accompanying the original LP sets includes a spirited defense of live recordings by H. W. Steinhausen.

Above all, this is the first *Ring* that begins to capture the unique sound of the Festspielhaus itself. We hear the singers with remarkable clarity, and the orchestra, sunken in the mystic abyss, rarely intrudes. The Bayreuth audiences, as usual, behave themselves; there is a minimum of extraneous sound. Yet it is peculiar, and something of a letdown, that applause at the end of each act is deleted.

Larger shortcomings are also apparent. The sound is generally flat, two-dimensional. There is little stereophonic exploitation of depth, or movement from right to left (as in the Solti). And there is still a regrettable lack of orchestral detail. The Bayreuth brass in particular struggles to be heard.

Böhm conducts with confidence and spirit. His and Boulez's are the only *Ring* recordings discussed here that are less than fourteen hours long. Yet Böhm never seems to hurry. He is as sure of himself as are Furtwängler and Krauss.

Böhm's cast closely resembles Solti's. His Sieglinde (Rysanek) may be preferred to Solti's (Crespin), and Stewart is a pleasant surprise as Gunther. Adam's intelligent reading of Wotan is on a smaller, less imposing scale than the authoritative god projected by Hotter; most listeners have preferred the latter.

In some smaller roles (Gutrune, the Wood Bird) there are problems. Windgassen again succeeds as Siegfried. The forging scene is sung well—no catastrophe here as in the Krauss. Yet the hammering is all off; can we really expect any tenor to hammer and sing well at the same time? Solti's studio version boasts perfect hammering, no doubt wielded by a timpanist, not a singer. This may be cheating, but the result is magnificent.

This *Ring* is likely to remain in the shadow of the Solti, for ironically the Solti studio work is more alive than this live recording: it projects a more vivid presence and articulates greater detail. The Böhm is an archive of mid-1960s Bayreuth, and that is important. It will survive principally as the second or third choice of serious enthusiasts.

Herbert von Karajan. Berlin Philharmonic. Deutsche Grammophon. Studio. 1967–1970.

R 415 141-2   V 415 145-2   S 415 150-2   T 415 155-2   Complete 435-211-2

Since 1970 the Karajan *Ring* has stood in apposition to the Solti and has been treated, as its creators intended, as an alternative approach to *The Ring*. Its advocates have chiefly praised its cerebral, refined, and lyrical aspects. These are among its greatest strengths; its musicianship and clarity always provide a safe haven for the listener.

Like Solti, Karajan exploited the skills of a great orchestra, with which he was uncommonly familiar, and a large pool of accomplished, even memorable, Wagner singers. The Berlin Philharmonic matches Solti's Vienna Philharmonic at the highest level. There are passages of astonishing virtuosity. Some have regretted a sense of detachment in the playing, as though the Berliners are attempting the perfect brass sound rather than the perfect sword motive, or the perfect technical crescendo rather than a seething rise in Wotan's emotional temperature. This emphasis may reflect the conductor's approach more than the players', but it remains another way of comparing the Karajan and the Solti recordings.

The singers, with more than a few exceptions, do not match those in the Solti. Solti called on historically important Wagner singers, even though some were past their physical prime. Karajan generally opted for very good singers in the middle of their careers, many of whom sang at his Salzburg *Ring* during this period. Karajan's Wotans—Fischer-Dieskau in *The Rhinegold* and Stewart in *The Valkyrie* and *Siegfried*—have sometimes been deemed lacking in weight and authority.

More obviously, Solti's Brünnhilde—Nilsson—is so strong that she seems unfairly to overshadow strong performances by Crespin in *The Valkyrie* and Dernesch in *Siegfried* and *Twilight*. Thomas takes the title role in *Siegfried*. His spectacular failure and replacement in the Solti, lavishly documented in Culshaw's *Ring Resounding*, was a blow to his career (even though Culshaw did not identify the tenor). Yet he is better than adequate, as is Brilioth's Siegfried in *Twilight*.

The tenor role of real interest is Vickers's Siegmund. The Canadian always had his detractors—the voice is frequently harsh—but his strong suits, dramatic sensibility and intelligently drawn characterizations, single-handedly elevate the production; in fact, the second act of *The Valkyrie* is Karajan's great triumph. This long and structurally problematic act, frequently tolerated by audiences as a bridge between the more obvious glories of the first and third, is the lynch pin of the entire *Ring*; Wotan's plans are dashed, and the process of Brünnhilde's transformation is initiated. Nowhere else is Karajan's measured conception more convincing, or Wagner's architecture better articulated. At the heart of the act is Siegmund's unflinching tenderness for Sieglinde, and his relentless integrity of purpose. Vickers and Karajan capture the heart of Siegmund.

Two other passages bear special mention: the Wanderer's scenes with Erda and Siegfried in S-3-i and S-3-ii, respectively. Stewart's interpretation here is as thoughtful and committed as Vickers's in V-2; he makes an unforgettable impression as he renounces his will and leaves his inheritance to the young ones. In these scenes, the Karajan projects a dramatic content that matches his technical prowess.

Reginald Goodall. English National Opera Orchestra. EMI. Live. 1973–1977.

R CMS7 64110-2   V CMS7 63918-2   S CMS7 63595-2   T CMS7 64244-2

The Goodall is of special interest as the only major English-language *Ring* recording. In fact, it is an achievement of historic importance on any level. Like the Bayreuth stage production of 1951 and the Solti/Decca studio recording of 1958-66, the early 1970s production at the Sadler's Wells (now the English National) Opera was among those postwar events that restored *The Ring* as a vital fixture of our contemporary musical lives.

This was no small feat for a small national company, one of secondary stature even in London. But its unanticipated success proved once again that a unified conception and a prodigious team effort can yield a result greater than the sum of its parts. There is mediocre singing throughout the set, and the Sadler's Wells orchestra hardly brought an international reputation to this production.

Yet the singing is at its best where it must be. Bailey's lustrous sensitivity as Wotan/The Wanderer launched a major career, which reached its greatest height in his Hans Sachs. More poignantly, Hunter gave us a glimpse of a Brünnhilde for a lifetime. She combines a sweet lyricism, an incandescent and feminine power, and an intelligent grasp of tempo and pacing that are rarely heard. Her performance in the tortuously complex S-3-iii love duet (with much help from Goodall and tenor Remedios) fully articulates the scene and is among the most impressive of all recorded *Ring* passages.

The largest praise, though, must go to Goodall himself for the unexpected power and expressiveness he elicits from the orchestra. To describe his reading as spacious seriously understates the matter. The Goodall runs to almost seventeen hours, two-and-a-half hours longer than the Solti and fourteen minutes longer even than the Knappertsbusch. There are indeed stretches in which he loses the dramatic thread and with it the momentum. But far more often he draws us into Wagner's musical arguments in a way that is appealing and revelatory.

Finally, a word about the text. Purists will argue that any *Ring* not sung in German is not truly *The Ring*, and they are correct. However, English-speaking audiences relying on surtitles are not perfectly engaged in Wagner's *Ring* either: we simply cannot read and listen (or look at the stage) at the same time. This recording provides the strongest evidence that *The Ring* in English can convey the meaning of the text without interrupting the visual and musical aspects. Andrew Porter's superb translation was especially crafted for the Sadler's Wells stage production.

Pierre Boulez. Orchester der Bayreuther Festspiele. EMI. Live. 1980.

R 434 421-2   V 434 422-2   S 434 423-2   T 434 424-2   Complete 434 421/4-2

It is at once liberating and limiting to listen to the Boulez recording on its own, disassociated from the visual aspects of the Chéreau production.

Some have argued erroneously that Boulez himself was somehow too un-Wagnerian to take on *The Ring*. To be sure, he brought a different (modern? French?) sensibility to the job. But Boulez is among the most cerebral of conductors, and his analyses of Wagner's musical methods are both compelling and admiring. His notes accompanying this set are especially fascinating for their technical insight.

Nor did Boulez, as has sometimes been suggested, merely suppress sound; there are passages of both great intensity and volume. But the pure musicality and detachment of Boulez's reading are both deliberate and appealing. Critic Edward Rothstein points out that "he understates the bass line, giving the music's aggressive restlessness an eerie disembodied character. . . . Filigree and details are crisply articulated without undue stress on the leitmotifs; nothing is made sentimental or obvious."[5]

Yet Boulez was leading a singing cast that was weaker than that of most major *Ring* recordings. McIntyre, for example, is an imposing and skilled presence. Yet he is strangely enfeebled here, as are others, perhaps a result of Chéreau's dramatic conception in which most characters are deliberately wretched if not ignoble.

The sound quality is at a level high enough to please proponents of live recording. Listeners must, however, put up with a good deal of dreadful banging as characters stomp upon set designer Peduzzi's grated stage flooring.

Boulez's approach to *The Ring*, like that of Knappertsbusch and Levine, is especially committed to its purely musical content. But while Levine relentlessly and Knappertsbusch more facilely focus the music on the mythic and heroic in the drama, Boulez steps back to a reading that is detached from those traditional moorings. It is a counterpoint, but one well worth hearing.

Marek Janowski. Dresden State Orchestra. Eurodisc. Studio. 1980–1983.
R GD 69004   V GD 69005   S GD 69006   T GD 69007   Complete GD 69003

It is tempting but unfair to link this recording with the former East Germany's impact on *Ring* stage productions since the early 1970s (see "Staging *The Ring*" in the Appendix). More than Karajan, more even than Boulez (whom this cycle closely follows in time), Janowski's reading is refined and disciplined. Like Levine, he pays uncommon attention to detail. Janowski's is also an articulate and unified conception of *The Ring*'s music, and the set is filled with wonderful moments.

The Dresden orchestra plays with pristine clarity. There are no histrionics here, no reaching for outsized effect. Nor is there any lingering; the Janowski is the third fastest *Ring* recording discussed here (after Boulez and Böhm). The effect can be disappointing; in the *Twilight* prologue, for example, Siegfried seems to be crossing the Moldau instead of the Rhine.

This kind of playing exposes Wagner's score to the most open kind of scrutiny, as if we were looking at an X-ray. We are rewarded by hearing familiar music played in a new way, again reminded of the inexhaustible pleasures of the score.

Janowski's approach works best at times of dramatic exposition—in the Gibichung plotting in T-1-i, for example. Yet a cerebral *Ring* can lack passionate involvement; especially at the colossal and unavoidable climaxes, the rendering is flat. Occasional weaknesses in the singing compound the problem. These center most often on Adam's Wotan. Janowski's tempo at Wotan's "Farewell!" to Brünnhilde is so rushed as to seem a deliberate dramatic diminishment. We are lucky to have a historical record of Norman, Jerusalem, Kollo, and Altmeyer at this stage of their careers.

There is a real danger that the Janowski *Ring* will become lost in the rising tide of new recordings. That would be unfortunate.

Bernard Haitink. Symphonieorchester des Bayerischen Rundfunks. EMI. Studio. 1988–1991.
R CDS7 49853-2   V CDS7 49534-2   S CDS7 54290-2   T CDS7 54485-2

This is a *Ring* of extremes. One of three recent complete cycles, it is a huge, aggressive effort, expansive and enthusiastic, in the tradition of the Solti. Haitink and the Bavarian Radio Orchestra lead its considerable assets. Known for his articulate, measured interpretations with the Amsterdam Concertgebouw, Haitink draws a response from the lesser-known Bavarians that is remarkably handsome and assured. Many passages, such as the Storm Prelude to V-1 and Siegfried's Rhine Journey, are orchestral *tours de force*.

This impact is closely aligned with the quality of the sound reproduction, the most spectacular of all *Ring* recordings. The EMI engineers embroil us in an explosive, lush, and vibrant sound. Individual instruments are clearly heard yet superbly blended. The music accomplishes a reverberating depth, a thrilling three-dimensionality.

For some, the booming bigness of the sound may not work. There is no cool detachment here, as in the Janowski or Karajan; the flood of sound can be overwhelming. More regrettable, the sound exposes singing that comes up short compared to that of other recordings. This is an international and accomplished cast, but some weaknesses are glaring. Marton's Brünnhilde struggles at times. Tomlinson, a superb stage presence and Bayreuth's Wotan as of 1995, is unduly raw as Hagen.

The Haitink is not fully satisfying. Although its impact is impressive and immediate, the conception here is less unified than that of other *Ring*s. Despite its energy, we are less consistently engaged in the drama: we return to this *Ring* for its shimmering beauty.

**James Levine. Metropolitan Opera Orchestra. Deutsche Grammophon. Studio.
1987–1989.**
R 427 607-2   V 423 389-2   S 429 407-2   T 429-385-2

Levine's deliberate pace recalls his *Parsifal,* yet his *Ring* is shorter than the Karajan and only eight minutes longer than the Furtwängler. (It is nearly two hours shorter than the Knappertsbusch and the Goodall, which are in a class by themselves in this regard. And the Levine video version is significantly shorter than the studio recording discussed here.)

Levine's sense of control is more relentless, conductor and music more exposed, than in any other *Ring*. Levine seems determined to miss nothing, to illuminate each measure of this long and daunting score.

The superb sound reproduction lacks the reverberating depth of the Haitink but is rich and lucid. In fact, unblended, individual instruments are sometimes heard all too clearly: an intrusive tuba disturbs the final moments of R-iv; in the same scene the lament of the Rhine Daughters, rather than floating up from the deep valley behind, as intended, comes directly at Wotan—and us. We wish for more subtlety here.

Levine's deliberate reading is inevitably linked with the Metropolitan Opera's stage production of the late 1980s and early 1990s, which he conducted and which was generally faithful to Wagner's directions. It was hugely successful with audiences, but some critics faulted the production as overly literal and dramatically inert; at times Levine's constancy mutes the dramatic contracts. Wagner himself knew when to step back, to relent, by taking us through occasional valleys in the journey from one emotional peak to the next. And by making his intention so clear, Levine sometimes loses the element of surprise; we tend to see what is coming.

Nevertheless, this recording is a huge achievement. To his great credit, Levine's enhancement of the orchestra has been among the signal contributions of his Met tenure. That effort seems to have been undertaken for this very *Ring*. The orchestra consistently responds to the huge demands of both composer and conductor. It is as confident in the quiet and gentle passages as in the cataclysmic. The playing might not boast the sheer virtuosity of the Vienna and Berlin groups (in the Solti and Karajan, respectively), but it stands proudly on its own.

As in the Karajan, the orchestra also provides a safety net over which the singers can perform comfortably. Levine generally assembled the best of contemporary *Ring* artists. Norman is again a glorious Sieglinde. Morris is the leading Wotan of this time, and his interpretive skills come close to matching his majestic voice. Behrens is stronger in this set, especially at T-3-iii, than on stage or on the video tape, demonstrating another advantage of the studio recording.

Levine, who is conducting the 1994–1998 Bayreuth cycle, has given us a most personal musical vision of *The Ring*. He takes huge risks in unfolding the score so patently. His success is further proof that measure by measure, the *Ring* score satisfies the most intense scrutiny; that measure by measure, the meaning of *The Ring* is in the music.

Daniel Barenboim. Orchester der Bayreuther Festspiele. Teldec. Live. 1991.
R 4509-91185-2   V 4509-91186-2   S 4509-94193-2   T 4509-94194-2

The Barenboim is the strongest case yet for live recordings. Teldec has met the technical challenge of optimum reproduction: this is a vibrant, animated sound. Extraneous noises have been substantially reduced, although there are still problems; the excessive footpadding of the Gibichungs at the introduction to the Funeral March in T-3-ii is particularly annoying, and a prompter is frequently heard talking to the singers. But occasionally stage noises add rather than detract: the vassals rush in to Hagen's call in T-2-iii like rolling thunder.

More important, the genius of the Festspielhaus acoustics is fully realized at last. The voices, as always at Bayreuth, are clearly heard, but they are also superbly balanced in relation to each another. And for once the orchestra—as ensemble and in its component parts—seems to benefit from the mystic abyss rather than be victimized by it. We hear what we are meant to hear.

The Bayreuth orchestra plays in all its glory, blending or individualizing sounds as the need arises, and with enthusiasm (perhaps energy pent up since the days of Boulez). The playing is especially theatrical in the best sense; whether lyrical, stark, dangerous, or noble, it is in keeping with Wagner's dramatic intentions.

Much credit for this achievement must go to the conductor. Barenboim's phrasing here seems more measured—consistent and not so quirky—than it was during the 1992 cycle that I attended. This effect may have been partly realized by splicing from multiple performances in June and July 1991.

The singing also exceeds expectations. On paper, this is among the least formidable *Ring* recording casts, and there are serious weaknesses. But in general the cast delivers an honest performance that we can both relish and admire. Most notable is Jerusalem, a more thoughtful interpreter than is generally credited (see his Loge in the Levine/Deutsche Grammophon *Rhinegold* video). Here his voice sheds the tired, foggy edge that has sometimes weakened other performances. Evans's Brünnhilde may not inspire, but it is a noble and attractive reading.

The Barenboim recording may benefit from its separation from the visual aspects of Kupfer's production. That highly personal and distracting vision may have prevented us from knowing the musical virtues of this cycle. In that, the Barenboim set is a liberation.

Recordings of Individual Ring Operas

Erich Leinsdorf. *Die Walküre.* **London Symphony Orchestra. Studio. 1962.**

V 430 391-2

Erich Leinsdorf's *The Valkyrie* of 1962, with the London Symphony, may be better than either Solti's or Karajan's. Combining Nilsson and Vickers at their primes, Leinsdorf also had the incomparable Brouwenstijn as Sieglinde and Gorr as Fricka. To many, London's Wotan is as handsome as Hotter's. Leinsdorf and the LSO bring a Solti-like combination of excitement and intelligence to the score. This record was the first installment of an abortive attempt to record the full cycle. One can only regret it was never completed.

Bruno Walter. *Die Walküre,* **Act 1. Vienna Philharmonic. EMI. Studio. 1935.**

V-1 CDH 7 61020-2

Everything about this recording is exemplary, but above all it demonstrates why Melchior has been regarded as the heldentenor of the century. He is strong, bold, and melodious. There is never a weak moment, much less a misstep. More than anything, Melchior makes equal and perfect sense of music and word. This must be all the tenor Wagner could have hoped for.

Cast Lists

	Karajan	Furtwängler	Krauss	Knapperts-busch	Knapperts-busch	Solti	Böhm
	Bayreuth 1951	RAI 1953	Bayreuth 1953	Bayreuth 1957	Bayreuth 1958	Decca 1958–1966	Bayreuth 1967

The Rhinegold

Alberich	Pflanzl	Neidlinger	Neidlinger	Neidlinger	Andersson	Neidlinger	Neidlinger
Wotan	Björling	Frantz	Hotter	Hotter	Hotter	London	Adam
Fricka	Malaniuk	Malaniuk	Malaniuk	von Milinkovic	Gorr	Flagstad	Burmeister
Freia	Brivkalne	Grümmer	Falcon	Grümmer	Grümmer	Watson	Silja
Fasolt	Weber	Greindl	Weber	van Mill	Adam	Kreppel	Talvela
Fafner	Dalberg	Frick	Weber	Greindl	Greindl	Böhme	Böhme
Froh	Windgassen	Fehenberger	Stolze	Traxel	Kónya	Kmentt	Esser
Donner	Faulhaber	Poell	Uhde	Blankenheim	Saedén	Wächter	Nienstedt
Loge	Fritz	Windgassen	Witte	Suthaus	Uhl	Svanholm	Windgassen
Mime	Kuen	Patzak	Kuen	Kuen	Stolze	Kuen	Wohlfahrt
Erda	Siewert	Siewert	von Ilosvay	von Ilosvay	von Ilosvay	Madeira	Soukupova

The Valkyrie

Siegmund	Trepton	Windgassen	Vinay	Vinay	Vickers	King	King
Sieglinde	Rysanek	Konetzni	Resnik	Nilsson	Rysanek	Crespin	Rysanek
Hunding	van Mill	Frick	Greindl	Greindl	Greindl	Frick	Nienstedt
Wotan	Björling	Frantz	Hotter	Hotter	Hotter	Hotter	Adam
Brünnhilde	Varnay	Mödl	Varnay	Varnay	Varnay	Nilsson	Nilsson
Fricka	Höngen	Cavelti	Malaniuk	von Milinkovic	Gorr	Ludwig	Burmeister

Siegfried

Mime	Kuen	Patzak	Kuen	Kuen	Stolze	Stolze	Wohlfahrt
Siegfried	Aldenhoff	Suthaus	Windgassen	Aldenhoff	Windgassen	Windgassen	Windgassen
The Wanderer	Björling	Frantz	Hotter	Hotter	Hotter	Hotter	Adam
Alberich	Pflanzl	Pernerstorfer	Neidlinger	Neidlinger	Andersson	Neidlinger	Neidlinger
Fafner	Dalberg	Greindl	Greindl	Greindl	Greindl	Böhme	Böhme
Wood Bird	Lipp	Streich	Streich	Hollweg	Siebert	Sutherland	Köth
Erda	Siewert	Klose	von Ilosvay	von Ilosvay	von Ilosvay	Hoffgen	Soukupova
Brünnhilde	Varnay	Mödl	Varnay	Varnay	Varnay	Nilsson	Nilsson

Twilight of the Gods

Siegfried	Aldenhoff	Suthaus	Windgassen	Windgassen	Windgassen	Windgassen	Windgassen
Brünnhilde	Varnay	Mödl	Varnay	Varnay	Varnay	Nilsson	Nilsson
Gunther	Uhde	Poell	Uhde	Uhde	Wiener	Fischer-Dieskau	Stewart
Hagen	Weber	Greindl	Greindl	Greindl	Greindl	Frick	Greindl
Gutrune	Mödl	Jurinac	Hinsch-Gröndahl	Grümmer	Grümmer	Watson	Dvořáková
Waltraute	Siewert	Klose	Malaniuk	von Ilosvay	Madeira	Ludwig	Mödl
Alberich	Pflanzl	Pernerstorfer	Neidlinger	Neidlinger	Andersson	Neidlinger	Neidlinger

Karajan	Goodall	Boulez	Janowski	Levine	Haitink	Barenboim
DG	EMI	Bayreuth	Eurodisc	DG	EMI	Bayreuth
1967–1970	1973–1977	1981	1980–1983	1988–1991	1988–1991	1991–1992
Kelemen	Hammond-Stroud	Becht	Nimsgern	Wlaschiha	Adam	von Kannen
Fischer-Dieskau	Bailey	McIntyre	Adam	Morris	Morris	Tomlinson
Veasey	Pring	Schwarz	Minton	Ludwig	Lipovšek	Finnie
Mangelsdorff	McDonall	Reppel	Napier	Haggander	Johansson	Johansson
Talvela	Lloyd	Salminen	Bracht	Moll	Tschammer	Hölle
Ridderbusch	Grant	Hübner	Salminen	Rootering	Rydl	Kang
Grobe	Ferguson	Jerusalem	Büchner	Baker	Seiffert	Schreibmayer
Kerns	Welsby	Egel	Stryczek	Lorenz	Schmidt	Brinkmann
Stolze	Belcourt	Zednik	Schreier	Jerusalem	Zednik	Clark
Wohlfahrt	Dempsey	Pampuch	Vogel	Zednik	Haage	Pampuch
Dominguez	Collins	Wenkel	Wenkel	Svendén	Rappé	Svendén
Vickers	Remedios	Hofmann	Jerusalem	Lakes	Goldberg	Elming
Janowitz	Curphey	Altmeyer	Norman	Norman	Studer	Secunde
Talvela	Grant	Salminen	Moll	Moll	Salminen	Hölle
Stewart	Bailey	McIntyre	Adam	Morris	Morris	Tomlinson
Crespin	Hunter	Jones	Altmeyer	Behrens	Marton	Evans
Veasey	Howard	Schwarz	Minton	Ludwig	Meier	Finnie
Stolze	Dempsey	Zednik	Schreier	Zednik	Haage	Clark
Thomas	Remedios	Jung	Kollo	Goldberg	Jerusalem	Jerusalem
Stewart	Bailey	McIntyre	Adam	Morris	Morris	Tomlinson
Kelemen	Hammond-Stroud	Becht	Nimsgern	Wlaschiha	Adam	von Kannen
Ridderbusch	Grant	Hübner	Salminen	Moll	Rydl	Kang
Gayer	London	Sharp	Sharp	Battle	Te Kanawa	Leidland
Dominguez	Collins	Wenkel	Wenkel	Svendén	Rappé	Svendén
Dernesch	Hunter	Jones	Altmeyer	Behrens	Marton	Evans
Brilioth	Remedios	Jung	Kollo	Goldberg	Jerusalem	Jerusalem
Dernesch	Hunter	Jones	Altmeyer	Behrens	Marton	Evans
Stewart	Welsby	Mazura	Nöcker	Weikl	Hampson	Brinkmann
Ridderbusch	Haugland	Hübner	Salminen	Salminen	Tomlinson	Kang
Janowitz	Curphey	Altmeyer	Sharp	Studer	Bundschuh	Bundschuh
Ludwig	Pring	Killebrew	Wenkel	Schwarz	Lipovšek	Meier
Kelemen	Hammond-Stroud	Becht	Nimsgern	Wlaschiha	Adam	von Kannen

Timings of Selected *Ring* Recordings

Times are in minutes, or hours and minutes, rounded to the nearest minute.

	Furtwängler 1953	Krauss 1953	Knappertsbusch 1958	Solti 1958–1967	Böhm 1967	Karajan 1967–1970
The Rhinegold						
i	29	25	–	24	–	25
ii	46	44	–	46	–	43
iii	28	28	–	26	–	27
iv	51	48	–	50	–	51
Total	2.35	2.25	2.37	2.26	2.16	2.26
The Valkyrie						
1	68	62	–	66	62	67
2	96	85	–	93	83	97
3	69	65	–	70	64	73
Total	3.57	3.52	3.54	3.49	3.29	3.57
Siegfried						
1	89	83	–	82	–	83
2	75	75	–	74	–	74
3	84	80	–	80	–	83
Total	3.48	3.58	4.57	3.57	3.43	4.00
Twilight						
Prologue and 1	–	115	–	120	111	125
2	–	67	–	67	61	69
3	–	78	–	78	73	82
Total	4.27	4.20	5.11	4.25	4.05	4.36
Tetralogy	14.47	14.35	16.39	14.37	13.33	14.59

Goodall 1972–1975	Boulez 1980–1981	Janowski 1980–1983	Levine 1989	Haitink 1992	Barenboim 1994
32	23	23	24	26	–
53	48	46	48	42	–
33	27	27	27	27	–
56	47	44	55	50	–
2.54	2.25	2.20	2.34	2.25	2.29
73	–	65	65	65	–
100	–	89	95	95	–
76	–	66	70	72	–
4.09	3.34	3.40	3.50	3.51	3.53
95	–	77	83	78	–
86	–	74	79	71	–
96	–	80	83	79	–
4.37	3.44	3.52	4.05	3.49	4.00
138	–	–	119	117	–
79	–	–	66	64	–
94	–	–	81	76	–
5.11	4.04	4.10	4.26	4.18	4.27
16.51	13.44	14.02	14.55	14.23	15.31

NOTES

Preface

1. From Richard Wagner's *The Artwork of the Future*, quoted in A. Goldman and E. Springhorn, eds., *Wagner on Music and Drama*, trans. H. Ashton Ellis (New York: E. P. Dutton & Co., Inc., 1984), 188.
2. Bryan Magee, *Aspects of Wagner*, 2nd ed. (Oxford: Oxford University Press, 1988), 9.
3. Deryck Cooke, *The Language of Music*, 2nd ed.(Oxford: Oxford University Press, 1989), 32. Cooke takes on the modernist theory, as expressed by Hindemith and Stravinsky, that there can be no inherent expression of emotion in music.
4. Terence Kilmartin, *A Reader's Guide to Remembrance of Things Past* (New York: Vintage Books, 1984), vii.

Introduction

1. Those seeking a challenging test of their *Ring* knowledge will enjoy William O. Cord's "201 Questions (and Answers) on Richard Wagner's *Der Ring des Nibelungen*," Wagner Society of Northern California, 1993.
2. Barry Millington, "Wagner's Revolutionary Musical Reforms" in Stewart Spencer, transl., *Wagner's "Ring of the Nibelung": A Companion* (New York: Thames and Hudson, 1993), 14. Try though he might, Wagner was never as convincing on the equality of poetry and music in practice as he was in theory. The primacy of the music was inexorable. See also chapter 3.
3. Deryck Cooke, *I Saw the World End: A Study of Wagner's "Ring"* (London: Oxford University Press, 1979), 12.
4. Cooke, *I Saw*, 12.
5. From Stewart Spencer's "A Note on the Text and Translation," in Spencer, *Wagner's "Ring,"* 13.
6. Andrew Porter, transl., *The Ring of the Nibelung* (New York: W. W. Norton), xvi.
7. Spencer, *Wagner's "Ring,"* 13.
8. Porter, *The Ring*, ix.
9. See Porter, *The Ring*, ix–xx.
10. Spencer, *Wagner's "Ring,"* 7.

Chapter One   Background

1. Robert Gutman, *Richard Wagner: The Man, His Mind, and His Music* (San Diego: Harcourt Brace Jovanovich, 1990), 120–121.

   Wagner's conception of *The Ring,* his writing of the texts and music, and the way these relate to each other and to his artistic theories, practices, and other works are immensely complicated subjects that are only summarized here. They have been explored in great detail by leading Wagner scholars. The notes throughout this book and the bibliography suggest useful sources for further review.

2. Deryck Cooke, *I Saw the World End: A Study of Wagner's "Ring"* (London: Oxford University Press, 1979), 10.

3. Cooke, *I Saw,* 88.

4. Cooke, *I Saw,* 91.

5. In *Richard Wagner and the Nibelungs* (Oxford: Clarendon Press, 1990), the British musicologist Elizabeth Magee meticulously charts Wagner's use of the Royal Library's resources and succeeds in demonstrating Wagner's substantial reliance on nineteenth-century works.

6. Cooke, *I Saw,* 84.

7. See Ernest Newman, *The Wagner Operas* (New York: Alfred A. Knopf, 1963), 393–450.

8. Ernest Newman, *Wagner as Man and Artist* (New York: Vintage Books, 1960), 213.

9. He wrote no music of importance after finishing the *Lohengrin* prelude in August 1847. In the summer of 1850 he composed a version of the Norn scene and a bit more, but perhaps "stopped upon finding his musical language and technique as yet deficient in the means to set forth the sounds heard in his inner ear," according to Robert Gutman. See Gutman, *Wagner,* 148.

10. With one exception: the prose plan for *The Rhinegold* was written before the prose plan for *The Valkyrie.* However, the poem for *The Valkyrie* was written before the *Rhinegold* poem. See also Barry Millington, *Wagner* (New York: Vintage Books, 1987), 194–202.

11. Gutman, *Wagner,* 120.

12. Millington, *Wagner,* 35.

13. Gutman, *Wagner,* 157.

14. Newman, *The Wagner Operas,* 416–417.

15. Newman, *The Wagner Operas,* 417.

16. Four rejected versions, written between 1848 and 1856, are included in Stewart Spencer, *Wagner's "Ring of the Nibelung": A Companion* (New York: Thames and Hudson, 1993), 360–363.

17. Quoted in Ernest Newman, *The Life of Richard Wagner* (Cambridge: Cambridge University Press, 1933), vol. 2, 359. Newman discusses this subject thoroughly (pages 347–362). His four-volume biography, first published in 1933, remains the first choice for those wishing to examine Wagner's life in 2500 pages.

18. Newman, *Wagner as Man and Artist,* 255.

19. Richard Wagner, *My Life* (New York: Tudor Publishing, 1936), 603. Originally published in 1911.

20. Gutman, *Wagner*, 149.
21. Charles Osborne, *The Complete Operas of Richard Wagner* (New York: Da Capo Press, Inc., 1993), 241.
22. Millington points out that *Siegfried* was not entirely out of mind throughout this period; during 1864–1865 Wagner completed the scoring of S-1 and S-2. Millington, *Wagner*, 201.
23. Gutman, *Wagner*, 177. It has been suggested that *Tristan* grew out of Wagner's romantic feelings for Frau Wesendonck, but Gutman is at his insightful best when he says "this famous affair . . . was the result, not the cause, of the *Tristan* theme coursing through him" (Gutman, 36).
24. Newman, *Wagner as Man and Artist*, 345.
25. Quoted in Bryan Magee, *Aspects of Wagner*, 2nd ed. (Oxford: Oxford University Press, 1988), 80.
26. For a discussion of Wagner's patrimony, see Gutman, *Wagner*, 1–6.
27. B. Magee, *Aspects*, 7. Magee's is a superb and concise summary of Wagner's aesthetic theories, distilled from thousands of pages of Wagner's frequently incomprehensible efforts to explain himself.
28. Rudolph Sabor, *The Real Wagner* (London: Sphere Books, 1989), 319.
29. John Deathridge and Carl Dahlhaus, *The New Grove Wagner* (New York and London: W. W. Norton & Company, 1984), 61.
30. Sabor, *The Real Wagner*, 323.
31. Kurt Saffir, "Mystic Abyss," *Opera News*, April 1974, 12.
32. Sabor, *The Real Wagner*, 335.
33. Gutman, *Wagner*, 348
34. Gutman, *Wagner*, 348.

Chapter Three   The Music

1. Bryan Magee, *Aspects of Wagner*, 2nd ed. (Oxford: Oxford University Press, 1988), 79.
2. Ernest Newman, *Wagner as Man and Artist* (New York: Vintage Books, 1960), 320 and 324.
3. From Boulez's remarkable description of the music of *The Rhinegold* in the notes accompanying his Philips recording of that opera, Philips 434 421-2, page 17.
4. Newman, *Wagner as Man and Artist*, 196.
5. Robert Jacobs, *Wagner* (London: J. M. Dent and Sons, 1965), 160.
6. Robert W. Gutman, *Richard Wagner: The Man, His Mind, and His Music* (San Diego: Harcourt Brace Jovanovich, 1990), 364.
7. Gutman, *Wagner*, 365.
8. Gutman, *Wagner*, 363.
9. Robert Donington, *Wagner's "Ring" and Its Symbols* (London: Faber and Faber, 1963), 275–276.
10. Donington, *Symbols*, 63.
11. For a fuller discussion of this matter, see Deryck Cooke, *I Saw the World End* (London: Oxford University Press, 1979), 2–12; and Donington, *Symbols*, 138–140.

12. Donington, *Symbols*, 63.
13. Deryck Cooke, *An Introduction to Wagner's "Der Ring des Nibelungen"* (New York: Time Inc., 1972), Example 61.
14. See Cooke, *I Saw*, 48–56.
15. Newman, *The Wagner Operas*, 463.
16. Cooke, *An Introduction*, Examples 63–79.
17. Cooke, *An Introduction*, Example 160.
18. Cooke, *An Introduction*, Example 84.
19. Donington, *Symbols*, 85.
20. Donington, *Symbols*, 114.
21. Cooke, *An Introduction*, Example 71.
22. Newman, *Wagner as Man and Artist*, 335.
23. This passage is also discussed in Cooke, *I Saw*, 2–12, and in Donington, *Symbols*, 138–140.
24. Newman, *The Wagner Operas*, 512.
25. Newman, *Wagner as Man and Artist*, 249.
26. Cooke, *An Introduction*, Example 115.
27. Newman, *Wagner as Man and Artist*, 360.
28. Cooke, *An Introduction*, Example 49.
29. Certainly the most droll criticisms of *Twilight of the Gods*, if not the most insightful, come from Bernard Shaw. See *The Perfect Wagnerite* (Chicago: Herbert S. Stone and Company, 1898), 116–117.

Chapter Four   The Characters

1. Elizabeth Magee, *Richard Wagner and the Nibelungs.* (Oxford: Clarendon Press, 1990), 61.
2. See E. Magee, *Wagner and the Nibelungs*, 63–67.
3. Robert W. Gutman, *Richard Wagner: The Man, His Mind, and His Music* (San Diego: Harcourt Brace Jovanovich, 1990), 453.
4. E. Magee, *Wagner and the Nibelungs*, 82.
5. Deryck Cooke, *I Saw the World End* (London: Oxford University Press, 1979), 84.
6. Cooke, *I Saw*, 117.
7. Cooke, *I Saw*, 12.
8. Cooke, *I Saw*, 150.
9. E. Magee, *Wagner and the Nibelungs*, 190.
10. Robert Donington, *Wagner's "Ring" and Its Symbols* (London: Faber and Faber, 1963), 74.
11. See Donington, *Symbols*, 75.
12. Cooke, *I Saw*, 152.
13. E. Magee, *Wagner and the Nibelungs*, 191.
14. For a fuller discussion of these motives, see Cooke, *I Saw*, 48–56, and Cooke, *An Introduction to Wagner's "Der Ring des Nibelungen"* (New York: Time Inc., 1972), examples 59 and 60.

15. Quoted in E. Magee, *Wagner and the Nibelungs*, 195.

16. Quoted in E. Magee, *Wagner and the Nibelungs*, 196.

17. Cooke, *I Saw*, 117.

18. Cooke, *I Saw*, 160.

19. Quoted in E. Magee, *Wagner and the Nibelungs*, 196.

20. E. Magee, *Wagner and the Nibelungs*, 197.

21. Karl Weinhold's article of 1849 on Loki, quoted in E. Magee, *Wagner and the Nibelungs*, 199.

22. See Cooke, *I Saw*, 105–106.

23. See E. Magee, *Wagner and the Nibelungs*, 113–114.

24. Cooke, *I Saw*, 199.

25. See E. Magee, *Wagner and the Nibelungs*, 113–114.

26. Cooke, *I Saw*, 226.

27. Cooke, *I Saw*, 226.

28. Cooke, *I Saw*, 229.

29. Quoted in Ernest Newman, *The Life of Richard Wagner* (Cambridge: Cambridge University Press, 1933), vol. 2, 359.

30. See E. Magee, *Wagner and the Nibelungs*, 69–71.

31. See Cooke, *I Saw*, 2–12, for his own interpretation along with those of Shaw, Newman, and Donington.

32. E. Magee, *Wagner and the Nibelungs*, 69.

33. E. Magee, *Wagner and the Nibelungs*, 154.

34. Friedrich von der Hagen, who translated *Thridiks Saga* and the *Poetic Edda* in 1814–1815, quoted in E. Magee, *Wagner and the Nibelungs*, 155.

35. Owen M. Lee, *Wagner's "Ring": Turning the Sky Round* (New York: Summit Books, 1990), 93.

36. Cooke, *I Saw*, 117.

37. E. Magee, *Wagner and the Nibelungs*, 166.

38. Cooke, *I Saw*, 344.

39. Ernest Newman, *The Wagner Operas* (New York: Alfred A. Knopf), 512.

40. Cooke, *I Saw*, 96.

41. Quoted in Cooke, *I Saw*, 98.

42. E. Magee, *Wagner and the Nibelungs*, 62.

43. Donington, *Symbols*, 254 and 260.

44. Donington, *Symbols*, 260.

45. Cooke, *I Saw*, 117.

46. E. Magee, *Wagner and the Nibelungs*, 86.

47. Cooke, *I Saw*, 91.

48. E. Magee, *Wagner and the Nibelungs*, 77.

49. Cooke, *I Saw*, 91.

50. E. Magee, *Wagner and the Nibelungs*, 93.

51. See Cooke, *I Saw*, 91.

Chapter Five Concordance

1. M. Owen Lee to J. K. Holman, 6 July 1993.
2. Deryck Cooke, *I Saw the World End* (London: Oxford University Press), 239.

Appendix

1. Lilli Lehmann, who was a Rhine Daughter and the Wood Bird in the 1876 Bayreuth *Ring* and sang Brünnhilde in Cosima's 1896 cycle, wrote: "All roads may lead to Rome, but to the Bayreuth of today there is but one—the road of slavish subjection. Cosima was not only very clever and well-informed. She also had assumed the authority of judgment peculiar to the aristocracy, so that what she announced was accepted as infallible." Gerald Fitzgerald and Patrick O'Connor, eds., *The Ring* (New York: Metropolitan Opera Guild, n.d.), 47.
2. See Charles Osborne, *The World Theatre of Wagner* (Oxford: Phaidon Press, 1982), 57; and Oswald Georg Bauer, *Richard Wagner: The Stage Designs and Productions from the Premieres to the Present* (New York: Rizzoli, 1982), 98–99.
3. Götz Friedrich, Metropolitan Opera/Texaco radio broadcast commentary, 4 March 1993. Private collection.
4. On the difficulty of staging *The Ring* according to Wagner's instructions, see John Culshaw, *Reflections on Wagner's "Ring"* (New York: Viking, 1975), 67–102.

Discography

1. Bryan Magee, *Aspects of Wagner*, 2nd ed. (Oxford: Oxford University Press, 1988), 71–72.
2. John Culshaw, in his notes for the Solti *Das Rheingold* CD, Decca 414 101-2, page 7.
3. Bernard Holland in "Worthy Versions of 'The Ring': A Critical Selection," *The New York Times*, 16 April 1993, C27.
4. John Rockwell in "Worthy Versions of 'The Ring.'"
5. Edward Rothstein in "Worthy Versions of 'The Ring.'"

BIBLIOGRAPHY

The literature upon Wagner's Nibelungen Ring *is so extensive
that it seems almost preposterous to add anything more.*

—Katherine A. Layton, "The Nibelung of Wagner"
(Ph.D. diss., University of Illinois, 1908), Introduction.

THIS BIBLIOGRAPHY is meant to provide an opening into the vast world of Wagner
and *Ring* literature. Though compiled for the serious reader and listener, it is highly
selective, limited to just twenty-five entries, all in English. Although the greatest body
of *Ring* scholarship is in German, the reader need not feel slighted; the Anglo-American
literature is extraordinarily strong—comprehensive, illuminating, readable, original,
and deeply satisfying.

Most selections here make a focused contribution to our understanding of *The Ring*
itself. Ernest Newman's classic four-volume biography, *The Life of Richard Wagner*, is ex-
cluded, for example, because its essential scope is outside *The Ring*. (Later biographers
have had the advantage of sources not available to Newman early in this century, but his
opus remains essential for those who want to pursue the composer's life in detail.) On
the other hand, three single-volume biographies are included because they clarify the
connections between Wagner's life and his creation of *The Ring*.

Many of the works cited below have their own extensive bibliographies. The reader is
encouraged to consult these, too.

Allen, Peter. *Talking about "The Ring."* Metropolitan Opera Guild, 1988. Audiocassettes.
No introduction to *The Ring* could be more enjoyable or effective than Peter Allen's
Talking about "The Ring." Widely known as the voice of the Metropolitan Opera's Saturday broadcasts, Allen has an elegant ability to simplify, entertain, and inform. He
covers an extraordinary amount of material in this four-part series. Musical examples
are taken from the Solti recording.

Bauer, Oswald Georg. *Richard Wagner: The Stage Designs and Productions from the Pre-
mieres to the Present.* New York: Rizzoli, 1983.
This is one of two lavish photographic histories on the subject of staging Wagner (see
Charles Osborne, *The World Theatre of Wagner*, below). Bauer provides a pictorial

history of productions of all Wagner's operas, even *Die Feen* and *Das Liebesverbot*, and he includes a large number of striking color and black-and-white photos and sketches of sets and costumes. Bauer also provides an extended background on the staging of each opera, paying particular attention to the problems posed by the original productions and the solutions favored by Wagner himself.

Bauer was for many years involved in the administration of the Bayreuth Festival, and the book includes an introduction by the festival's director—the composer's grandson—Wolfgang Wagner, which articulates much of Wolfgang and brother Wieland's approach to their historic stagings.

Burbridge, Peter, and Richard Sutton, eds. *The Wagner Companion*. New York: Cambridge University Press, 1979.
This is a collection of essays covering Wagner's life and work, arranged by subject and covering a wide range of significant issues. The chapters on the German intellectual and literary background, rarely explored in English, are especially useful.

The gem is Deryck Cooke on Wagner's development of revolutionary harmonic techniques to articulate a coherent musical language. Cooke remarks that the obsession with leitmotifs has bedeviled our understanding of the way Wagner's music is constructed to convey not just concepts, but the "profound emotional and psychological realities" behind them.

A comprehensive index of Wagner's works and a bibliography are included.

Cooke, Deryck. *An Introduction to Wagner's "Der Ring des Nibelungen."* New York: Time Inc., 1972. CD London 443 581-2.
Cooke's in-depth analysis of the musical motives of *The Ring* was included with Time-Life Records' reissue of the London/Solti *Ring* recording. The *Das Rheingold* set included recordings of Cooke reading his text, along with recorded musical excerpts illustrating 193 motivic examples (cassette tapes and CDs of this reading are available from the Wagner Society of New York). Cooke's interpretation of Wagner's musical architecture occasionally seems forced—it is highly systemic, especially with regard to "families" of motives generated by a basic, "originating" motive—but this work nevertheless provides a superb overview of *Ring* motives.

———. *I Saw the World End: A Study of Wagner's "Ring."* London: Oxford University Press, 1979.
Cooke's purpose was to create what he considered an objective interpretation of *The Ring*, and his work remains among the most authoritative in the *Ring* literature. Unfortunately, he completed only half his task; *I Saw the World End* interprets only *The Rhinegold* and *The Valkyrie*. Cooke died in 1976, leaving behind only fragments on the last two *Ring* operas.

Cooke intended to refute the Jungian Robert Donington (see below) and other *Ring* analyses that Cooke considered nonobjective. "After all," he wrote, "the question is not 'What meaning can *we* find in *The Ring*?', but 'What did *Wagner* really *mean* by

The Ring?"' Cooke believed that "the overt meaning of each element in the drama must be accepted as what it is (and what Wagner intended it to be), and not explained away or made to mean something else." One can only imagine Cooke's reaction to the era of personal-vision *Ring*s that gained ascendance at Bayreuth in the same year he died (see "Staging *The Ring*" in the Appendix).

Fortunately Cooke did not allow himself to become the victim of his own prescriptions. He understood as well as anyone the difficulty of articulating meaning in music (his other major work is *The Language of Music*), and he knew that, despite the most communicative text and music (and essays and letters), Wagner nevertheless "was unable to communicate his intentions clearly."

Cooke's own approach is based on the assumption that *The Ring* is primarily symbolic. Understanding its symbolism, he argued, requires a thorough understanding of the way Wagner used, and did not use, the German and Scandinavian mythological sources to fashion his story. This book and Elizabeth Magee's (see below) provide the most fulsome assessments of the myths and their place in *The Ring*.

Culshaw, John. *Reflections on Wagner's "Ring."* New York: Viking, 1975.

Culshaw set a standard in *Ring* writing for brevity, insight, plain speaking, and common sense. Producer of the monumental London/Solti *Ring* (see Culshaw, *Ring Resounding*, below), Culshaw gave four short talks on the *Ring* operas on the Texaco/ Metropolitan Opera Saturday radio broadcasts. Hugely popular, these essays are reprinted here, together with a fifth chapter on the problems of staging *The Ring*'s demanding and spectacular special effects.

Culshaw's perspective was unique among *Ring* analysts: his job was to reproduce electronically only the audible aspects of *The Ring*, not the visual. He understood that Wagner's music, like all music, describes emotions that cannot be put into words or stage actions and that Wagner evokes powerful emotional reactions in *The Ring* by connecting the audience's response to the music with "the response to the retelling of a myth, which is something all of us share." This book and Culshaw's account of making the Solti recording (described immediately below) should be required reading for those responsible for producing *The Ring*.

————. *Ring Resounding.* New York: Viking Press, 1967.

A triumph about a triumph. Culshaw describes the monumental London/Solti project to produce the first studio high-fidelity recording of the complete *Ring*, in the years 1958 to 1966. The recordings themselves are the most honored in recording history, and for his efforts as producer Culshaw was knighted.

A good behind-the-scenes account of an artistic collaboration, this book documents with wit and charm the successes and trials of the immense effort. Moreover, by showing us how musical problems were faced and solved, Culshaw sheds much light on the meaning of *The Ring* itself.

But the book is more, even, than this. It is a blueprint for excellence, reminding us that superior results are got by great talent, hard work, and an unwavering commitment to standards. Especially today, Culshaw's book should be seen more as a lesson than a reminiscence, and not just for *Ring* recordings.

Ring Resounding was included in the 1972 Time-Life Records reissue of the London/Solti recording.

Deathridge, John, and Carl Dahlhaus. *The New Grove Wagner*. New York and London: W. W. Norton & Company, 1984.

This work is lifted from *The New Grove Dictionary of Music and Musicians* (London 1980), and it shows. Deathridge's biographical section is cursory. It presupposes a prior knowledge of the major events of Wagner's life and often reads as a commentary on unresolved biographical issues.

Dahlhaus is an insightful Wagner essayist, and his sections on Wagner's aesthetics, musical-dramatic practices, and individual operas are more than just good reference materials. The book includes much other useful information, including comprehensive lists of Wagner's writings and compositions and a bibliography.

DiGaetani, John L., ed. *Penetrating Wagner's "Ring."* New York: Da Capo Press, 1978.

A compendium of short pieces on a broad range of *Ring* topics by many of its most gifted analysts and performers, such as Georg Solti, Adolphe Appia, Wieland Wagner, Culshaw, Donington, Porter, and G. B. Shaw. Most of the thirty-five pieces are reprinted from other sources, including Joseph Wechsberg's account of his personal "liberation" of the Bayreuth Festspielhaus on V-E day in 1945.

DiGaetani's own contribution is to describe *The Ring* as comedy rather than tragedy, not in its abundant but generally overlooked humor, but as an expression of Wagner's faith in the ability of his operas to improve society, in the ultimate triumph of nature, and in the demise of a society, like Wotan's, that must, morally, give way to the new.

Donington, Robert. *Wagner's "Ring" and Its Symbols*. London: Faber and Faber, 1963.

Donington's is a masterpiece of *Ring* commentary. The best of all efforts to explain the meaning of *The Ring* in clinical psychological terms, it is also among the most warmly compelling *Ring* commentaries on any level.

Linking the inner meaning of *The Ring* with the psyche of its composer has been an obvious course of inquiry from the time of the first festival at Bayreuth. Wagner invited such analysis because he never stopped writing and talking about himself, and great slices of his life were an open and often scandalous book. More important, Wagner's works probed his own and his characters' inner drives and conflicts, much as Freud's self-analysis served as a basis for his own works. It is little wonder that Wagner has been the subject of endless psychological speculation.

In Donington's Jungian view, *The Ring* represents no less than the development of a single personality—Wagner's. However, the greatest value of Donington's argument is not in its adherence to clinical psychological methods, but rather in the moving and elegant way it relates these to the overarching humanity of the music of *The Ring*. And by orienting his interpretation around the symbolism in *The Ring*, as any Jungian would, he draws with great effect on the mythological cornerstones of the work. In this, Donington articulates the inner workings of *The Ring* in the same way that Wieland Wagner's austere stage productions directed us to them visually.

Goldman, Albert, and Evert Sprinchorn, eds. *Wagner on Music and Drama.* New York: E. P. Dutton, 1964.

A compendium of Wagner's prose writings, translated by Ashton Ellis. No composer wrote more, on more subjects, than Wagner. His racial and other diatribes would be ludicrous had they not caused such pain. But on conducting, on nineteenth-century music and drama, on the Greek ideal, and on his own "art work of the future," he wielded great influence, despite frequently impenetrable language and significant divergences between theory and practice. The book, recently reissued, is a necessary reference tool for those who wish to read Wagner as well as hear him.

Gutman, Robert W. *Richard Wagner: The Man, His Mind, and His Music.* San Diego: Harcourt Brace Jovanovich, 1990. (Originally published in 1967.)

The most expansive and provocative of the single-volume biographies. The authoritativeness of Gutman's book is built on prodigious scholarship unvarnished by any sentimentality. Gutman also benefited from access to significant materials unavailable to biographers earlier this century.

Gutman's language is complex but worthy of careful reading. There is a kind of tension throughout, as Gutman struggles to keep his judgments of Wagner's behavior and art skeptical but objective; his admiration for Wagner's work is so matter-of-fact as to seem grudging. It is a tension that, on the whole, adds rather than detracts.

At the end, however, Gutman appears to lose his grip. In documenting Wagner's "moral collapse" late in life into an especially vicious advocacy of pro-Aryan and anti-semitic theories, Gutman interprets *Parsifal* as nothing more or less than a clear expression of such nonsense. This is an extreme and unpersuasive indictment of Wagner's final, most spiritual, and still ambiguous work.

A lavishly illustrated version of the Gutman biography was included with the 1972 Time-Life reissue of the London/Solti recording.

Lee, M. Owen. *Wagner's "Ring": Turning the Sky Round.* New York: Summit Books, 1990.

This book grew out of Father Lee's radio intermission talks during the Metropolitan Opera's 1990 *Ring* performances. A professor of classics at the University of Toronto, Lee views *The Ring* as evolutionary, both inwardly in terms of a soul in crisis and outwardly as the prevailing religious cosmos gives way to a higher level of ethical consciousness. This may be a doctrinal interpretation, but it is made as elegantly and persuasively as any *Ring* analysis.

This volume includes brief but provocative synopses and a useful annotated bibliography and discography. Lee's book has immediately entered the ranks of required *Ring* reading.

Magee, Bryan. *Aspects of Wagner.* 2nd ed. Oxford: Oxford University Press, 1988. (Originally published 1968.)

Upon its original publication in 1968, this thin volume of short essays represented something of a milestone in its attempt to establish an objective and common-sense approach to Wagner. For example, Magee provides a concise and intelligible summary of Wagner's theories on opera and drama.

A research fellow in the history of ideas at King's College, Magee also illuminates the Wagner literature's disproportionate focus on nonmusical aspects of the artist: his theories, antisemitism, megalomania, political views, or sex life. Magee is most vehement about Wagner in performance: staging should be "from the music outwards." Especially after the political upheavals in Europe of 1968, stage directors initiated a "great wave of left-wing political consciousness [making] Wagner's operas vehicles for comment on contemporary and recent history," a maze from which we may only now be emerging.

Magee, Elizabeth. *Richard Wagner and the Nibelungs.* Oxford: Clarendon Press, 1990.

This is an impressive academic achievement: Magee meticulously examines Wagner's study and use of the mythological sources of *The Ring*, as well as documenting his ambitious personal collection of the mythologies. She chronicles his research in Dresden in 1843 and 1844, his writing of the initial poem in 1848, and the evolution of the final *Ring* text.

Magee's definitive work allows us to make no mistake about two specific aspects of Wagner's remarkable invention of the *Ring* story. First, he consumed a huge number of sources, deeply and comprehensively. Second, he used the primary sources but drew even more upon secondary sources, including academic and fictional works written after 1800. Especially important among these were the encyclopedic writings of Jacob Grimm, Fouqué's dramatic poem, *Sigurd der Schlangentödter*, and Simrock's modern language versions of the myths.

Millington, Barry. *Wagner.* New York: Vintage Books, 1987.

Millington's work has become a fixture among the one-volume biographies, falling between the compact Deathridge-Dahlhaus work and Gutman's intricate and more exhaustive exploration discussed above. Although Millington covers Wagner's life in only 123 pages, he does so with authority. The rest is devoted to the operas themselves, of which thirty-seven pages describe the music of *The Ring*.

Newman, Ernest. *Wagner as Man and Artist.* New York: Alfred A Knopf, 1924.

Ernest Newman (1868–1959, born in Liverpool as William Roberts) is the father of modern Wagner criticism in English. He cleared away a vast underbrush of inadequate Wagner commentary, usually written by rabidly pro- or anti-Wagnerians, to establish a credible basis for Wagner scholarship. He separated fact from fiction with respect to aspects of Wagner's personal life, which had been rigidly protected and/or extravagantly reinvented by the composer himself in the autobiography *Mein Leben*, and subsequently by his wife, Cosima.

Newman also separated sense from nonsense in Wagner's extensive theoretical writings, for Wagner wrote brilliantly on music and drama and repugnantly on other subjects. Newman also analyzed the composer's artistic practices as they evolved throughout his creative life. Newman's patent enthusiasm never stands in the way of his objectivity. He explores Wagner's musical failures as well as the many gaps that evolved between theory and practice.

In fact, the final section of this book, "The Artist in Practice: The Mature Artist," has never been improved upon as a survey of Wagner's craft. It can be read and reread for its insight, style, and passion.

————. *The Wagner Operas.* New York: Alfred A. Knopf, 1963.
Also available under the title *Wagner Nights*, this is still the standard survey of Wagner's ten mature masterpieces. Newman devotes some seventy pages to each opera, describing both the evolution of the work from its initial sketch and the story itself with musical examples. Owen Lee's description is apt: "Any Wagnerite in good standing knows it by heart."

Osborne, Charles. *The World Theatre of Wagner.* Oxford: Phaidon Press, 1982.
One of two picture books on the Wagner operas (see Bauer, above). Osborne is well known for other works on Wagner (and Verdi, Puccini, and Strauss), and this book is more a survey of the operas themselves than a focused analysis of their staging. The photographs emphasize British productions. The book also includes a useful biographical dictionary that describes leading Wagnerian singers, conductors, and producers of the past hundred years.

Porter, Andrew, transl. *The Ring of the Nibelung.* New York: W. W. Norton, 1976.
Porter wrote this landmark translation for the Sadler's Wells Opera (now the English National Opera) *Ring* of the early 1970s: his chief concern was that the singers' words would be readily comprehensible on first hearing. The translation is therefore looser than its more literal predecessors. Porter also established cadences consistent with the musical mood and flavor of the German text. This is a work that was intended to be heard but should be read as well.

For those pursuing the subject of *Ring* translations, Porter's introduction is essential reading for its historical survey of earlier *Ring* translations and for its examination of the peculiar challenges and choices Wagner's text presents to anyone brave enough to take on the translator's task. (See also "The *Ring* Texts and Their Translations" in the Introduction.)

Sabor, Rudolph. *The Real Wagner.* London: Sphere Books, 1989.
Sabor's book is an informal, impressionistic, often insouciant view of Wagner's life, emphasizing its flavor and color rather than its chronology. It succeeds; Wagner's most attractive and repulsive traits are presented boldly but conclusively. The book is arranged around issues important in Wagner's life: Ludwig, Cosima, Bayreuth and *The Ring*, financial matters, and love life.

Many bad books have been written by enthusiastic admirers of Wagner. Sabor, who has given live entertainments called "An Evening with Richard Wagner," is among the few who carry the day. He draws on letters so telling on Wagner's career that they seem manufactured. For example, Wagner's breathtaking conceit is aptly illustrated in his 1861 letter to Baron von Hornstein, who had rejected the composer's request for both villa and stipend with the advice that he approach "*really* wealthy persons":

> I would be wrong not to rebuke you for your answer to my letter. It will probably not happen again that a man like me will have contact with you, but it should be a wholesome lesson to you to be made aware of the impropriety of your lines. It is not your place to advise me in any way whatever.

Shaw, George Bernard. *The Perfect Wagnerite*. Chicago and New York: Herbert S. Stone and Company, 1898.

Shaw's interpretation seems more misguided today than ever. The great playwright shoehorns *The Ring* to conform to his own Fabian socialist precepts, and his resulting rejection of *Twilight* as inconsistent and inferior to the first three operas, understandable on Shaw's terms, nevertheless runs counter to every contemporary view.

All this is rather beside the point. Shaw's argument is appropriately provocative, exploring aspects important to *The Ring*, especially Wagner's political and social views during his revolutionary period (1848–1853) when he wrote the *Ring* texts. Shaw's wit, as always, is a source of pleasure in its own right.

Moreover, we are fortunate to have this *Ring* commentary from an intellectual giant of the post-Wagner generation. As we try to come to terms with Wagner's art and the issues it raises, the explorations of Shaw, Nietzsche, Mann, and other luminaries only enrich our own efforts.

Spencer, Stewart, transl. *Wagner's "Ring of the Nibelung": A Companion*. New York: Thames and Hudson, 1993.

Spencer's fine translation is accompanied by a wealth of useful materials—brief commentaries by other analysts, chronology, glossary, photos, notes on the process of translation, and bibliography. Spencer also provides text versions ultimately rejected by Wagner, including four versions of Brünnhilde's peroration written between 1848 and 1856.

Spotts, Frederic. *Bayreuth*. New Haven and London: Yale University Press, 1994.

Spotts's new work is bound to replace Geoffrey Skelton's 1965 book as the standard history of Bayreuth, and not only because so much has happened there in the past thirty years. Spotts thoroughly explores the establishment of the house and festival, its administration, and its performances.

His examination of Bayreuth's Nazi period is unflinching and insightful. While cataloguing Hitler's involvement in degrading the festival, he also makes it clear that Hitler saved Bayreuth, financially and even artistically, from the Nazi *nomenklatura*, who hated opera, Wagner, and Bayreuth's continuing use of liberal, internationalist, and Jewish artists. While many conductors, singers, and musicians shunned or fled Bayreuth, many did not, and the 1930s under Tietjen and Pretorius was a period of undoubted artistic achievement.

Spotts also tackles controversial subjects of more recent vintage, including both the problems of personal-vision *Ring*s since 1976 and the continuing challenges and tensions, especially within the Wagner family, regarding the administration of the festival, especially as the long tenure of Wolfgang draws to a close.

Wagner, Richard. *The Ring of the Nibelung.* New York: G. Schirmer, Inc., 1906. These vocal scores were first transcribed for piano by Wagner's accompanist, Karl Klindworth. Frederick Jameson's English translations, frequently incomprehensible to today's readers, nevertheless prevailed for half a century. These scores, available in paperback, are indispensable as a musical reference; all musical examples and most stage directions quoted in this book are taken from them. I would add a personal note and confession: no other *Ring* experience, including most stage productions, affords the pleasures that come from being alone with a good recording, earphones, and the Schirmer Vocal Scores.

PHOTO CREDITS

The author is very grateful and extends his sincere appreciation to all those who have provided photographs for this book.

Front and back of dust jacket: Metropolitan Opera/Winnie Klotz.
Frontispiece: The British Library.
Photos of the Bayreuth Festspielhaus, chapter 1: Bayreuther Festspiele GmbH/Wilhelm Rauh.
Stage set photos, chapter 2: Metropolitan Opera/Winnie Klotz.
Photos of the Rolf Langenfass costume designs, chapter 4: Metropolitan Opera/Winnie Klotz and Herr Langenfass.
Photos of *Ring* productions in the Appendix:
  1 Bayreuther Festspiele GmbH/Schwannicke
  2 Bayreuther Festspiele GmbH/Siegfried Lauterwasser
  3 Bayreuther Festspiele GmbH/Wilhelm Rauh
  4 Bayreuther Festspiele GmbH/Rudolph Betz
  5 Bayreuther Festspiele GmbH/Wilhelm Rauh
  6 Bayreuther Festspiele GmbH/Wilhelm Rauh
  7 Bayreuther Festspiele GmbH/Wilhelm Rauh
  8 Bayreuther Festspiele GmbH/Wilhelm Rauh
  9 Bayreuther Festspiele GmbH/Jean-Marie Bottequin
  10 Bayreuther Festspiele GmbH/Jean-Marie Bottequin
  11 Bayreuther Festspiele GmbH/Wilhelm Rauh
  12 Bayreuther Festspiele GmbH/Siegfried Lauterwasser
  13 Bayreuther Festspiele GmbH/Siegfried Lauterwasser
  14 Bayreuther Festspiele GmbH/Siegfried Lauterwasser
  15 Bayreuther Festspiele GmbH/Wilhelm Rauh
  16 Bayreuther Festspiele GmbH/Wilhelm Rauh
  17 Bayreuther Festspiele GmbH/Wilhelm Rauh
  18 Bayreuther Festspiele GmbH/Wilhelm Rauh
  19 Bayreuther Festspiele GmbH/Wilhelm Rauh
  20 English National Opera/Anthony Crickmay
  21 English National Opera/Anthony Crickmay

22 Seattle Opera/Ron Scherl
23 Seattle Opera/Ron Scherl
24 Berlin-Washington/Joan Marcus
25 Österreichischer Bundestheaterverband/Hannes Gsell
26 Österreichischer Bundestheaterverband/Axel Zeininger
27 Lyric Opera of Chicago/Dan Rest
28 Lyric Opera of Chicago/Dan Rest
29 Lyric Opera of Chicago/John Reilly
30 Châtelet/Théâtre Musical de Paris/Marie Noëlle Robert
31 Châtelet/Théâtre Musical de Paris/Marie Noëlle Robert

INDEX

This index is limited to names not otherwise easily located in the text. As a reference work, this book has been designed with detailed lists of contents and headings throughout to help readers find the *Ring* operas, stories, music, characters, words, books, recordings, and even events in Wagner's life. The Concordance (chapter 5) is itself an index of principal words from the *Ring* librettos.

Aeschylus, 32
  Oresteia, 32
Alfrik, 176
Alpris, 176
Andvari, 26, 176, 180, 189, 190, 196
Attila, 24, 231, 235, 240

Bayreuther Blätter, 104
Beethoven, Ludwig van, 32, 37, 132
Bergman, Ingmar, 374
Berlioz, Hector, 105
Bismarck, Otto von, 39
Boulez, Pierre, 20, 21, 104, 374
Böhm, Karl, 20
Brandt, Carl, 40
Brecht, Bertold, 375
Bruckner, Anton, 43
Brückner, Gotthold and Max, 43
Brückwald, Otto, 40
Burgundians, 24, 214, 221, 231, 232, 235, 237, 240
Bülow, Hans von, 34, 35, 38

Chéreau, Patrice, 104, 374, 375
Cochrane, Peggie, 20

Cooke, Deryck, 18, 23, 24, 25, 27, 107, 116, 119, 121, 125, 129, 139, 165, 180, 193, 202, 204, 205, 220, 221, 231, 237
  An Introduction to Wagner's "Der Ring des Nibelungen," 107

Donington, Robert, 24, 106, 107, 121, 125, 128, 160, 186, 227, 234
  Wagner's "Ring" and Its Symbols, 24, 106, 107
Dorn, Heinrich, 25
  Die Nibelungen, 25

Edda (see also *Poetic Edda* and *Prose Edda*), 173, 184, 187, 195, 204, 222
English National Opera (Sadler's Wells Opera), 20
Etzel, 231, 232, 235
Eugel, 176

Fafnir, 26, 180, 189, 190
Faust, 182
Felsenstein, Walter, 375
Fouqué, Baron Friedrich de la Motte, 26, 200, 222, 229
  Sigurd der Schlangentödter, 200, 229

Frauer, Ludwig, 220
  Die Walkyrien, 220
Frederick the Great, 38
Freud, Sigmund, 24
Frey, 187, 193
Freyja, 180, 187
Friedrich, Götz, 375, 376
Frigg, 184, 187, 193
Furtwängler, Wilhelm, 21, 42

Gautier, Judith, 36
Geyer, Cäcilie (sister), 31, 32
Geyer, Ludwig (stepfather, possibly bio-
    logical father), 31, 32
Gibicha, King, 231, 232, 233, 234, 235, 237,
    238, 240
Gounod, Charles, 43
Grieg, Edvard, 43
Grimhild, 238
Grimhildur, 238
Grimm, Jacob and Wilhelm, 25, 26, 173,
    176, 184, 185, 189, 190, 196, 204, 207,
    220, 222
  Die deutsche Heldensage, 189, 207
  Deutsche Mythologie, 173
Gunnar, 235
Gunthaharius, 24, 231, 234, 240
Gutman, Robert W., 23, 28, 29, 105

Haitink, Bernard, 21
Hamlet, 399
Hogni, 220, 235
Hreidmar, 188, 189, 190
Huns, see Attila

Iago, 236
Ibsen, Henrick, 18, 183
Idunn, 187
Ildico, 24, 231

Jameson, Frederick, 19, 20, 46
Jord, 195, 204
Jung, Carl Gustav, 24, 175, 186

Karajan, Herbert von, 20
Klindworth, Karl, 19, 34, 46
Kriemhild, 25, 215, 235, 238
Kupfer, Harry, 375

Langenfass, Rolf, 172
Laussot, Jessie, 33
Lear, King, 182
Lee, M. Owen, 107, 140, 219, 244
  *Wagner's "Ring": Turning the Sky
    Round*, 107
Leipzig University, 32
Levine, James, 21
Levi, Hermann, 44
Lex Burgundiorum, 24, 231, 240
Das Lied vom hürnen Seyfrid, 176, 238
Lizst, Franz, 19, 32, 33, 38, 43
Loki, 26, 176, 189, 190, 196
Louis Napoleon (Napoleon III), 29
Ludwig II, King of Bavaria, 30, 35, 36, 38,
    40, 43

Magee, Bryan, 31, 103
Magee, Elizabeth, 25, 26, 27, 176, 185, 187,
    197, 200, 210, 213, 220
Mann, William, 20, 21, 46, 106, 135, 243,
    244, 397, 399
Margravine Theater, Bayreuth, 39
Metropolitan Opera, 46, 172, 375
Meyerbeer, Giacomo, 32
Mjollnir, 195
Mone, F. J., 26
Müller, W., 189
  Altdeutsche Religion, 189

Nazi, 375
Neumann, Angelo, 36, 45
Newman, Ernest, 27, 28, 31, 103, 104, 107,
    118, 135, 139, 152, 221
  The Wagner Operas, 27, 107
Der Nibelunge Nôt, 222
Das Nibelungenlied, 24, 25, 26, 173, 176,
    202, 207, 210, 215, 222, 232, 235, 238

Nidung, King, 213
Nietzsche, Friedrich, 35, 36, 43
Nornir, 229

Odin, 26, 176, 180, 184, 187, 189, 190, 193, 195, 204, 215, 220
Osborne, Charles, 30

Pedro II, Emperor of Brazil, 43
Poetic Edda, 19, 25, 26, 180, 184, 188, 193, 200, 204, 207, 213, 215, 228
    "Baldr's Dream," 204
    "Wise-Woman's Prophecy," 204
Porter, Andrew, 19, 20, 243
Prose Edda, 25, 26, 180, 184, 188, 193, 220, 229

Don Quixote, 182

Regin, 188, 189, 190
Royal Library, Dresden, 25, 32

Saint-Saëns, Charles Camille, 43
Salter, Lionel, 20, 21, 46, 106, 243, 244, 397, 399
Schirmer, G., 19, 46, 106, 109, 397, 399
Schnieder-Siemssen, Günther, 375
Schopenhauer, Arthur, 29, 34
B. Schotts Sohne, 46
Semper, Gottfried, 38, 40
Shakespeare, William, 37
Shaw, George Bernard, 18, 183
Siggeir, King of Gothland, 210, 212, 213
Signy, 210, 212
Sigurd, 189, 215
Simrock, Karl, 26, 213, 222, 232
    Amelungenlied, 213, 232
    Heldenbuch, 26
Sinfiötli, 210
Skuld (Norn), 230
Solti, Georg, 20, 109
Spencer, Stewart, 18, 19, 20, 243
Sturluson, Snorri, 26, 220, 229

Tchaikovsky, Peter Ilyich, 43
Teutons, 24, 179
Thidriks saga af Bern, 25, 26, 173, 176, 199, 210, 213, 215, 222, 228, 235
Thor, 193, 195, 204
Triebschen, 30, 35, 38

U.S. Independence Celebration Committee, 36

Vaterlandsverein, 33
Vendramin, Palazzo, 37
Verdi, Giuseppe, 236
Vishcher, F. T., 25
Volsung, King, 210, 212
Volsunga Saga, 25, 26, 179, 188, 199, 200, 206, 210, 212, 222, 238

Wagner, Carl Friedrich (legal father), 31
Wagner, Cosima (second wife), 30, 34, 35, 38, 39, 373
Wagner, Eva (second daughter), 35
Wagner, Isolde (first daughter), 35
Wagner, Johanna Rosine Pätz (mother), 31
Wagner, Klara (sister), 32
Wagner, Minna Planer (first wife), 32, 33, 34, 35, 185
Wagner, Ottilie (sister), 32
Wagner, Richard, Works (other than the *Ring* operas)
    "Art and Revolution," 25, 33
    "The Art Work of the Future," 25, 33
    The Ban on Love (Das Liebesverbot), 32
    A Communication to My Friends, 222
    "Centennial March," 36
    The Fairies (Die Feen), 32
    The Flying Dutchman, 32
    Jesus of Nazareth, 23, 33
    Lohengrin, 23, 25, 32, 33, 34, 105
    The Mastersingers of Nuremburg, 27, 30, 34, 35, 38
    My Life (Mein Leben), 29, 35
    "The Nibelung Myth as Scheme for a Drama," 25, 27, 28, 33, 37

Wagner, Richard, Works (other than the
    Ring *operas), continued*
"Opera and Drama," 25, 33
Parsifal, 18, 27, 35, 36, 37, 44, 163
"A Project for the Organization of a
    German National Theater for the
    Kingdom of Saxony," 33, 37
Rienzi, 32
Siegfried Idyll, 35, 154, 155
Siegfried's Death (Siegfrieds Tod), 25, 27,
    28, 33
Tannhäuser, 30, 32, 34, 375
Tristan and Isolde, 18, 27, 30, 34, 35, 38
The Victors (Die Sieger), 34
The Wedding (Die Hochzeit), 32
"Wesendonck Lieder," 34
"The Wibelungs," 25, 28, 33
Wieland the Smith, 213
Young Siegfried, 27, 33

Wagner, Rosalie (sister), 32
Wagner Siegfried (son), 35, 373
Wagner Societies, 39
Wagner, Wieland (grandson), 373, 374
Wagner, Winifred, 373
Wagner, Wolfgang (grandson), 373, 374
Wahnfried, 36
Wala, 204, 245
Washington, D.C., 39
Weinhold, Karl, 197, 198
    Die Sagen von Loki, 197
Werdandi (Norn), 229
Wesendonck, Mathilde, 30, 33, 34
Wilhelm II, Kaiser, 39, 43
Wilhelmine, the Margravine (sister of
    Frederick the Great), 38
Wolzogen, Hans von, 104
Wurdur (Norn), 229